Praise for THE

"A vivid and at times startling reappraisal of one of the most ~~~~ ~~~~ ties in history. If you thought you knew the Borgias, this book will surprise you." —TRACY BORMAN, author of *Queen of the Conqueror*

"A fascinating look into the lives of the notorious Italian Renaissance family and its reputation for womanizing, murder and corruption. Meyer turns centuries of accepted wisdom about the Borgias on its head, probing deep into contemporary documents and neglected histories to reveal some surprising truths. . . . A gripping history of a tempestuous time and an infamous family." —*Shelf Awareness*

"The mention of the Borgia family often conjures up images of a ruthless drive for power via assassination, serpentine plots, and sexual debauchery. This is partially owing to propaganda spread by contemporary rivals of the Borgias, nineteenth-century Renaissance historians, and even films and television shows. . . . Meyer . . . convincingly looks past the mythology to present a more nuanced portrait of some members and their achievements. . . . [The] Borgias are treated with . . . evenhandedness in this well-researched and surprising study." —*Booklist*

"Many accounts of the Borgias focus on the most scandalous stories about this powerful Renaissance family. . . . Meyer argues that many of these salacious tales are untrue and the result of slander. Through a logical and thoughtful examination of sources . . . he shows that claims of corruption, poisoning, incest, and murder are untrue or greatly exaggerated."
—*Library Journal*

"As a follow-up to his previous book, *The Tudors*, Meyer brings his considerable skills to another infamous Renaissance family, the Borgias. . . . [A] fascinating . . . fresh look into the machinations of power in Renaissance Italy."
—*Historical Novel Society*

Praise for THE TUDORS

"[A] sweeping history of the gloriously infamous Tudor era. Unlike the somewhat ponderous British biographies of the Henrys, Elizabeths and Boleyns that seem to pop up perennially, Meyer displays some flashy, fresh irreverence [and cuts] to the quick of the action. . . . Energetic and comprehensive."
                                        —*Kirkus Reviews*

"Meyer brings a fresh, and not at all admiring, perspective on this story. . . . He certainly knows how to strip an immense subject down to its essentials and bare the hard realities that underlie history's romance and melodrama."
                                        —*The Dallas Morning News*

"Meyer's book is a rich and vibrant tapestry depicting England's most notorious—and most remembered—monarchs."—*The Star-Ledger*

"*The Tudors* is graphic proof that truth is stranger—and more horrific—than fiction. If you've read books about individuals of the period, read Meyer's book to tie the loose ends together. . . . [It provides] a world view of this historical period."—Huntington News Network

"Intelligent, discerning, and professionally responsible history of the family's century-long occupation of the English throne. As [Meyer] removes layers of false image, far more realistic portraits emerge: [The Tudors] were cold and efficient figures, far less glorious than Hollywood would have it."—*Booklist*

"History buffs will savor Meyer's cheeky, nuanced, and authoritative perspective on an entire dynasty, and his study brims with enriching background discussions, ranging from class structure and the medieval Catholic Church to the Tudor connection to Spanish royalty."
                                        —*Publishers Weekly* (starred review)

"A thoroughly readable and often compelling narrative." —Associated Press

Also by G. J. Meyer

The Tudors: The Complete Story of
England's Most Notorious Dynasty

A World Undone: The Story of the Great War, 1914–1918

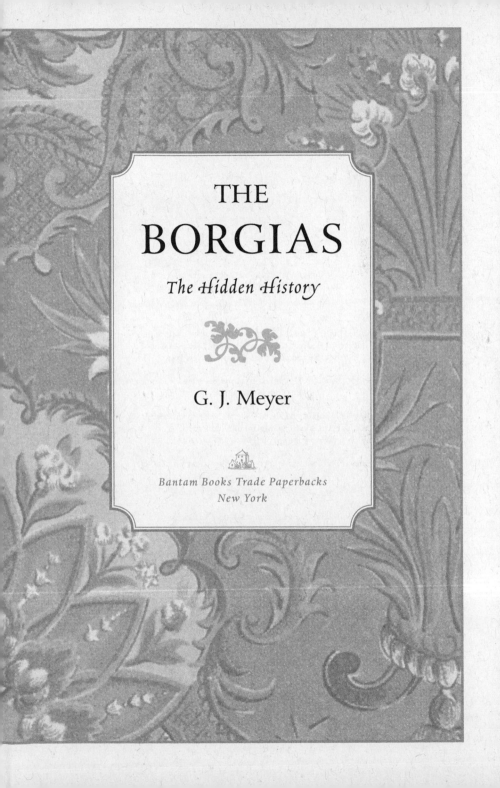

THE
BORGIAS

The Hidden History

G. J. Meyer

Bantam Books Trade Paperbacks
New York

Published in the United States by Bantam Books, an imprint of
Random House, a division of Random House LLC,
a Penguin Random House Company, New York.

BANTAM BOOKS and the HOUSE colophon are registered trademarks of
Random House LLC.

Originally published in hardcover in the United States by
Bantam Books, an imprint of Random House,
a division of Random House LLC, in 2013.

LIBRARY OF CONGRESS CATALOGING-IN-PUBLICATION DATA

Meyer, G. J.
The Borgias: the hidden history / G.J. Meyer.
pages cm
Includes bibliographical references and index.
ISBN 978-0-345-52692-2 (acid- free paper) — ISBN 978-0-345-52693-9 (eBook)
1. Borgia family. 2. Nobility—Italy—Biography. 3. Renaissance—Italy.
4. Italy—History—15th century. 5. Italy—History—1492–1559. I. Title.
DG463.8.B7M49 2013
945'.060922— dc23
[B]
2012037777

Printed in the United States of America on acid-free paper

www.bantamdell.com

2 4 6 8 9 7 5 3 1

Book design by Virginia Norey

For Eric, Ellen, and Sarah

Who have always made everything meaningful, and worthwhile

Contents

A Traditional Genealogy

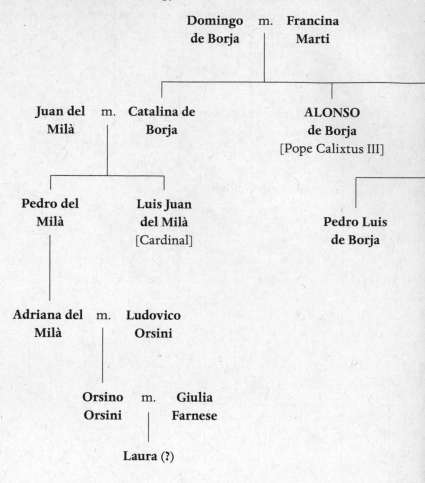

Domingo de Borja — m. — Francina Marti

Juan del Milà — m. — Catalina de Borja

ALONSO de Borja [Pope Calixtus III]

Pedro del Milà

Luis Juan del Milà [Cardinal]

Pedro Luis de Borja

Adriana del Milà — m. — Ludovico Orsini

Orsino Orsini — m. — Giulia Farnese

Laura (?)

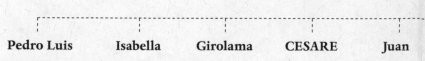

Pedro Luis   Isabella   Girolama   CESARE   Juan

(A dotted rule denotes illegitimate children.)

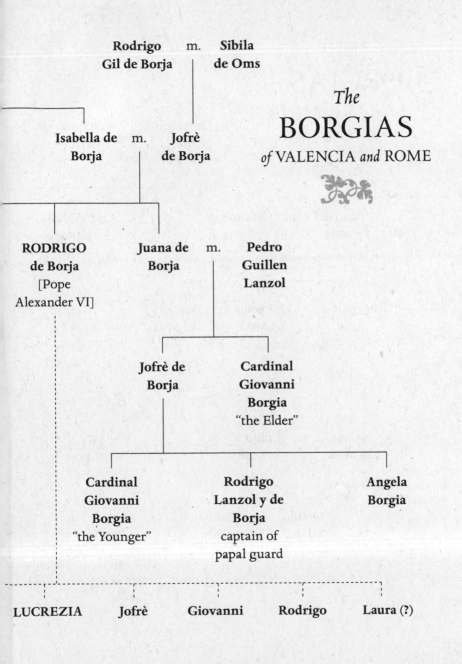

Rodrigo m. Sibila
Gil de Borja de Oms

The
BORGIAS
of VALENCIA *and* ROME

Isabella de m. Jofrè
Borja de Borja

RODRIGO   Juana de m. Pedro
de Borja   Borja   Guillen
[Pope   Lanzol
Alexander VI]

Jofrè de   Cardinal
Borja   Giovanni
                 Borgia
              "the Elder"

Cardinal   Rodrigo   Angela
Giovanni   Lanzol y de   Borgia
Borgia   Borja
"the Younger"   captain of
                 papal guard

LUCREZIA   Jofrè   Giovanni   Rodrigo   Laura (?)

The
BORGIAS
of VALENCIA *and* ROME

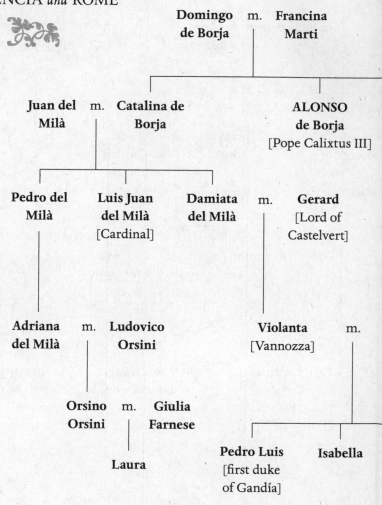

Domingo m. Francina
de Borja | Marti

Juan del m. Catalina de   ALONSO
Milà | Borja   de Borja
    [Pope Calixtus III]

Pedro del   Luis Juan   Damiata m. Gerard
Milà   del Milà   del Milà | [Lord of
   [Cardinal]   Castelvert]

Adriana m. Ludovico   Violanta m.
del Milà | Orsini   [Vannozza]

Orsino m. Giulia
Orsini | Farnese

Laura   Pedro Luis   Isabella
    [first duke
    of Gandía]

An Alternative Genealogy

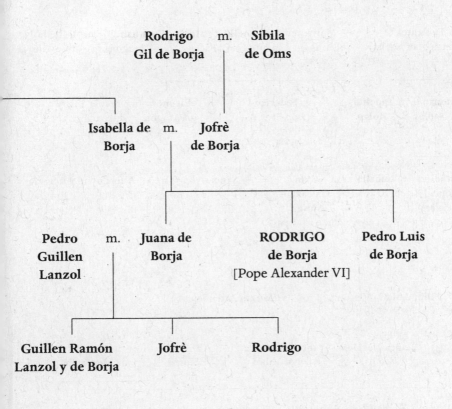

Rodrigo Gil de Borja m. Sibila de Oms

Isabella de Borja m. Jofrè de Borja

Pedro Guillen Lanzol m. Juana de Borja

RODRIGO de Borja [Pope Alexander VI]

Pedro Luis de Borja

Guillen Ramón Lanzol y de Borja

Jofrè

Rodrigo

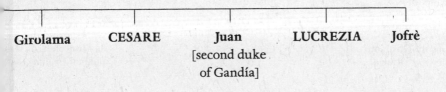

Girolama   CESARE   Juan [second duke of Gandía]   LUCREZIA   Jofrè

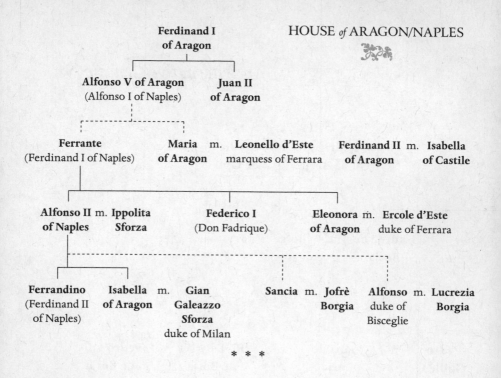

HOUSE *of* ARAGON/NAPLES

**Ferdinand I
of Aragon**

Alfonso V of Aragon
(Alfonso I of Naples)　　**Juan II
of Aragon**

Ferrante
(Ferdinand I of Naples)　　**Maria
of Aragon**　m.　**Leonello d'Este**
marquess of Ferrara　　**Ferdinand II**　m.　**Isabella
of Aragon**　　　**of Castile**

Alfonso II　m.　**Ippolita
of Naples**　　　**Sforza**　　　**Federico I**
(Don Fadrique)　　**Eleonora**　m.　**Ercole d'Este
of Aragon**　　duke of Ferrara

Ferrandino
(Ferdinand II
of Naples)　　**Isabella
of Aragon**　m.　**Gian
Galeazzo
Sforza**
duke of Milan　　**Sancia**　m.　**Jofrè
Borgia**　　**Alfonso**　m.　**Lucrezia
duke of**　　　**Borgia**
Bisceglie

* * *

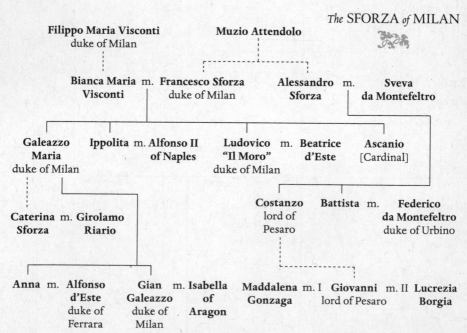

The SFORZA *of* MILAN

Filippo Maria Visconti
duke of Milan　　**Muzio Attendolo**

Bianca Maria　m.　**Francesco Sforza**
Visconti　　　duke of Milan　　**Alessandro
Sforza**　m.　**Sveva
da Montefeltro**

**Galeazzo
Maria**
duke of Milan　　**Ippolita**　m.　**Alfonso II
of Naples**　　**Ludovico**　m.　**Beatrice
"Il Moro"**　　**d'Este**　　**Ascanio**
duke of Milan　　　　　[Cardinal]

Costanzo
lord of
Pesaro　　**Battista**　m.　**Federico
da Montefeltro**
duke of Urbino

Caterina　m.　**Girolamo
Sforza**　　**Riario**

Anna　m.　**Alfonso
d'Este**
duke of
Ferrara　　**Gian**　m.　**Isabella
Galeazzo**　　**of**
duke of　**Aragon**
Milan　　**Maddalena**　m. I　**Giovanni**　m. II　**Lucrezia
Gonzaga**　　lord of Pesaro　　**Borgia**

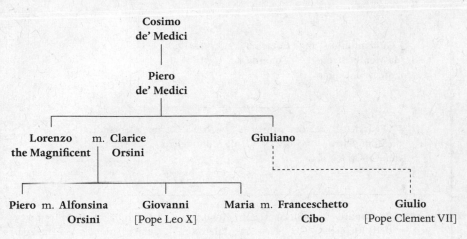

**Cosimo
de' Medici**

**Piero
de' Medici**

Lorenzo m. **Clarice**
the Magnificent | **Orsini**

Giuliano

Piero m. **Alfonsina
Orsini**

Giovanni
[Pope Leo X]

Maria m. **Franceschetto
Cibo**

Giulio
[Pope Clement VII]

* * *

HOUSE *of* ESTE (FERRARA)

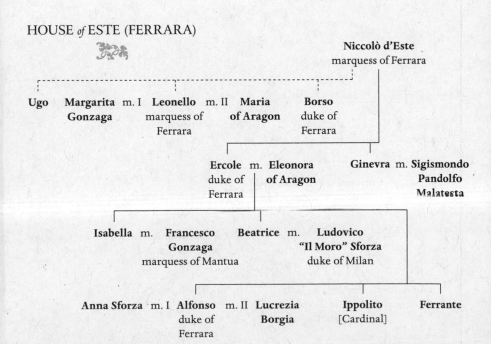

Niccolò d'Este
marquess of Ferrara

Ugo **Margarita** m. I **Leonello** m. II **Maria** **Borso**
Gonzaga marquess of **of Aragon** duke of
Ferrara Ferrara

Ercole m. **Eleonora**
duke of **of Aragon**
Ferrara

Ginevra m. **Sigismondo
Pandolfo
Malatesta**

Isabella m. **Francesco
Gonzaga**
marquess of Mantua

Beatrice m. **Ludovico
"Il Moro" Sforza**
duke of Milan

Anna Sforza m. I **Alfonso**
duke of
Ferrara

m. II **Lucrezia
Borgia**

Ippolito
[Cardinal]

Ferrante

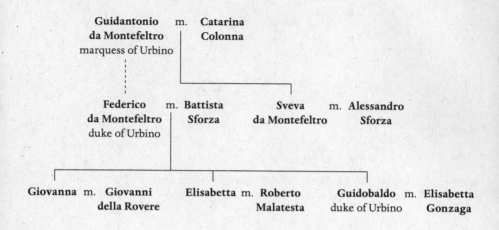

Guidantonio da Montefeltro — marquess of Urbino — m. Catarina Colonna

Federico da Montefeltro — duke of Urbino — m. Battista Sforza

Sveva da Montefeltro — m. Alessandro Sforza

Giovanna — m. Giovanni della Rovere

Elisabetta — m. Roberto Malatesta

Guidobaldo — duke of Urbino — m. Elisabetta Gonzaga

* * *

DELLA ROVERE/RIARIO

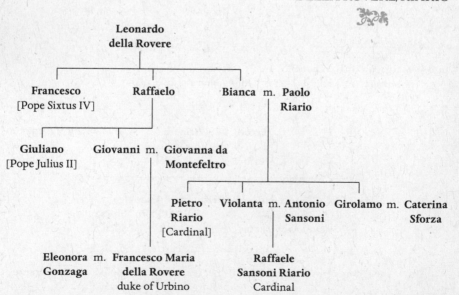

Leonardo della Rovere

Francesco [Pope Sixtus IV]

Raffaelo

Bianca — m. Paolo Riario

Giuliano [Pope Julius II]

Giovanni — m. Giovanna da Montefeltro

Pietro Riario [Cardinal]

Violanta — m. Antonio Sansoni

Girolamo — m. Caterina Sforza

Eleonora Gonzaga — m. Francesco Maria della Rovere — duke of Urbino

Raffaele Sansoni Riario — Cardinal

Timeline

1378   Alonso de Borja born at Játiva in Valencia, Spain.

Start of Great or Western Schism, dividing Roman Church.

1416   Alfonso V becomes king of Aragon.

1417   Alonso de Borja enters service of Alfonso V.

Oddone Colonna elected Pope Martin V.

1420   Martin V returns papacy to Rome, ending long exile.

1431   Rodrigo de Borja born at Játiva.

Gabriele Condulmer elected Pope Eugenius IV.

1442   Alfonso V drives Angevins from Naples, assumes Neapolitan crown.

1444   Alonso de Borja appointed to College of Cardinals, moves to Rome following year.

1447   Tommaso Parentucelli elected Pope Nicholas V.

1451   Birth of Isabella, future queen of Castile.

1452   Birth of Ferdinand II, future king of Aragon.

1453   Constantinople falls to Ottoman Turks.

1455   Cardinal Alonso Borgia elected Pope Calixtus III, appoints Rodrigo Borgia protonotary apostolic and Pedro Luis Borgia commander of Castel Sant'Angelo.

1456   Rodrigo Borgia is made a cardinal, Pedro Luis captain-general of papal army.

1457   Rodrigo appointed vice-chancellor of Church.

1458   Rodrigo appointed bishop of Valencia.

Alfonso V dies, to be succeeded as king of Naples by son Ferrante (Ferdinand I).

Calixtus III dies; Enea Silvio Piccolomini succeeds as Pope Pius II.

Death of Pedro Luis Borgia.

Athens falls to Turks.

1460   Cardinal Rodrigo rebuked by Pius II following garden party
        in Siena.

1462   Birth of Louis of Orléans, future Louis XII of France.

1463   Start of sixteen-year war between Venice and Ottoman Empire.

1464   Pietro Barbo elected Pope Paul II.

1470   Negropont captured by Turks.

        Birth of Charles VIII of France.

1471   Francesco della Rovere elected Pope Sixtus IV.

        Rodrigo Borgia appointed papal legate to Iberian peninsula.

1475   Probable year of Cesare Lanzol y de Borja's birth in Spain.

1476   Probable year of birth of Cesare's brother Juan Lanzol y
        de Borja.

1478   Pazzi Conspiracy against Medici family in Florence.

        Beginning of Pope Sixtus's Italian War, which will continue
        two years.

1480   Lucrezia Lanzol y de Borja born.

        Ottoman Turks occupy Otranto in southern Italy.

1481   Probable year of death of Guillen Ramón Lanzol, father of Pedro
        Luis, Cesare, Lucrezia, and others.

        Ludovico Sforza, as regent, wins control of the duchy of Milan.

        Death of Ottoman Sultan Mehmed II; son and successor Bayezid II
        withdraws Turkish troops from Otranto.

1484   Giovanni Battista Cibo elected Pope Innocent VIII.

1485   Pedro Luis Lanzol y de Borja is made duke of Gandía by
        Ferdinand and Isabella of Spain.

1488   Murder of Girolamo Riario, nephew of Sixtus IV and husband
        of Caterina Sforza.

1491   Charles VIII of France marries Anne of Brittany.

        Cesare Borgia appointed bishop of Pamplona.

1492   Death of Lorenzo de' Medici.

        Election of Rodrigo Borgia as Pope Alexander VI.

        Archbishopric of Valencia is conferred on Cesare.

        Christopher Columbus sails west from Spain, seeking Japan,
        China, and India.

1493   Borgia marriages: Juan to Maria Enriquez de Luna of Spain, Lucrezia to Giovanni Sforza, Jofrè to Sancia of Aragon.

Cesare is appointed to College of Cardinals.

Columbus returns from his first voyage of discovery.

Papal bull divides newly discovered territories between Spain and Portugal.

1494   Death of Ferrante of Naples; succeeded by son Alfonso II.

French invasion of Italy by Charles VIII.

Expulsion of Medici family from Florence.

1495   Alfonso II of Naples abdicates; succeeded by son Ferrandino (Ferdinand II).

Charles VIII meets Alexander VI in Rome, enters Naples in triumph.

Holy League formed to resist French occupation.

Following Battle of Fornovo, Charles withdraws to France.

1496   Death of Ferrandino of Naples; succeeded by uncle Don Fadrique (Federico I).

1497   Friar Girolamo Savonarola of Florence is excommunicated after calling for a council to depose Alexander VI.

Alexander makes war on Orsini; death of Virginio Orsini.

Murder in Rome of Juan Borgia, second duke of Gandía.

Annulment of Lucrezia Borgia's marriage to Giovanni Sforza.

1498   Murder of Pedro Calderón, Lucrezia's alleged lover.

Death of Charles VIII; succeeded by Louis XII, who later agrees with Venice to partition Milan.

Lucrezia wed to Alfonso of Aragon, duke of Bisceglie.

Cesare is allowed to resign from College of Cardinals; travels to French court at Chinon, France; is made duke of Valentinois; wed to Charlotte d'Albret.

Savonarola, discredited, is executed by Florentine civil authorities.

1499   Louis XII marries Anne of Brittany, seizes Milan and Genoa.

Pope Alexander excommunicates Romagna lords, seizes territories of the Gaetani.

Vasco da Gama returns to Lisbon from voyage to India.

Cesare's first *impresa* captures Imola, besieges Forlì.

Lucrezia gives birth to son, Rodrigo of Aragon.

1500   Cesare captures Caterina Sforza.

Duke of Bisceglie is attacked and gravely wounded, subsequently strangled.

Cesare launches second *impresa*, besieges Faenza.

Spain and France agree to partition kingdom of Naples.

1501   Alexander creates Cesare duke of Romagna.

Don Fadrique abdicates as king of Naples, retires to Anjou.

Lucrezia is married to Alfonso d'Este.

1502   Arezzo rebels against Florence.

Cesare launches third *impresa*, captures Urbino and Cesena.

Machiavelli and Soderini meet Cesare at Urbino.

Conspiracy of *condottieri* against Cesare.

Cesare makes surprise visit to Louis XII at Milan, renews alliance.

Machiavelli visits Cesare at Imola.

Cesare resumes offensive, advances to Senigallia.

1503   Vitelli and Oliverotto strangled at Senigallia.

Alexander and Cesare launch war on Orsini.

Gonsalvo captures city of Naples for Spain.

Death of Alexander VI, election of Francesco Todeschini Piccolomini as Pope Pius III.

Death of Pius III, election of Giuliano della Rovere as Pope Julius II.

1504   Having earlier become the prisoner of Julius II at Ostia and subsequently freed, Cesare is again arrested, at Naples, this time by Gonsalvo, transported as prisoner to Spain.

Death of Isabella of Spain.

1505   Lucrezia becomes duchess of Ferrara upon death of Ercole d'Este.

Cesare transferred from Chinchilla to Medina del Campo.

1506   Cesare escapes from Medina del Campo, makes way to Navarre.

1507   Cesare killed in battle.

1519   Death of Lucrezia.

ITALY
IN THE 15TH CENTURY

SWISS FED.

HOLY ROMAN EMPIRE

KINGDOM OF HUNGARY

FRANCE

Milan

Venice

ISTRIA

Asti

Mantua

DUCHY OF MILAN

Modena

Ferrara

Imola

Ravenna

Bologna

Forlì

Faenza

Cesena

Genoa

REPUBLIC OF VENICE

DALMATIA

OTTOMAN EMPIRE

Pisa

Florence

Rimini

Pesaro

Ancona

Arezzo

Urbino

Siena

TUSCANY

APENNINES

PAPAL
STATES

Adriatic Sea

Ligurian Sea

Piombino

ELBA

Tiber River

ABRUZZI

CORSICA

Civitavecchia

Rome

Ostia

Gaeta

Capua

Naples

KINGDOM
OF
NAPLES

APULIA

Otranto

KINGDOM
OF
SARDINIA

Tyrrhenian Sea

CALABRIA

Squillace

Ionian Sea

0 Miles   100   200
0 Kilometers   200

Mediterranean Sea

KINGDOM
OF
SICILY

© 2013 Jeffrey L. Ward

London

Paris

Chinon

HOL

Atlantic
Ocean

DUCHY OF MILAN
Geneva

FRANCE

Milan

Pamplona
Viana

Avignon

NAVARRE

Marseilles

Geno

ARAGON

CORSICA

Madrid

Barcelona

Lisbon

PORTUGAL

Toledo

CASTILE

Valencia

SARDINIA

GRANADA

Mediterranean Sea

0   Miles   200   400

0   Kilometers   400

EUROPE
IN THE 15TH CENTURY

POLAND-
LITHUANIA

OMAN EMPIRE

Vienna

HUNGARY

Venice

Bologna

Ravenna

orence

Rimini

Urbino

sa

Siena

PAPAL STATES

Civitavecchia

Ostia

Rome

Adriatic Sea

Black
Sea

OTTOMAN EMPIRE

Constantinople

KINGDOM
OF
NAPLES

Naples

Otranto

Tyrrhenian
Sea

Athens

Ionian
Sea

SICILY

CRETE

MALTA

Mediterranean Sea

© 2013 Jeffrey L. Ward

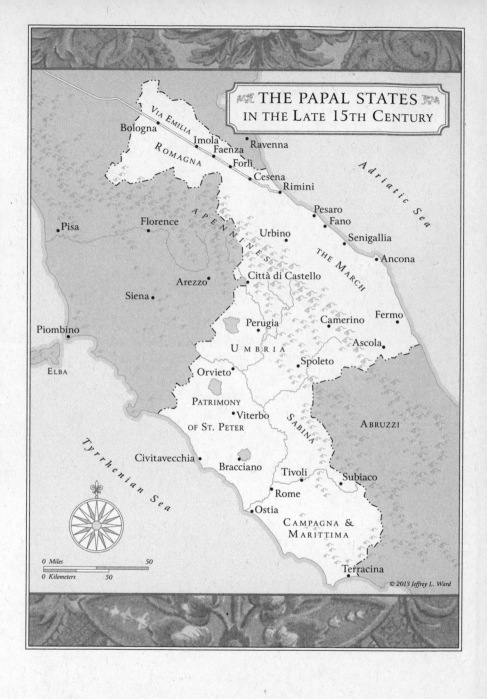

THE PAPAL STATES
IN THE LATE 15TH CENTURY

VIA EMILIA

Bologna

Imola

Faenza

ROMAGNA

Ravenna

Forlì

Cesena

Rimini

Adriatic Sea

Pisa

Florence

APENNINES

Pesaro

Fano

Urbino

Senigallia

THE MARCH

Ancona

Arezzo

Città di Castello

Siena

Perugia

Camerino

Fermo

Piombino

UMBRIA

Ascola

ELBA

Orvieto

Spoleto

PATRIMONY
OF ST. PETER

Viterbo

SABINA

ABRUZZI

Tyrrhenian Sea

Civitavecchia

Bracciano

Tivoli

Subiaco

Rome

Ostia

CAMPAGNA &
MARITTIMA

0 Miles   50

0 Kilometers   50

Terracina

© 2013 Jeffrey L. Ward

The Borgia Problem:

An Introduction

T his is not the book I set out to write.

    My expectation, at the start, was simple: that by digging more deeply into the story of the Borgias than other writers appeared to have done, I might be able to put new flesh on that story's old bones—all the thrilling tales of murder and incest and horrors beyond numbering. Thereby bringing the whole thing to life in more entertaining, possibly more meaningful ways.

A year of research on both sides of the Atlantic did generate that new flesh—more fresh material than I had hoped, as the following pages will show. But I found something unforeseen as well: evidence that the Borgia story, when one pursues it far enough, turns out to be vastly different from what the world supposes and vastly more interesting than I myself had imagined.

I found myself confronted not only with new flesh but new bones—an entirely new understanding of who the Borgias were and what they actually did. As my book began to take shape, it did so in stunningly unexpected ways.

I send the result out into the world on the two wings of a promise and a hope.

My promise is that any reader who has some knowledge of the Borgias will be surprised by the pages that follow. That, in fact, the more familiar you are with the version of the Borgia story that centuries ago hardened into legend, the greater your surprise will be.

My hope is that the appearance of this book may encourage others—by provoking incredulity or indignation, if that's what it takes—to look anew at its subject. Popular interest in the Borgias never flags, which is as it should be in view of the extraordinary personalities of the family's leading members, the high drama of their lives, and above all the light their story casts on the world of the Renaissance. But scholarly interest has been so dormant for so long that a revival is badly overdue.

Nearly seven decades have passed since J. H. Whitfield of Oxford University, in an article in *History,* called attention to what was even then the decrepit state of the established Borgia myth. The evil reputation of the family, Whitfield observed, had appeared to be confirmed beyond possibility of doubt by such once-magisterial nineteenth-century historians as Jacob Burckhardt and Ferdinand Gregorovius. But in the twentieth century it became clear that those same historians were so wrong about so many things that they were, in effect, largely discredited. Whitfield not only regarded "a revision in favor of the Borgias" as necessary but appears to have expected it to come soon.

Though his optimism was misplaced, he put his finger on what has always been the core of the Borgia problem: the acceptance as true, on the basis of laughably insubstantial evidence or no evidence at all, of accusations of the darkest kind. Examples abound in Gregorovius's treatment of the central figure in the Borgia story, the Rodrigo Borgia who in 1492 became Pope Alexander VI. In the seventh volume of his *History of the City of Rome in the Middle Ages,* Gregorovius acknowledges that "the secrets of [Rodrigo's] life as cardinal are unknown, no one having spoken on the subject," and in his biography of Lucrezia Borgia he observes again that "nothing is known" of Rodrigo's private life during the thirty-six years between his elevation to the College of Cardinals and his election as pope. But immediately after the first of these statements Gregorovius describes Rodrigo as "passionately sensual," and immediately after the second he asserts that "insatiable sensuality ruled this Borgia . . . until his last years. Never was he able to cast out this demon." These words are bizarre, coming as they do from someone who has just admitted that his subject's personal life remained a complete blank until, at age sixty, he took center stage as head of the Roman Catholic Church.

It is much the same with Burckhardt, who in his long-revered *The Civilization of the Renaissance in Italy* accepts as true one outlandish anecdote after another, informing his readers that Rodrigo/Alexander was defined by "devilish wickedness," that Cesare had an "insane thirst for blood," and that the two saved the world from themselves by inadvertently imbibing some of the mysterious "white powder of an agreeable taste" with which they had previously decimated the elite of Rome. The present volume will, I trust, demonstrate the absurdity of these opinions.

The Borgia problem is rooted in the fact that from the early sixteenth century forward, for reasons ranging from Pope Julius II's hatred of his predecessor, Alexander VI, to the eagerness of Reformation polemicists to depict the papacy in morally horrific terms, "every conceivable crime was credited to the Borgias." By a process of gradual accumulation the scant contemporary record came to be covered over by a thick blanket of invective, with Victor Hugo contributing his play about a monstrous Lucrezia Borgia and Donizetti turning the play into grand opera. Finally even the Catholic historian Ludwig Pastor, whose *History of the Popes from the Close of the Middle Ages* fills forty fat volumes, evidently could see no point in even questioning the legend. That the Borgias were indefensible had come to seem self-evident.

"Burckhardt and Gregorovius have had their day," said Whitfield in 1944. But since then: almost nothing. Little beyond the endless repetition of the same old shopworn tales, unsupported and insupportable as many of them are.

In writing the present volume I have done two things that are unusual in the treatment of the Borgias, though neither should be unusual at all. I have asked obvious if long-neglected questions, and I have declined to accept answers generally accepted as settled when those answers turn out to have little or no factual foundation. I have also rejected the old practice, where evidence is lacking, of opting for the ugliest hypothetical explanation of a puzzling event.

I make no claim to providing definitive answers to all the questions I raise. Some are probably unanswerable after five hundred years, but simply pointing out that they are unanswerable is worthwhile under the circumstances. Others cry out for the attention of investigators with unusual skills (in the regional dialects of medieval Spain, for example, or the record-keeping practices of Vatican archivists half a millennium ago, or the detection of forged papal bulls).

Much work remains to be done. If this book serves to encourage the undertaking of some part of that work, I will regard my own efforts as richly rewarded. If other writers can show—not just complain, but *show*—that I have gone too far in being skeptical about alleged Borgia crimes, I will welcome their achievement. Every time another of the old tales is shown to be at least probably true or untrue, another step will have been taken in a process that should be much further along than it is: lifting the Borgia story out of the realm of fable and turning it into history.

I wish to express particular thanks to Oxford's Bodleian Library, where I spent many fruitful days over a period of many months. Without its magnificent resources and the helpfulness of its staff, this book would have been immeasurably more difficult if not impossible to complete in its present form. Also to my superb editor, the acutely perceptive and tirelessly helpful Tracy Devine.

G. J. Meyer
Mere, Wiltshire, England

THE BORGIAS

Prologue

One Whom All Did Fear

The dates and some of the other details are hopelessly uncertain, but the story's essential elements appear to be beyond dispute:

One day the bishop of Calahorra paid an official visit to the church of Saint Mary of the Assumption in the little city of Viana, in what was by then northern Spain but had long been part of the kingdom of Navarre. If the visit happened in 1527 as some of the accounts have it, or in 1537 as is also said, the church was already more than two centuries old, its origins as distant for the bishop as those of the White House, say, are for us. It was a tall, gauntly cavernous specimen of Gothic stonework, with pointed arches everywhere and ceilings so high as to be shrouded in gloom even on the brightest days.

If as is commonly said the visit didn't take place in the 1500s at all but in the closing years of the seventeenth century, it may have happened in connection with the renovations the church is known to have been undergoing at that time. A high tower was being erected above the main entrance, its design baroque rather than Gothic. Inside, the original altars and alcoves were disappearing under extravagant carvings in the newer, more fashionable rococo style. It would have been natural for the bishop, whose diocese included Viana, to make a tour of inspection while all this work was in process.

Whenever it happened, *what* happened is that His Excellency the bishop was shocked to come upon, just in front of the high altar and therefore in a position that could hardly have been more conspicuous, the bulkily ornate tomb of one of the most famous sons of one of Spain's most famous families. And to find displayed upon it an epitaph, written in regional dialect, that translates as follows:

> *Here in a little earth*
> *Lies one whom all did fear,*
> *One whose hands dispensed both peace and war.*
> *Oh, you that go in search of things deserving praise,*
> *If you would praise the worthiest,*
> *Then let your journey end here,*
> *Nor tremble to go farther.*

The body inside the tomb was that of a young man, and if intact it bore the signs of a horrifically violent death. In life it had worn the red hat of a cardinal of the Roman Catholic Church, made its home in the papal palace in Rome, ridden into proud cities as their conqueror, been joined in marriage to a princess, and had honors heaped upon it by kings of France and Spain. Not once but twice it had held in its hands the power to decide who would be elected pope. For thirty years it had been inhabited by a spirit of such force and originality as to inspire one of the immortal classics of world literature.

Perhaps most remarkably, all these things had been done by the time the man was twenty-eight years old. By that age he had become one of the legendary figures of European history, as feared and admired—as his epitaph attested—as anyone living in his time.

The bishop of Calahorra, however, was offended to find such a man memorialized not only in this way, not only in a church, but in a church for which he, as prelate, was responsible. It seemed to him a scandal. And so he ordered the tomb demolished—literally eradicated, broken into bits with heavy hammers—and the body removed. Even that was not enough. Declaring the exhumed remains to be unfit for interment in consecrated ground, the bishop had a hole dug at the foot of the stone staircase leading down from the church to the busy road below. He then had the body deposited in the hole and paved over. So that, he is supposed to have said, it would be "trampled on by man and beasts forever."

Whose body *was* this? What kind of man, having risen to eminence in so many ways in the course of such a short life, would leave behind a name capable of provoking such a powerful reaction from a churchman who could never have known him—and doing so decades, possibly generations, after his obscure and rather mysterious death?

To answer that question is one of the purposes of the story that follows. In order to answer it, we must look first at the world, and the family, out of which the young man rose.

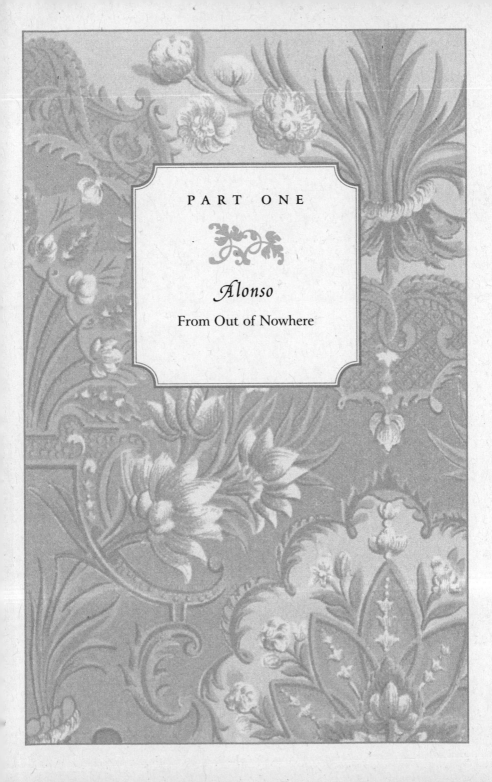

PART ONE

Alonso

From Out of Nowhere

1

A Most Improbable Pope

It is the third of April, and springtime is in full force.

We are in Rome, which in this year of 1455 is neither the glorious world capital it had been under the emperors of old nor the great city it will become once again in a few generations. Instead it is a dilapidated backwater of thirty or perhaps forty thousand souls.

At the Vatican, dominated by the thousand-year-old and slowly disintegrating St. Peter's Basilica, the cardinals are assembling. They are doing so because ten days have passed since the death of Pope Nicholas V. Of "apoplexy," the attending physicians have declared, thereby revealing that they haven't the faintest idea of what it was that caused him to grow feebler week after week until finally, aged only fifty-seven, he himself announced that his end was at hand.

The death of this particular pontiff at this particular time is a deeply worrisome thing. As for the fact that the time has come to elect his successor—it is so snarled up in difficulties and dangers as to scarcely bear thinking about.

Officially and as usual, the first nine days after the pope's death were reserved for the obsequies with which deceased pontiffs are launched into the afterlife: one requiem mass per day, each presided over by a different cardinal. But in fact, and inevitably, the days and the nights as well have been filled with backstairs politicking, mainly to see who can put together the most potent blocs of votes. In the midst of all this,

Nicholas's wizened little body has been sealed up in the traditional three coffins, one of cypress inside another of lead inside still another of fine-grained and polished elm. It was then laid to rest in the crypt under the basilica, a structure so alarmingly decrepit that in the last few years of the pope's reign 2,500 cartloads of stone had been stripped from the Colosseum and hauled across the Tiber for use in shoring it up.

By the time the last *Ite, missa est* brought the last mass to an end, the windows of one wing of the pontifical palace were boarded up in the customary way. Austere little cells, each containing a cot, a stool, and a small table, have been hammered together inside. The fifteen available cardinals (six others are too far from Rome to attend) are now reporting for duty. As they file inside, the doors are bolted behind them. Guards are posted, and the conclave of 1455 is formally in session.

Deprived of natural light, the cardinals are dependent on candles and oil lamps for illumination. With no ventilation and wood fires the only source of morning warmth, the air they breathe will soon be foul. But conclaves are not supposed to be pleasant. Physical discomfort long ago proved its value. It encourages the princes of the Church to get on with their business, announce the results, and go home.

Every part of the process is governed by customs that have evolved over a millennium and a half. At various times the choosing of popes has been under the control of Roman emperors, Byzantine emperors, and Holy Roman emperors from beyond the Alps. Sometimes popes have been able to nominate their successors, and there have been periods when no one would dare take the throne without the approval of the clergy—even the people—of Rome. But in 1059 a papal decree conferred the right of election on the College of Cardinals. Eighty years later another decree gave that right to the cardinals *exclusively,* meaning that no further approvals were needed once the Sacred College had made its choice. Forty years after that, a two-thirds majority of votes cast became necessary for election.

With that, the pattern was set. Though there have been other changes—an attempt, for example, to force fast action by reducing the cardinals' rations if they fail to reach a decision within three days and reducing them again if a pope has not been elected after five—the essential rules could hardly be simpler. Whoever can get the votes of ten of the men now locked together inside the palace will assume the full powers of the papacy from the moment of his election. He will do so even if the whole outside world disapproves.

Simple rules are no assurance of an easy outcome, however. Choosing a pope is always a complicated affair, because much is always at stake and so many competing forces invariably come into play. Things rarely go smoothly. As the cardinals settle into their cubicles and begin to talk among themselves, they know that this election is unlikely to be an exception.

Not that Nicholas has left them with a mess. To the contrary, he was in no way a bad or even a careless pope. By the standards of the time he was a good one. Anyone comparing him with his immediate predecessors might find reason to call him an almost great one. Raised in humble circumstances in northwestern Italy, he had risen in the Church purely on the basis of merit—first as one of the leading humanist scholars of his time, then through success as a diplomat. His election was a fluke; he became a cardinal only a few months before the conclave that made him pope, and it never could have happened if the most powerful factions in the College of Cardinals had not deadlocked. But the eight years of his reign proved to be rich in achievement and free of scandal. He contributed greatly to bringing peace and a measure of stability not only to Italy but to Germany as well, ended a last outbreak of schism, found honest ways to replenish the Vatican's treasury, and resumed the oft-interrupted process of trying to restore the decayed city of Rome to its lost splendor.

Even more remarkably, he appointed only a single relative, a half-brother, to the College of Cardinals and did nothing to enrich his kin. All in all, his reign has been an impressive step forward in the rebuilding of the papacy—in restoring its ancient importance and prestige. Whether this will continue or now come to a stop is likely to depend, everyone knows, on who is chosen to succeed him.

The problems facing the cardinals go much deeper than anything Nicholas did or failed to do. They are the residue of the century and a half of discord that preceded his reign: generation after generation of exile, of schism, of a deeply damaging struggle to decide whether the pope is the supreme head of the Church or subordinate to general councils. Some of the great questions are by now settled, or at least appear to be, but ugly memories are still fresh, deep wounds unhealed. Nicholas's election came only four years after the return of the last exiled pope to Rome, and it was not until two years after his election that the last antipope abandoned his claim to the throne. A mere two years separate Nicholas's death from the latest plot to overthrow papal rule and restore republican government in Rome. That he escaped unharmed does not mean that all danger has passed. That too is likely to depend, at least in part, on who takes his place.

If all Italy is at peace in 1455, this again is a departure from recent history and a fragile one. The peninsula last erupted in general war as recently as 1452, when Venice attacked Milan; Florence, Genoa, Bologna, and Mantua all came to Milan's assistance; and Naples threw in with Venice. The pope, to his credit, kept Rome neutral, thereby leaving himself free to help broker a settlement and bring the belligerents together in what he called the Italian or Most Holy League. This league is without precedent in Italian history, a defensive alliance encompassing the whole peninsula, obliging longtime enemies to embrace each other as friends and aimed at establishing a balance of power stable enough to preserve the peace. It became effective only weeks before Nicholas's death, when the troublesome king of Naples finally signed on, and was the crowning achievement of the pope's career. It is supposed to remain in effect for twenty-five years, but the realities of Italian political life make its chances of doing so vanishingly small. The part that Nicholas played in making it all happen, coupled with his departure from the stage, adds to the sense that the conclave now in session matters more than most.

The existence of the league requires the most powerful princes in Italy to pledge to do things that they are unaccustomed to doing: respect existing frontiers, join forces to punish any state that breaks the peace, and work together to keep foreign powers out. It obliges the most ruthless and ambitious of these princes to abandon—to defer, anyway—long-cherished dreams of subduing their neighbors and seizing their domains. Few of them would have agreed to any such thing if not for one of the supreme political catastrophes of the late Middle Ages: the capture by the Ottoman Turks, just twenty-three months before Nicholas's death, of the fabled city of Constantinople.

For eleven hundred years Constantinople had been the capital of the Eastern or Byzantine Empire, and incomparably richer and more important than Rome. It had also, for half a millennium, been the seat of the Orthodox Church. But after centuries of decline and generations of being dismantled piecemeal by the relentlessly expanding empire of the Turks, nothing remained but a pale shadow of what it had been at its zenith. Its end was tragic: after a siege of less than two months, a defense force of seven thousand troops was overwhelmed by eighty thousand Islamic invaders. This was followed by three days of horror, as Sultan Mehmed II ("Mehmed the Conqueror," only twenty-one years old) rewarded his men by allowing them to pillage, rape, and kill at their pleasure. As many as fifty thousand of the proud old city's inhabitants were put to the sword, and the survivors disappeared into the slave markets of the East. It was a world-changing event, and it chilled the blood of every Christian who understood its significance.

The West had no right to be shocked, actually; its leaders could not claim to have been caught off guard. They had stood by passively through all the years when the Turks drew ever closer to Constantinople. The city's emperors had sent ever more desperate appeals for help, and Europe not only failed to respond but contributed to making collapse inevitable. If at midcentury the Turks controlled much of the Balkan peninsula and Hungary south of the Danube, this was not a new state of affairs: all of Bulgaria, along with much of Serbia, had been seized more than fifty years before. That Constantinople itself had become the Turks' prime objective could not have been more obvious. When they cut off the Bosporus, the great waterway connecting Constantinople to the Black Sea and the world beyond, the city was caught in a stranglehold, its doom clearly imminent. Its last emperor—whose name, rather sadly, was Constantine, and who would die fighting when the Turks came swarming over his walls—got little from the West except bombastic words of encouragement and promises that meant nothing. Nicholas V made some effort to organize a rescue expedition, but nothing came of it. His failure to do more would be seen by many as the one disgrace of his reign.

In taking Constantinople the Turks gained not only a glorious new capital for their empire—the Hagia Sophia, one of the architectural wonders of classical times, was converted from a church to a mosque— not only one of the world's most magnificent harbors, but a platform from which to threaten central and southern Europe. Venice, its fabulous wealth dependent on access to eastern markets, is the most threatened of the Italian states, but this too has long been the case, and Venice has been slow to take alarm. Its merchant princes grew up thinking of Constantinople as their principal commercial rival, not as a bulwark against Muslim aggression, and they took foolish satisfaction in its decline. They nursed hopes of taming the Turks and turning them into business partners. The folly of such thinking was not exposed until the Turks sank a Venetian ship trying to pass through the Bosporus, beheaded all the crewmen who had not drowned, and put the body of its captain on display after killing him by impalement. But by then, at least where Constantinople was concerned, it was already too late.

That Venice is not alone in its peril became clear when Sultan Mehmed, after taking Constantinople, added "Roman Caesar" to his list of titles. No one has mistaken this for a joke; if Constantinople could fall, so could Rome. And if Rome fell, who could say that Christian civilization was not doomed? It is questions like this, and the grimness of the only credible answers, that have caused the leading Italian powers to put aside their quarrels and come together in the Holy League.

These are the issues that hang over Italy, the Church, and Europe in April 1455, creating an urgent need for leadership. Human nature being what it is, however, they are not necessarily the issues that matter most to the cardinals sequestered in the Vatican. Domestic rivalries loom larger, and some at least of the cardinals can be depended upon to care more about getting an advantage over their rivals, or stopping their rivals from getting an advantage over them, than about anything as abstract as the fate of Western civilization. Coiled like a serpent at the heart of the conclave, capable of poisoning everything, is the blood feud that almost from time immemorial has kept Rome's two greatest families at each other's throats. Without the hatred of the Orsini for the Colonna and the Colonna for the Orsini, the seven Italians who make up the conclave's largest national contingent could expect to have little difficulty recruiting the three additional votes needed to deliver the papacy to one of their own. Because of that hatred, the election of an Italian is going to be difficult at best.

This is no trivial matter. Since the return of the papal court from what is called the Babylonian Captivity, when for sixty-seven years it remained at Avignon in Provence and so completely under the thumb of the kings of France that seven consecutive popes were Frenchmen, there has been a return also to the assumption that popes should be Roman, and if not Roman then at least Italian. The people of the Eternal City take this idea seriously indeed. The cardinals know that the election of an outsider is likely to bring angry crowds into the streets, and that the election of someone from what the Romans regard as the barbarian world beyond the Alps would be certain to do so. Though the city has been fairly tranquil since the failure of the republican conspiracy of 1453, thanks largely to the pains taken by Nicholas V to deal even-handedly with the ever-jealous Orsini and Colonna and other baronial clans, not a great deal is ever needed to spark an explosion in Rome. The separation of the Italian cardinals into irreconcilable camps, and the consequent possibility of a non-Italian pope, are further causes of anxiety.

The Italians cannot be unified because of the presence of two of the Sacred College's most formidable members, both of them Roman nobles, both in their mid-forties, and both able to draw on enormous reserves of political, financial, and even military power. Latino Orsini occupies the seat in the college that his family has held for so many centuries that its leaders regard it as theirs by right, as practically their personal property. Among the ornaments on his family tree are three Orsini popes, the first elected in 1191, and the second so notorious for corruption that Dante gave him a small speaking role as one of the damned souls in *The Inferno*. Latino need look no further than to his clan's history for lessons in what a boon it can be to put a relative, or someone dependent on one's relatives, on the papal throne. And for equally compelling examples of how badly things can go when that throne is occupied by an enemy—worst of all, from the Orsini perspective, by a Colonna or a friend of the Colonna.

Proud and potent though Latino is, he is outmatched by his most dangerous rival, Cardinal Prospero Colonna. A nephew of the Oddone Colonna who became Pope Martin V in 1417 and used his office to heap wealth, high office, and noble titles on his kinsmen, Prospero has had a colorful career. He was made a cardinal while still in his teens, was excommunicated after his uncle's death changed the Colonna from Vatican insiders to undesirables, won his way back into favor, and then was very nearly elected himself. Through three tense days at the conclave of 1447, Prospero remained just two votes short of victory. His inability to get those two votes and the subsequent melting away of his support were due to the loyalty to the Orsini of several cardinals and the uneasiness felt by others because of Prospero's notorious readiness to use violence in pursuing his objectives. It was this Orsini-versus-Colonna deadlock that led to the surprise election of the conclave's newest member, the scholarly Tommaso Parentucelli, who had thus become the now-deceased Nicholas V.

The conditions that led to deadlock in 1447 are all in place in 1455. As the cardinals prepare to cast the first round of ballots, it becomes clear that the Italian Domenico Capranica is favored by a number of his colleagues. Objectively, this is an understandable, even a commendable, development. There is nothing objectionable about Capranica and much to recommend him. At fifty-five he is a seasoned senior churchman, having been a bishop for thirty years and a cardinal for more than twenty. He is also one of the Vatican's leading diplomats and administrators, a humanist scholar of note, a champion of ecclesiastical reform, and so blameless in his personal life that historians of the early Renaissance will one day describe him as saintly.

By the measures that should matter most he is an exceptional candidate. No one could find good grounds for complaining of his election, and his colleagues like the fact that he has been one of them for nearly a generation; many of them feel that, because the late Nicholas had entered the Sacred College mere months before his election, he never developed a proper respect for its importance.

Capranica has a problem all the same, and it proves to be disabling. He began his career as secretary to the Colonna pope Martin V—had been chosen for the post because of his exceptional abilities and outstanding promise—and because of this the Orsini early classified him as an enemy and always treated him accordingly. Over the years he and the Orsini clashed so often and so seriously that there can be no hope of his election in any conclave over which Latino Orsini holds veto power.

Capranica's cause being thus lost, Latino now puts forth his choice: Pietro Barbo, nephew of the Pope Eugenius IV who had died in 1447 (and who himself had been the nephew of a still earlier pope). Barbo is a fifteen-year veteran of the college in spite of being only thirty-eight years old, and though not as distinguished as Capranica, he is in no way unworthy of consideration. He has the support not only of the Orsini but of Venice and the king of Naples as well. But he too has no chance, and for reasons unrelated to anything he himself has ever said or done. The problem is his late uncle. When Eugenius made Barbo a cardinal at age twenty-three, he did so in Florence, and he was living in Florence because six years earlier he had fled Rome for his life, and his flight from Rome had become necessary when he tried to break the power of the Colonna and instead was overpowered.

The result was humiliation. Three years after his election Eugenius found himself disguised as a monk and floating downstream in a Tiber barge, cowering under a shield as wrathful Romans shouted their contempt and hurled stones, sticks, and rubbish down on him from the banks above. He found refuge in Florence, which welcomed him because its dominant family, the Medici, was closely affiliated with the Orsini, who were always happy to embrace an enemy of the Colonna.

Rome was ultimately retaken by force, not by Eugenius himself but by a commander of the papal army named Giovanni Vitelleschi, who was both a cardinal and one of the most savagely aggressive soldiers of the age. The leader of Rome's short-lived, Colonna-sponsored republic was dismembered alive by men wielding red-hot tongs, and the city was put under a military occupation designed to make resistance impossible and life intolerable for any Colonna foolish enough to remain. The provinces belonging to the papacy and known as the Papal States were ravaged as well, even the churches of towns disloyal to the exiled pope were razed, and the city of Palestrina, seat of one of the Colonna family's most powerful branches, was obliterated.

Pietro Barbo had nothing to do with any of this—it is unclear whether even his uncle the pope intended or approved the atrocities committed in his name—but in the eyes of the Colonna he is fatally tainted, absolutely and forever unworthy of trust. If in 1455 Prospero Colonna no longer has sufficient clout to stand as a credible candidate himself, he certainly remains capable of blocking the election of anyone suspected of being a danger to his clan. He is helped by Barbo's relative youth. Not without reason, cardinals tend to think it unwise to bestow the crown on someone who might possibly wear it for twenty or thirty years. In Barbo's case a forty-year reign would not be inconceivable.

With Capranica and Barbo eliminated, clearly a compromise is needed, one that Latino and Prospero will accept. Days are passing, and as the cardinals look about them for a solution, several find their attention fixing on an ecclesiastical anomaly. This is Basilios Bessarion, who with his compatriot Isidore of Kiev is one of two Greeks present at the conclave. Both began their careers in the Orthodox Church, rose high in the hierarchy at Constantinople, and in 1434 were appointed delegates to the Roman Church's Council of Basel, where they showed themselves to be strongly in favor of ending the centuries-old split between the Eastern and Western rites. In 1439, when the council was meeting in Florence, Bessarion and Isidore delighted the papal court and became traitors in the eyes of their Orthodox brethren by defecting to Rome. In short order they were made cardinals. Over the next decade and a half Bessarion won a reputation as one of Europe's leading humanists and promoters of the new learning, and as a man of solid competence and impeccable moral character. Also in his favor, in the opinion of many cardinals, are the appreciation of the Turkish threat that his Eastern origins have given him and his insistence that the West must respond forcefully.

But he too has no chance of election. The conclave's French members, no longer keeping silent because what is under discussion is no longer a strictly Italian quarrel, take the lead in complaining that Bessarion is an alien. They make much of the fact that, contrary to the conventions of the Sacred College, he continues, in the Byzantine fashion, to wear a long beard. Even those cardinals who most admire Bessarion find it necessary to agree that expecting him to rule Rome and its Church could end in nothing but calamity.

So . . . some *other* compromise has to be found. The cardinals, frustrated and weary and wanting to be set free, find it quickly. Find *him* quickly. The desire to be done with this tiresome business awakens them at last to the fact that there is in their midst a man of whom no one has a bad word to say. A man who, if not a champion of the new humanism in the manner of Capranica or Bessarion or Pope Nicholas, is an esteemed scholar nevertheless, with two doctorates in law and an international reputation as an authority on the subject.

A good man, untouched by scandal and known to all Rome for his sponsorship of hospitals, his generosity to the elderly and the poor, and the simplicity of his life.

A statesman too, with an impressive career behind him and decades spent at the right hand of one of the greatest kings in Europe.

A peacemaker of the first order, a key player in bringing the Western Schism to an end and settling a long conflict between Naples and Rome.

Known to be loyal to popes rather than councils, and to understand the Turkish threat.

Not greedy—not even ambitious.

And, what matters more in this deadlocked conclave, free of politics: unaffiliated with any of the Sacred College's factions after ten years as a member, so detached from the intrigues of the papal court that no one—no Orsini, no Colonna, no anyone—has reason to regard him with distrust.

And finally—what's best of all, the clincher—seventy-six years old and in declining health. It is inconceivable that he will live much longer. This makes him perfect.

And so when Cardinal Bessarion rises to his feet and declares in solemn tones that he is giving his vote to Alonso Borgia, his compeers all but fall over themselves in their haste to do the same. They do so with joyful relief, confident that they are settling on a man who will reign benignly, passively, and above all briefly, soon departing for the hereafter having distressed no one and changed nothing.

Little do they know.

THE ROAD TO ROME

IT IS CURIOUS THAT ALONSO DE BORJA CHOSE A LIFE IN THE Church. Being an only son of landowning parents, he must have been expected to marry, inherit his father's estate, and carry on the family name. That name carried considerable weight in the old kingdom of Valencia, where Alonso's life began. A hundred and forty years before his birth, when King Jaime of Aragon drove the Muslims out of Valencia, among the *conquistadores* in his army were eight men who called themselves de Borja. Possibly they, or some of them, were descended from an ancient family of that name. No less possibly, they just happened to be from the old Roman city of Borja near Zaragoza and had taken its name in the customary way.

The records show that one of Jaime's Borja soldiers was given responsibility for parceling out conquered lands in and around the Valencian town of Játiva, or Xátiva. He was generous with himself and his kinsmen. Their name became common among the gentry of the neighborhood. The estate of Torre del Canals, where Alonso was born on the last day of 1378, was neither the humblest nor the grandest of the numerous Borja households.

Through much of his long life Alonso was a lawyer more than a churchman, remaining in minor orders rather than being ordained a priest. He entered the University of Lérida at age fourteen, staying to earn doctorates in canon and civil law and in time becoming a lecturer. At age thirty he was a respected and respectable academic—not a whiff of scandal was ever attached to his name—but still a deeply obscure provincial. He was not an intellectual in any true sense of the term, showing no interest in the revival of classical learning that was sweeping across Europe early in the fifteenth century. By all accounts he was honest, hardworking, and able, but one searches in vain for evidence of a colorful personality.

At age thirty-seven, doubtless because of his legal expertise and the appointment he held as a canon of the local cathedral, Borja was chosen as the diocese of Lérida's representative at the Council of Constance. This assembly of the Church had been convened mainly to deal with the Great Schism, the split in Western Christendom that had begun in 1378 with the almost simultaneous election of two competing popes. (Considering the importance that the schism would play in Borja's life, it is an interesting coincidence that the two entered the world in the same year.) During the four years of its existence the council deposed two men judged to be "antipopes" because never legitimately elected, accepted the resignation of the claimant whose election was recognized as legitimate (he quit voluntarily in the interests of unity), and chose a single successor, the Colonna who became Martin V. This did not end the schism, however, because a Spaniard calling himself Benedict XIII refused to abandon his claim and was supported by the royal House of Aragon.

Though there is no evidence that Alonso de Borja participated in the council's debates—no evidence, even, that he attended any of its sessions—its actions presented him with vexing questions. As a loyal subject of Aragon and a junior member of its clergy, he had always been disposed to follow the lead of its rulers, and Benedict like himself was a respected legal scholar and above reproach in his personal life. That Benedict had been repudiated by a general council of the Church, however, was not to be shrugged off lightly. Further complications included the council's assertion, even as it made Martin V pope, that he was subject to it because councils were the highest authority in the Church, and Martin's rejoinder that he and not the council was supreme. The result was the greatest challenge to papal authority until the Reformation, which was still a century in the future. The uncertainty to which these disagreements gave rise was offensive to Borja's lawyerly mind and must be one reason why, at about this point, he began to express two convictions. First, that Church unity was the only alternative to chaos. Second, that unity was impossible if the pope was not supreme.

These beliefs were firmly in place when, in 1417, the fortyish Borja made his first visit to the court of the charismatic young Alfonso V, whose kingdom of Aragon had long since absorbed Valencia. Possibly he had been summoned to explain the decrees coming out of Constance; this would have been natural in light of the support that Alfonso and his father before him had extended to the Spanish antipopes, and the questions of law stirred up by the contest between the council and Martin V. Whatever the reason for the visit, it proved to be important in the king's life and the great turning point in Borja's.

Alfonso V at twenty-one was ruler not only of Aragon but of Sicily too. That was enough to make him as powerful as any monarch in Europe, and he was already launched upon the campaigns that would add Corsica and Sardinia to his empire. And he was glamorous as well as important. Short but strongly built, with a small hawklike nose and the penetrating gaze of a born predator, he had a grace and a flair for the theatrical gesture that would win him the honorific "Alfonso the Magnanimous." He was also intelligent and witty (happy marriage, he said, required that the wife be blind and the husband deaf) and radiated a sunny self-assurance. Clearly he saw something that he liked in the lawyer from Lérida, even if that lawyer was dry and cautious and nobody's idea of a man of action. Borja for his part must have been flattered to find himself attracting the interest of such a *kingly* young king, even one whose views were not entirely compatible with his own. When the visitor was offered employment at Alfonso's court, there can have been little hesitation. His whole life, his place in the world, was utterly transformed. In short order he was the king's secretary and principal counselor and therefore at the center of European affairs.

Alfonso no less than Borja faced delicate questions. Ridiculous as the current Spanish claimant to the papal crown might appear to be (he called himself Clement VIII and had been elected by three men whom Benedict XIII had proclaimed to be cardinals shortly before his death), he continued to be recognized by the House of Aragon, and a faint aura of prestige clung to him as a result. Though Alfonso stood to gain nothing by keeping the schism alive, abandoning a cause with which his family had long been identified would have been no simple step. If not taken carefully, it could look like an admission of failure. Alfonso had no tolerance for failure.

It fell to his new secretary to find a way forward. And so when in 1421 Alfonso arrived in Naples in response to Queen Joanna II's appeal for help in fending off a French attack—the childless and only dubiously sane queen had found the perfect way to recruit him, declaring him to be her heir—he immediately and at Borja's suggestion sent off a letter offering Pope Martin his friendship. He had every reason to expect a positive response. Martin, having recently returned the pontifical court to the Eternal City after many years of exile, seemed unlikely to want to continue an old and costly feud. He had barely begun the hard task of restoring order in Rome and the adjacent Papal States, and he was encountering enough opposition from the Orsini and others to need no trouble with Spain. Alonso de Borja, who had remained behind in Aragon as head of a council advising Queen Maria, her husband's regent, must have waited hopefully for word of a rapprochement—and been taken aback to learn that the pope had instead allied himself with Queen Joanna's enemy, the Frenchman Louis of Anjou, who claimed to be rightful king of Naples. Worse news followed: Alfonso had retaliated by reaffirming Clement VIII as pope. Borja's plan for reconciliation had come to nothing—had, if anything, made things worse. He had learned that the politics of Italy were too tricky to be managed, or even understood, from where he sat in Spain. Prudent lawyer that he was, he turned his attention to business closer to home and tried to keep it there.

Alfonso V meanwhile threw himself into a war for Naples that dragged on year after year. Its complexities and reversals would require a chapter of their own, and even then would be barely comprehensible. After two years of fighting, Joanna announced that Louis of Anjou, not Alfonso, was now her heir, and therefore her erstwhile rescuer was now an interloper and a foe. As the advantage shifted sporadically from side to side, it began to seem that the bloodshed might continue forever. Atrocities and outrages became almost commonplace. Mercenaries in Louis's service, having killed Alfonso's beloved brother Pedro with a lucky shot, celebrated their success by firing his corpse out of a cannon. When in 1423 Alfonso had to return to Spain to deal with an outbreak of hostilities between another brother, Juan king of Navarre, and his brother-in-law Juan king of Castile, he interrupted his voyage to pay a call on Marseilles, the capital of the House of Anjou. He tried twice to set it afire and both times was foiled by rain. He declared that if it happened a third time, he would accept failure as God's will and move on, but there was no more rain, and Alfonso had the rare satisfaction of reducing a major city to ashes before weighing anchor and continuing on his way.

He was still in Spain when, a year later, news of the defeat of his army in Naples and the killing of its commander had an improving effect on his view of the situation. He decided that fighting a pope who had the support of most of Europe and insisting on the legitimacy of a powerless and largely forgotten Spaniard were never going to get him anywhere, and that a fresh approach was in order. Alonso de Borja agreed heartily— had long, in fact, been suggesting a change of course. He appealed to the king not by invoking Church unity, which was unlikely to matter greatly to an energetic young monarch bent on conquest, but by pointing to the practical advantages of getting the pope to endorse his claim to Naples. There was nothing to be lost, and so the king freed his secretary to see what diplomacy might accomplish.

It accomplished great things. Negotiations began, the pope was receptive, and a tentative settlement was worked out. Martin conceded, somewhat obliquely, that Alfonso just might have a valid claim to Naples. Borja, and through him Alfonso, acknowledged that Martin just might be the true pope. Building on this, in 1429 Borja went to the trouble of seeking out Antipope Clement at his hideaway in the remote Valencian town of Peníscola. There, offering as inducement the bishopric of Palma on the island of Mallorca, he persuaded Clement to make submission to Rome. With this, the royal House of Aragon abandoned its long repudiation of the Roman popes, king and pontiff were reconciled, and after almost half a century the Great Schism was at an end at last. A grateful pope announced Borja's appointment as bishop of Valencia. This must have been deeply gratifying: Valencia was not only one of Spain's richest sees but the Borja family's home diocese. The appointment raised the Borja name to an eminence never before achieved, and it made Alonso a hero to his relatives. Among these relatives were his widowed sister and her children, who took up residence in Valencia's grand episcopal palace. In order to become bishop, he had to take a step he had until now neglected: have himself ordained a priest.

The leaders of the Council of Constance had been ready to adjourn since 1418, but they feared that by disbanding they would free the pope to repudiate everything they had done. As a preventive measure they decreed that a new council must be convened after five years, with another seven years after that, and others every ten years thereafter. Pope Martin, though no friendlier to councils than his predecessors had been and his successors would be, found it impossible to avoid calling one in 1423. This new assembly, however, was so paralyzed by political divisions as to be unable to act. It accomplished little beyond reaffirming the supremacy of councils and scheduling another gathering for the Swiss city of Basel in 1431.

Martin died early in 1431 and was succeeded by the wealthy and handsomely aristocratic Cardinal Gabriele Condulmer of Venice, who became Eugenius IV. He was only forty-seven, some six years younger than the fledgling bishop of Valencia. Devoid of political experience and gifts, almost from the first day of his reign he began committing blunders. Ultimately, as we saw earlier, he so undermined his own position as to be obliged to depart Rome under a barrage of sticks and stones.

After years in exile, an exasperated Eugenius excommunicated everyone associated with Basel and called for an alternative assembly to convene at Ferrara. In response, the council denounced him as a heretic and voted to depose him. As replacement, it elected a new antipope, the onetime duke of Savoy, who had taken holy orders after the death of his wife and now styled himself Felix V. In all this the council was supported by the duke of Milan and, to the chagrin of Alonso de Borja, by Alfonso V. Everything the bishop had accomplished late in the reign of Martin V was thus in ruins, and disorder seemed to be spreading by the day. Fate almost seemed to be mocking him for attaching such importance to unity and a strong papacy.

When Alfonso V returned to Italy and took up once again the war for Naples, he brought Borja with him. Unhappy with almost everything that was happening, the bishop nevertheless continued the management of his master's affairs and undertook a reform of the judicial system in the territories Alfonso controlled. Among his responsibilities was overseeing the education of Alfonso's illegitimate son Ferdinand, who was in his early teens. This boy, known as Ferrante, was already a significant figure because his father's marriage to the sickly and sadly unattractive Princess Maria of Castile had produced no offspring. Alfonso, resigned to the fact that when he died most of his sprawling empire would be inherited by his brother Juan or Juan's son Ferdinand, was becoming obsessed with the thought that the great kingdom of Naples, if he could win it, should go to Ferrante. Meanwhile Borja was getting to know Ferrante and forming an opinion of the boy's character that would have consequences in years to come.

The bishop refused to conceal his disapproval of the king's friendliness toward the Council of Basel and its antipope. When Alfonso appointed him envoy to Basel, he took the astonishing step of refusing to go. When Eugenius ordered the council to move to Florence and some of the delegates obeyed while others remained defiantly in Basel, Borja signaled his support of the pope by going to Florence in person, possibly without the king's approval. It is testimony to how much Alfonso valued the bishop's services that he retained him as chief minister in spite of their differences on such a painfully divisive question.

The war for Naples appeared to have ended in disaster for Alfonso when, in the mid-1430s, another lost battle caused him to become the prisoner of Milan's vicious Duke Filippo Maria Visconti, a supporter of Louis of Anjou and always an eager troublemaker. Almost miraculously, considering that to fall into the sadistic Filippo Maria's hands often meant either a gruesome death or lifelong imprisonment under unspeakable conditions, Alfonso talked the duke into releasing him. He did so by arguing—his success shows the force of his personality—that it would be better for Milan if he became king of Naples and the Angevins were expelled.

Alfonso's release marked a turning point in his fortunes. When in 1442 he finally crushed his Angevin rivals and sent them scurrying back to France, the way was cleared for the resolution of an array of long-festering issues. By the time he entered the city of Naples, the Council of Basel had lost all credibility. Though it remained in session, even Felix V had tired of its sterile debates and departed. With both council and antipope reduced to near-irrelevance, Alfonso V (now Alfonso I of Naples as well) and Pope Eugenius were free to turn their attention to each other. What they saw—what Alonso de Borja encouraged them to understand—was that they had more to gain by coming to terms than by continuing their dispute. Because Naples was recognized by all Europe as a papal fief, no one could legitimately rule it without the approval of—without being formally invested in it by—the Roman pontiff. Alfonso would never be accepted as its king until some pope recognized him as such, the sooner the better. Felix, from Geneva, offered to do the investing, but he had so little standing by this time that the suggestion could not be taken seriously.

Eugenius for his part would be denying reality if he refused to accept the Aragonese conquest of Naples. Nothing could come of that but more years of trouble. All the elements needed for agreement were obviously in place, and so negotiations got under way with Borja once again representing the king. By the terms of the resulting Treaty of Terracina, Alfonso recognized Eugenius as pope and received investiture as king of Naples. For the second time in a decade and a half, Alonso de Borja had reunited the Western Church. Eugenius felt it safe to return to Rome, which during his years of exile had sunk into a wretched state of lawlessness.

Pope and king embarked upon a political honeymoon. In 1444 the grateful Eugenius made Borja a cardinal and presbyter of the church of Santi Quattro Coronati on Rome's Coelian Hill. He did so not in response to any appeal from Alfonso V or as a political favor to Naples but in recognition of Borja's services to the Church. That same year, assenting to something that his new royal friend desired almost as urgently as he had wanted Naples, Eugenius legitimated the twenty-one-year-old Ferrante. Alfonso celebrated this as a coup, one that opened the way for Ferrante to succeed him on the throne of Naples. Cardinal Borja was not the only legal scholar to find this a dubious proposition; there were old and widespread doubts about whether legitimization brought with it a right of succession.

In 1445 Borja took up residence in Rome. Presumably he was expected to serve as Alfonso's representative at the papal court, but it is likely that he felt he had done quite enough for an insatiably ambitious king and was weary of being asked to untangle his affairs. In any case, once settled in an old palace in a quiet quarter between the ruins of the Colosseum and the almost as ancient Basilica of St. John Lateran, he showed less interest in political matters than in his gardens. The only issue that could still draw him out was the old, perennially unresolved question of papal authority. When a dispute between the Vatican and the German Church was settled toward the end of Eugenius's life, Borgia (as his name was now spelled in Rome) was one of only two cardinals to complain that too much had been conceded that rightfully belonged to the pope. For the most part he lived the life of a retired and beneficent dignitary, a patron of charitable institutions rather than of artists, architects, and scholars. As a Spaniard he was very much an outsider, but he seems to have been content with that. He kept to the margins of Roman society, staffing his residence with countrymen from Spain and opening it, unenthusiastically on the whole, to the relatives who were migrating to Italy in the hope that having a kinsman who was a cardinal could put opportunities in their path.

When in February 1447 Eugenius IV died at age sixty-two, Borgia was already sixty-eight. And though he now was, because a cardinal, eligible for election, at no point in that year's conclave was he mentioned as a possible candidate. Nor does he appear to have taken any significant part in the politicking, even when the Orsini-Colonna deadlock made it impossible for either family's candidate to be chosen. The winner who ultimately emerged, the famously brilliant Cardinal Tommaso Parentu-celli, was only forty-nine years old, young enough to be Borgia's son. Though small and oddly shriveled in appearance, with tiny dark birdlike eyes, the new Pope Nicholas was in good enough health, lived simply, and had great plans both for the papacy and for the city of Rome. There could have seemed little possibility that the elderly Cardinal Borgia would live to see another conclave, and no possibility at all that he would ever be in contention for the papal crown.

2

Surprises,
Disappointments, Hope

There is reason to surmise that one man only may have been less than flabbergasted by Cardinal Alonso Borgia's elevation to the pontifical throne, and that the man in question was Alonso himself.

This possibility arises out of virtually the only interesting story about Alonso's early life to have come down to us—a tale that must have some sort of basis in fact, because Alonso himself appears to have believed it.

According to this story, at some point in his boyhood Alonso crossed paths with a famous holy man and preacher named Vincente Ferrer, a Spanish friar descended through his father from Scottish nobility. That such an encounter took place is in no way implausible. Ferrer, famous for working wonders and for converting huge numbers of Jews using methods that would raise eyebrows in later centuries, was a celebrated figure in Valencia in the late fourteenth century, attracting crowds wherever he appeared. He also took a doctorate in theology at the same University of Lérida where Alonso would later study and teach law.

Be all that as it may, upon meeting Alonso, Ferrer is supposed to have declared that the child would one day achieve "the highest authority which mortal man can obtain"—words that any educated European of the time would have understood as referring to the papacy. Alonso is said to have taken the prophecy to heart, and to have waited serenely for its fulfillment as men younger and still younger than himself were elected instead. All we know with certainty is that, as one of his first acts after becoming Pope Calixtus III, he saw to it that Vincente Ferrer was canonized. Today a handsome church on the Upper East Side of Manhattan bears his name.

Calixtus's reign got off to a fast start. It was also a rocky start: on the day of the new pope's coronation, packs of toughs affiliated with the Orsini and the Colonna roamed the streets of Rome claiming to be offended that a "Catalan" had become pope, looking for opportunities to make trouble. They so disrupted one procession that the aged pontiff was nearly thrown from his horse. The trouble was worst, predictably, wherever rival prowling gangs collided. It rose to a fever pitch when the chief of the Bracciano branch of the Orsini, Napoleone by name, tried to use the growing disorder to take revenge on an old foe. By the time the papal retinue with its eighty bishops all dressed in white had moved past the ruins of the Forum and the Colosseum and reached the Basilica of St. John Lateran, it was inching its way through something between a full-blown riot and a miniature war. Houses were being looted and set on fire. Onlookers were being attacked, even killed.

The former Alonso Borgia, a man known for nothing so much as for being "peaceable and kindly," the dark-horse candidate who had been made pope precisely because none of his fellow cardinals could imagine him interfering in their affairs, turned to the proud and powerful Cardinal Latino Orsini, who as it happened was Napoleone's brother, and ordered him to control his family. *Now. Or else.* Order was restored, the pope had put his mark on his first day in office with a forcefulness he had rarely if ever displayed in Rome, and the Orsini had been given a foretaste of the half-century of Borgia difficulties that lay in store for them.

That was nothing compared to the surprises that followed, and the speed with which Calixtus began producing them. His health so poor that on many mornings he was unable to get out of bed, he nevertheless began drawing upon previously unsuspected reserves of energy—and upon a long agenda of things he was determined to accomplish. He summoned secretaries to his bedside one after another, gave them instructions or dictated letters and bulls in a seemingly endless flow, and sent them bustling off on a bewildering variety of missions. At the center of this whirlwind, overshadowing everything else, was a subject to which Calixtus's predecessor Nicholas V had paid the necessary lip service but rarely given real priority: the Turks.

By the time of Calixtus III's election, the Turks had been in Europe for more than a century. With the exception of a brief period around 1400, when Mongol hordes swept through the Middle East on a vast raid that threw everything into disorder until the invaders abruptly turned around and galloped back to eastern Asia, the Ottoman armies were as voracious and seemingly unstoppable as a plague of locusts. By stages they devoured so much of the old Byzantine Christian Empire that at midcentury almost nothing remained of it except the capital, Constantinople, enfeebled almost to the point of helplessness.

Sultan Mehmed II, only twenty-three when Calixtus became pope but already as feared as anyone then living, was a worthily warlike link in a chain of land-hungry fathers and sons whose empire would ultimately encompass substantial parts of three continents and last more than six hundred years. His forefathers had emerged in the thirteenth century as heads of one of the ten or so little principalities that came to dot Anatolia (in what is now Turkey) as the Eastern Christian Empire lost its grip there. The dynasty that would take its name from the second man to head it, the emir Osman I, was consistently both more aggressive and more successful than its neighbors and began absorbing them one by one. Osman's grandson Murad I achieved such eminence that by the 1370s he was minting his own coins and using the title "sultan"—a word connoting sovereignty, and religious as well as political authority.

Mehmed II was Murad I's great-grandson, and by the time of his birth in 1432 the unique phenomenon that was Ottoman culture was pretty much fully formed. Among the striking features of that culture were a pervasive and remarkably creative use of slavery, polygamy on an epic scale, royal fratricide as government policy, and ingenious ways of controlling subject populations vastly more numerous than the Turks themselves. Slavery, so integral to the empire that at its zenith one in every five residents of Constantinople was officially in bondage, took such novel forms under the sultans that it became a major source of their strength. Osman I and his descendants made the improbable discovery that prisoners of war, especially the youngest of them, could be turned not only into useful fighting men but into fiercely loyal ones.

This led to the creation of a system for recruiting talent on a massive scale through systematic abduction. Every five years the sultan's troops would scour his Christian domains (Serbia and Bulgaria, for example, and the Greek communities of Anatolia), round up thousands of boys between ten and perhaps fifteen years of age, select the strongest and brightest, and carry them off. They would be lodged with Turkish families long enough to learn the language and receive basic instruction in Islam, and then be placed on the bottom rungs of career ladders leading to the most powerful positions in the army and navy, the imperial bureaucracy, and municipal and provincial government. Legally these youngsters remained slaves, but they were slaves with far more opportunities than most of the supposedly free people of the time. Eventually the empire came to be managed mainly by men whose careers had begun with their being stolen from their parents. They could be considered slaves only in the sense of being—like everyone else in the empire—absolutely subject to the will of the sultan.

This system didn't merely work, it worked brilliantly. The harvesting of children gave the Turks a force of so-called janissaries that was one of the wonders of the age: not only the first large-scale standing army to be seen in Europe since classical times, but the first recognizably modern army. The janissaries were salaried, wore uniforms, lived in barracks, marched in time to music, and were trained to a level of discipline and efficiency that had no equal elsewhere. They also became great innovators, pioneers, for example, in the use of muskets and artillery. (The walls of Constantinople, during the siege that ended in the city's fall, were reduced to rubble by huge stone balls fired from the Turks' twenty-six-foot cannons, the doomsday weapons of their time.) What was perhaps most improbable, janissaries were as a rule almost fanatically faithful to their masters. And why not? The most talented and ambitious of them could achieve high rank at an early age and all the good things that success brought with it.

The Turks trafficked in women as well—they would continue to do so into the twentieth century—but the world of their female slaves was vastly more limited than that of the janissaries. The capture of young women was one of the primary objectives of the sultan's troops when they went plundering, and their raids on foreign territory yielded bountiful supplies of salable flesh. The most attractive girls naturally came into the possession of senior officers, who in turn would pass some of them further up the chain of command until a tiny minority were selected for the sultan's harem. Thus was perpetuated perhaps the most peculiar characteristic of the Ottoman dynasty: the fact that it was not a family at all in any ordinary sense, but a line of men who had, instead of queens, platoons of women whom they owned and who lived as their pampered prisoners.

Infidelity was made impossible for these women by another famous feature of the sultan's Topkapi palace: a harem guard force made up of black African slaves who, because their sexual organs had been removed, could not cuckold the monarch. Because Islamic law forbade castration, the Turks purchased these eunuchs as children from such places as Ethiopia, Abyssinia, and Sudan, where slave traders were happy to perform the necessary alterations. The palace also employed white eunuchs drawn from European sources, but these were used in administrative functions rather than as harem guards. Eunuchs, like janissaries, sometimes became the most powerful officials in the empire.

The claustrophobic world of the harem, and the inhabitants' competition for the attention of the sultan, made it a hotbed of vicious intrigue. The first harem girl to present the sultan with a son, whether before or after he inherited the throne, became by doing so the mother of the imperial heir. This gave her superiority over her harem-mates no matter how lofty their origins—and not a few were daughters of conquered rulers—or how many sons they ultimately produced. The true ruler of the harem, however, was always the sultan's mother. She was empowered, among other things, to order the execution of her son's women if she deemed this advisable. She could also, if her son was weak or more interested in self-indulgence than in the duties of his office, become de facto ruler of the empire. Obviously this was a recipe for trouble, producing in every generation a huge supply of surplus younger sons whose frustrated and jealous mothers encouraged their resentments. The results, predictably dire, included rebellion and warfare among the sons of deceased sultans.

Mehmed II, the conqueror of Constantinople and disturber of the peace of Calixtus III, was the son of a sultan who had had to defeat and kill an uncle and a younger brother in order to make himself secure on the throne. Mehmed's grandfather too had had to fight his own brothers to the death in order to become sultan, his great-grandfather had ordered the strangulation of a younger brother to nip trouble in the bud, and so on back through the generations. This grim history prompted Mehmed to institute a practice that would persist for centuries: whenever a new sultan took the throne, his younger brothers and half-brothers were put to death. As time passed this answer to the succession problem would be refined in grisly ways. It would become customary for the pregnant members of a dead sultan's harem to be bundled together in sacks and dropped into the sea. The survivors, whether young or old, spent the rest of their lives in celibate confinement.

Mehmed was often a good deal less savage in dealing with his Christian subjects than with his own relatives. As continued conquests caused the Turkish portion of the empire's population to be numerically overwhelmed by Christians, he found it advantageous to extend a degree of toleration that was unusual for the time but not without cost to the beneficiaries. He heavily taxed the Christians—almost all of them members of the Orthodox rather than the Roman Church—in return for allowing them to retain their clergy. And of course they were expected to submit without question to the Islamic political regime.

The bitter division that separated the Roman and Orthodox churches abetted the Ottomans in expanding their frontiers. It had begun with the unspeakable savagery with which the Fourth Crusade, organized for the purpose of retaking Jerusalem, sacked Constantinople instead and then made it the seat of a short-lived Latin empire. Then came the failure of the West to come to the assistance of the Byzantines when they stood on the brink of destruction, and the willingness of some Western powers to prey on Constantinople themselves. Against this background, and however much it may have baffled and infuriated Calixtus III and others in Rome, it is not really surprising that Orthodox Christians such as the Bulgarians and the Serbs sometimes sided with the Ottoman sultan rather than with the Christian West.

But it is also not surprising, considering the seriousness of the threat, that stopping the advance of the Ottoman Empire into Europe became the defining purpose of Calixtus's papacy, practically his reason for existing. The first need was for ships—galleys—with which to engage the seagoing forces of the sultan. Naval engineering in the mid-fifteenth century was remarkably unchanged from what it had been two thousand years before. Across all the centuries since the time of Pericles the state-of-the-art warship had remained the trireme, a long, narrow vessel of shallow draft propelled by three banks of oars on each side, as many as 150 oars in all, each powered by a single crewman. In short bursts these galleys could skim forward at great speed, and in all navies the basic tactic was to grapple with enemy vessels, board them, and butcher their crews. The first sailing ships capable of tacking into the wind were still decades in the future, and even after they appeared, galleys would remain dominant in the Mediterranean for another century.

Before he had been in office a month Calixtus was hiring galleys and crews wherever they could be found, asking the Italian powers and the crowned heads of the north to contribute their fleets to the cause, and turning Rome's Ripa Grande embankment into an enormous bustling shipyard. Craftsmen brought to Rome for the purpose were laying down the keels of all the new galleys for which space could be found. The papal treasury or camera, restored to solvency by Nicholas V, was again emptied to make this possible. Calixtus's lifestyle, always simple, was now imposed on the Vatican's entire establishment and staff. Spending for nonmilitary purposes was slashed almost in half, largely by slowing or halting Martin V's construction projects and reducing the number of scholars and artists employed at the Vatican. The displaced men complained that this was what came of electing a foreign pope, a barbarian of low tastes and rude values, but Calixtus was undeterred. The books in the Vatican library, though not sold off, were stripped of their gold and silver bindings and jeweled adornments. Possessions ranging from country estates to Nicholas's silver service went on the auction block. Plain earthenware was all that he required, the pope declared. He set May 1, 1456, just under a year off, as the day on which the new fleet would embark, and in the course of that year he spent 150,000 ducats on the preparations.

All the resources of the Vatican were not going to suffice, however. Calixtus dictated appeals to the rich and powerful in every corner of Europe; the pontifical archives contain thirty volumes of these messages, which relays of legates carried to their addressees. Churches everywhere were instructed to ring their bells daily to remind the faithful to pray for the success of the crusade. (This would become the Angelus, the universal and still-practiced ringing of church bells every day at noon.) Tithes were imposed on ecclesiastical revenues, collections were taken up among the laity, and rulers were urged to put aside their disputes and focus on saving Christendom from being overrun. Preachers offered indulgences—release from punishment in the hereafter—to all who contributed the prescribed amounts of support.

The response was rarely what Calixtus hoped. Throughout Europe the very idea of crusades had grown tiresome. The glory of the first crusade more than 350 years earlier, with its expulsion of the Muslims from Jerusalem and the establishment of a Christian kingdom there, had been followed by eight subsequent expeditions that cumulatively produced little except defeat, disgrace, and tragic loss. Two centuries of sacrifice ended not only with the surrender of everything that had been gained in the beginning but with such horrors as the Children's Crusade (during which thousands of young volunteers disappeared into slavery in the East) and the sacking of Christian Constantinople by invaders from the West.

The crusading ideal had been further degraded by popes who abused it to make war on political enemies close to home. By 1455 such things were a fading memory, but not a happy one. For most Catholic Christians, who had never seen a Turk, the Ottoman conquests in the eastern Mediterranean were remote to the point of seeming not quite real. Outright hostility to the pope's appeals was rare except in Germany, where resentment lingered about the great sums sent to Rome in the past to pay for crusades that never happened. Not many of the pope's envoys encountered the kind of anger that erupted when one of their number tried to sell Calixtus's crusade to a congregation gathered in Cologne Cathedral—he was sent running for his life—but not many were received with enthusiasm either. Stony indifference was the usual reaction.

Nor did Calixtus get what he wanted from the rulers. In England, where King Henry VI had just emerged from one of his bouts of catatonic insanity, the Wars of the Roses were just heating up, and not even many churchmen cared about what was happening in Italy and beyond. Charles VII of France promised thirty warships but then decided to keep them at home for use against the English. The fearsome soldier

Francesco Sforza, having made himself master of Milan only a year before, declined even to pretend to be interested in putting either his own skills or the resources of his duchy at the pope's disposal. Though Venice above all had reason to fear the expanding reach of the Turks, as usual it was pursuing its own priorities in its own arcane ways and was unable to view the other Western powers as potential allies rather than as rivals.

But the odium that today attaches to the word *crusade* notwithstanding, the danger was clear and present, the need for action urgent. From Constantinople the Turks were pushing deeper into the Balkan peninsula, bearing down on Greece, and impinging upon the sea routes that had long brought wealth to Italy. It is testimony to Calixtus's understanding of the magnitude of the crisis, and the energy with which he responded despite his feeble health, that he had a first squadron of galleys ready for deployment by September 1455, barely five months after his election. He ordered this squadron to station itself south of Sicily, where its assignment was to intercept any Turkish moves into the western Mediterranean and against Rome while the main fleet was still under construction there. But the entire exercise was turned into a disaster and a humiliation by the squadron's commander, Pietro Urrea, bishop of Tarragon. Calixtus found himself deluged with complaints that Urrea was operating as nothing better than a pirate, using the vessels entrusted to him to plunder Christian shipping. If Urrea had been selected for command because like Calixtus he was a Spaniard, the pope had made a mistake that would have painful ramifications.

Hope was to be found in one place only—in Naples, whose king, Calixtus's onetime master Alfonso of Aragon, appeared to be the one happy exception to the indifference and cynicism that pervaded all of Europe. Alfonso not only promised a fleet of galleys but actually assembled one. The pope's agents reported that this fleet lay at anchor in the Bay of Naples, ready to join the new Roman fleet as soon as it deployed. A hard blow against the Turks seemed possible after all.

IL REGNO—*THE* KINGDOM

THE FIRST THING TO UNDERSTAND ABOUT NAPLES AND ITS place in the story of the Borgias is that it was not then what it is today. Its name did not stand for a city only—ancient and vibrant and fascinating, but just a city all the same—but for a kingdom covering almost the whole southern half of the Italian peninsula. Until France proved otherwise when a second Borgia pope sat on the throne of St. Peter, Naples was believed to rank among the leading powers not only of Italy but of all Europe.

Its stature is evident in the willingness of no less a figure than Alfonso V, already the ruler of Aragon and a number of the greatest Mediterranean islands including Sicily, to devote much of his life to making himself Alfonso I of Naples as well.

Alfonso was motivated in part by the thought—he was not the first to have it—that possession of Naples would position him for further and greater gains, possibly even mastery of all Italy and the extension of his empire eastward toward Asia. Hence the price he was willing to pay to continue his campaign for Naples, and the risks he was willing to take.

Naples had always been such a great prize that there was nothing remotely unique about the three decades of struggle that culminated in Alfonso's victory. To the contrary, his long war was only the most recent in an almost uninterrupted series of conflicts that had been soaking southern Italy in blood since the fall of the Roman Empire. Nor could there be anything astonishing, for anyone who knew the Naples story, in the way that Alfonso's success, rather than leaving him satisfied, inflamed his hunger for *more*. He was the third Neapolitan king in two centuries not only to want all of Italy but to appear to have a real chance of getting it. The threat that he posed to his neighbors to the north, to Rome and Florence and even faraway Venice and Milan, was a natural function of the power of his new kingdom—or of its perceived power, at any rate. When combined not only with the great island of Sicily but with Alfonso's other possessions in the Mediterranean, and with his

Spanish domains as well, the crown of Naples made him a terrifying force.

It also, not incidentally, gave him one of the world's oldest and greatest capital cities, the largest in all Europe in the fifteenth century with a population that can only be estimated but was well in excess of a hundred thousand. Naples was so old that its origins were Greek rather than Italian—it began as Neapolis or New City, one of the main strongpoints of the adventurers who colonized southern Italy before the rise of Rome and called it Greater Greece. Over the ensuing millennia Naples had seen not only rulers and dynasties but whole civilizations rise and fade away. It saw no reason to think itself inferior to Italy's other leading states, Rome included. Its people are not likely to have been greatly impressed with the arrival of the Spaniard Alfonso V, or to have felt particularly honored by his decision to make Naples, rather than Sicily or Corsica or Sardinia or Aragon itself, the capital of his empire. The choice would have seemed merely natural. Neither is it likely that the Neapolitans gave Alfonso much chance of having any more success, or making a more lasting impact, than the kings who had ruled them before him. They had watched them all come, and watched them all go.

In the years following the collapse of the Roman Empire, Naples had fallen into the hands of that branch of the invading northern barbarians known as the Ostrogoths. In the sixth century it became an outpost of Constantinople, in the eighth a duchy subject to the popes in Rome, and in the ninth an independent entity much troubled both by outside enemies and internal contests for power.

In the eleventh century, at nearly the same time the nobles of Normandy were invading England under William the Conqueror, other Norman warriors were moving to southern Italy to take up employment as soldiers for hire. By the twelfth, having awakened to the fact that they were more powerful than their employers, these Normans took control of both Sicily and Naples and joined them in a single kingdom. Their regime became the most impressive in all of western Europe, north or south, with a court unrivaled in culture and magnificence. It was under the Normans, as the historian Benedetto Croce observed, that southern Italy gave rise to "the state as a work of art."

The Norman kings gave way in the mid-twelfth century to the Hohenstaufen dynasty from Swabia in Germany. Generation after generation, this remarkable family produced such epic figures as Frederick Barbarossa and his grandson Frederick II, called in his own time Stupor Mundi, the Wonder of the World. These men spent their lives in Sicily and Naples, neglecting their home base in the north, and their rising power brought them into conflict with the popes in Rome. Fear of Frederick II caused Pope Urban IV to invite Charles of Anjou, brother of King Louis IX of France, to come to Italy and take charge of his war with the Hohenstaufen. After a long struggle during which he was excommunicated four times, Frederick was finally bested in battle and politically destroyed. In 1266, after Charles of Anjou finished off the Hohenstaufen by defeating and killing Frederick's illegitimate son Manfred, Pope Innocent IV crowned him Charles I of Naples.

France and the other future great kingdoms of the north being still backward, fragmented, and weak, Charles's coronation vaulted him into the first rank of European monarchs. He was able to dictate the outcome of papal elections, and he aspired to more than that. He had acquired Provence through marriage, made himself king of Albania by conquest, and was planning to reconstitute the onetime Latin empire in the eastern Mediterranean when, in 1282, the bloody phenomenon known as the Sicilian Vespers brought his ambitions to an end. This was a plot to expel the Angevins from Sicily, and it turned into a massacre of the island's French population. By the time Charles died three years later, Sicily had become the property of Aragon in Spain, and he, though still king of Naples, was a spent force.

Though Angevin rule continued through the fourteenth century and nearly half of the fifteenth, it brought nothing but conflict and disorder. Partly because of the legacy of the Norman and German and French invaders, partly too because Naples had no major cities other than its capital and therefore almost no urban middle class, what emerged was a feudal society on the northern European model, one more dominated by hereditary landholding barons than any of the other major Italian states. In all of mainland Italy it was the only state whose ruler had royal status, causing it to become known as Il Regno—*The* Kingdom. As in the territories near Rome, here too the power of the barons became a chronic source of instability. Charles I's heirs were barely able to hold together their inheritance and could not have done so without the *fisc*— the financial tribute that the barons owed to the king as overlord. In the fourteenth century the barons, a wild and unruly lot under any circumstances (Machiavelli would describe them as "men inimical to any kind of civilization"), became completely uncontrollable. The weak rulers of the time had no choice but to grant them repeated concessions and yield to their escalating demands. The result was mayhem on a grand scale and a draining away of Naples's importance in international affairs.

In 1382 Charles I's great-great-grandson Charles, who thanks to the dynastic maneuvers of his ancestors was king of Hungary, murdered his much-married but childless cousin Queen Joanna I of Naples and seized her throne. Four years later he was succeeded by his son Ladislas, who needed until the end of the century to consolidate his control and then set about to reestablish Naples as a major power. Though often irresponsible in his management of Il Regno's internal affairs, selling favors to the barons to raise the money with which to finance his campaigns of conquest, he was relentless in encroaching on his neighbors to the north. The conditions of the time favored his ambitions: this was the period of the Great Schism, so that a weakened papacy was unable to maintain control over its Italian territories, and Milan too had been temporarily enfeebled by the premature death of its duke. Ladislas made himself dominant in central Italy. He might have done so in the north as well if he had not died at age fifty-eight. He had been preparing fresh conquests when his health suddenly failed.

Ladislas's successor was the climactic Angevin disaster, his sister Joanna II. Like the first Joanna she was childless, and her willingness to hand power over to various lovers contributed to making her two decades on the throne yet another period of violence and confusion. We saw earlier how she made Alfonso of Aragon her heir and invited him to move to Naples and help her fend off her Angevin cousins, then changed course and declared successive Angevins to be her heirs instead, thereby ensuring that her death would be followed by continued war for the crown.

When the popes returned to Rome, it became their policy to do everything possible to keep Naples weak. We have seen how Eugenius IV, in order to secure Aragonese support of his claim to be sole legitimate pope, departed from this policy by recognizing Alfonso as king of Naples.

It was a fair enough trade, justified by the circumstances and offering significant benefits to pope and king alike. But it was also dangerous, and its long-term consequences would be momentous. By granting Naples to a strong, capable, and ambitious king who already ruled much of the western Mediterranean, Eugenius's recognition of Alfonso made Il Regno as powerful as it had ever been, thus setting the stage for generations of further conflict.

3

Pope and King,
Friends No More

In May 1456, meeting the deadline that Calixtus had set a year earlier, a Christian war fleet made up of sixteen newly built triremes set forth from the papal port at Ostia, where the Tiber enters the sea some twenty miles downstream from Rome. In command was Cardinal Ludovico Trevisano, known as Scarampo and, as it happened, the same ferocious prelate who, a decade and a half before, had so thoroughly subdued the Papal States and the city of Rome as to make it possible for Pope Eugenius IV to return from exile. By this time Scarampo, vastly rich thanks to the booty from his campaigns, had for some years been peaceably occupied as chamberlain at the papal court. It is not surprising that a man of his aggressive temperament was eager for a return to action.

He sailed first for Naples, where he expected to be joined by Alfonso V's fleet and perhaps by Bishop Urrea's wayward squadron as well. He found no one waiting for him, however, because by then the king's and Urrea's ships had joined forces and sailed off to the north, launching an unprovoked attack on the city-state of Genoa. Not only would Naples not be contributing to Calixtus's crusade, therefore, but Genoa, which Alfonso regarded as an obstacle to the expansion of his empire, was now out of the picture as well. Scarampo had no choice but to embark for the East alone. Calixtus, when he learned what had happened, took King Alfonso's actions as not only a violation of Naples's responsibilities as a member of the Italian League but as a personal betrayal.

Alfonso was emerging as second only to the Turkish sultan as an obstacle to the fulfillment of Calixtus's hopes, and the relationship between him and the pope was turning venomous. But the king too felt betrayed: Calixtus, far from being the compliant tool of Naples that Alfonso had expected and others had feared, was proving to be entirely his own man and showed no inclination to take direction from anyone, Spanish or Italian or otherwise. The two were clashing not only over war against the Turks but across a wide array of issues. In the very month that Scarampo's fleet disappeared over the horizon, Calixtus found it necessary to use thousands of his desperately needed ducats to pay off a mercenary chieftain named Jacopo Piccinino, to get him to break off a siege of Siena that had disrupted the peace in Tuscany. Along the way the pope discovered that from the start, Piccinino had been acting with Alfonso's encouragement and support. It was another violation of the Italian League, and another betrayal.

It must by this time have seemed to Calixtus that he could expect nothing from those whose help he needed except disappointment and double-dealing. Even the captain-general of the papal forces, one Giovanni Ventimiglia, turned out to be a traitor. He had somehow contrived to get himself taken prisoner just as he stood at the threshold of victory over Piccinino, who was thus able to escape with his forces intact.

It is understandable that Alfonso found it difficult to accept that his onetime secretary, whom he had lifted out of obscurity and put on the path to the papacy, was now his liege lord. The fact that he, proud head of the greatest family in Spain, was obliged as king of Naples to pay a vassal's obeisance to a mere Borja of Játiva must have seemed a violation of the natural order. To be defied by this same Borja must have seemed an outrage. Frustrated and indignant, Alfonso clearly thought himself justified in stirring up trouble not only in Tuscany and Genoa but in the pope's own territories. He continued to meddle in the Papal States, encouraging the local barons in their habitual defiance of Rome's authority. He saw the Orsini in particular as a conduit through which to extend his influence northward, and he made himself their patron in order to do so.

The alienation of pope from king deepened step by painful step. Calixtus alarmed Alfonso by declining to ratify the bulls of legitimization conferred on young Ferrante by his two predecessors, thereby reviving the old question of whether the king's bastard was entitled to inherit the Neapolitan crown. Next he declared that Alfonso had no right to Benevento and Terracina, two strongholds that lay in the disputed borderlands between Naples and Rome and that the king claimed as rightfully his. The rift became unbridgeable when Alfonso sent a beautiful young woman with whom he had become infatuated, Lucrezia d'Alagna, to Rome to ask Calixtus to annul his forty-year marriage to Maria of Castile. Calixtus had already shown himself willing, within broad limits, to help the king with his wooing. He had agreed to the appointment of a cousin of Lucrezia's as cardinal-archbishop of Naples, and to the marriage of her sister to Ausias del Milà, one of his own young kinsmen. The annulment of a royal marriage of almost forty years' duration, however, was more than he felt able to give. Pressed for an answer, he told the young lady, who had been accompanied to Rome by an extravagantly costly entourage and was obviously hoping to become Naples's queen, that he could not do as she asked because he did not wish to accompany her to hell. That marked the end of civil communications between Naples and Rome.

Before long Calixtus was warning Alfonso that "Your Majesty should know that a pope can depose kings," and Alfonso was replying that "Your Holiness should know that, should we wish, we shall find a way of deposing a pope." When Calixtus refused to appoint a bastard son of the bastard Ferrante to the bishopric of Zaragoza in Spain—frustration was driving Alfonso to make increasingly outlandish demands—old resentments hardened into a cold hatred that would last until pope and king were both dead. Alfonso, in a quest for allies among the other rulers of Italy, began arranging what would become a set of marriage alliances with the Sforzas of Milan. His grandson and namesake was married to a daughter of Duke Francesco Sforza, and later a daughter of that union would be married to the third Sforza duke of Milan. The eventual consequences of these arrangements would have horrified Alfonso and Francesco alike had they been able to foresee them.

The pope's continuing appeals for unity and resistance to the Ottoman onslaught received the friendliest reception, not unnaturally, in those places that were most directly threatened. One such place was the Serbian capital of Belgrade, an Orthodox bulwark against Turkish conquest of the Balkan peninsula and, as long as it could hold out, a shield protecting the rest of eastern Europe. Its survival at this juncture was in large measure the achievement of three extraordinary individuals, two of them sent by Calixtus from Rome. One was possibly the nearest thing to a military genius that Europe produced in the fifteenth century, the Hungarian János Hunyadi, who understood what a catastrophe the fall of Belgrade would be for his homeland and threw himself wholeheartedly into what many others saw as a cause already lost. The second was the Franciscan friar Juan Capistrano, who had been sent to Germany to preach Calixtus's crusade and, upon learning that a showdown was approaching in Belgrade, recruited his own army of volunteers and, at age seventy, marched it the five hundred miles from Frankfurt to Serbia. The third was a veteran Vatican diplomat, Cardinal Juan de Carvajal, whom Calixtus had dispatched to Hungary to help in whatever way he could. Together, the Hungarian general, the Neapolitan friar, and the Spanish cardinal managed to get the various nationalities and factions gathered at Belgrade to put their differences aside and focus on the threat outside the city's gates. Drawing on resources made available by Calixtus's order that all monies collected outside Italy for crusade purposes should be sent directly to Hungary rather than to Rome, they were able to assemble and arm enough men—albeit largely untrained men—to reduce the sultan's numerical advantage to two against one. On July 22, 1456, a masterful counterattack by Hunyadi so shattered the Ottoman army that the sultan, himself wounded, had to abandon the siege. It was as great a defeat as Mehmed II would suffer in a career studded with victories, and when news of it reached the Vatican, it sparked wild jubilation.

Calixtus, convinced that a miracle had occurred, ordered it to be celebrated annually, thereby making the Feast of the Transfiguration a permanent feature of the liturgical calendar. Good news rarely lasted long where the conflict with the Turks was concerned, however. Just a month after his victory, Hunyadi fell victim to an outbreak of plague probably precipitated by the heaps of rotting corpses in and around Belgrade. Capistrano died of the same cause in October. Nevertheless, what they and Carvajal had achieved stood as proof that the Ottomans were not invincible and that much could be achieved if the Christians learned to cooperate.

The same lesson could be drawn from the accomplishments of Scarampo and his fleet during the eighteen months that they were active in the eastern Mediterranean. In the course of 1457, from their base on the island of Rhodes, the cardinal's men drove Ottoman forces from the Aegean islands of Lemnos, Thassos, and Samothrace, briefly took possession of the city of Corinth and even of the Acropolis at Athens, and defeated a Turkish fleet at Mytilene. These were inspiring achievements for a small force operating far from home, or should have been. Scarampo sent repeated appeals for more ships, more men, more money. Calixtus tried to help but had little left to give. When he summoned the nations of Europe to a general congress to open in Rome that December, the result was fresh disappointment. Not enough delegates were on hand for discussions to begin in earnest until March, and two months after that the congress was abandoned, having accomplished nothing. Still unsupported, unable to deliver a decisive blow, Scarampo performed a great service nevertheless. Until finally obliged to return to Italy, he kept the sultan's navy distracted, divided, and off balance. His expedition, like the defense of Belgrade, became a painfully vivid lesson in what might have been.

It is likely that much of Europe owed its safety and survival, at this juncture, to what was happening in the East. The regions where Roman Christianity gave way to the Orthodox faith became the setting for exploits of an epic character. Though most Italians paid little attention, great things were accomplished decade after decade and made an immense and lasting difference. One of the most brilliant of the heroes was Stephen III, who in 1457 at age twenty-four was crowned prince of Moldavia in what is now Romania and immediately launched into a career that over the next forty-seven years would see him defeat one invasion after another by various, always numerically superior, enemies. He won forty-six of his forty-eight battles, repelling a lifelong series of Turkish attacks while also having to fight off the attempts of his Roman Catholic neighbors, Hungary and Poland in particular, to take possession of his homeland. Somehow he managed to improve the prosperity and enrich the cultural life of Moldavia in the midst of end-less peril, and after his death he would be canonized a saint by the Orthodox Church.

Better remembered today, for macabre and not entirely imaginary reasons, was Vlad III of Wallachia, like Moldavia an independent prin-cipality in the fifteenth century and today part of Romania. Known even in his own time as Dracula (son of the dragon), and to the Turks as "the impaler prince" for his favored method of dispatching enemies, he became *voivode* or ruler of Wallachia a year before Stephen took charge of Moldavia and was about the same age. Despite his lurid repu-tation, he was on the whole a good if severely firm ruler, and the inten-sity of his hatred for the Turks is explained by his life story. In boyhood he had become a hostage of the sultan, his father surrendering him and a brother as security for good behavior, and he was regularly beaten for recalcitrance. The Turks ultimately killed his father and blinded and buried alive an elder brother. Though after achieving his freedom Vlad succeeded in retaking Wallachia from the invaders, this early success simply opened the way to a life of unceasing conflict. Like Stephen, he became an immovable obstacle to Turkish progress west of the Black Sea, and he continued to stand firm until his death in battle at age forty-five. The West owed him, as it owed Stephen, an immense debt. The two kept whole Ottoman armies tied up for decades.

Even more important, and with an even more remarkable story, was the Albanian George Kastrioti, known as Skanderbeg. He, like Vlad Dracula, was given over to the Turks as a hostage in his youth, and in contrast to the Impaler he converted to Islam, entered military service as a janissary, and rose to be a general of cavalry fighting, among other Christian leaders, Hunyadi of Hungary. But in 1443 he switched sides, and a year later won the first of what would ultimately be his more than twenty victories over his erstwhile Turkish comrades. And again the Christian states demonstrated their chronic inability to support, even to refrain from undercutting, one another. Venice, at first delighted with Skanderbeg's repeated thrashings of the Turks, by 1447 was begin-ning to be wary of Albania's growing strength. And so it declared war on Skanderbeg, offering a lifetime pension to anyone who succeeded in killing him and encouraging the Turks to attack him in his rear. In 1448, in the space of a few days, Skanderbeg so completely crushed first the Turks and then the Venetians that the latter were obliged to come to terms. Then, his little nation exhausted and desperately in need of support, Skanderbeg offered to become a vassal of Alfonso V, promising to take an oath of fealty as soon as the last Turk had been expelled from Albania (something that was, in fact, never achieved).

Alfonso, so blithely indifferent to Pope Calixtus's efforts to mount a crusade, was nevertheless happy to take Albania under his wing. Doing so gave him, in the person of Skanderbeg, a brilliantly able ally in his long campaign to elbow Venice aside in the eastern Mediterranean and establish an empire of his own there. It provided benefits closer to home as well. When a baronial rebellion erupted in Naples, Skanderbeg sent some of his famously ferocious light cavalry, the *stradioti,* to help Alfonso put it down. He repeated the favor in Sicily a year later, both suppressing an uprising and helping Alfonso to show enough strength to discourage a threatened invasion by the Turks. Cynical self-interest, however, remained endemic among the Italians. When the Albanian capital came under siege at one point, Venetian merchants happily sold supplies to the Turkish invaders.

By a cruel irony, Skanderbeg's success became a factor in the fall of Constantinople: his ability to turn back one invasion after another encouraged other princes to resist Ottoman expansion as well, and this persuaded the Turks that the ancient Christian capital could not be allowed to survive. Four years after they took it, in 1457, they felt ready to attack Albania again and did so with an army of seventy thousand men. On September 2 of that year, true to form, Skanderbeg whipped them so thoroughly that the sultan agreed to a five-year truce. Once again, however, Albania was exhausted physically and financially, and this time Skanderbeg's appeals to Alfonso V were ignored. He next appealed to Rome, and though Calixtus's response was pathetically feeble, it appears to have been the best he could do: the immediate dispatch of the only available galley, a gift of money so inadequate as to be practically irrelevant, and a promise of more at the earliest opportunity. Skanderbeg cannot have been greatly consoled to have conferred upon him the meaningless title *Athleta Christi*—Champion of Christ. He was essentially alone, facing the dead certainty that, truce or no truce, the Turks would be back in their scores of thousands.

Without question Alfonso had it within his means to help Skanderbeg substantially, and without question he was greatly in Skanderbeg's debt. There being no particular need to care about the fate of Albania at the moment, however, it was not in the king's nature to be distracted from his own immediate priorities, especially the status of his son Ferrante in the aftermath of Calixtus's refusal to issue a bull (a document bearing the papal seal and therefore official) declaring the young man to be legitimate. It was by now clear that so long as Calixtus remained alive, Ferrante's path to the crown would be anything but assured.

Lurking in the background through all this was the question of whether Ferrante was actually Alfonso's son. Doubts about his paternity had stalked Ferrante all his life. From his infancy people had whispered that his real father was a half-Moorish functionary at the Aragonese court, and alternatively that Ferrante's supposed mother had pretended to give birth to him in order to spare the wife of one of the king's brothers the humiliation of being exposed as an adulteress. Whatever the truth—and the rumors may have been rooted in nothing more substantial than a belief the great Alfonso couldn't possibly have fathered such an unappealing human being—by the late 1450s Calixtus was in as good a position as anyone still living to know it. At the time of Ferrante's birth he had been Alfonso's secretary, and at the center of Aragonese court life, for some five years.

There being nothing in Calixtus's life story to cast doubt on his integrity or his respect for the prerogatives of royalty, his unbending opposition to Ferrante remains an enticing mystery. Niccolò Machiavelli, who was still eleven years from being born when Alfonso died and appears to have had little evidence to draw on, would later allege that the pope was scheming to make one of his own nephews the king of Naples. This is implausible for many reasons, not least the existence of other, far more formidable claimants. Perhaps by this point Calixtus's hatred for Alfonso had grown so powerful as to overwhelm his usual equanimity. Possibly he was repelled by the prospect of a bastard becoming anointed king of the great kingdom of Naples; having been born and raised in a culture far more feudal than Italy's, he is likely to have taken a sternly disapproving view of illegitimate birth. Additionally, he had seen enough of the world to understand the threat to stability that sons born out of wedlock could pose when they laid claim to thrones, and the wisdom of the ancient precept that no bastard should ever become king. And it is in no way impossible that he believed—and had reason to believe—that Ferrante was not even Alfonso's bastard.

Finally and most interestingly, there is the fact that the pope knew Ferrante intimately: had overseen his education, functioned as a kind of guardian, and personally escorted him to Italy when Alfonso summoned him there. Ferrante's own life story, as we shall see, makes it possible to suspect that Calixtus, knowing what kind of man he was, foresaw what kind of ruler he would be and found the prospect horrifying.

AMAZING ITALY

THE ITALY FOR WHICH ALONSO DE BORJA LEFT SPAIN IN THE 1440s, and to which many of his relatives later began migrating in hopes of benefiting from his exalted position, was a place that lightning had struck twice. A full thousand years after the collapse of the Roman Empire, it was once again the wonder of the world: the richest region in all of Europe because by a wide margin the most economically advanced. Its cities were incomparably the biggest, most beautiful, and most vibrant, and in fields as diverse as education and architecture, banking and art, it was leading the way to modernity.

In one area only was Italy conspicuously backward. Politically it was so fragmented, in such disarray, that strictly speaking there was no such thing as "Italy." From the Alps southward the peninsula was a crazy quilt of large and small city-states, some of which were more or less autonomous while others were subject to domineering neighbors. They differed vastly in character and had long since shown themselves to be incapable of sustained cooperation. To the extent that their people saw themselves as members of a single Italian nation, they did so by virtue of more or less sharing a common language ("more or less" because that language was splintered into a babel of dialects) and a culture unlike any to be found elsewhere. But their nationhood, such as it was, had never come close to producing unity. That this remained true while France and Spain were beginning to coalesce under increasingly powerful monarchs meant that Italy, for all its achievements, was year by year growing comparatively weaker. It was becoming vulnerable.

How Italy had come to be such a stunning place—and that is literally what it was, newcomers from the north consistently describing themselves as stunned upon experiencing it for the first time—is of course a complicated story. Probably it starts with the fact that much of the Italian peninsula, having been the heart of the empire of the Caesars, continued during what we call the Dark Ages to cling to two things that were disappearing in places more distant from Rome. One was the town as the core around which society was organized. Whereas throughout northern Europe cities of any significance became rare, with the nobility withdrawing into often-remote fortresses from which they could dominate populations of peasants, the most vital parts of Italy remained distinctly town-centered.

Except in the region around Rome and the sprawling kingdom of Naples, both of which developed a feudal order similar to the one prevailing beyond the Alps, the survival of the towns and the evolution of some of them into great cities became an essential element in Italy's unique character. Class and caste distinctions grew faint and porous as nobles and merchants, artisans and soldiers and clergy, learned to live together on terms approaching equality in their crowded, lively streets. More than in any other place in Europe, the townsfolk of Italy were not oppressed, could not even be looked down on, by the hereditary nobility. To the contrary, some of the greatest cities came to be ruled by their commercial classes. It was not uncommon for nobles to be excluded from public life, and for noble families to be forced to abandon their rural strongholds and move to town.

The other fragment of the classical past that set Italy apart was the Roman law, which was not swept away in favor of rigid, status-focused feudal codes as happened elsewhere. This proved to have a profound impact intellectually, culturally, and socially. While the scholars of a slowly reviving northern Europe were focusing on theology and philosophy, in the early twelfth century their Italian counterparts discovered and undertook the study of digests of imperial law compiled under the Emperor Justinian six hundred years earlier. Italy's traders found in the old code an ideal framework for their bustling commercial life: practical rules and regulations and guidelines, ways of doing business, that grew ever more relevant as the economy developed. The Italian universities, the first to appear anywhere on earth, attached an importance to the study of the law not to be found in France, Germany, or Spain.

Italy was shaped also, even long after Rome ceased to be the hub of the known world, by an astonishing diversity of outside influences. The Eastern Christian Empire, from its capital at Constantinople, early put its cosmopolitan stamp on Sicily and the southern part of the peninsula as well as on its main outpost on the northern Adriatic coast, the port of Ravenna. Sicily was an Arab possession until late in the eleventh century, the Normans then came from northern France to make themselves kings of Naples as well as Sicily, both places fell next into the hands of the Spanish, and from the Dark to the High Middle Ages a succession of German chieftains and kings descended regularly upon Italy and laid claim to various parts of it. Meanwhile the bishops of Rome were evolving into popes, declaring themselves the spiritual leaders of all Christendom, and becoming the overlords of much of central Italy.

The peninsula became an arena in which the popes and Germany's so-called Holy Roman emperors fought each other for dominance. Both sides, in seeking the support of the cities, granted them liberties and favors that ultimately, if inadvertently, helped them to become autonomous. Those cities, in turn, were developing in strikingly different ways, sometimes adopting republican forms of government that at a distance could almost be mistaken for democracy. Many fell under the dominion of warlords, and even the republics came to be run by elites that rarely constituted more than a fraction of their populations.

By the time Alonso Borgia became Calixtus III, the peninsula had long been dominated by five "great" (by Italy's modest standards) powers:

Venice, a republic dominated by an oligarchy of merchant families that had grown immensely rich and risen to a position of international importance by trading throughout the eastern Mediterranean, building there a great network of colonies and commercial alliances.

Florence, also a republic and ruled by families that had made their fortunes in banking, manufacturing, and trade, the jewel in Italy's golden crown by virtue of the astonishing artistic and intellectual flowering that, before the end of the fifteenth century, would make it one of the most dazzling cultural phenomena in all of human history.

Rome, a theocracy dominated by the pope, gradually recovering some of its long-lost strength but still an administrative center only, without a commercial middle class capable of challenging the baronial clans.

Milan, the giant of the north, an industrial powerhouse and master of the vast fertile plain of Lombardy, politically a tyranny, long in the grip first of its Visconti and then of its Sforza dukes.

And of course Naples, Il Regno, a kingdom encompassing the whole southern half of the mainland, the most feudal state in Italy and therefore also the most backward, fatally weakened by an endless struggle between its great capital city and rural barons unwilling to be ruled by anyone.

The greatest of Italy's cities—Naples, Venice, and Milan—all had populations of well over a hundred thousand when London was still the only city in England with as many as twenty thousand residents. And all of them controlled great expanses of countryside, staking out broad spheres of influence by conquest, intimidation, and bribery. All of them but Naples, which stagnated under the oppressive rule of a series of more or less vicious and decadent monarchs, possessed a vitality to be found almost nowhere else. They took for granted things that remained unknown or unwelcome elsewhere: rapid change, steady growth, and wide-open social mobility—even, in some places, educational opportunities for women comparable to those available to men.

The absence of a functioning feudal system, and of feudalism's arrangement of the population into commoners who owed loyalty to nobles who in turn owed loyalty to kings, had one unfortunate consequence. Some of the greatest of the city-states, along with innumerable smaller communities including tiny hilltop villages, came to be dominated by local strongmen who could make no claim to political legitimacy—to having any real right to the power they wielded. In the fourteenth century, when the papacy was absent from Rome and utterly incapable of stopping thugs from seizing pieces of the Papal States and setting themselves up as tyrants, authority based on force alone became virtually the norm. Thus the masters of one city-state after another were in a vastly less justifiable position than, say, an English baron whose title and landholdings had been formally conferred upon him in a Church-sanctioned ceremony by an anointed king. Even when the usurpers were able to win recognition as papal vicars, governing their domains in the pope's name, such titles were little more than legal fictions. They signified almost nothing—certainly not a willingness to be loyal to the pope. To the extent that vicariate status gave the warlords a shred of the legitimacy they craved, it was a shred too scanty to remove their insecurity or make them more responsible in the use of their power or make the so-called Papal States more peaceful.

Misrule and instability thus formed the dark underside of the Italian Renaissance, with almost every regime recurrently under threat from internal as well as external enemies. It was far from uncommon, and at times was almost commonplace, for the lords of Italy's cities to be bloodily overthrown—often by their own kinsmen, with brother killing brother either to gain or to retain power. Men who had become rulers through violence could find little grounds for complaint, and often nowhere to appeal, when their turn came to be violently overthrown. Might made right: this became a fact of life and was the one utterly inglorious element in Renaissance Italy's otherwise magnificent heritage. Betrayal and murder became endemic even at the most exalted levels of society, even within the greatest families. This was the world in which the Borjas of Valencia had to learn to make their way.

4

Family Matters

During the years when an increasingly feeble Calixtus III was bringing unexpected vigor to meeting the Turkish threat, managing a Church that was the largest and by far the most complex institution in Europe, and struggling to cope with the never-ending schemes and squabbles of strongmen far and near, another and more personal dimension of his life was becoming burdensome as well.

This was his relationship with his family, which in addition to being numerous and eager for advancement had become binational as more and more of its members left Spain for Rome to see what advantage could be wrung from having a relative who was first a cardinal and then—miracle of miracles—the supreme pontiff.

We don't know how many Borgias were in Italy during Calixtus's reign, only that their demands for favors provoked him to complain. But he complained too of relatives who had not left Spain at all, instead remaining there while appealing for help in achieving a lifestyle appropriate to a family whose name he had made grand. Among the stay-at-homes was his sister Isabella, who as a young woman had married their kinsman Don Jofrè de Borja, son of a wealthier branch of the family with better connections to the aristocracy. This Jofrè had died in 1437, leaving Isabella with a family of at least two sons and four daughters, possibly more. By that time Alonso was bishop of Valencia and living in Italy in the service of Alfonso V. He permitted Isabella to move with her brood into Valencia's episcopal palace, which put her on a level with the city's proudest families.

In terms of bloodline, Isabella's children stood above their mother and her brother the cardinal. Their paternal grandmother, Don Jofrè's mother, was a child of the de Oms family, which occupied a higher perch in the Valencian nobility than any of the Borjas. It was partly because of his marriage to Sibila de Oms that Jofrè's father, Rodrigo Gil de Borja, had risen to be chief counselor of Játiva and a member of the court of King Pedro of Aragon. Isabella's marriage to Jofrè had been a significant step up, and Alonso always took an interest in her children. He saw to it that advantageous marriages were arranged for the daughters and that the sons were provided with the kinds of educations and connections that could get young careers off to a fast start. Alonso had another sister, Catalina, who had made a good marriage to the Valencian baron Juan del Milà, and he was generous with assistance to their numerous progeny as well.

Several of Alonso's nephews and cousins, Isabella's son Rodrigo and Catalina's Luis Juan del Milà among them, were steered toward careers in the Church. This was customary because practical: it was in the ecclesiastical field that an uncle who was first a bishop and then a cardinal could be most helpful. Vatican records show Rodrigo and Luis Juan being singled out, as early as the reign of Eugenius IV, for benefices, offices generating ecclesiastical income, that would have been unimaginable without the intervention of a patron who had access to the pope's ear and the king of Aragon's as well. We see Rodrigo, still no more than a schoolboy, becoming the recipient of ecclesiastical revenues first from his hometown of Játiva, then from the cathedral of Barcelona, and finally from the cathedral of Valencia. In 1449, when Rodrigo was about eighteen and his uncle was in his fifth year as a cardinal resident in Rome, Pope Nicholas V issued a bull allowing him—in contravention of the rules, which is why a bull was necessary—to keep his benefices (all of which were in Spain) even if he resided at a university or in Italy. This cleared the way for the youth to leave Spain for study at one of the great universities of Italy without sacrificing the income that permitted him to live in the style of a young lord—a cardinal's nephew. Again there was nothing scandalous, even unusual, about any of this. Everything known about Rodrigo makes it reasonable to suppose that he was both an able student—not even his enemies would ever deny his intelligence—and a conscientious one, consistent hard work being one of his defining characteristics throughout his life.

Rodrigo thus spent the next six years in Italy, along with his brother Pedro Luis and their cousin del Milà, but little is known of their lives. Rodrigo and del Milà were almost certainly studying law at the University of Bologna, and in 1453 the latter, who was probably the elder of the two by a few years, was given the bishopric of Segorbe in Spain although still short of the required canonical age of twenty-seven. Two years later, when Alonso became pope, the nephews, in their mid-twenties now, found their lives dramatically transformed. On May 10, 1455, just twenty days after his coronation, Calixtus appointed all three to positions of importance. Rodrigo was given the high office of protonotary apostolic, with duties appropriate to his legal training. Bishop Luis Juan del Milà became papal legate, representative, in the great city of Bologna, a fief of the papacy. Pedro Luis Borgia, the trio's sole non-churchman, took command of the Castel Sant'Angelo, the massive and ancient circular fortress that stood on the bank of the River Tiber overlooking the Vatican. This was no mere honorary appointment. The Castel, thirteen hundred years old, was an impregnable stronghold and the cornerstone of papal security in Rome. As its governor and commander of its troops, Pedro Luis became a power in the city and a potential adversary of the baronial clans, the Orsini and Colonna and others, whose unruly behavior kept Rome endlessly on the verge of violent disorder.

Upon receiving these promotions Rodrigo and Luis Juan returned to Bologna, where the latter took up his duties as legate and the former returned to his studies, completing his doctorate in the autumn of 1456. Before that happened, there had come a flurry of further and even more significant appointments. On February 20, in consistory, Calixtus announced his first three appointments to the Sacred College: his two clerical nephews and, as part of his efforts to win support for the campaign against the Turks, a twenty-two-year-old member of the Portuguese royal family who was also a nephew of Alfonso V. It would later be said that several cardinals objected to the elevation of such young men to such high positions, but in fact there is no contemporary evidence of any such reaction—none provided by anyone in a position to

know, certainly. The scholarly diplomat Enea Silvio Piccolomini, a respected figure and destined to become pope himself, wrote at the time
that "Cardinal Rodrigo is young, it is true, but his conduct and good
sense add years to his age." Every cardinal present signed the bull of
appointment. By the time the promotions were made public, Calixtus
had also named Pedro Luis Borgia captain-general, commanding officer, of the papal army.

These actions, though obviously nepotistic, raised no eyebrows.
Such things were not only accepted but expected—Nicholas V had been
the exception rather than the rule—and the reasons for them were
clear. Calixtus, still new in office, was surrounded by the same men
who had assented to his election only because their own choices had
been blocked, and they expected him to do nothing while waiting
quietly for his own death. These were hardened veterans of the Vatican's political wars, cynical and self-serving, and to a man they were
professing to be the pontiff's best friends while pushing for the advancement of their own agendas and the thwarting of their rivals. At
the center of this tangle of hypocrisy and intrigue, isolated and probably lonely, Calixtus faced immense problems and was in urgent need of
deputies he could trust. There were such men among the cardinals
who elected him—the Greek Bessarion, the Spaniard Carvajal—and he
took them into his confidence. But he needed others too, and he was far
from being the first pope to look to his own family. Not even the Orsini
or the Colonna could complain when he did so.

Especially not the Orsini or the Colonna. Both families owed much
of their wealth and power to the success of their ancestors in capturing
and exploiting the papal crown. And they must have understood that
not only Calixtus but the Church itself was fortunate that he had capable and responsible young nephews to place in the Sacred College. As
for the appointment of Pedro Luis as captain-general, if it is not excused
it is certainly explained by the treachery of the previous incumbent,
Giovanni Ventimiglia, who at Siena had snatched defeat from the jaws
of what should have been an important papal victory by arranging to
have himself taken prisoner by a beaten foe. Beyond that, the promotion is most fairly judged on the basis of Pedro Luis's subsequent performance in office.

Calixtus's elevation of his young nephews reflects his determination, once a campaign against the Turks had been set in motion, to attack other problems as well. Foremost among his other problems were the Papal States, those huge expanses of the Italian landscape that the Church had begun accumulating in the time of the Emperor Constantine but by the dawning of the Renaissance were in the hands of an assortment of warlords and petty despots, few of whom were willing to acknowledge, much less yield to, the authority of Rome. The city-states ruled by these despots and warlords spread across a great part of northern and central Italy. At their core was the thousand-year-old duchy of Rome, which extended from the border with Naples northward into Tuscany, but they also included the Romagna and the March of Ancona on the Adriatic coast, the province of Umbria between the March and Tuscany, the duchies of Spoleto and Benevento, the former papal capital of Avignon in what is now France, parts of Corsica, and a long list of scattered cities and towns. All this might have been a source of immense wealth and power for the papacy, but it had rarely been anything of the kind. By the ninth century, barely a hundred years after its possession by the popes had been confirmed by Pepin king of the Franks and reconfirmed by his son Charlemagne, virtually the whole inheritance was completely out of control. And things went downhill from there, reaching their nadir in the fourteenth century when the popes were in exile and the warlords were left free to do as they pleased. By the time of Calixtus the lawlessness of the Papal States and the brutality of their rulers were accepted as normal almost everywhere except inside the Vatican. In determining to put things right, to begin the process of restoring order, Calixtus was challenging some of the most murderously dangerous families in Italy. No one could have been surprised that, in selecting lieutenants to whom he could entrust this domestic crusade, he looked to his sisters' sons.

The appointment of Luis Juan del Milà as legate to Bologna made sense as an early step. Ancient and rich, more important than any northern city except Milan and Venice, Bologna had for centuries been a papal fief and therefore subject, in theory, to the temporal authority of Rome. In practice, the families that made up its ruling oligarchy had long since grown accustomed to being accountable to no one, and naturally they had no interest in submitting to Rome. As legate, armed with instructions from his uncle to reassert Rome's authority, the young

Cardinal del Milà was undertaking an assignment that would have been a challenge for the most gifted and experienced of Vatican diplomats. Calixtus, aware that he had no time to spare, was teaching his nephew to swim by throwing him into deep water.

He did much the same with the Borgia brothers, and for them the waters were deeper and more treacherous. Pedro Luis was instructed to muster the pope's troops and lead them into the hill country immediately north and west of Rome, territory that had been the property of the Church since before the fall of the Roman Empire but that generations of Orsini had learned to think of as theirs alone. There he was to assert his uncle's lordship and deal with the resistance that such a claim was certain to provoke. He would be making war not only on the Orsini but also, by unmistakable implication, their patron and semi-secret partner, Alfonso of Aragon and Naples. It would have been a daunting assignment for the best general in Italy.

Cardinal Rodrigo's turn came on the last day of 1456, when Calixtus signed a bull appointing him vicar general in matters temporal—matters pertaining to civil governance—in the March of Ancona. Roughly a hundred miles north of Rome on the eastern side of the Apennine Mountains that run down the Italian peninsula like a high ragged spine, the March was not as wild and lawless a part of the Papal States as the Romagna, which lay immediately to its north, but it was wild and lawless enough. It too had long been beyond the reach of papal power and ravaged by the endless petty wars of the local strongmen. Early in his career the brilliant mercenary Francesco Sforza had won control of much of it. Later, when Sforza's ambitions sent him northward to the far greater prize of Milan, he left pieces of the March in the hands of various members of his family. Alfonso V, always happy to trouble any waters in which he saw the possibility of profitable fishing, later and rather brazenly proposed that Calixtus turn the whole province over to him. In his sixties by this point, a monarch of international importance for nearly half a century, Alfonso had developed such a massive ego that he was able to regard this suggestion as reasonable or at least feasible. He had also probably not entirely stopped hoping that his onetime faithful servant Alonso de Borja would prove willing to do his bidding. The pope, however, was insulted and alarmed. If the

March were not brought back under Roman control, he concluded, it might soon be lost forever.

Calixtus was prodded into action not only by Alfonso's presumption but by reports of what was happening in the March town of Ascola (Ascoli Piceno today). A young nobleman known to history only as Josias had murdered the town's resident tyrant, one Giovanni Sforza (whose place in the large tangled family of that name is not clear). After trying to take over as tyrant himself and being expelled by the citizenry, this Josias seized the local *rocca* or fortress—the property, as it happened, of the papacy—and began using it as a base from which to prey on the neighborhood as head of a gang of bandits. When Josias's victims appealed for help to their overlord in the Vatican, Calixtus decided that the time had come to intervene. The job of managing the intervention was going to be immensely complex, with prickly political, diplomatic, and military dimensions. In giving it to the untested young Cardinal Rodrigo, the pope was taking yet another huge risk.

What followed was an early demonstration of Rodrigo's precocious competence. The failed tyrant Josias was soon a failed bandit chieftain as well, a prisoner on his way to Rome. The people of Ascola found themselves under an administration more rational and benign than anyone then living in the area had ever experienced. As the cardinal extended his control and his reforms into other parts of the March, he became a popular figure, celebrated as a liberator. His uncle, in sending him north, had equipped him with extraordinary powers, not least with respect to bringing the region's churchmen under control. He had the authority to bestow any benefice upon any recipient of his choice and also—what could be very useful in bringing ecclesiastical practice into alignment with the needs and realities of the hour—to accept the surrender of benefices. During almost a year in the March he threaded his way through a maze of difficulties, and there is no record of his putting a foot wrong.

His one unsolvable problem was money. It was expected at this time, in Europe generally, that a churchman in a role of secular administration like Rodrigo's would pay his own expenses. This was a justification for the heaping of multiple benefices upon senior clergy: in many cases it was not only the simplest but almost the only way of providing a ruler's senior lieutenants with the revenues they needed to be effective. A famous example is Cardinal Thomas Wolsey, who for many years ran the government, the foreign policy, and the Church in England under his master Henry VIII and was able to do so on the grandest scale thanks entirely to the enormous revenues generated by his ecclesiastical offices. Those revenues paid not only for Wolsey's lavish lifestyle but for the sprawling bureaucracies he headed. The income of the crown itself, at the time, could not have sufficed even to provide Wolsey and his fellow ministers with satisfactory salaries. It was the same in France, in Spain, and elsewhere and is one of the reasons (education being another) why bishops, archbishops, and cardinals were so often top government officers. Their benefices made it unnecessary for the monarchs to pay them—at least in any direct way.

Rodrigo, however, soon found the costs of bringing new management to the March beyond his ability to pay. His uncle, in financial extremis himself, tried to help in the only way he could: by appointing Rodrigo to the vacant bishopric of Girona in the northeastern corner of Spain, thereby opening up an additional stream of income. Even this, however, proved to be insufficient.

We will see this sort of thing happening again, and it is something to be taken into account when considering the accusations of greed that have always been directed at Rodrigo. While his income did rise in time to stunning levels, it ceases to seem quite so disgraceful when measured against his expanding responsibilities, the expenses that they entailed, and the need for him to pay most of the bills himself. Throughout most of his life his income would not be *his,* strictly speaking, but that of the sectors of the Vatican machinery it was his duty to operate.

During the nine or ten months that he spent in the March, his financial situation was dire. He found it necessary, in order to carry out the mission on which his uncle had sent him, to mortgage—borrow against—his entire projected income for the next three years.

Worrisome as such problems were, however, they sank into insignificance when orders reached the March for Rodrigo to return to Rome, because he was again being promoted.

THE MEN IN THE RED HATS

THE IMPORTANCE OF THE COLLEGE OF CARDINALS IN THE STORY
of the Borgias—the fact that if Alonso had not been made a cardinal, he
would never have moved to Rome and certainly could never have been
elected pope—raises the question of what exactly a cardinal *was* in
those days, and how it was that becoming one mattered so much.

The short answer is that, as the fifteenth century advanced and the
popes reestablished themselves in Rome, the cardinals became a kind of
papal royal family—"princes of the church." They lived lives of extraordinary privilege, with unique access to power and splendid sources of
income. All of which added to the allure of membership in the tiny
group that elected the pope and from which new popes were invariably
chosen. It also helps to explain why the most powerful families in Italy
came to regard it as essential always to be represented in the college.

Like the papacy itself, like the Church generally, the college was a
long time evolving. The first cardinals, when they appeared in the fifth
century, were not princes in any sense but simply the chief priests of
Rome's parish churches. Their name was derived from the Latin *cardo,*
which means "hinge" and indicated that cardinals were the main point
of connection between the bishop of Rome—*il papa*—and the people.
A century later these cardinal-priests were joined by a new group of
cardinal-deacons (deacons being clerics but not ordained priests and
therefore not empowered to say mass) with their own distinct responsibilities. After another two hundred years cardinal-bishops appeared as
well. This newest group, being made up of men of higher rank than the
others, was the most prestigious but had no more power or authority.

In the eleventh century the three groups, each of which had functioned separately under its own elected dean, increased their clout by
combining into a single body, the Sacred College. It established its own
small bureaucracy, assumed responsibility for the management of papal
elections (though not yet for actually doing the electing), and secured
for its members all the top positions in the Curia, the papal administra-

tive machinery. In such ways it gave itself a foundation from which it would become capable of challenging the authority of the popes. In the 1170s, when the election of a six-year-old Holy Roman emperor made it transparently absurd for emperors to choose popes, the Third Lateran Council handed the entire process over to the Sacred College, where it has remained to this day. The years following saw the emergence of the consistory: pope and college meeting together as a governing council. The *galero,* a wide-brimmed red hat with tassels, had become the sign of membership in the college.

The rivalry between popes and councils that shaped the career of Alonso de Borja was paralleled by a similar contest between the papacy and the Sacred College. This was, essentially, a struggle to determine whether the Church was going to be a nonhereditary monarchy, ruled by a single supreme leader, or an oligarchy governed by the men with red hats. Both the Babylonian Captivity and the Western Schism happened in large part because of the refusal of the college to accept the pope as monarch. More than a few cardinals showed themselves willing to split the Church, if necessary, to reduce the pontiff to a figurehead.

As early as 1352, the cardinals' distrust of papal power introduced yet another new element into the selection of popes. This was the "capitulation," a promise to which all participating cardinals were expected to subscribe before voting. Many elections came to be preceded by the drafting and adoption of long lists of capitulations. Typically, the cardinals pledged that if elected they would not do certain things: dilute the power of their colleagues by increasing the size of the college, appoint new cardinals without approval of two-thirds of the membership, imprison any cardinal without unanimous approval, or appoint relatives to certain important positions. Such promises figured conspicuously in conclaves throughout the Western Schism and beyond, but the results were practically nil. New popes consistently ignored them, making use of the many ways they had of making their former colleagues dependent upon them for money, for appointment to coveted positions, for any number of things.

Appointment to the college remained a great prize all the same and attracted the interest of even the greatest of kings. Inevitably in a world where noble and even royal families consigned children to careers in the

Church for political purposes, the red hat could become the penultimate goal (the pontifical throne being the ultimate one) for power-hungry, greedy men with no interest at all in the religious life. In a Church whose supreme head doubled as the monarch of one of Italy's most important states—a state that was, inevitably, sometimes in conflict with its neighbors—cardinals who knew how to make war could be worth their weight in holy relics. Thus in the fourteenth century, when Pope Innocent VI wanted to return from Avignon but didn't dare do so before clearing Rome and the adjacent territory of the ruffians who had taken control, the man he chose for the job was Cardinal Gil Álvarez Carrillo de Albornoz, archbishop of Toledo. He proved a good choice. A veteran of Spain's wars against the Moors, Albornoz took Rome back from the bandit who had established himself as tyrant there and not only subdued most of the Papal States but imposed on them a constitution that would remain in effect into the nineteenth century. It was only his sudden death, and the unraveling of his gains, that obliged the pope to forget about a triumphal return to Rome.

Albornoz's successor was another warrior-cardinal, one who if not his equal as a general or administrator definitely surpassed him in savagery. Like Albornoz of royal blood (he was a cousin of the king of France), Robert of Geneva came to be known as the "butcher of Cesena" for allowing some four thousand of that little city's citizens to be slaughtered in retribution for a rebellion. This, however, did not prevent his being elected the first antipope of the Western Schism (again in contrast to Albornoz, who at the pinnacle of his career refused the papal crown). His reign as Clement VII was undistinguished but free of further atrocities. Mainly he confined himself to selling ecclesiastical offices and doing the bidding of the French crown.

He was not the last of the fighting cardinals, but from the time of the popes' return to Rome they were a disappearing breed. Gradually the Sacred College was domesticated, its members abandoning the idea of becoming at least equal to the pope and accepting high status in compensation. This new status would become official in the 1460s when the pope of the time, Paul II, conferred on all cardinals the official rank of prince, so that they were recognized across Europe as equal to dukes in the feudal hierarchy and inferior only to the pope and his fellow crowned heads. Thenceforth they would dress in resplendent red robes and be the star performers in a whole new theater of pomp and circumstance. They were not to appear in public except "in state," accompanied by as many as three hundred uniformed attendants.

But they were never just puppets in a meaningless bigger-than-life play. They sat with the pope in consistory and so had the opportunity to influence important decisions. Most of them had charge of at least one of the Vatican's numerous courts, which dealt with cases from every corner of Europe. They also directed the Curia's most important departments; high rank, good education, and lofty family connections made them useful as diplomats; and they were often employed as legates and governors in the Papal States. Rulers throughout Europe found it advantageous to employ cardinals as advisers or petitioners when favors were wanted from Rome, and often put them on retainer.

For all these reasons the Sacred College became a hotbed of political and diplomatic intrigue, especially for the states of Italy as they maneuvered for advantage. This was never more true than when the cardinals gathered to elect a new pope; many arrived as agents of whatever secular state had secured their appointment in the first place and were expected to support candidates not unfriendly to that state or even—the best of all possible outcomes—its native sons. History is a trickster, though, and it mocks the best-laid plans. Thus Alonso Borgia was elected precisely because, during his decade in Rome, he had refused to become a player in the politics of the Vatican. It was by becoming the least visible and least feared of cardinals, ironically, that he turned himself into the man of the hour. He was, however, one of those exceptions that prove a rule. The rule in this case was the unsurprising fact that success both in college and in conclave required skill, strength, and clear, practical goals.

Perhaps the most surprising development of the fifteenth century was the way in which the College of Cardinals gradually became less, rather than more, international. Of the fifteen cardinals at the conclave that elected Alonso Borgia, seven were Italian. Thirty-seven years later, when another conclave elected a second Borgia pope, twenty-three cardinals participated, but only two were not Italian. The Italians had taken over in part because their most powerful families, the rulers of the peninsula's leading states, had more at stake than their counterparts in more distant places. It had come to seem essential, in the interim between the two elections, that every.princely house in Italy not only be represented in the college but place one of its own sons there. It was taken for granted that the college could never be without a Sforza from Milan, a Medici from Florence, an Este from Ferrara, a Gonzaga from Mantua, and an Orsini and a Colonna from Rome and its environs. Among the things demanded of cardinals was, above all, that they live in princely fashion— that they expend their wealth on the construction and adornment of great palaces, the building or rebuilding of the churches and piazzas of Rome, and the recruitment of artists and artisans capable of carrying out such work at the highest level of perfection. Thus could they contribute to fulfilling the dream that Martin V had for Rome when he returned the papacy from its long exile in 1420: that it would again become the glory of the world, a monument in stone to the greatness of the Church.

That contradictions lay embedded in all this could go without saying. To recruit cardinals from the richest and most powerful families in Italy, to make them both the political instruments of their houses and Rome's new royalty—these things were easily accomplished. But that these same men should also function as religious leaders, as models of rectitude—that was expecting too much.

This whole line of discussion inevitably gives rise to questions about the moral standards of the cardinals and other clergy—their sexual behavior in particular—in the fifteenth century. Salacious anecdotes are available in abundance and in a vast array of sources. What is less easy is to determine how meaningful these anecdotes are, how typical of the cardinals, bishops, and priests of the time, and even how true. Alonso Borgia was elected pope 332 years after the First Lateran Council settled a thousand-year debate about clerical celibacy by making it mandatory throughout the Western Church. All clergy thenceforth took vows of chastity. In a milieu where many positions of leadership were held by men who had been assigned to ecclesiastical careers for political and dynastic reasons and where much of the clerical rank and file was without education or training, it is hardly surprising if lapses were commonplace. Complaints about lapses were likewise not rare and came, as often as not, from the clergy itself. The only valid generalization, probably, is that exemplary behavior and gross misbehavior were to be found almost anywhere one looked, and that the College of Cardinals itself was rich in saints and sinners.

The complex ironies of the situation are encapsulated in what Ludovico Gonzaga, marquess of the city-state of Mantua, told his son in 1460:

"Although you are a cardinal, be religious."

5

The End of the Beginning

Don Pedro Luis de Borja—Pierluigi Borgia to the Italians—was still in his mid-twenties when he became the first member of his family to be the most hated man in Rome. He did so not by behaving badly in any way of which a credible record has survived, but by carrying out an assignment that made him the enemy of some of the most badly behaved Romans of his time.

That assignment, simply described, was to lead an army into the countryside north and west of Rome and take control of it in his uncle the pope's name. By every measure this was a lawful and legitimate objective, the territories in question having been the property of the Church for fully a thousand years. In practical terms too, it was entirely justified, even necessary, involving as it did a long-overdue challenge to the misrule of the Orsini. For generations—for centuries, actually—the leaders of the Orsini clan had been left free to do whatever they chose in places to which they had no rightful claim without having to account to anyone.

What they consistently chose, as it happened, was contrary to the interests of everyone involved except the Orsini themselves. The people who worked the land had sunk into a state of profound demoralization after generations of being treated as little better than livestock. In Rome itself disorder and danger became chronic, the Orsini turning the parts of the city that they controlled into killing zones. They showed no reluctance to shut down the highways leading to the city's gates and so cut off its supplies of food, fuel, and other essentials whenever it served their purposes to do so.

Though Calixtus III was by no means the first pontiff to set out to regain control of at least some part of the Papal States, his approach was novel in one important respect. In the regions closest to Rome in particular, his predecessors had commonly used one baronial clan as a weapon with which to bludgeon another into submission, supporting now the Colonna against the Orsini, now the Orsini against the Colonna. Almost invariably this turned out to be a self-defeating strategy, because whatever could be taken from the clan targeted for attack tended to end up in the hands not of the Church but of the clan that had done the attacking in the pope's name. The result was an endlessly repeating pattern in which, as pope succeeded pope, the fortunes of the Orsini and the Colonna became like two pistons in a reciprocating engine, with one side up whenever the other was down. Where the Church was concerned nothing really changed: the Papal States, and much of the old capital, remained out of control.

By appointing his nephew captain-general and sending him against the Orsini, Calixtus gave himself a chance, at least, of holding on to the fruits of any victories the campaign might achieve. The only serious disadvantage affected Pedro Luis personally: he became a marked man, conspicuous as both the leader and the symbol of his uncle's war. By contrast, his brother Cardinal Rodrigo and their cousin Cardinal Luis Juan del Milà—the former far away in the March of Ancona when Pedro Luis took the field, the latter even farther away in Bologna—could take comfort in being almost forgotten men.

The process by which the wrath of the Orsini came to be focused on Pedro Luis unfolded very gradually. The first favor that his uncle bestowed on him upon becoming pope, the governorship of the great citadel of Castel Sant'Angelo, caused little concern if any. At this early point in his reign Calixtus appeared to have no objectives except to mount a crusade against the Turks, and there was no reason to suspect that in disposing of the Castel he had anything more in mind than to raise a young favorite to a position of some prestige. Later, when Pedro Luis became the Vatican's captain-general, it again seemed nothing more than a harmless act of nepotistic largesse, without political significance and no threat to anyone. But soon Pedro Luis was not merely enjoying an impressive title and the handsome income that went with it, but actually making war. On the Orsini. At that point everything changed.

The campaign went surpassingly well. Advancing out of Rome, Pedro Luis took control, generally at the direct expense of the Orsini, of more towns and fortresses than can be named here. Of Terni, Narni, and Rieti; Todi, Orvieto, and Foligno; Nocera, Assisi, and Amelia; not only the whole of the province called the Patrimony of St. Peter but the part of Tuscany that belonged to the popes; finally even the duchies of Spoleto and Benevento and the great fortress of Terracina far to the south. This culminated in Pedro Luis's appointment, in April 1457, to the important post of prefect of Rome. The position had become vacant with the death of the latest in an unbroken line of Orsini prefects reaching back so far that the family had come to regard it as theirs by hereditary right. With the office they lost also—were obliged to surrender to Pedro Luis—the coastal city of Civitavecchia and much of the territory abutting Lake Vico north of Rome. These were serious losses; things were getting difficult for the Orsini, even alarming, as one possession after another was being torn out of their hands and Pedro Luis continued to press on. Cardinal Latino Orsini, long one of the most powerful men in Rome, found his situation so uncomfortable that he slipped away to the countryside.

The Colonna, of course, were delighted with everything that was happening and delighted also with Calixtus and his captain-general. His connection to the pope, his victories, and his growing number of offices made Pedro Luis the most attractive marital prize in central Italy, and soon there was talk of his betrothal to a Colonna bride. Everything he had gained and everything he still hoped to accomplish depended, however, on the survival of his uncle, and Calixtus was growing steadily more frail and finding it increasingly difficult to leave his bed. He continued to send out streams of instructions, exhortations, and appeals, willing himself to generate more activity than many of his younger, healthier predecessors, but that he was in serious decline is suggested by a letter sent to Rodrigo in the March of Ancona. It was written not by Calixtus himself but by his old friend Enea Silvio Piccolomini, a seasoned Vatican diplomat who had recently been made a cardinal at the urging of Germany's Holy Roman emperor and the king of Hungary.

Boiled down to its essence, the letter was an appeal to Rodrigo Borgia to return to Rome. "Would to God that this were granted," Piccolomini wrote, "the sooner the better; for your return would be very useful; you would be a comfort to the great aged Pontiff, your uncle, who, absorbed by constant anxieties, finds no relief. Your very presence would be an enjoyment for him, since it is sweet to mind and heart to be with one of your own blood."

It was not for Rodrigo to decide when he should return to Rome, of course. But the question was soon decided for him, and a lonely old man's wish to have someone of his "own blood" near at hand may have had something to do with the startling way in which it happened. In the autumn of 1457 Calixtus sent a letter "to our beloved son, Rodrigo," informing his nephew that he was again being promoted, this time to a post that would elevate him above all other members of the College of Cardinals. He was to report to Rome and take up the duties of vice-chancellor of the Church, the highest position in the hierarchy after the papacy itself. If the pope could be thought of as in effect the Church's chairman and chief executive, and the College of Cardinals as analogous to a board of directors, the vice-chancellor was the pope's right hand, a chief operating officer responsible for managing much of the Curia's vast administrative apparatus as well as overseeing the collection of revenues and the granting of benefices and favors. The office also gave Rodrigo—fittingly enough, insofar as he had a doctorate in law—charge of the Sacred Romana Rota, the Vatican's highest court with twelve judges and a large staff of advocates and notaries. If some cardinals were surprised at seeing a position of such reach and power conferred upon a twenty-six-year-old, the fact that the nominee was a relative of the pope's appears to have offended no one. As Cardinal Piccolomini's letter to Rodrigo showed, the pontiff's need for lieutenants in whom he could place firm personal trust was understood. The last man to serve as vice-chancellor—the post had been vacant since 1453—had been a nephew of Eugenius IV.

As if all this were not more than enough, Rodrigo was simultaneously appointed "chief and general commissary of the pontifical army." This amorphous title, suggestive to modern ears of procurement and

food service, in fact conferred upon the young cardinal not only command over all the officers of the papal armed forces, his brother the
captain-general included, but responsibility for overseeing whatever
wars the Vatican might be engaged in and authority to enter into treaties with the warlords whose little domains studded the map of the
Papal States. It made Rodrigo not so much a field general—never in his
life would he claim to have either experience or competence as a
soldier—as his uncle's minister for war. Thus when he finally departed
the March of Ancona, probably in November 1457, it was to take up in
Rome an astonishingly heavy array of responsibilities. He took with
him, as the residue of almost a year of restoring order in the March,
direct experience of the lawlessness that poisoned life in the Papal States
and new, well-earned confidence in his own ability to deal with such
matters. It was a time of extraordinary personal growth for Rodrigo, as
his uncle heaped more and more work on his shoulders and he showed
himself capable of handling it. The process of being tested and tested
again and never found wanting was lifting him to a position of primacy
among the pope's three nephews.

The months following his return to Rome appear to have been a
comparatively quiet time for Rodrigo. He gets little mention in the reports of the ambassadors at the Vatican, which is not surprising in light
of the time and attention that must have been required for him to take
up the reins of the chancery with its many departments, the Rota, and
the papal military. He also had to set up a household, one both appropriate to his new eminence and big enough to provide working space
for his suddenly enormous number of subordinates. His brother Pedro
Luis was ill that winter of 1457–58, so that the papal army was even less
active than it ordinarily would have been at that time of year. Calixtus
from his bed continued to try to muster reinforcements for Scarampo's
little force in the eastern Mediterranean and continued to be rebuffed.
He and Rodrigo would have spent many hours conferring.

New popes, upon taking office, were required to surrender whatever
offices and benefices they had held at the time of their election, distributing them as administrative or political considerations required or as
their personal preferences suggested. Calixtus of course had conformed
to this rule, but in the two years following his coronation he had done
nothing to fill the vacant see of Valencia, the only bishopric he had held

when a cardinal. Because Valencia was the Borgia family's home diocese, and also no doubt because it was one of the richest and most prestigious sees on the Iberian peninsula, Calixtus wanted to give it to
Rodrigo, whose mother was presumably still living in its episcopal palace. Though from a Roman perspective vastly less important than the
vice-chancellorship or the war ministry, the see turned out to be much
more difficult for the pope to bestow as he wished, because others had
designs on it. Calixtus's old master and now-nemesis Alfonso V wanted
it for one of his son Ferrante's numerous offspring, while Alfonso's
brother King Juan of Navarre saw it as a suitable perch for one of *his*
sons. This was not an unusual conflict; disagreements over who had
the right to appoint bishops and archbishops had been setting kings and
popes at odds with each other almost as long as Europe had had kings
and popes, sometimes with disastrous consequences. Confronted with
such formidable competition, Calixtus sensibly hesitated to act. There
were limits to how far even a pope could go in defying the family that
ruled much of the Mediterranean world.

Everything changed in May 1458 when Alfonso V fell ill. Still boiling
with vitality and ambition, until suddenly obliged to retire to his bed he
had been preparing the next of his attacks on Genoa, whose colonial
outposts he had never stopped coveting. He declined rapidly but lingered for some forty days, the royal physicians trying every available
remedy to no avail. When death came on June 27 it removed from the
scene the mightiest monarch and one of the most brilliant personalities
of his time. King of Aragon and Valencia, of Majorca and Sardinia and
Corsica and Sicily and Naples, count of Barcelona and Rousillon, he was
as fascinatingly paradoxical a character as any biographer could hope to
find: sincerely religious but also utterly untrustworthy; kindly and generous but also ruthlessly, insatiably ambitious; a great patron of the arts
and an endless source of trouble for Italy's other rulers. He might have
been the man to unify Italy—he certainly intended to be—if at various
times and in various ways he had not been thwarted by the Sforzas of
Milan, the Medici of Florence, and the popes in Rome. Blocked by Venice and the Turks from creating the empire that he hungered for in the
East, he had retaliated by creating endless difficulties for both. He had
dominated the political stage for so long that his disappearance, which
the embalming process showed to have been the result of an abscess on

his lung, left everyone in a state of stunned uncertainty. The kingdom of Naples, which during his reign had been inexhaustibly aggressive, suddenly went limp.

Alfonso's intended heir Ferrante, his claim to the crown seriously in doubt, was immediately thrown on the defensive. This brought a sense of deliverance in many quarters. Almost overnight Venice found that it had one fewer rival in the Aegean and other eastern places; thus it felt free to be less hostile toward Skanderbeg of Albania. This freed the Albanians, in turn, to focus on rebuilding their strength in anticipation of renewed Turkish aggression. Genoa felt that a black cloud had been removed from over its head, and for a while politics became less thorny for the Italian states generally.

No one was more delighted than Calixtus. "The bond is broken," he exclaimed, "and we are free!" Free not only of Alfonso's endless meddling in the affairs of Rome and the Papal States, but free also to set Naples on an entirely new course in which Ferrante would have no part. The legal complexities of the succession question were enormous, but in all Europe there was no one better prepared to deal with them than the onetime legal scholar Alonso de Borja. Drawing upon his professional knowledge, he found a sound basis for arguing that, when Eugenius IV invested Alfonso with the crown of Naples, the king had been granted life tenure only, with no right of succession. No less significantly, Europe's feudal code made it virtually indisputable that legitimization did not carry with it the right of inheritance, especially with respect to thrones. Calixtus issued a bull declaring that with Alfonso's death the fief of Naples had reverted to the Holy See. He said that as pope he was at liberty to bestow the crown wherever he wished—or to bestow it on no one. Ferrante, who had long shared the responsibilities of rule with his father and at age thirty-five was a seasoned and formidably shrewd politician, sent envoys to Rome to argue his case. To the extent that they were given a hearing, it was a distinctly frosty one.

Suggestions that the pope had a hidden agenda—that he hoped to make the Borgias the ruling dynasty of Naples—are not easily squared with what we know of Calixtus's character, the existence of several candidates possessing both royal blood and powerful support, and the certain fact that any attempt to confer the crown on Pedro Luis or any other Borgia would have aroused ferocious opposition not only throughout Italy but across Europe. Ferrante's most obvious rival was Juan of Navarre, whose entitlement to every part of his brother Alfonso's empire except—just possibly—Naples was beyond possibility of challenge. The thought of Juan inheriting Naples was not a comfortable one for Rome, however, because the vast reserves of manpower and wealth available to him as ruler of Aragon and Sicily and numerous other places would enable him to become the same kind of danger Alfonso had been. To the Aragonese argument that Sicily and Naples went together, so that if Juan was king of Sicily he was entitled to Naples as well, Calixtus replied that the so-called Union of Two Sicilies had been created for the benefit of Alfonso alone and was dissolved by his death.

Yet another twist was the fact that Juan had two sons who were not churchmen, were both legitimate though born to different mothers, and had rival claims to be their father's heir. The elder of the two, Carlos of Viana, was not only alienated from his father, who favored his younger half-brother Ferdinand, but literally at war with him. It was undoubtedly for this reason that Calixtus declared Carlos's claim to Naples to be worthy of consideration; it was a way of keeping Juan off balance. The pope said similarly encouraging things about the claim of the House of Anjou, the branch of the French royal family that Alfonso had driven out of Naples fifteen years before. He pledged to "do my utmost to deliver my successor" by excluding Ferrante not only from the throne but even from the list of candidates. Clearly this was his main objective where Naples was concerned. His second was to keep the kingdom from falling into the hands of anyone as powerful as Juan.

On June 30 he cut the Gordian knot, assembling the cardinals in consistory and securing their approval of Rodrigo as bishop of Valencia. At the same time, in an effort to placate the House of Aragon, he got consent to the bestowal of the archbishopric of Zaragoza upon a third son of King Juan. The gesture failed; the new archbishop's royal father was neither satisfied nor grateful. Being now in possession of his late brother's international empire, he believed himself entitled to choose his own bishops, especially on his home ground in Spain. And there were practical reasons for his discontent. The bishopric of Valencia was substantially more lucrative than the *arch*bishopric of Zaragoza, producing as it did an income of nearly twenty thousand ducats per year. Calixtus, however, had made up his mind. He was determined to keep Valencia in the family and not to let the opportunity created by Alfonso's death slip away unused.

In Naples, meanwhile, Ferrante was showing his determination to become king regardless of what the pope thought. When Calixtus repeated his old assertion that neither Ferrante nor Naples had any claim to Benevento or Terracina or the territories surrounding, Ferrante moved to secure both places with his troops. Pedro Luis then moved the papal army southward to the frontier, where he paused to await developments. A further move by either side would be the start of a war.

By that time July was well advanced, bringing with it the heat and humidity that invariably descended upon Rome in midsummer. Daily life became a punishment even for the young and healthy, and malaria and plague began to ravage the population. For an eighty-year-old pope who had long been an invalid it was murderous, making the long days nearly unendurable and sleep difficult even at night. From ancient times it had been part of the rhythm of Roman life for everyone who could do so to withdraw to the cool of the hill country. But in 1458, either because he had so much to do or because he was too weak to travel, Calixtus did not go. The result was predictable: he became seriously ill and soon was unable to attend to business. Reports that he was dying spread. The members of the baronial clans who had not left the city, already short-tempered thanks to the oppressive weather, began to make plans for taking advantage of his passing.

On July 26, upon receiving unsettling reports about his uncle's condition, Rodrigo left his hilltop retreat in Tivoli and hurried the twenty-five miles back to the Vatican. Pedro Luis may have done likewise, because in the course of the next several days Calixtus rallied sufficiently to dictate a bull making him vicar—not duke, but governor—of Benevento and Terracina. The pope must have believed, or hoped at least, that he was not dying, because he certainly understood that such a bull could mean nothing in the event of his death.

As August began, the imminence of the pope's death was taken for granted everywhere. This brought to the enemies of the Borgias the liberating conviction that they no longer had anything to fear. That the hour of vengeance had arrived. For the Orsini especially, but for some of the city's lesser clans as well, the effect was exhilarating. They took to the streets and summoned their rural kinsmen to join them. It became dangerous to be a Spaniard, never mind a Borgia, anywhere in Rome. The Spanish were attacked if they left their homes, and at least a few were killed. Houses were set afire, along with the warehouses of Spanish merchants. Many of the papal household's Spanish employees stopped showing up for work.

The danger was greatest for Pedro Luis; the Orsini hated no one as they hated him. It became impossible for him to show his face in public. As Calixtus faded into unconsciousness, many of the cardinals turned against his captain-general, demanding that he relinquish control of the Castel Sant'Angelo and other key fortresses. The Orsini and their henchmen grew bolder by the hour. It had become questionable whether Pedro Luis—whether any member of his family—could survive either by remaining in the city or by trying to get away.

The Borgias of Rome had arrived at their first great crisis.

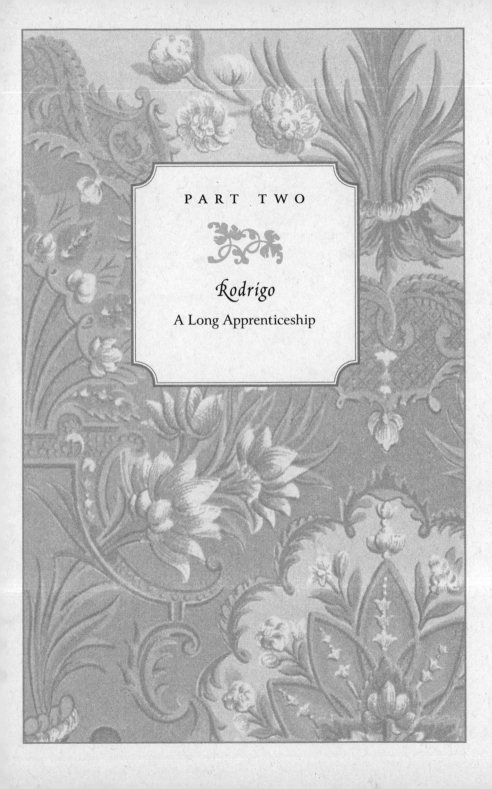

PART TWO

Rodrigo

A Long Apprenticeship

6

Surviving

Calixtus was not yet dead when the contempt of the Roman citizenry for the Spanish interlopers they called "Catalans" rose to a murderous pitch.

The pontiff was not himself an object of this hatred or of the bloodlust to which it gave rise. Though the Romans sometimes called him a "barbarian" pope, this was less because he had done anything to give offense—or was perceived as an offensive figure, even—than because he was not Italian, had come to Rome as a man of advanced years, and so would always be an outsider. Against a man who lived as simply and virtuously as Calixtus did, one so determined to go on doing his duty as the infirmities of old age bore down on him, not even the Romans could work up much hostility.

Although he was left to die almost alone as the members of his largely Spanish household slipped fearfully away, Calixtus was therefore never in danger. No one objected to letting him expire in peace.

It was different for his countrymen, most different of all for the young Borgias whom he had raised to princely status. They were marked men. Pedro Luis, prefect of Rome and captain-general of the papal troops, master in his uncle's name of more towns and territories than anyone could readily name or even count, was in danger from the moment the pope's illness became widely known. By the first days of

August it was no longer possible to be confident that Pedro Luis was going to escape with his life.

This part of our story would be simpler if more were known about what kind of man Pedro Luis actually was. But the evidence is too thin and too dubious to bring him into focus. That he was raised high at a precocious age, and was bitterly resented by those who saw his advancement as an affront and a threat, we have already seen. What is not clear is whether and to what extent he had done anything to justify the hatred that was directed at him. Did it happen simply because he was a Spaniard and a Borgia and conscientious in the execution of the duties assigned to him by the pope? Or was he in fact the kind of man who would have been hated even if he had been Roman from birth?

Down the centuries, Pedro Luis has often been depicted as everyone's image of a Spanish nobleman-warrior in the age of the conquistadores: proud, arrogant, cruel, and therefore despised by decent people. He has also been described as self-defeatingly stupid—a defect not often found among the Borgias—and doomed for that reason. Possibly he was all these things, but it is equally possible that he was none of them. Practically all of the unflattering accounts of his character can be traced no further back than to people who had never met him, people who were not alive when he was but had political or religious reasons to think him a typically evil member of a uniquely vicious clan. In Pedro Luis we encounter for the first time the great challenge of Borgia history: the need to distinguish between what can be accepted as true or at least probable on the basis of credible evidence and what was fabricated after the fact but has been endlessly repeated because of its usefulness in showing yet another Borgia to have been odious. What is known for sure about Pedro Luis is sufficient neither to condemn him nor to declare him grievously misunderstood. It is difficult to judge even his performance as a military commander, so little being known about the opposition he faced, the resources he had at his disposal, or how he conducted himself while in action.

On August 5, 1458, in any case, the truth about Pedro Luis's character and conduct was far less urgent than the question of his survival. On the previous day, with Calixtus visibly losing his grip on life and the clans rampaging in the streets, a delegation of cardinals had called on the captain-general and demanded that he surrender the one absolutely secure place of refuge in Rome, the Castel Sant'Angelo. He had agreed, but only after being promised the twenty-two thousand gold ducats that he claimed were owed him by the pontifical treasury. (There is no way of judging the legitimacy of this debt, but it is entirely plausible that Pedro Luis expended this much or more out of his own pocket in the discharge of his many duties.) A deal having been struck, attention shifted to getting him out of Rome.

This turned out to require both guile and a show of force. Between them, Cardinal Rodrigo as de facto Vatican war minister and Pedro Luis as captain-general were able to muster some three thousand mounted troops and two hundred infantry. This little army, after being formed into a protective phalanx around the mounted Pedro Luis, was paraded with attention-compelling ostentation out of the Vatican and across the Milvian Bridge, obviously headed out of the city. But as it approached the Porta del Popolo, a major exit point known to be in the hands of the Orsini, Rodrigo and a friend from the College of Cardinals, Pietro Barbo, slipped away with a smaller, less conspicuous company of troops, taking a disguised Pedro Luis with them. Upon reaching the Porta San Paolo, having determined that the road ahead was clear, the two cardinals bade Pedro Luis farewell and turned back into the city. Pedro Luis galloped downriver toward Ostia on the coast, taking his gold with him. There he waited to be picked up by a galley that never came, finally hiring a fishing boat that took him the forty miles up the coast to the papal fortress of Civitavecchia, which he commanded as captain-general.

Rodrigo returned to the Vatican—an act of some courage under the circumstances—and was with his uncle when he died the following day. Rome was in a state of near-anarchy. Rodrigo did nothing to protect his "palace"—still little more than a strung-together assortment of recently derelict buildings, used mainly as a workplace for the employees of the papal chancery—and so it was stripped bare. He must have had relatively little worth stealing at this point, and trying to hold off the mob could only have inflamed its wrath. By in effect throwing open his doors he relieved some of the hostility directed at him as a Catalan, a Borgia, and the dead pontiff's fellow barbarian.

Attention now turned, to the extent that anyone could focus his attention in the midst of so much disorder, to the ceremonials involved in burying a pope and preparing for the election of a successor. It could go without saying that there was not the smallest possibility of Rodrigo Borgia being chosen or even considered; his youth would have disqualified him had there been no other negatives. By the time of Calixtus's interment, those cardinals hopeful of election were well along with their campaigning. There was considerable expectation—probably proclaimed most strongly by the candidate himself—that the all-but-certain winner was Guillaume d'Estouteville, cardinal of Rouen. He was fabulously wealthy, a cousin of the king of France, openly ambitious for the throne, haughty, vain, of dubious moral character—and for all these reasons disliked by more of his fellow cardinals than he appears to have understood. In the days just after Calixtus's death, the most popular contender had been Domenico Capranica, the same admired theologian whose candidacy had been blocked by Latino Orsini at the conclave of 1455. This time his chances looked better, but just three days before the opening of the conclave he threw everyone's calculations into confusion by unexpectedly dying, aged fifty-eight. No doubt this confirmed for Estouteville that God himself was clearing a path to his election. The next five days, however, would demonstrate the wisdom of an ancient proverb: he who enters the conclave a pope, exits a cardinal.

The first secret ballot, taken after two days of discussion, produced a surprising result. Estouteville received not a single vote, meaning that he hadn't voted for himself. This may have been an obscure strategic move on the Frenchman's part, but it also sheds light on just how little his election was desired. Enea Silvio Piccolomini of Siena and Filippo Calandrini of Bologna received five votes each. The remaining ballots were scattered among an essentially random assortment of cardinals, none of whom had a chance of being elected.

That night Estouteville went into action, lobbying hard, offering bribes, and threatening retribution to any who declined to cooperate. He told his colleagues one by one, in feigned confidence, that he was a single vote short of the needed two-thirds majority, and he painted an enticing picture of the rewards that awaited the man who put him over the top. Obviously he was setting the stage for an overwhelming show of support in the next day's voting. What happened next cannot be told better than in the words of the man who was about to emerge as Estouteville's sole rival, Cardinal Piccolomini. In his written account of the conclave—a document unique in history, no cardinal before or since having produced anything comparable— Piccolomini refers to himself in the third person as "Enea." He recounts how offended he was, on the night of August 18, to discover that Estouteville had stationed himself in the latrine ("a fit place for such a pope to be elected!" he exclaims) and was using every possible promise and threat in a bare-knuckles push for votes. And how, after being warned that he himself had better get on the bandwagon before it was too late, Piccolomini went to bed resolved to launch a stop-Estouteville campaign upon rising the next morning. His memoir continues:

> Enea went at daybreak to Rodrigo, the vice-chancellor, and asked whether he had sold himself to Rouen. "What would you have me do?" he answered. "The thing is settled. Many of the cardinals have met in the privies and decided to elect him. It is not for my advantage to remain with a small minority out of favor with a new pope. I am joining the majority and I have looked out for my own interests. I shall not lose the chancellorship; I have a note from Rouen assuring me of that. If I do not vote for him, the others will elect him anyway and I shall be stripped of my office."
>
> Enea said to him, "You young fool! Will you then put an enemy of your nation in the Apostle's chair? And will you put faith in the note of a man who is faithless? You will have the note; Avignon [another French cardinal] will have the chancellorship. For what has been promised you has been promised him also and solemnly affirmed. Will faith be kept with him or with you? Will a Frenchman be more friendly to a Frenchman or to a Catalan? Will he be more concerned for a foreigner or for his own countryman? Take care, you inexperienced boy! Take care, you fool! And if you have no thought for the Church of Rome, if you have no regard for the Christian religion and despise God, for whom you are preparing such a vicar, at least take thought for yourself, for you will find yourself among the hindmost, if a Frenchman is pope."

He notes that Rodrigo "listened patiently to these words of his friend." He had certainly given the vice-chancellor much food for thought.

Filippo Calandrini, one of the two leaders in the previous day's balloting, dropped out before the next vote was taken. A hardworking but undistinguished Curia official who owed his place in the Sacred College to his half-brother Pope Nicholas V, Calandrini threw his support to Piccolomini. The next surprise, when the results of the latest round of voting became known, was that Estouteville, far from winning election or being barely short of victory as he had been telling everyone, received only six votes. The leader was his indignant antagonist Piccolomini, whose nine votes left him three short of the needed total.

At this point the conclave voted to try to bring matters to a conclusion "by accession," a traditional recourse when secret balloting failed to produce a winner. It involved sitting together in silence and waiting to see if any of the electors found themselves moved to change their minds. Estouteville needed to double his vote, making his prospects dim at best. Even Piccolomini, needing three, appeared to have limited prospects against so intimidating an opponent. The cardinals sat for what seemed a long time, the tension building, no one speaking or making a move. Then at last Rodrigo Borgia rose to his feet. "I accede," he said, "to the cardinal of Siena." To Piccolomini, that is, moving him to within two votes of election. At that point, in a desperate attempt to disrupt the proceedings, Cardinals Isidore of Greece and Torquemada of Spain (an enemy of Piccolomini's since the two had clashed over questions of theology at the Council of Basel) bolted from their seats and flounced out of the room. When no one followed, they decided that they had better return. They did so in time to see Cardinal Tebaldi of Santa Anastasia, a longtime protégé of Calixtus III and brother of the late pope's favorite physician, stand up and repeat Rodrigo's words.

One vote more was still needed. When Cardinal Prospero Colonna started to rise, Estouteville on one side and Basilios Bessarion on the other seized him by the arms and literally tried to drag him away. He threw them off, shouting that he too acceded to the election of Cardinal Piccolomini. Until that moment Colonna had opposed Piccolomini, but when he saw an opportunity to deliver the decisive vote and so put the next pope in his debt, he was too good a politician not to seize it. It was Rodrigo, however, who had broken the deadlock, acting first, alone, and at greatest risk to himself. Piccolomini—now Pope Pius II— understood what a difference he had made. If he had stayed with Estoute- ville, the whole accession process might have led to a very different result.

One must make of this episode what one will. It can be interpreted as showing Rodrigo to be a self-serving cynic, initially lining up with Estouteville for no nobler reason than the expectation that by doing so he would bring himself the most good. It is likewise possible to see him as showing weakness of character, a willingness to vote for the French- man when he seemed unbeatable and then to abandon him as soon as his vulnerability became plain. It is nonetheless true that in the end he voted for the clearly better man, and that he did so when no one else would and his action could have carried a high cost. When one consid- ers the effect of this election on Rodrigo's own career—he came out of it a favorite protégé of the new pope—it can fairly be considered an early demonstration of his political skill. What is most striking in Pic- colomini's account of their early morning conversation is the candor with which Rodrigo acknowledged not only that he was supporting Estouteville but that he was doing so out of sheer self-interest. Such candor is disarming even in an adversary. It will be characteristic of Rodrigo over the next forty-five years, helping to explain his almost uncanny ability to win the affection of almost everyone who came within his reach.

Rodrigo and Piccolomini had first become friends during the reign of Calixtus, both of them having open and affectionate natures com- bined with a voracious appetite for work. What had happened in con- clave propelled their relationship to a deeper level. It took on something of the character of a father-son connection. The new pope was not only the older of the two by a quarter of a century but had vastly more expe- rience of the world. He had much to teach, and the physically big, un- failingly cheery Rodrigo was nothing if not an eager and able learner. The liking that the two had for each other, the respect that each had for the other's character and ability, removed any possibility that Pius might prefer a different vice-chancellor.

The new pope was a remarkable man with an unusual background. Fifty-two years old at the time of his election, a cultivated lawyer with no personal wealth to speak of, he had not embarked upon a clerical career until he was well into his thirties (by which time he had, in Germany and Scotland, fathered illegitimate children who died in infancy). He had grown up the eldest of the eighteen children of a couple who, though of noble origins, were so poor that as a boy he had to labor in his father's fields. After schooling by a local priest he began university at age eighteen, late for those times, and went on to spend most of the next decade studying first literature and then the law. A revealing episode occurred when he was twenty-five: he announced that he wanted to enter the monastic life, but was dissuaded by friends who dismissed the idea as absurd for someone with the young Piccolomini's attraction to the pleasures of the flesh. Obviously he took the religious vocation seriously—so much so that he was unwilling to commit himself to it until he was satisfied that he could observe the required vows. While serving first as legal counsel to prominent figures at the Council of Basel, then as a diplomat handling assignments across Europe, he remained unmarried but a layman. In 1435 a winter voyage to Scotland, at the northernmost edge of the known world, proved so hair-raisingly hazardous that he vowed, if delivered safely ashore, to walk barefoot to the nearest shrine to the Virgin Mary. Keeping this pledge turned out to involve a ten-mile trek through ice and snow, causing so much tissue damage that he walked with a limp for the rest of his life.

Though at Basel he had served men hostile to Pope Eugenius IV and actively supported the antipope Felix V, ultimately joining the entourage of Felix's patron the Hapsburg emperor Frederick III, when about forty he yielded to the old call to the religious life. A year after taking his first, conditional vows, he played a significant role in negotiations that settled long-standing disputes between Eugenius and the princes of Germany. By 1452, when he returned to Italy for Frederick III's marriage and coronation, he was not only a priest but bishop of Siena. Thereafter he remained in Italy, representing the emperor at the papal court, and in 1456, at the urging of Frederick and the king of Hungary, he was appointed by Calixtus to the College of Cardinals. When elected pope just twenty months later, he was both a man of the world, accustomed to doing business with some of the most powerful people in Europe, and a devoted son of the Church, certain of its unique importance. There is significance in the fact that such a man showed no hesitation in making the young Cardinal Borgia not only one of his closest companions but virtually a junior partner. That Pius II embraced Rodrigo so unreservedly is the best indication we have of what kind of man the latter must have been, in terms not only of talent but of conduct, as he entered his thirties.

Pius and Rodrigo were a team from the day of the election and went into action quickly. Among the matters requiring immediate attention was the Pedro Luis problem. Pius dispatched Rodrigo to Civitavecchia to persuade his brother of the impossibility, in a climate of such intense resentment, of his holding on to the offices and properties that his uncle had conferred upon him. This accomplished, the brothers presumably agreed that Pedro Luis should return to Spain. Both surrendered their positions in the papal military, which went to a nephew of Pius's. One of the Colonna succeeded Pedro Luis as prefect of Rome. Whether or not this was a gesture of thanks for Prospero Colonna's climactic vote, Rodrigo must have been relieved that the job had not been returned to the Orsini. So soon after Calixtus's death, a papacy allied with the Orsini would have made Rodrigo's situation impossible.

Instead, his situation was enviable indeed. By remaining vice-chancellor, Rodrigo kept sole charge not only of one of the three largest branches of the Curia but of the only one whose functions were so essential that it could not be shut down for summer holidays. It included the office known as the Dataria, which received all requests and petitions and drafted letters and grants; the more than one hundred *scriptori,* expert in the preparation of various pontifical documents; and the notaries, lawyers responsible for preparing papal bulls and maintaining registries of all the correspondence and official documents arriving at and being sent out from the Vatican. The vice-chancellor's oversight of the Rota, the supreme court, gave him control of judicial favors, platoons of lawyers and clerks, and considerable sums of money.

Anyone who used this great office skillfully could make himself one of the most important men in Europe. No one would ever use it more skillfully than Rodrigo Borgia, or do so for such a long time. And it was far from his only responsibility; he was repeatedly given other major assignments as well, evidence of the confidence he inspired. When on September 26 news reached Rome of the death of Pedro Luis, probably of malaria, Pius sent the suddenly twice-bereaved Rodrigo back to Civitavecchia to see to the interment of his brother's remains, settle his affairs, and take possession of the fortress in the pope's name. It has long been said that what the cardinal inherited from his uncle and his brother provided the foundation of his later colossal wealth. There is in fact no evidence that even together the two left enough to place Rodrigo among the wealthiest cardinals—or for that matter, that Rodrigo ever managed to hold on to much of his very impressive income. Great as his revenues would be from all the offices conferred on him during his years as vice-chancellor, he appears to have spent them—usually for official or at least political purposes—at least as fast as they came in and sometimes alarmingly faster.

Among the issues carried over from Calixtus's reign, two were particularly vexing: the unsettled questions of who should succeed Alfonso V as king of Naples, and what should be done about the Turks. Perhaps because the second question was growing more urgent every year—in 1458 Athens fell to the Turks—Pius decided to put the first to rest. Having been persuaded by Francesco Sforza of Milan that life would be easier for both of them if the royal families of France and Spain were kept out of Naples, he put aside Calixtus's objections and invested Ferrante with the crown. This did not spare Ferrante from being challenged on two fronts; France's House of Anjou launched a fresh military campaign for the conquest of Naples, and Il Regno's barons rose up in rebellion. But these were not the pope's problems, at least not directly. He joined with Sforza in sending troops to aid Ferrante and trusted that that would suffice.

The problem of the Ottoman Turks, by contrast, would torment Pius to the end of his life. He addressed it first by preparing a letter to Sultan Mehmed, offering to recognize all the Turks' conquests in return for their conversion to Christianity. The Vatican's archives contain no indication that this offer was ever sent, or that if sent it received an answer. In all likelihood Pius set it aside upon realizing that it was futile to the point of absurdity and more likely to make him seem desperate and foolish than to produce a positive result. Next he wrote to all the nations of Europe, inviting them to send representatives to the city of Mantua in the summer of 1459. As conceived by Pius, this was to be the first meeting of the whole of Europe's secular leadership ever called for

a single purpose—that purpose being the planning of a three-year crusade. The crusade was to be financed by a special levy on every churchman and church in Europe, and by contributions from the various
crowned heads. Pius chose Mantua because, being in the far north of
Italy, it was convenient for the great figures he hoped to attract from
beyond the Alps. Also, the enormous palaces of Mantua's prince,
Ludovico Gonzaga, could accommodate not only the papal court but
all the dignitaries to whom Pius expected to be playing host.

When Pius set out for Mantua early in 1459, Rodrigo was among the
five cardinals who went with him. The journey became a festive procession, with people lining the roadside to cheer the pontiff as he
passed. It took them to his birthplace, the hamlet of Corsignano in the
Tuscan hills. There he stopped for a long sentimental visit, in the course
of which he took actions that would raise doubts about just how serious
he was in demanding shared sacrifices for the sake of his crusade. He
gave Corsignano the new name Pienza, a derivation of Pius, and promoted it from village to town. He declared it the seat of a diocese,
meaning that henceforth it would have a bishop and require a cathedral. He pledged himself, or rather the pontifical treasury, to pay for
building the cathedral and made it known that he expected all the cardinals to build summer retreats there. Rodrigo as vice-chancellor found
himself committed to financing the construction of an episcopal palace. It was a strange episode, an early, autocratic, and ill-timed exercise
in urban renewal, recognizable to anyone ever pressured to contribute
to a boss's pet cause.

When the papal party pushed on to Mantua, it found that not one of
the invited rulers had arrived or even sent a representative. Pius and the
cardinals had to wait all through the summer, and even when enough
delegates had assembled for formal discussions to begin, their number
remained low and few showed any real enthusiasm. The Venetians
were opposed to a crusade, clinging to the hope of reaching an understanding with the Turks. The French were uncooperative because
they were offended by Pius's failure to support the Angevins in Naples,
and when René count of Anjou showed up in person, he provoked indignation by trying to recruit allies for his war on Naples. Francesco
Sforza, though his capital of Milan was less than a hundred miles from

Mantua, was four months late in arriving. By the end of the year nothing had been accomplished, and there was clearly no hope that anything would be. In January 1460, just before departing, Pius issued two bulls. One was a proclamation—a somewhat forlorn one under the circumstances—that against all odds there was in fact going to be a crusade, and it would embark from the east coast of Italy in the summer of 1464.

The other bull, destined to be known by its opening word *Execrabilis,* dealt in bold terms with a matter that had been preying on Pius's mind since the years when he was involved in the squabbles at the Council of Basel. It declared that anyone appealing over the head of the pope to a council of the Church was, simply by virtue of having done so, a heretic and a traitor. It was prompted—an example of the arcane quarrels that plagued the reign of every pope—by an old and exasperating dispute with France over what was called the Pragmatic Sanction of Bourges. In signing this irksome document, dating back to 1438, France's king had endorsed the Council of Basel's declaration that councils were superior to popes. He had also happily agreed with the council that the selection of bishops should rest with the crown, not with the Vatican, that a king's decisions could only rarely be appealed to Rome, and that various revenues traditionally sent to Rome should go to the king instead. By Pius II's time the Pragmatic Sanction had been a source of friction for a generation. When King Charles VII sent ambassadors to Mantua rather than attending himself, and when those ambassadors made a display of their disdain for Pius's crusade, the pope vented his frustration by declaring the Sanction to be null. The aged Charles, at the end of his life now and disgruntled by the pope's support of Ferrante in Naples, responded by threatening to summon a new council. *Execrabilis* was Pius's answer. While not ending the dispute—the French received it with snorts of contempt—the bull would not be without effect. It drew a line under the generations of conflict between popes and councils. From now on the great battles would be between popes and kings, and sometimes between popes and cardinals.

Pius II was a restless spirit who had spent much of his life on diplomatic missions, and he loved to travel and had no affection for Rome. He also loved the land of his birth, Tuscany. Upon leaving Mantua, having no wish to return to a Vatican from which he had already been absent for some eight months, he now led his party to Siena. Like the previous year's visit to his home village, this was a sentimental journey; Pius had spent happy if impoverished years as a student in Siena, and much later he had been the city's bishop, albeit a usually absent one. He settled in for what he hoped would be a long and pleasant stay, seeking relief for his damaged feet at the nearby hot baths. He paid little attention to reports that Rome, as invariably happened in the absence of the pope and his court, was showing signs of disorder. Rodrigo cannot have shared his relaxed attitude; as vice-chancellor he had to keep abreast of developments back in Rome. The chancery's affairs were too essential to the papacy itself, and raised too many questions of policy, to be left in the hands of functionaries. Couriers would have been galloping to and fro between Siena and Rome, carrying Rodrigo's paperwork.

The disappointments of Mantua turned out to be almost trivial compared with the troubles that came down on Pius's head during this second sojourn in Tuscany. His chances of mounting a crusade of sufficient magnitude to accomplish anything of importance were dealt a serious setback—though Pius refused to admit it, probably even to himself—when Duke Philip of Burgundy (then an autonomous and immensely wealthy state) sent word that he would not be able to join the other participants until a year after the projected launch. Actually this was a polite way for Philip to drop out without admitting that he was doing so; he was being pressed to withdraw by his kinsman the king of France. Everyone understood that his postponement was actually a thinly veiled cancellation.

Other disappointments followed. Ferrante of Naples had met the Angevin invaders and his rebellious barons in battle and been whipped by them soundly; he was in serious jeopardy as a result, raising the possibility that Pius had made a costly mistake in recognizing him as king. And suddenly, up in the Romagna, the pope had a war of his own to fight, thanks to a troublesome vassal named Sigismondo Pandolfo Malatesta, lord of Rimini. Worse still, from Rome came reports of a new conspiracy to expel the papal government and declare a republic. If the pope didn't return soon, he was warned, he could find himself in exile like Eugenius IV twenty years before.

As a crowning blow—the reader familiar with the reputation of the

Borgias has perhaps been expecting something of this kind—Pius was visiting the healing waters of Petriolo when word reached him that back in Siena his right hand, his brilliant and beloved young vice-chancellor, had become embroiled in an absolutely outlandish scandal.

The dark side of the Borgia legend was at last beginning to unfold.

THE ETERNAL CITY, ETERNALLY REBORN

NO ONE SHOULD HAVE BEEN SURPRISED THAT SUCH PUBLIC order as the city of Rome enjoyed at the end of the 1450s began to disintegrate when Pius II removed the papal court to Mantua and did not return for almost a year and a half.

It was becoming all too clear, by this time, that Rome could not function—could not even survive as more than a crime-infested backwater—in the absence of the papal court. That whenever a pope was away for more than brief interludes, the city actually began to die. And that when the popes returned, its heart began to beat again. The so-called Eternal City was, ironically, the least stable, least vital, and least self-sufficient of Italy's great capitals.

The Rome of Pius II's time would not be recognizable to visitors from the twenty-first century any more than to visitors from the first. Its population, which totaled a million or more in the days of the Caesars and had dwindled to a pathetic twenty-five thousand at the start of the fifteenth century, cannot have been much more than fifty thousand in the 1460s. The remains of the old imperial capital were of course in ruins, most of the oldest palaces and churches having been either dismantled for their stone or transformed into makeshift fortifications behind which frightened families huddled for protection. Most of the people lived in squalor, crowded into the tangle of dark, narrow, and filthy streets that had taken shape helter-skelter around the Pantheon. Only one of the magnificent viaducts that once had supplied the city with water was still in working order, and few of the churches and palaces that are the glory of the city today had yet been built. St. Peter's Basilica was falling apart, and most of the fabled Roman hills had been given over to crops and livestock. Anyone looking down from one of those hills would have been struck first by the innumerable towers that studded the landscape. There were towers at the ends of the bridges across the Tiber, towers on what remained of the city wall, towers rising out of the fortress-homes of every family that could afford one. They were expressions of fear, these towers—of the need for vigilance in a chronically lawless place.

"The city is for the most part in ruins," the poet Giannantonio Campano reported upon seeing it for the first time at midcentury, "and in such terrible condition that tears came to my eyes. The inhabitants are more like barbarians than Romans; they are repellent of aspect and speak the most different dialects." Such words become all the more striking when one realizes that they were written fully a generation after Pope Martin V began the city's revival. At the time they were written Nicholas V's drive to restore Rome's splendor was fully under way.

The Rome of the early Renaissance did have one important thing in common with the capital of the Caesars. Both were parasite cities, devourers rather than creators of wealth. As the historian Theodor Mommsen observed, "there has perhaps never been a great city so thoroughly destitute of the means of support as Rome." Through all the centuries when it was the center of the known world, it gave rise to no important banking institutions or manufacturing operations or anything except the bureaucracies needed for the management of a great empire. And so when the empire ceased to exist, there was no longer much reason for Rome. It was far from alone in imploding—that was the fate of urban Europe generally, one of the things that made the Dark Ages dark. But when other cities once again began to show signs of economic life, growing and generating wealth, Rome was left behind. Lacking merchants and bankers of consequence, it failed to share in the benefits brought to other places by the emergence of a commercial middle class. Finally nothing much remained but a semirural population scattered rather wretchedly among decaying ruins and at the mercy of gangster-like clans.

These clans were a constant of Roman history from the Dark Ages onward. They accumulated wealth and power while successive popes were occupied with beating back German emperors as they invaded Italy and beating down attempts to establish republican government in the city. By the late thirteenth century the clan chiefs, titled nobility or "barons" now, had nearly succeeded in making the papacy their personal property and were exploiting it ruthlessly to their own advantage.

The endless, grinding street wars in which the clans fought one another for dominance made Rome literally ungovernable for a very long time.

The withdrawal of the papacy to Avignon allowed the barons to go unchallenged except by one another through much of the fourteenth century. A chronicler described the Rome of that time as "everywhere lust, everywhere evil, no justice, no law; there was no longer any escape; the man who was strongest with the sword was the most in the right. A person's only hope was to defend himself with the help of his relatives and friends; every day groups of armed men were formed." And every night those same groups ventured out to kill one another in the streets.

The feeble communal government that was pretending to rule Rome collapsed when Martin V brought the papacy back to the city in 1420. The clans, however, remained strong, and would plague every pope for the next two centuries. Conditions began to improve all the same; by introducing a modicum of law and order, Martin sparked a process of recovery. That process gathered momentum until 1434, when the Colonna drove Eugenius IV into his eight years of exile. He had not been gone long when the city again began descending into anarchy, but a measure of stability was restored with his return. As the papacy gradually recovered its strength, drawing money to the Vatican and creating increasing numbers of jobs, Rome recovered with it. Its evolution into a leading center of Renaissance culture was interrupted briefly by the republican conspiracy against Nicholas V in 1453, more seriously at the end of that decade when Pius II departed for Mantua and stayed away too long.

Eventually the people of Rome, even the barons, resigned themselves to the truth: the city had no place in the world except as the seat of a monarchy sufficiently important to bring riches from the outside world, a monarchy on which its subjects could feed. Thus there was no substitute for the papacy, and the republican dream was pure folly, leading to nothing but disorder and decline. This was not a particularly welcome truth, but it was inescapable all the same. Once it was understood, opposition to papal rule was finished. It became impossible to muster popular support for any other kind of regime.

The barons, however, remained determined to preserve their power. Every new pope had to work out his own way of dealing with them.

7

Pius II: Troubles
Rumored and Real

It surely makes sense, before arriving at conclusions about the first accusation of scandalous misconduct ever leveled at Cardinal Rodrigo Borgia, to pause and consider just what it is that we actually *know* about the incident.

We know that in June 1460 Pope Pius II was still lingering in Tuscany, where he and his entourage had stopped en route back to Rome from Mantua. And that on the eleventh day of that month, from the retreat where he was taking the waters, the pope sent a letter to Rodrigo in Siena. This letter is unique; we know of no similar communication, no comparably stern and explicit rebuke, ever addressed by a reigning pope to a member of the Sacred College on a matter of personal behavior. The matters with which it deals, the things it reveals, and the ease with which editing can manipulate its meaning require that it be considered in full.

Beloved Son,

We have learned that three days ago a large number of the women of Siena, adorned with all worldly vanity, gathered in the gardens of our well-beloved son Giovanni de Bichis, and that your Eminence, in contempt of the dignity of your position, remained with them from one o'clock until six o'clock in the afternoon; and that you had in your company another Cardinal to whom at least his age, if not the honor of the

Holy See, should have recalled his duty. We are told that the dances were immodest and the seductions of love beyond bounds and that you yourself behaved as if you were one of the most vulgar young men of the age. In truth I should blush to set down in detail all I have been told of what happened. Not only these things themselves, but the mere mention of them, are a dishonor to the office you hold. In order to have more freedom for your amusements you forbade entry to the husbands, fathers, brothers, and relations who came with these young women. You two, with a handful of attendants, were the sole organizers and instigators. It seems that at this moment no other thing is spoken of in the town of Siena and that you are the laughingstock of everybody. Assuredly here, in the baths, where there is a great crowd of ecclesiastics and laymen, you are on everybody's tongue. If I said I was not angry at these matters, I should commit a grave error. We are more angry than we can say, for it is a cause of dishonor to the ecclesiastical state and contempt for our ministry; it gives a pretext to those who accuse us of using our wealth and our high office for orgies, it is such things as these that cause the small esteem in which we are held by princes and powers, the daily mockery of the laity, and the reprobation hurled at our own conduct when we undertake to reprove others. The Vicar of Christ himself is an object of scorn because it is believed that he closes his eyes to these excesses.

You preside, my dear son, over the Church of Valencia, one of the most important in Spain; likewise you rule over the pontifical Chancellory; and what renders your act more reprehensible is that you are stationed close to the Sovereign Pontiff as Counselor of the Holy See. We leave it to your own judgment to say if it befits your high degree to pay compliments to women, to be sending them fruit, to drink a mouthful of wine and then have the glass carried to the woman who pleases you most, to spend a whole day as a delighted spectator of all kinds of games; and finally, for the sake of your liberty, to exclude from the gathering the husbands and relations of the women who are invited.

Your faults reflect upon us, and upon Calixtus, your uncle of happy memory, who is accused of a great fault of judgment for having laden you with undeserved honors. Your youth is not to be alleged in your defense, for it is not so tender and you are capable of realizing the responsibilities that your dignity places upon your shoulders. It behooves a cardinal to be irreproachable, to be a salutary example to all in the morality

*of his life, and the model of an existence which not only is edifying and
profitable to the soul but is so exteriorly as well. We are indignant when
secular princes approach us for dishonorable reasons, when they do us
wrong by coveting our properties and our benefices, and when we must
bend to their demands. It is ourselves who inflict upon us the wounds
from which we suffer when we so act that the authority of the Church is
less respected from day to day. We bear the shame of our conduct in
this world, and we shall suffer the punishment we have deserved in the
world to come.*

*Let your Eminence then decide to put an end to these frivolities;
you must remember your dignity and cease to appear among your
youthful contemporaries in the likeness of a man of pleasure. If such acts
were repeated we should be obliged to show that they happen totally in
spite of us and against our will; and our reproaches would be cast in
such terms as would put you to the blush. We have always loved you and
regarded you as worthy of our protection, because we have taken you for
a model of gravity and modesty. Let us long keep this opinion and this
conviction, and to this end you must without delay enter upon a much
more serious way of life. Your youth, the pledge of amendment, causes us
to warn you paternally. If you had allowed yourself such things at the
age of your companion, we should no longer be able to do you this
charitable service.*

The explosive word here, the one that seizes attention by crystalliz-
ing things otherwise left implicit, is of course *orgies*. Is it possible to read
it without imagining two clerics, naked perhaps except for their red hats,
flitting from one giggling lady to another among Signore de Bichis's
shrubs while the husbands, fathers, and brothers of those same ladies
loiter disconsolately on the other side of the garden wall? Could we
hope for better proof of the libertine that Cardinal Rodrigo was in his
prime—of his inability to keep his appetites in check even when the
failure to do so put his future at risk and betrayed the pope who had
become almost a father to him?

We could, actually. To understand why, it is necessary to distinguish
between what Pius himself knew when, in a burst of understandable
anger, he wrote his letter, and what he was supposing to be true. And
between what we as readers actually learn from his letter, and what his

words merely lead us to surmise. The first thing to note is that, though Pius's pain at what he has been told about the conduct of his "beloved son" has so destroyed not only his composure but the usual polish of his Latin prose that the letter has sometimes been dismissed as a forgery, he acknowledges even as he unburdens himself that he is dealing with hearsay—with what "I have been told."

Note also what Pius, who cares passionately about maintaining high standards and has been living and working in close association with Rodrigo for perhaps five years, reveals in his letter about what experience has taught him to expect of his young protégé. Far from saying that enough is enough and habitual mischievous antics have crossed a line and become intolerable, he declares that one reason for his shock is the fact the reported outrages have been committed by a man who has always seemed to him "a model of gravity and modesty."

Consider finally the inherent credibility of the tale that Pius in his anger has leaped to believe. We know from other sources that the party had been arranged because a child was being baptized—one whose parents were of sufficient status to have their invitations accepted by two of the cardinals who had accompanied the pope to Tuscany. Because of the rank of the people involved, the party took place in the gardens of an esteemed friend of the pope's, a "well-beloved son." But we are asked to believe that, upon arriving for the festivities, the male guests (individuals of considerable social standing) were turned away while their ladies (including unmarried girls) were allowed to enter. And that for the next five hours these ladies disported themselves with the cardinals—one of whom at least has long been known to the pontiff to be a man of good character—in ways that Pius would "blush to set down in detail." These were the womenfolk of the Sienese elite, mind you, at a time when gentlemen carried swords and were prepared to kill over questions of honor. Yet this horrific episode somehow became merely Tuscany's joke of the hour, with no harm done except to the already sullied reputation of the clergy.

The best that can be said of such a story is that it pushes credulity to the breaking point. It sounds ludicrous to twenty-first-century ears and would have been even more implausible in Renaissance Italy. And it is, for that matter, pretty thoroughly undermined by what happened after Pius's explosion. A few days later he sent a second message, this time in response to something Rodrigo had written after receiving the first. It shows the pope to be in a considerably altered frame of mind. He has, he says,

> *received your Eminence's letter and taken note of the explanation you give. Your action, my dear child, cannot be free from fault, though it may perhaps be less grave than I was first told. We exhort you to refrain henceforth from such indiscretions and to take the greatest care of your reputation. We grant you the pardon you ask; if we did not love you as a son of predilection we should not have uttered our affectionate reproaches for it is written: "Whom I love, him I rebuke and punish." So long as you do good and live in modesty, you will have in me a father and a protector whose blessing will be showered likewise upon those who are dear to you.*

We still don't know what happened at that party—the ladies' displays of their dancing skills touched the bounds of propriety, perhaps?—but Pius is satisfied that it was not what he had first been told. Orgies have been demoted to indiscretions, and instead of hurt and anger the pope is directing "affectionate reproaches" at Rodrigo. Any suspicion that something truly scandalous has transpired, or that Pius has decided after reflection that boys will be boys and not too much should be expected of his young favorite, now looks distinctly implausible. It cannot be without significance that, in the weeks following the notorious garden party, Pius II saw no need to depart Siena or send Rodrigo away. They did not go until the end of September, after the summer heat had loosened its grip on Rome, and departed then only because called away by developments too serious to be ignored.

It is likewise impossible to believe that, if anything seriously offensive had occurred, Pius in the years following would have taken Rodrigo with him when returning to Siena. But he did, and without hesitation. And it is curious that, when the pope's two letters came to light many years later, Rodrigo's answer or answers were not found with them. It would have been customary for the letters from both correspondents to remain together in the archives. When one considers the extent to which various records came to be tampered with in order to blacken the Borgia legend—see About the Character of Alexander VI, page 419—it is not far-fetched to wonder if whatever Rodrigo wrote in his own defense may have been intentionally destroyed.

This episode merits such close examination because of the light the pope's comments throw on the reputation of the clergy at this time and his high regard for Cardinal Rodrigo, and also because, as the only Borgia scandal of which there will be even a hint until many years later, it serves as a kind of prototype for the rough ways in which the reputations of Rodrigo and his kin will be handled through the centuries. For now, one further example must suffice. There has probably never been a detailed account of Rodrigo's life that did not—quite understandably—include this description of him by a man who had once been his teacher, one Gaspar of Verona: "He is handsome, of a most glad countenance and joyous aspect, gifted with honeyed and choice eloquence. The beautiful women on whom his eyes are cast he lures to love him, and moves them in a wondrous way, more powerfully than the magnet influences iron." Such a dazzling word-picture, rich not only in detail but in innuendo, merits repetition. But in the truncated form in which it usually appears it encourages rather lurid speculation. This renders inexcusable the omission, by one writer after another, of Gaspar's concluding sentence: "But it is admitted, to be sure, that he sends them off untouched."

Gaspar's description is typical of those left to us by people who knew Rodrigo. Without exception they emphasize the magnetism, the extraordinary vitality and appeal, of his person. Witnesses comment repeatedly on how multidimensional he was, and how fascinating to know. Physically he was imposing, tall and athletically built in his prime, and he carried himself with a dignity that must have been intimidating. But this simply added to the surprise of what he revealed in interacting with others: he turned out to be affable, accessible, kindly, and unfailingly charming. No one ever accused him of being less than a dutiful and hardworking vice-chancellor and cardinal. It has often been noted that he was never absent from consistories except when out of Rome or ill—which, thanks to his hardy constitution, he almost never was. But even when immersed in work he remained good-humored, even jovial. He was rather stolidly conservative in his religious beliefs—entirely comfortable with established dogma and no friend of theological or philosophical innovation—but he showed

marked tolerance in dealing with those whose views were not as orthodox as his own, on one occasion making the lame joke that "the Lord
requires not the death of a sinner, but rather that he may pay and live."
Late in his career, when the Jews were being expelled from Spain,
Rodrigo would annoy Ferdinand and Isabella by making the refugees
welcome in Rome.

Throughout his life he seemed incapable of taking offense at even
the most outrageous slanders, even when their source was a figure as
incendiary as Friar Savonarola, whom we shall encounter later. His
reputation has suffered permanently from his indifference to an anonymous pamphlet that appeared a few years before his death and declared
him to be a "monster" and "an abyss of vice" under whose influence
"the bestiality and savagery of Nero and Caligula are surpassed." The
ease with which he laughed such things off, brushing aside the complaints of relatives who urged him to forbid their circulation and punish
the parties responsible, shows one of the most attractive sides of his
personality. It has also, however, freed other writers to come to the
unwarranted assumption that Rodrigo failed to defend himself because
he knew his conduct to be indefensible. This encouraged further and
more specific slanders—for example, the preposterous assertion of
the Florentine historian Francesco Guicciardini (who was still twenty-
three years from being born when the Siena garden party took place)
that Rodrigo was "mightily lustful of both sexes, publicly keeping boys
and girls, but mostly girls."

All his life Rodrigo had an almost childish love of pomp, ceremony,
and public splendor, and he agreed with the popes he served that it was
part of a cardinal's duty both to maintain the dignity of the college by
maintaining a splendid front and to help make Rome the most magnificent city in the world. He could be reckless in his spending for such
purposes. On Palm Sunday 1461, when all Rome turned out for the arrival of what was supposedly the long-lost head of the apostle Andrew,
St. Peter's brother, Rodrigo became the talk of the town by turning not
only his own palace but its surroundings into a display of magnificent
extravagance. Pius II in his *Memoirs,* after describing the contributions
to the celebration by other cardinals and dignitaries, notes delightedly
that "all were far outstripped in expense and effort and ingenuity by
Rodrigo, the vice-chancellor. His huge towering house which he had

built on the site of the ancient mint was covered with rich and wonderful tapestries, and besides this he had raised a lofty canopy from which were suspended many and various marvels. He had decorated not only his own house but those nearby, so that the square all about them seemed a kind of park full of sweet songs and sounds, or a great palace gleaming with gold such as they say Nero's palace was."

If all this was wasteful, it had the ecstatic approval of the man to whom Rodrigo owed his position and his income. If it was foolish, it was also expected—practically required. If it was self-serving in the sense of enhancing Rodrigo's prestige in an era when it was considered shameful for holders of high office not to indulge in ostentatious display, it also carries a note of generosity. Certainly it was not the mark of a greedy, still less a miserly, man. And behind these bursts of ostentation, Rodrigo lived simply, even abstemiously. It comes as a surprise to learn that associates regarded it as a misfortune to be a guest at his table. The fare was so plain, Ferrara's ambassador reported, that "it is disagreeable to have to dine with him." So much for bacchanalian feasts.

The word that sums up Rodrigo Borgia is *gusto*. He loved life, enjoyed people, and found satisfaction even in the most challenging duties, but he was capable also of putting the cares of his work out of mind whenever time permitted. *Zest* would suit him also. And *joie de vivre*. The German Ludwig Pastor, who spent most of his life in Rome and wrote a forty-volume history of the papacy, observed that "nothing can be more false than the ordinary conception of Borgia as a morose and inhuman monster." A twentieth-century historian, Michael Mallett, summed up the consensus of five hundred years in writing of how even people with reasons to dislike Rodrigo "were often reconciled by his friendliness and boisterous good humor."

To round out the picture it is worthwhile to return to Guicciardini, who hated what he knew or thought he knew of Rodrigo and went far beyond the bounds of fairness in attempting to sully his name. Even Guicciardini conceded that as vice-chancellor Rodrigo was "prudent, vigilant, and maturely reflective," as well as exceptionally persuasive and effective in the management of difficult matters. Juxtaposed against how Rodrigo is usually depicted, even by Guicciardini himself, such words become rather baffling. It may have been bafflement that caused a more recent historian to throw up his hands at what he took to be Rodrigo's "strange many-sidedness" and call him "an enigma to his contemporaries." He was no such thing. People who knew him appear to have taken him at face value, and with few and explainable exceptions they liked what they saw.

When Pope Pius finally consented to bid adieu to Siena, three years remained to his life. They would be consumed by two things that commonly come together: war and money trouble. There was a continuing war in Naples, where Ferrante, with the help of reinforcements sent by Pius, Milan, and Skanderbeg of Albania, was clawing his way back from the brink of ruin. As the rebellious barons and the Angevin invaders slowly ran out of fight and Ferrante's situation became less dire, he was freed to reveal facets of his character that earlier had been concealed—except, perhaps, from those who knew him best, onetime intimates like Alonso Borgia. It was at about this time, according to stories from credible sources, that he created the prison-cum-museum in which the embalmed bodies of defeated foes were displayed alongside cages in which living captives were either starved to death or left to slowly go insane. As his political position became secure, Ferrante became nearly as powerful a force in Italian politics as his father Alfonso had been. It would become clear soon enough that he was also just as meddlesome.

War went on in the Romagna too, where the rebellious warlord Sigismondo Pandolfo Malatesta of Rimini was proving to be a maddeningly able soldier and impossible to bring to heel. But the conflict that was costing Pius the most, both financially and in emotional terms, was not a real but a hoped-for one. It was the fight he wanted to carry to the Ottoman Turks, the crusade he had pledged to launch in 1464 in spite of the failure of the congress of Mantua. It became the source of his, and then of Rodrigo's, worst money troubles. The sending of envoys to every part of Europe on a fund-raising campaign proved a serious financial drain—the crowned heads would have been insulted if the pope's men failed to arrive in grand style—and the returns were scarcely commensurate with the costs. Pius like Calixtus before him was meanwhile emptying the papal treasury to build galleys and hire crews. He found himself in such financial straits that he introduced a practice that would continue to have a corrosive effect on the Church long after his reign was over: he began selling positions in the Curia, the Vatican's bureaucracy.

Rodrigo was not merely feeling the pinch—he appears to have been going broke. He was doing so in spite of the fact that Pius, even more than his uncle Calixtus, rained benefices on him: bishoprics, abbeys, a share in the revenues generated by the sale of offices, sources of ecclesiastical income of almost every possible kind. Once again, it was a matter of his income being needed for the discharge of his responsibilities. At this time as much as at any in his life, that income was proving to be woefully inadequate for the purpose.

Cumulatively, the demands on Rodrigo's purse were of crushing weight. He was paying to construct the episcopal palace that he had "volunteered" to contribute to Pius's remaking of Pienza, and to provide a fully equipped galley with crew for the pope's crusade. (Such a warship was so costly that only the wealthiest entities in the Papal States—the city of Bologna, for example, and the duke of Ferrara—could possibly be asked to finance one.) He was also expected to contribute a troop of thirty armed men and ten horses to the pope's war with Sigismondo Pandolfo Malatesta, and it was taken for granted that as one of Rome's most prominent cardinals he would maintain himself in a style worthy of a prince—a style involving the establishment and maintenance of a residence, a palace, that reflected glory on the Church and its capital. Beyond all this it was his responsibility to provide salaries, workplaces, and perhaps even accommodations for a good many of the men employed in the chancery and the Rota as well.

While Calixtus was still alive, Rodrigo had purchased from the Vatican for two thousand florins a row of old buildings across the Tiber from St. Peter's between the Piazza di Spagna and the bridge at the Castel Sant'Angelo. He then began converting these buildings, among them a derelict structure that once had housed the papal mint, into a suitably grand home with space for his subordinates and the conduct of the chancery's business—a palace. This became yet another chronic and painful financial drain.

It all proved to be too much. In 1462, unable to meet his obligations, Rodrigo offered to sell his unfinished palace back to the papal treasury, the camera, for the original purchase price plus what he had spent on improvements. But the camera too was insolvent. Rather than letting what had become the chancery's headquarters go to a third party, Rodrigo mortgaged it. A year later he was still under such pressure financially that Pius granted him temporary permission to tax the beneficiaries of his diocese of Valencia—those clergymen receiving stipends as deans, canons, and the like. He was also allowed to sell at a discount, in return for an immediate infusion of cash, the next three years of his own revenues as Valencia's bishop. We will see him resorting to similar expedients in decades to come even as he is supposedly amassing a fortune of almost inconceivable size.

With the kings and high churchmen of all Europe reluctant to contribute more than token quantities of money and men, the pope's dream of a crusade would have had to be abandoned except for an event so unexpected, indeed so utterly improbable, that Pius declared it a miracle. It was the discovery, on land belonging to the papacy in the wooded hills of Tolfa about sixty miles north of Rome, of huge deposits of high-quality alum—potassium aluminum sulfate, the same humble substance sold today in the form of styptic pencils to stop the bleeding from shaving cuts.

Until some two hundred years ago, when a way of synthesizing it was discovered, alum was a quasi-precious substance with many uses, the most important involving the tanning of leather and the dyeing of wool and other fibers. Mines at the southern end of the Balkan peninsula had long been Europe's only source, and after the Turks moved into the Balkans, it could be obtained only at extortionate prices. This came to an abrupt end in the spring of 1462, thanks to a onetime dyer named Giovanni di Castro, who had fled Constantinople when it fell to the Turks and become a minor official in the Papal States. One day, exploring the hills inland from Civitavecchia between Florence and Rome, Castro noticed the prevalence of a species of tree rarely seen in Italy but common around the alum mines of the Balkans. Investigating further, he made his great discovery. He hurried to Rome and in great excitement announced to the pope that "today I bring you victory over the Turk. Every year they wring from the Christians more than three hundred thousand ducats for the alum with which we dye wool . . . But I have found seven mountains so rich in this material that they could supply seven worlds . . . This mine will supply you with the sinews of war, money, and take them from the Turks."

About the value of what he had found, Castro was not exaggerating. In short order thousands of men were at work in new mines at Tolfa; they would remain in operation for three and a half centuries. The profits climbed rapidly toward a hundred thousand ducats per year. Pius decreed that all of it was to be spent to make war on the Turks.

Thus it became possible for the crusade preparations to continue. The need remained obvious: a year after Castro's discovery, Sultan Mehmed invaded Bosnia and conquered it with frightening ease, taking his empire another step closer to Vienna, to Italy, to the nerve centers of southeastern Europe. Even after this loss, however, Pius could find support in only two places. First in Venice, resigned at last to the inevitability of war with the Turks, and then among the common people of the north. Even in places where the leaders of church and state had no interest in sacrificing anything for the sake of a distant campaign—in Germany and the Low Countries, in France and Spain, and as far away as Scotland—ordinary people responded to the pope's call. From pulpits across Europe, preachers dispatched from Rome were telling the faithful that all available men should prepare to report for duty in the summer of 1464. They should assemble in Venice, or better yet they should make their way farther down Italy's east coast and join the pope at the port city of Ancona. There—so the plan went—they would be taken aboard a great fleet of mostly Venetian galleys for transportation to the East and the great showdown with Islam.

It was a doomed enterprise, insufficiently funded and without political support. It was kept alive by little more than the pope's refusal to admit that the obstacles were too great to be overcome. In September 1463, with his launch date now less than a year away, Pius called the cardinals together in a consistory at which he complained in angry, bitter terms that neither Europe's leaders nor its people were rallying to the cause. He was right about the leaders and undoubtedly should have called the whole thing off, but he had become a man obsessed. In an act so deeply foolish that it can only have been intended to shame the crowned heads of Christendom, Pius announced that he was going to lead the crusade personally. He had already recruited the brilliant Skanderbeg to take charge of military operations; this new pledge to inject himself into the expedition in spite of his complete lack of military experience and indifferent health looks less like an effort to inspire than an outburst of spite and defiance.

Nine months later, on June 18, 1464, Pius set out for Ancona and the fulfillment of his great dream. Some of Rome's leading citizens, the memory of the disorders that had erupted during the pope's previous long absence still fresh in their minds, had objected with considerable heat when informed of his plans. To placate them he promised to leave the pontifical administration at home, its leadership intact. This removed any possibility that Cardinal Borgia, the central figure in that administration, might be expected to go with the pontiff to war. He did, however, set off to accompany the pope to Ancona. It was a brutally hot summer, and Pius, who had been feverish for some time, found himself capable of traveling only in short, slow stages with frequent stops for recuperation. Rodrigo caught up with him at Terni, and they pushed on together from there. They arrived at Ancona on July 19 to find it a boiling cauldron of confusion and pestilence, overrun with amateur crusaders from all parts of Europe. The town had no way to shelter so many visitors, too little food, even a desperate shortage of drinking water. There was no sign of the Venetian fleet, which was overdue, and as plague broke out, many of the volunteers who did not fall sick began to flee. The pope, too weak to leave his room overlooking the harbor, watched for the arrival of Venice's galleys as his ragtag volunteer army melted away. By August 9 Rodrigo too was ill—which fact has given rise to another ridiculously insubstantial Borgia scandal.

This one rises out of a letter written on August 10 by the marquess of Mantua's ambassador to the papal court. He informs his master of Rodrigo's sickness, adding that "the physician who saw him first says that he has little hope for him, principally because he had, shortly before, not slept alone in bed." This has been interpreted as meaning that Rodrigo had been indulging in sexual adventures since arriving in Ancona and was dying as a result. But of course there never has been a venereal disease that kills or even incapacitates in a matter of days, and the most dangerous of such diseases, syphilis, is generally believed to have been unknown in Europe before Columbus's return from his first voyage of discovery in 1493. As for the cardinal's not sleeping alone, as recently as the nineteenth century it was not uncommon even for men of importance to share beds, and it may very well have been necessary for senior members of the pope's entourage to do so in the grossly overcrowded conditions of Ancona that summer.

Rodrigo's symptoms, in any case, are on record. They included earache and a swelling under his left arm. These are consistent with the bubonic plague, which was rampant in the March of Ancona at this time and gets its name from the phenomenon called buboes, a swelling of the lymphatic glands in armpit and groin. Here again we see that no stick is too crooked to be used in whipping a Borgia.

Four days after the Mantuan envoy wrote his letter, the Venetian fleet sailed into Ancona's harbor with the doge Cristoforo Moro in command. On that same day, the death of Pope Pius was so obviously imminent that those cardinals not too sick to move were called to his bedroom to say their goodbyes. He died the next day, and it was probably with deep relief that Moro, after seeing the state of affairs in Ancona and conferring with the cardinals who remained able to function (Rodrigo was not among them), declared that proceeding to the East had become impossible. He returned to his fleet and was rowed home to Venice.

It was necessary for the cardinals to return to Rome, for the burial of Pius and the election of the next pope.

IL PAPA

IN ROME IN THE FIRST CENTURY OR TWO OF THE CHRISTIAN ERA, the Church may or may not have been led by a man who functioned more or less as a bishop even if not yet bearing that title.

The first Roman bishops—assuming that there were such things in the generations following the death of Saint Peter—may have regarded themselves as the apostle's successors and therefore as leaders not only of the local church but of all Christians everywhere.

Or they may not have. The idea of a single head of the whole Church may not have emerged until centuries later, inside the heads of Dark Age bishops eager to fill the vacuum created by the killing of Rome's last emperor.

These questions have answers. The problem is that the answers vastly outnumber the questions. Catholics have their answers, various Protestant denominations have theirs, et cetera ad infinitum. It is inconceivable that these conflicting interpretations of early Christianity will ever be reconciled.

Anyone acquainted with the facts, however, is likely to agree that the story of how the papacy of the Renaissance came into existence is, for better or worse, one of the most colorful in all history. It can be inspiring and disgusting, exciting or depressing, beautiful or horrible, depending on which part of it is under examination and the preconceptions of the examiner. No one wanting to prove that the papacy is the Whore of Babylon will ever be embarrassed by a lack of supporting evidence. Much the same is true for anyone wanting to believe that the pope is everything he claims to be.

The story of the popes can be taken up, for our purposes, early in the fourth century, by which time there was indeed a bishop of Rome. When the Emperor Constantine departed to establish a new capital in the ancient Greek city of Byzantium (and rename it after himself), he left the Eternal City in the charge of its bishop and gave him the imperial palace, the Lateran, as his residence. Constantine being among the greatest of all

Roman emperors, and Rome at this point being still the capital of the world, this act of delegation radically increased the bishop's prestige. It added to the stature he already possessed as prelate of the only apostolic church in the Western Empire—the only one established by one of the twelve apostles—at a time when Christianity's birthplace, Jerusalem, was in ruins.

This prestige was further enhanced in the following century when the Western Empire collapsed. In the absence of an emperor, and with the European kingdoms of the Middle Ages not yet in existence, almost no unifying principle was available to the Church's scattered bishops except their colleague in the old capital. And so Rome's bishop, once not much more than the custodian of pilgrimage sites, became a unique source of support and guidance. Gradually he began to claim to be, and to be accepted as, the man in overall command.

Rome, helpless, was sacked three times in the fifth century. But even then the intruders from the north showed themselves to be in awe of the great city, if no longer terrified of its might, and to regard it as quasi-sacred. Their reverence grew rather than diminished with the passage of time. When the Lombards made themselves masters of much of Italy in the sixth century, they kept clear of Rome, putting it off limits even to themselves. When they were converted to Christianity, their respect for the place was extended to its overlord as well, and as the number of Christendom's bishops increased, the title *Il Papa* was reserved for the one who presided in Rome.

When in the eighth century Pepin the Short led his Frankish warriors southward to supplant the Lombards, he did so not as just another barbarian intruder but at the invitation of Pope Stephen II, who had given him the title Patrician of Rome. Pepin then introduced a new element into history by bestowing an extensive portion of his newly conquered territories on the pontiff. He thereby transformed the bishop of Rome into what his successors would remain into the nineteenth century: one of the most important temporal rulers in Italy, monarch of the Papal States, capable of joining in the power games of Venice, Naples, and Milan. Papal prestige rose to unprecedented heights. When Pepin's son Charles the Great—Charlemagne—was crowned as *imperator* in Rome in 800, he received his crown from Pope Leo III after approaching the pontiff on his knees and kissing his slippered feet.

The next seven centuries were a wild ride in which bursts of real glory alternated with episodes of appalling degradation. The prestige that had brought Charlemagne to his knees was taken away and recovered, thrown away and recovered again, lost and regained repeatedly in a cycle that seemed destined to continue to the end of time. Few things on earth were rarer than a happy and successful papal reign. Eight decades after the death of the pontiff who crowned Charlemagne, Pope Stephen VI was strangled in Rome's Castel Sant'Angelo by people infuriated at him for having his predecessor's body dragged out of its tomb, put on trial, and thrown into the Tiber. In 974 Benedict VI died in the same way in the same place, and ten years later John XIV perished in the Castel of poisoning or starvation.

The deaths of Stephen VI and John XIV bracketed the so-called "Pornocracy," a long and ugly interlude during which the papacy was virtually the property of a family of Roman consuls and senators called the Theophylacti. The tenor of the period can be inferred from the career of a member of this family named Marozia. She is alleged—by hostile sources, it must be acknowledged—to have been the lover first of Pope Sergius III (by whom she supposedly had a son who grew up to become Pope John XI) and later of John X (whom she is supposed to have had murdered). She was the grandmother of John XII (himself a murderer, elected at age eighteen and said to have made his niece his mistress and blinded his confessor), the great-grandmother of Benedict VIII and John XIX (who was a layman when elected), and the great-great-grandmother of Benedict IX. This last pontiff, no more than twenty when given the crown, has several distinctions. He is the first pope known with certainty to have been homosexual, and the only man ever to become pope three times. He was deposed in favor of an antipope twenty years after his election, was restored to his office a year later only to sell it, then changed his mind and took the crown back from the buyer. In the end he was deposed permanently.

Such depths were never to be reached again. The reigns of even the most admired and formidable popes, however, were invariably laden with grief if not outright tragedy. In 1077 the reformer Gregory VII, whose zeal for purging the Church of corruption bordered on fanaticism, triumphed so completely over his archenemy Emperor Henry IV that the poor man was reduced to donning a hair shirt and standing barefoot in the snow for three days in a desperate bid to win release from a bull of excommunication. It was a never-to-be-forgotten display of papal power, but it did not save Gregory from later being deposed (as was Henry) and dying in exile. The tragic futility of the centuries-long struggle between papacy and Holy Roman Empire was again made clear in the mid-thirteenth century, when Innocent IV defeated and destroyed the spectacularly brilliant Emperor Frederick II, known to contemporaries as the Wonder of the World, only to find himself at the end of his life losing a war with Frederick's illegitimate son. Another peak was reached in the reign of Boniface VIII, who at the dawn of the fourteenth century was so engorged with pride and self-importance that he would greet pilgrims in Rome by shouting *Ego, ego sum imperator!* ("I, I am the emperor!") In 1302 he issued the bull *Unam Sanctam,* which declared that no one who failed to submit to the authority of the pope could achieve salvation. This sparked such a violent reaction—from the king of France, among others—that Boniface found himself languishing in prison.

Just seven years later the so-called Babylonian Captivity began, with the pope resident at Avignon and becoming almost an adjunct of the French crown. During this period 113 of the 134 appointees to the College of Cardinals were French, and so much Church money went into the French king's treasury that German relations with the papal court were permanently poisoned. After that came the Great or Western Schism, which began in 1378 with the election of an antipope and over the next four decades never offered the faithful fewer than two men simultaneously claiming to be the rightful pontiff.

The papacy that Martin V brought back to the wrecked city of Rome in 1420 was itself, therefore, a scarred and tattered thing. It was virtually bankrupt, had barely escaped being discredited beyond possibility of repair, was unloved by the people of Rome, and controlled almost none of its supposed territories. Those of its neighbor states that were not its enemies were also not its friends.

It was from these wretched beginnings that the papacy of the Renaissance would rise for another period in the sun.

8

Paul II: The Poisoned Chalice

The conclave that followed the death of Pius II was the second in which Rodrigo Borgia took part, and it came at a time when his role in the hierarchy was subtly changing. He was entering his mid-thirties now, and he had proved himself as vice-chancellor and right hand to two successive pontiffs. Though still much too young to be considered *papabile,* a possible candidate for elevation to the throne, he was no longer either a green novice or quite the Spanish alien that he had seemed during the reign of his uncle.

He was, to the contrary, very much a Vatican insider and a consummately skilled ecclesiastical politician. Though the conclave of 1464 was the only one he would ever attend without playing a significant part, his passivity in this one instance was entirely the result of physical incapacity: he remained so debilitated by the bout of bubonic plague that had brought him low in Ancona that he was reported as attending one session of the conclave with his head bound up in cloths.

Fortunately for Rodrigo, there was no great need for him to exert himself because there was never much danger that anyone hostile to him would be chosen as Pius's successor. Among the cardinals who appeared to have support as the conclave opened, two, Carvajal and Torquemada, were Spaniards and could be depended upon to embrace Rodrigo and his kin as allies if by some chance either of them was elected. Guillaume d'Estouteville, who had tried so hard to bluff, bribe,

and bully his way to the throne in 1458, remained France's most powerful churchman and a highly visible presence in Rome, with apparently
unlimited financial resources and a gnawing hunger for the papal tiara.
He had reason to blame Rodrigo for the worst of his disappointments,
his failure at the conclave that had turned Enea Silvio Piccolomini into
Pius II, but his chances of pulling together a two-thirds majority were
now smaller than ever. As for the bloc from which the new pope was
almost certain to be chosen, the ten Italians who made up more than
half of the cardinals present, there was only one among them whom
Rodrigo had reason to fear. This was Latino Orsini, on whose family
Calixtus III had made war. But Latino was not the fountain of energy
and wrath he once had been, and in the six years of Pius's reign the
membership of the Sacred College had changed to such an extent that
he no longer had the power either to elect a candidate of his own choosing or to veto anyone he disliked. As for his own election, like Estouteville's it was out of the question.

Rodrigo, in eight years as a cardinal and seven in the most important
post in the Church after the pope, had learned a good many things
about papal conclaves and the papacy itself. Of conclaves he had learned
that once the doors were locked anything could happen, that what did
happen was often totally unexpected, that great wealth and power
were not only no guarantee of election but if clumsily employed could
be self-defeating, and that promises made in the pursuit of votes could
safely be forgotten once the voting was done. Of the papacy he had
learned that nepotism was not only acceptable but understood to be
desirable if not carried to extremes, that popes never had enough money
and therefore were well advised to be coldly self-interested in the management of their finances, and that as a general rule it was best not
to trust anyone—certainly not the rulers of the Italian city-states or
crowned heads anywhere.

What he would be a long time learning was the difficulty, seemingly
the near impossibility, of ruling successfully and bringing a reign to a
satisfying conclusion. Almost the whole history of the papacy could
have been drawn upon as evidence that the institution was a poisoned
chalice and that whoever drank from it was doomed to disillusionment,
failure, and grief. Such words describe the fate of Calixtus III and of
Pius II and of earlier pontiffs beyond numbering. That intelligent men

continued to fight for such an office is testimony both to the human hunger for power and, less often, to the price some good men were willing to pay in order to extract the Church from its recurrent calamities.

The cardinals present at the conclave of 1464 were for the most part concerned not with great issues but with extracting themselves from their own predicament and concluding their business at the earliest possible moment. Their predicament was the sense of being trapped in a dangerous situation in a dangerous place. Their hurry was propelled by fear: of the Roman mob, which was using the death of a Tuscan pope as an excuse to ransack the homes and businesses of the city's Tuscan residents; of Pius's ambitious nephew Antonio, recently elevated to duke of Amalfi, who remained captain-general of the papal army and seemed poised to interfere in the election; of the very office the cardinals had come together to fill.

The last-mentioned fear is, paradoxically, the one that gripped the conclave most fiercely. The cardinals could and did extract from Duke Antonio a pledge that he would surrender both his office and the Castel Sant'Angelo as soon as the election was concluded and that he would meanwhile do what he could to maintain some measure of order in the streets of Rome. The contest between papacy and Sacred College was a far more worrisome matter and not so easily resolved. Many of the cardinals were uneasy, to say the least, about the extent to which the power of the popes had been growing at their expense. Therefore they made it their first order of business to draw up a list of the most challenging capitulations ever adopted by a conclave. With one obscure exception, every cardinal affixed his signature to this list, thereby pledging to do the following if elected:

Convene a general council of the Church to meet three years after the election (it being understood that the purpose of this council would be to put constraints on the pope).

Limit the Sacred College to twenty-four members (so as not to dilute the power of individual members).

Appoint no cardinal under the age of thirty.

Appoint only one nephew.

And appoint only "learned men."

Additionally, and far more radically, the capitulations stipulated that without the approval of the college the pope could thenceforth appoint no cardinals, enter into no political alliances, declare no wars, and dispose of no Church territory.

Finally, and least controversially, there was a pledge to make war on the Turks.

These capitulations were intended to effect a profound change in the character of the papacy and the constitution of the Church. They amounted to a blunt rejection of the notion that the pope was not only a monarch but an absolute monarch, and that he ruled *over,* rather than *with,* the Sacred College. For those who rejected the monarchical principle, the acceptance of the capitulations by every cardinal with any chance of being elected must have seemed to presage a long-sought, epic victory: the demotion of the pope to a kind of chairman of the board, presiding over but not dictating to an oligarchy of cardinals.

This accomplished, the conclave got down to the business of voting. A first ballot, in which each cardinal was permitted to cast three votes, produced seven for the fierce old warrior Scarampo, nine for the tirelessly self-promoting Estouteville, and eleven for the colorless but unobjectionable Pietro Barbo of Venice. This Barbo was the same nephew of Pope Eugenius IV who in 1455 had been put forward as the candidate of the Orsini only to be blocked by Prospero Colonna. Prospero, however, was now in his tomb, the Sacred College was for the time being without a Colonna, and Barbo had reached an age, forty-seven, at which he could be considered marginally ready to receive the papal crown. Still in a hurry to be finished, sensing that a conclusion had come within reach, the cardinals immediately moved on to the process of accession. Barbo had no difficulty in securing the additional votes needed for election—in fact he quickly had fifteen of the nineteen votes cast—and it was done. The conclave had lasted little more than forty-eight hours.

It is reasonable to surmise that Rodrigo must have voted for Barbo at the end and was probably doing so from the beginning. The two were friends of long standing (the reader will recall that it was Cardinal Barbo who had helped Rodrigo spirit Pedro Luis Borgia out of Rome as Calixtus III lay dying), and Barbo's actions after his election do not suggest that Rodrigo had done anything to damage the relationship. Be all that as it may, there was nothing startling about how the election turned out and no evident reason for anyone to be alarmed. Though not particularly distinguished intellectually or extravagantly well endowed with political connections, Barbo was an attractive enough candidate, tall and handsome with a dignified demeanor, known for his kindness, gentleness, and generosity. He was honest as well, and though somewhat chilly in demeanor had never shown much appetite for conflict. Apart from indulging a passion for ancient coins and precious stones and spending huge sums on transforming the Roman residence of Venice's cardinals into the city's first great Renaissance palace, he had always lived simply and kept himself free of scandal.

After the failure of his candidacy in 1455, Barbo had remained sufficiently well thought of to again receive notable support in the conclave of 1458. The factor that made the difference in 1464 was his Venetian birth. Venice by this juncture was enmeshed in a costly and open-ended war with the Turks and therefore was eager for an alliance with Rome and almost desperately enthusiastic about the idea of a great pan-European crusade. Thus the Roman faction in the Sacred College had reason to regard Venice as a friend rather than as a nuisance unwilling to admit the gravity of the Ottoman menace. The cardinals could now expect a pope whose family was rooted in Venice to pursue the fight against the Turks with all possible vigor.

One thing, however, could not possibly have been understood within the conclave or Barbo would never have been elected. The new pope carried within him an uncompromising belief in the papacy as supreme, in the pope as sovereign over cardinals, councils, emperors, and all other challengers. Like many and probably most of his fellow cardinals, he had signed the capitulations without any intention of honoring them if he became pope. This became clear almost immediately after his election, when three days passed without his publishing—as the capitulations themselves required—a bull confirming everything that had been pledged. The new Pope Paul II did, however, go to some lengths to soften his betrayal. (If betrayal it was; not only had capitulations been regularly ignored by Paul's predecessors, but it was not difficult to find scholars who declared them to be so fundamentally invalid as to have no binding force.) It was Paul who introduced the practice of dressing cardinals in silken red robes and officially elevated them to the status of "princes of the Church," the equals of dukes and lower than no one except popes (of course) and hereditary royalty. He ordered that cardinals when in public should always be surrounded by platoons of retainers and conferred generous stipends on those lacking independent means. An implicit bargain was being struck: the cardinals could be among the most exalted personages in all Europe, but only by acknowledging that the pope was their master. Appointment to the Sacred College would be a guarantee of wealth, influence, and a life of privilege, but only by providing access to the one man empowered to dispense such prizes. This proved an effective strategy. It became a prototype for the process by which, generations later, secular rulers such as Louis XIV of France would seduce once-dangerous nobles into submitting to central—meaning royal—authority.

For Cardinal Rodrigo, Paul II's reign became an advanced course in just how poisonous the papacy could be even for a well-intended pope, and how much bitterness and humiliation the fates could heap upon those who won the throne. Paul's exalted view of his office embroiled him in conflicts of many kinds: with the baronial clans in and near Rome, with the warlords who ruled the more distant Papal States, with the leading Italian princes, and even with his fellow monarchs beyond the Italian peninsula. This is one reason why history has not dealt kindly with him, but there are other reasons as well. Biographers never fail to note that his motives in embarking on an ecclesiastical career had been unedifying if not really ignoble. He had been a youth of good family preparing for a life as a Venetian trader—in fact was about to leave home for a position overseas—when news reached Venice that Cardinal Gabriele Condulmer had been elected pope. Condulmer being his mother's brother, young Pietro decided that his prospects would be brighter in the Church than in business and so took holy orders. He was not wrong in his calculations, becoming a cardinal when scarcely more than a boy, but the authenticity of his religious vocation was always open to question.

As pope he alienated his former colleagues by not only ignoring the capitulations but flouting one of their key provisions, appointing three young nephews to the Sacred College. That the three in the course of long careers would prove themselves worthy of their high positions could of course not be known at the time of their appointment, and so it did nothing to ease the annoyance of the men who had elected their uncle. Paul also raised eyebrows with the eccentric lifestyle he adopted upon taking office, sleeping during the day and granting audiences in the middle of the night only. It seems possible, in light of his compassionate nature and the seriousness with which he embraced his new responsibilities, that his upside-down schedule was intended to reduce the number of supplicants coming to ask favors, thereby sparing him the pain of having to say no. Whatever the motive, his schedule was a headache for those with business that required his attention. It was also unhealthy for the pope himself, increasing his isolation and aggravating his inclination to be distrustful.

Long after his death, historians would depict Paul II as an egomaniac, neurotically hungry to aggrandize himself, insistent on excessive display, and draping himself in flamboyant attire on ceremonial occasions. Such complaints are true enough as far as they go—Paul certainly went to extremes in demanding that his ceremonies be splendid—but it is also possible to see his behavior less as frivolous waste than as a political technique. In Renaissance Europe no less than in the Middle Ages, power had to be *displayed* to be credible. Even in distant England, a ruler as parsimonious as Henry VII would spend lavishly on grand palaces and grandiose courtly displays and would do so for baldly political reasons. Much the same can be said of the increasing elaboration of the Church's ceremonies and celebrations in the same century: susceptible to being depicted as disgraceful, explainable as a cost of doing business.

Even as a young man Pietro Barbo had struck people who did not know him as haughty, even cold. A story often told about him is that, upon being elected pope, he declared his intention to take the name Formosus, not in honor of a ninth-century predecessor of that name but because it meant "good-looking." The cardinals, it is said, had to argue hard to dissuade him from this frivolous display of self-love. The truth is that Barbo was complicated in ways bound to produce misunderstanding, an introvert whose stony demeanor concealed a soft heart. All his life he had been openhanded with his wealth, funding hospitals for the needy and the distribution of free medicines. He continued these benefactions as pope, giving particular attention to widows, invalids, and displaced persons. He was repulsed by violence of whatever kind, war and lawful executions included, and throughout his papacy he would be an active supporter of monastic reform. He attacked official corruption by forbidding legates, governors, and judges to accept gifts and applied the prohibition to himself.

In short, Paul made a serious and sustained effort to be everything he thought a good pope should be. Even his critics—who have always been legion and have rarely stopped short of hinting at an irregular sexual orientation—uniformly acknowledge that he maintained high standards in choosing his associates and distributing favors. They concede also that during his reign offices and benefices were awarded on the basis of merit rather than cronyism or bribery. It reveals a certain largeness of spirit that the cardinals who became his closest confidants and advisers were his former rivals for the papacy, Bessarion and Carvajal. The two were universally recognized as among the finest churchmen of the time, not only untouched by any hint of corruption but unwilling to keep silent about corruption when they encountered it. That they became and remained central figures in Paul's administration is a point to be taken into account when judging the character of his reign. Similarly, his attitude toward the vice-chancellor is the best clue we have to what kind of life Cardinal Borgia was living as he approached age forty. Paul like Pius and Calixtus displayed high confidence in Rodrigo, significantly expanding his responsibilities and authority, increasing the number of Curial offices he was empowered to fill, and conferring upon him a number of benefices (all of them in Spain, to avoid angering the Italians). Everything we know about Paul II makes it difficult to believe that he could have shown so much favor to a subordinate whom he so much as suspected of inappropriate conduct.

Neither high standards nor worthy companions, however, were sufficient to make Paul a successful or even a popular pope. The opposition he aroused in asserting his own supremacy was simply too substantial to be overcome. He began, logically enough, with the Papal States, it being his belief that he had not only the right but the duty to make himself their ruler in fact as much as in principle. And things went reasonably well in the early going. In the Romagna, after experiencing some early setbacks, he had had the good sense or good luck to employ the services of Federico da Montefeltro, duke of Urbino, who quickly broke the power of the rebellious Malatesta of Rimini.

Things went even better when Paul chose, as his next objective, a piece of papal territory less than a day's journey north of Rome. This had for years been the domain of Eversus Anguillara, patriarch of a family of ruffians and bandits that had taken advantage of the weakness of the papacy to seize a number of towns and impose on them a brutishly harsh regime. Eversus having died, Paul again hired Montefeltro, along with Napoleone Orsini, lord of Bracciano, and dispatched them to drive out Anguillara's sons. In short order thirteen castles were taken and the tyrants put to flight. The end result, however, was not what the pope had in mind: the Orsini took over many of the properties from which the Anguillara had been expelled, strengthening their position north of Rome and with it their own ability to make trouble. This was another step in the education of Rodrigo Borgia, looking on from Rome. It demonstrated anew both the need to deal with the warlord clans and the difficulties of doing so in ways that made a meaningful difference.

The attack on the Anguillara was, in any case, the end of Paul's good luck. When he turned his attention to a more ambitious target, the great papal fiefdom of Bologna, things quickly went wrong. Bologna, rich and powerful since the days of the Roman Empire, was in the grip of a tight little circle of dominant families. The pope regarded this flagrantly self-serving oligarchy as a disgrace to the papacy, which as overlord was supposed to be in charge. But when he demanded reforms, he met with more resistance than he had the means to overcome, and in the end he agreed to a settlement that served no purpose except to allow much of the power of the oligarchs to pass into the hands of a single family, the Bentivoglii. Once again, intervention had produced unintended and distinctly unwelcome consequences. As a result, Bologna would be an even more intractable problem for Paul's successors than it had ever been for his predecessors.

Mistake followed mistake, failure begot failure. Most humiliating of all was a crisis that erupted at home, within the Curia. Paul was unusual among Renaissance pontiffs in having no perceptible interest in humanistic studies. He disliked the classicists' celebration of pagan antiquity and therefore resented the costs of maintaining the Vatican's College of Abbreviators, a privileged clique of literary men, officially scribes or secretaries, whose membership had been increased to seventy by Pius II. Paul suspected the abbreviators, not without reason, of harboring heretical beliefs and dreams of making Rome a republic once again. When reports reached him that they were involved in a plot to imprison or kill him and take command of the city, Paul's response was to declare the college abolished. Their jobs disappeared with it, and as many of them had paid hard cash for their positions, the ferocity of their resentment is not hard to understand.

Though the rebellion that ensued was a tiny one with no possibility of accomplishing anything, it did leave Paul besieged in his palace for some three weeks. The outcome was inevitable—the rebels were subdued and taken prisoner, Paul liberated—but the whole thing had been a profound embarrassment. It showed the pope to be so weak that he could be put in peril by fewer than a hundred of his own scribbling scholars. The episode also assured that Paul would be known as a bad man and bad pope more or less forever. The leading troublemaker among the abbreviators, Bartolomeo Platina, somehow expected to be reemployed upon his release from confinement, and when this did not happen, he was freshly offended. He took his revenge years later by writing *Lives of the Popes,* which depicted Paul II as a monster of cruelty and sexual depravity. His description has long since been shown to bear little connection to the truth, but the damage to its subject's reputation proved to be lasting.

Still worse was to come. In 1469 word reached Rome that the tireless Sultan Mehmed II was assembling an army of eighty thousand men and an enormous fleet of galleys for a fresh offensive and that his target this time was to be the city of Negropont in the Aegean Sea. Negropont was a key Venetian stronghold, one of the serene republic's essential colonial possessions, and its loss would be a disaster of the first order. Venice tried to rise to the challenge, extracting forced loans from its wealthier citizens and using the money to hurriedly expand its war fleet. By the time the Turkish attack came in 1470, the Venetians were ready. Negropont was under siege but holding out, its walls being slowly reduced to rubble by the Turks' guns, when Venice's fleet came racing over the horizon. The plan was to sever the Ottoman lines of supply, which would force the attackers to withdraw. Success seemed certain when suddenly the inexperienced Venetian commander lost his nerve and ordered his galleys to turn back. Negropont fell to the Turks just a day later, and its population was slaughtered. The city's governor, who had surrendered on condition that he not lose his head, was cut in half at the waist instead. It was the greatest Turkish success since the conquest of Bosnia in 1463. Coming on the heels of the death of Skanderbeg of Albania, who had fallen victim to malaria, it awoke all Italy to just how great the danger now was. The peninsula's leading powers and a number of the secondary ones came together once again in the new League of Lodi, a nonaggression pact akin to the one that had brought peace to Italy in the last days of Nicholas V. Peace was once again assured, at least for the time being, but it was a peace of a fearful and demoralized kind.

One evening a year after the fall of Negropont, Pope Paul, still only fifty-four years old, became ill after a hard day that had included six hours spent in consistory. He canceled the audiences scheduled for that night and retired to his bedchamber. Hours later his attendants found him dead, the victim of "apoplexy" according to his baffled physicians, probably of a stroke. It was said that he died from overindulging in melons, which must be a medical first of some kind, and stories of how he had suffered a fatal seizure while being sodomized by a young favorite would years later make their way into print. There is no contemporary testimony to any such thing, and no reputable commentator believes it today.

It makes more sense to suggest that Paul II had drunk too deeply from the supposedly great prize he had won seven years before and had become its latest victim.

THE INEXTINGUISHABLE EVIL-HEADS

THE STORY OF THE POPES AND THE ROMAGNA REGION OF northeastern Italy, from early times part of the Papal States, is a long, dismal chronicle of bloodshed, betrayal, and tragic outcomes. And it appears in perfect capsule form in the story of one family: the Malatesta of Rimini.

Malatesta: the word translates as something like "evil-head." It is not necessary to delve very deep into the family's history to get some understanding of why this came to be its name. Generation after generation over a period of two centuries, the Malatesta repeatedly shocked even their violent age with the extravagance of their crimes. They came to embody much of what was worst, along with a little of what was best, in the Italy of their time.

They first appear in history in the twelfth century as one of the first families to become noteworthy as soldiers-for-hire. Early in the thirteenth century they took a decisive step up, playing one side against the other as the popes in Rome fought the Holy Roman emperor Frederick II for supremacy in Italy, and establishing themselves as masters of several towns. Before the end of that century they were the lords of Rimini, which from that time forward would be the capital and main stronghold of the family's senior branch.

A rich lore would grow up around any princely family that stayed in power very long, but the tales told of the Malatesta were different: singularly horrific, and also generally true. The oldest and most famous of these tales—Dante included it in *The Inferno,* and it has been the subject of dozens of operas and plays—is that of Francesca da Rimini. She was the bride of a physically deformed Malatesta lord, fell in love and had an affair with her husband's charming brother, and was butchered along with her lover when the husband found them out. History repeated itself more than a century later when the fourteen-year-old Parisina Malatesta was married to Niccolò d'Este lord of Ferrara, twenty years her senior. This Niccolò had an illegitimate son a year younger than his bride, and again an affair ensued. When the lovers were discovered and young Ugo d'Este was put to death, Parisina cried out, "Now I no longer want to live!" Her husband obliged her by cutting off her head.

If these were the most romantic episodes in the history of the Malatesta, they were by no means the bloodiest. But ruthlessness and cruelty were useful in their world, and as the Malatesta went on with murdering their enemies and one another, they also gradually came into possession of a little mini-empire of cities and towns scattered across the Romagna and the March of Ancona. As they did so—here we touch on one of the paradoxes of Renaissance Italy—they also showed themselves to be improbably cultivated, lovers of literature and patrons of the arts. They built up a great library, which survives today, and early in the fifteenth century one of the lords of Rimini came to be known as "Malatesta of the sonnets."

The most notorious and in his way the greatest of the Malatesta was born in 1417 and grew up to become the plague of popes and kings. This was Sigismondo Pandolfo Malatesta, tall and powerfully built, blue-eyed and golden-haired, with the moral code of a sociopath. He first went soldiering at age thirteen, a year later took command of Rimini's defenses and fought off an attack by some Malatesta cousins, and succeeded to the lordship of the city one year after that. He was intelligent, a poet, a patron of artists and architects, so talented a general as to be described by some as a military genius. He was also so unscrupulous, so hungry for conquest, that finally no one could trust him. The stories told about him defy belief; he was said to have murdered two wives, copulated with his daughters, and been stopped at knifepoint from raping his son. The worst of these tales are almost certainly fabrications—Pope Pius II, who hated him as he hated no one else on earth, was the source of many of the most hair-raising of them—but it is nonetheless certain that he was capable of atrocious acts. The same cousins whom he had bested at Rimini at age fourteen later became so terrified of him that to escape his wrath they sold their home city of Pesaro to the duke of Milan.

The assortment of enemies that Sigismondo accumulated would have caused most men to reconsider their conduct, but he was fearless quite literally to a fault. Among those who sought his destruction were Alfonso V of Aragon and then his son Ferrante, Pope Pius II and then his successor, Paul. What would ultimately matter more, Federico da Montefeltro, a general who was an even better soldier than he and a far cooler head, came to hate him bitterly. Montefeltro's home city of Urbino was not distant from Malatesta's Rimini, which meant that, both men being ambitious to expand their domains, they were fated to collide. Things first turned seriously ugly in the late 1450s, when the two became embroiled in a dispute over the towns of Mondavio in the March of Ancona and Senigallia on the Romagna coast. Pope Pius was invited to arbitrate, but his decision left Malatesta convinced that he had been cheated. His response was to seize Mondavio and lay siege to Senigallia, thus putting himself at war with Rome and drawing down upon himself charges of heresy and treason.

In July 1462 Malatesta met a superior papal force at Castel Leone and subjected it to such a humiliating defeat that he expected Pius to come to terms. But the pope was unwilling to give up. Instead he again hired Montefeltro, who had not been present at Castel Leone, and in one of the weirdest exercises in the history of the papacy had Malatesta burned in effigy and canonized in reverse as a damned soul. ("I am Sigismondo Malatesta, king of traitors," a sign on the blazing dummy said. "Enemy of God and man, by sentence of the Sacred College condemned to the flames.") In short order Montefeltro and Malatesta had their showdown, and the latter was defeated so thoroughly that the war was over.

Pius wanted to drive the now-helpless Malatesta out of his last remaining stronghold, Rimini, and take possession of it himself. But Milan and Venice intervened, declaring that they could not tolerate the establishment of a papal outpost so far north. Malatesta had to pay a hefty annual tribute and pledge to fast on bread and water every Friday for the rest of his life. He lost almost all of his territories but was allowed to keep Rimini and a bit of the adjacent countryside for as long as he lived. His brother Domenico remained lord of Cesena on the same terms. Satisfied, Pius lifted the three bulls of excommunication earlier laid on Sigismondo and approved his departure for Greece, where he became a commander of Venetian forces in the war against the Turks.

The Malatesta, it appeared, were finished. This seemed all the more certain when, in 1465, Domenico died without an heir and the lordship of Cesena became vacant. Paul II, just a year into his papacy, moved quickly to take possession. Under ordinary circumstances such a step would have been opposed by the leading powers of the north, all of which coveted the Romagna and none of which wanted to see Rome entrench itself in the region. But Paul was lucky in his timing. Sigismondo Pandolfo Malatesta was in no position to do anything, obviously. Florence was distracted by upheavals following the death of its leader Cosimo de' Medici; Milan's Duke Francesco Sforza was incapacitated by dropsy and gout; and the Venetians, locked in their war with the Turks, were unwilling to risk offending their ally the pope. In short order Cesena's government was in the hands of a legate from Rome, and it had all been accomplished without bloodshed.

Three years later, when Sigismondo died in Rimini (he had returned from Greece sometime earlier and shortly before his death had visited Rome with the apparent intention of murdering Paul II), the pope made ready to repeat his success at Cesena. But his luck had run out. Sigismondo had left two sons, the legitimate Sallustio and the bastard Roberto, who promptly showed himself to be a true Malatesta by murdering his half-brother (he probably killed Sigismondo's widow as well) and declaring himself lord. When the pope laid claim to the city, he was met with defiance. Roberto immediately received pledges of support from Ferrante of Naples, the Sforzas of Milan, and finally even Venice, which could see nothing good in allowing even a Venetian pope to acquire a foothold on the north Adriatic coast.

Paul preferred to avoid war even when he had the advantage, and the opposition now facing him would have made going to war an act of political suicide. And so he tried diplomacy, and the great ever-turning wheel of alliances made and alliances broken began to spin as dizzyingly as only Italy could spin it. When it came to rest in the summer of 1469, another general war was getting under way, Rome and Venice were once again allies, and on the other side were Naples, Milan, and Florence. This was the weirdest war yet, constantly throwing up surprises. Montefeltro took Rimini from Roberto Malatesta, decided to keep it for himself rather than handing it over to the papacy, then changed course again by doing what no one could possibly have imagined him doing. He switched sides and joined forces with Roberto Malatesta. Sudden and baffling changes of allegiance were common in fifteenth-century Italy, as we have seen and will see many times more, but this one seemed to come out of nowhere. That Montefeltro would come to the rescue of the son of the one man he had hated all his life was crazily improbable even by the standards of the time.

It all ended in calamity for the pope. An army jointly commanded by Montefeltro and young Malatesta went out in search of their Roman and Venetian adversaries, found them, and inflicted on them a defeat so total that Paul gave up all thought of taking Rimini. The Malatesta were back, stronger than ever, and Roberto marked his triumph by marrying one of Montefeltro's numerous daughters. The pope could only lick his wounds, perhaps consoling himself with the thought that he was not the first pope to have failed ignominiously in the Romagna and was not likely to be the last.

9

Sixtus IV: Disturbing the Peace

None of the cardinals who voted for Francesco della Rovere in August 1471 could possibly have imagined, never mind expected, the torrent of blood and grief that, as Pope Sixtus IV, he was going to bring down on Italy in the course of a thirteen-year reign.

Rodrigo Borgia was one of those cardinals—he played a conspicuous part in rounding up the votes needed for della Rovere's election, actually—and there is no reason to think that his motives were any different from those of his colleagues. What they wanted, most of them, was a pope who would put an end to the turmoil of Paul II's last years.

Della Rovere seemed a perfect choice: a man unlikely to stir up trouble and likely to do good instead. A native of Liguria, the tiny province that is now the Italian Riviera but five centuries ago was a place of little consequence, in his fifty-seven years he had risen high from extraordinarily humble beginnings, managing while doing so to give offense to virtually no one. He was the son of a poor fisherman and at an early age had entered the Franciscan order of mendicant or begging friars— hardly a promising path to the highest levels of the Church. He proved to be academically gifted, however, and emerged from years of study and deep poverty as a professor of theology and philosophy, a respected author, and one of the leading members of his order. His promotion to cardinal was characteristic of what was best about Paul II. It was done not for any political purpose, or as compensation for any favors rendered, but in recognition of merit.

His election as pope came about in the same way. The conclave of 1471 is often described as a conflict between two hostile parties, one made up chiefly of men named to the Sacred College by Paul (the *Paoleschi*), the other of Pius II's appointees (the *Pieschi*). This way of explaining what happened, however, turns out to have limited value. The opening of the conclave found eighteen cardinals present; the fact that only three of them were not Italian meant that for the first time in more than two centuries the Italians had an opportunity—if they were united, which inevitably they were not—to elect one of their own without outside help. In any case the Italians were going to elect the pope, and it was almost inevitable that their choice would be Italian. When the conclave's first ballot produced a result that was curious under the circumstances, giving the lead to the Greek Bessarion and that tireless self-promoter Estouteville of France, the obvious explanation was that almost no one present was ready to show his hand.

This was certainly true of Rodrigo. He gave his first-round vote to Bartolomeo Roverella, the archbishop of Ravenna, a respectable enough choice but with no possibility of being elected. This was a delaying tactic, a way of concealing his intentions while waiting for the other cardinals to reveal theirs. Having cast it, he began lobbying actively for della Rovere, who on the third day received thirteen votes—five *Paoleschi* and three *Pieschi* among them—and so became pope. It is not clear why four cardinals—three *Pieschi* but also a solitary *Paoleschi*—refused to give della Rovere their votes even after his election became a certainty, thereby making it impossible to tell the world that the election had been unanimous. Perhaps those four knew della Rovere better than their colleagues.

Della Rovere's supporters knew that their choice was intelligent, immensely learned, and pious, and as Pope Sixtus IV he continued to be all those things. He showed himself to be other things as well. He quickly revealed not only a previously unsuspected toughness but a ruthlessness that could turn under pressure into outright brutality. Also completely unsuspected, and equally troubling when it manifested itself, was a devotion to his family that went almost beyond the bounds of reason. At the time of his election, most of that family was living in modest circumstances, even in near poverty, back in Liguria. With the stunning news that their kinsman had become pope, they descended upon Rome in a swarm, hoping to transform their lives. Not many were disappointed. Within a month of his election, Sixtus was dispensing favors to his relatives with a profligacy rarely if ever equaled in papal history.

Among his brother Raffaelo's offspring were three sons in their twenties: Giuliano, who thanks to his uncle the cardinal's patronage was already bishop of a diocese in France; Bartolomeo, who had followed the future pope into the Franciscans; and Giovanni, a layman in search of a career. In short order the brilliant, hot-tempered, and blazingly ambitious Giuliano was made a cardinal. A place was found for Giovanni in the service of the best soldier in Italy, Federico da Montefeltro, and he was also appointed vicar, governor, of the papal town of Senigallia on the Adriatic coast. Friar Bartolomeo, for whatever reason, had to wait to be given a bishopric, but the wait took barely a year. The father of this trio found himself vaulted from the obscure penury of his old life into eminence as senator of Rome.

Sixtus also had sisters, two of whom produced offspring destined to figure in the Borgia story. One of Luchina Basso's five sons became a cardinal while all of his brothers were raised to the nobility, but none of them would be nearly as important as two of Bianca's sons, the Franciscan friar Pietro Riario and his brother Girolamo. Their father, Paolo Riario, had been generous when his brother-in-law was a penniless young student, which may explain why Sixtus singled out the Riarii for special treatment. He gave the twenty-five-year-old Pietro the revenues of a rich abbey in northern Europe and appointed him to the College of Cardinals simultaneously with his cousin Giuliano della Rovere. Girolamo was a carefree young ruffian who in adolescence, after declining to take advantage of the educational opportunities made available by his uncle, had supported himself by selling oranges and raisins in the streets of his hometown. When his uncle was elected pope, he joined the southward stampede to Rome, and even he—arrogant lout that he was—must have been surprised by what happened next. He found himself captain-general of the papal army, a position for which he had no qualifications, and ennobled as count of Bosco. He was also put forward as a bridegroom for an illegitimate daughter of the duke of Milan, but as the girl was only eight a wedding was not yet possible.

What would have been most apparent to the senior members of the Sacred College, in the early going, was not Sixtus's nepotism but his gratifying willingness to do as they had hoped, first by ending the conflicts to which Paul II's assertiveness had given rise, then by succeeding where his predecessors had failed in mounting a campaign against the Turks. These goals the cardinals approved heartily, of course, and the pope so intertwined the things he did to achieve them with the advancement of his family's interests that the former tended to camouflage the latter. His success in marrying one of the least impressive of his nephews to a princess (albeit an illegitimate princess) of Naples's royal family was an astonishing coup for the *arrivistes* from Liguria, but it was no less plausibly explained as a necessary step in dissolving the ill feeling that remained from Pope Paul's reign. The marriage of another young della Rovere into the ducal family of Urbino, and the opening of negotiations over a possible union of the onetime fruit vendor Girolamo Riario with a Sforza of Milan, also had multilayered ramifications. Such unions raised the pope's family to a level that until recently would have been unimaginable, but their possible political value for the Church transcended even this and made criticism difficult.

Sixtus was businesslike in setting out to organize a pan-European counteroffensive against the Turks. Instead of doing the usual thing and announcing an international conference to be held in some city in or near the Alps, hoping that at least some of the powers would show up, he arranged to carry his appeal into every major capital in Europe. He announced the appointment of five cardinals who, armed with the powers of legates, were to fan out across the continent to enlist support. His choices for this assignment showed the seriousness with which he approached the challenge: able and respected men, each particularly well suited to the part of the world for which he was given responsibility. The aging and revered Bessarion was dispatched to Louis XI of France, Edward IV of England, and Charles the Bold of Burgundy. Cardinal Marco Barbo, the son of a brother of Paul II, was sent to central Europe: to Germany and the two short-lived kingdoms of Hungary-Bohemia-Croatia and Poland-Lithuania. The veteran diplomat Angelo

Capranica got the thankless job of making the rounds of all the Italian principalities north of Naples and persuading them to put aside their endless quarrels and join the pope's crusade. Naples was assigned to Oliviero Carafa, who was the son of a noble Neapolitan family and had managed through his career to stay on good terms with the devious Ferrante. Upon winning Ferrante over, Carafa was to add the Neapolitan triremes to the papal fleet and set off for Ottoman waters.

The selection of Rodrigo Borgia as legate in the Iberian peninsula was all but inevitable. He was now the only Spanish cardinal in Rome— the only Spanish cardinal alive, aside from his cousin Luis Juan del Milà, who had long since withdrawn to his diocese of Lérida and was never seen in Italy—and was also the obvious choice by virtue of the pope's high regard. Not only in this instance but throughout his reign, Sixtus would rely heavily on Rodrigo as vice-chancellor and turn to him when needing help in areas unrelated to work of the chancery. There would be no assignment more daunting than the one he now took on, because the prospects of finding substantial support for a crusade were even worse in Iberia than in the rest of Europe. What would eventually become the kingdom of Spain did not yet exist. Granada in the south remained a Muslim emirate and an outpost of Islamic North Africa, and though the peninsula's Christian regions were no longer as politically fragmented as they once had been, they were still divided into the four kingdoms of Aragon, Castile, Portugal, and Navarre. Aragon and Castile were both ruled by branches of the House of Trastámara, but this did not keep them from being recurrently at odds.

In returning to the land of his birth Rodrigo would be stepping into a tangle of dynastic and ecclesiastical disputes, all of them involving dangerous questions of money and power. It is a measure of the pope's confidence that, rather than cautioning Rodrigo to limit himself to the proposed war on the Turks and keep clear of other, thornier issues, he empowered him to deal with almost anything he might encounter in whatever way he thought best. He was granted authority to dispense papal indulgences in return for support of the crusade, pardon crimes other than murder, settle property disputes, impose a special tithe on the incomes of Spanish clerics, and even offer appointments to the College of Cardinals. Later, when these powers appeared to be insufficient for dealing with the problems Rodrigo encountered, Sixtus would send out new bulls granting him still more. Among them was authority to excommunicate, though there is no evidence that Rodrigo ever used it.

Such a high-level diplomatic mission involved transporting all the people and matériel required for a grand display of ecclesiastical splendor. It was therefore vastly expensive, which brings us back to the subject of Cardinal Borgia's finances. When Pope Sixtus, upon taking office, followed the established practice of distributing the benefices he had held at the time of his election, he triggered as usual a game of musical chairs: many of the cardinals had to surrender offices they already possessed in order to accept others. Rodrigo was given the rich abbey of Subiaco near Tivoli and the bishopric of Albano in central Italy. Finally and more remarkably, a papal bull dispensed him from having to give up the see of Valencia or any of the other benefices bestowed on him by earlier popes.

Setting aside the obvious undesirability of allowing any single individual to be bishop of two or more cities (a practice that would not be ended until the Council of Trent in the sixteenth century), it was no proof of wickedness or indeed of simony. To the contrary, when not used as a way of capriciously enriching family and favorites, it could be not only practical but nearly unavoidable. The test, surely, is whether the incomes in question were used to good purpose or simply to indulge the recipient. Sixtus fails that test badly in some instances—grossly where his favorite nephews are concerned—but not in the case of Rodrigo Borgia. What happened in the two months following his appointment as legate indicates that, far from getting rich, Rodrigo was once again seriously short of funds. On January 17, 1472, Sixtus signed a bull permitting him to auction the income due from his benefices over the next three years. On March 6, with his departure for Spain only two months off, he was authorized to mortgage the revenues of the chancery as well. Such favors would never have been granted if Rodrigo had not requested them. Because their net result would be a significant reduction in his income over several years, he would not have asked if his need had not been serious.

His arrival at Valencia on June 17 was treated as a great event, with the governor-general heading a reception committee of dignitaries and the walls of the city draped in crimson cloth. Rodrigo was a quadruply noteworthy guest of honor: Valencia's absentee bishop, a cardinal, the pope's personal representative, and a native son returning home in glory. As soon as the formalities had been completed and Rodrigo had delivered an address to the assembled clergy of his diocese, he moved up the coast to the Catalonian province of Tarragona. There he met for the first time King Juan of Aragon, the complexity of whose character is reflected in the fact that he was called by some Juan the Great, by others Juan the Faithless. Younger brother of the late Alfonso V, uncle of Ferrante of Naples, Juan was tough and ambitious, a ruthless political infighter. Having arrived at his court, Rodrigo was able to get down to the business that had brought him to Spain.

At the top of his agenda, of course, was bringing the kingdom of Aragon and its satellites into an international coalition to fight the Turks. Juan, predictably uninspired by the idea, replied that he had far too many problems to do any such thing. He had a war on his hands, thanks to the refusal of the people of Catalonia to accept absorption into Aragon on his terms. At the time of Rodrigo's arrival he had been besieging Barcelona for almost a year without result. What was at least as frustrating, his attempt to unite Aragon and Castile by marrying his son and heir Ferdinand to the king of Castile's half-sister and supposed heir Isabella had gone so badly wrong that it was no longer certain that Isabella was in fact her brother's heir—or that her marriage to Ferdinand was valid.

Seeing that he had no chance of accomplishing the pope's purposes unless Juan were somehow extracted from these difficulties, Rodrigo undertook to perform the extractions personally. He obtained the king's permission to go to Barcelona and talk with the defenders, searching for terms on which the siege might be satisfactorily concluded. When he came away, it seemed that he had failed, that the Catalans were unwilling to compromise. But soon thereafter—whether because their situation inside the besieged city was becoming unsustainable, or because of the new options that Rodrigo had opened to them—the Catalans made themselves available for talks. Juan, accepting the cardinal's counsel, responded in encouraging terms. The result was peace—a peace that had been inaccessible until Rodrigo's intervention. No account of how he accomplished this exists, but the engaging frankness that he brought to all his relationships—the openness and candor with which, for example, he had responded when Cardinal Piccolomini challenged his decision to vote for Estouteville in 1458—must surely have been a factor. As we shall see, his life story is studded with instances in which his ability to connect even with adversaries affected the course of history. Barcelona accepted Aragonese rule, and in keeping with Rodrigo's proposal its defenders were granted a general pardon. Juan pledged to uphold the Catalan constitution, and the city's French commandant was allowed to depart unharmed. Problem solved.

Next, Rodrigo used the authority given him by Sixtus to dispense Ferdinand and Isabella from the canon law that prohibited the marriage of near relations. (The two were cousins in multiple ways, thanks to numerous intermarriages among the royal families of Aragon, Castile, and Portugal.) He thereby validated the marriage that they had entered into three years earlier, when Ferdinand was seventeen and Isabella a year older. Another problem solved.

This left the question of whether Isabella was in fact heir to the throne of Castile, so that her marriage could serve its intended purpose of uniting that kingdom with Aragon. Rodrigo moved on to Castile and to the Madrid court of King Enrique IV. There he found a kind of low-grade war in process between nobles demanding that Isabella be recognized as heir and those supporting the claim of the king's supposed daughter, Juana. This struggle was fueled by the widespread suspicion that Juana was not Enrique's daughter at all and therefore not entitled to inherit. Her enemies, and Enrique's, referred to her as *La Beltraneja*, a jibe reflecting the belief that she was the product of an adulterous affair between Enrique's queen and one Béltran de la Cueva, duke of Albuquerque. Rodrigo found it surprisingly easy to persuade Enrique to repudiate the princess he had always acknowledged as his daughter. The Castilian king, as weak as his sobriquet "Enrique the Impotent" suggested, was willing to acknowledge Isabella as heir in return for nothing more costly than the promotion of his favorite bishop to the Sacred College. Rodrigo arranged that, when in 1473 Pope Sixtus appointed a slate of new cardinals, the list would include Enrique's favorite. Delighted as he was, Enrique cannot have been more pleased than Juan of Aragon and his son and daughter-in-law.

Before departing Castile, Rodrigo summoned the bishops of Castile and León to meet with him in Segovia. There he launched a program of reform that would, among other things, make Spain the home of some of Europe's first diocesan seminaries, ending the ordination of priests who knew nothing of Latin or theology. The time that Rodrigo devoted to Church business while in Spain—his instituting of reforms at a number of monasteries being another example—is not easily reconciled with claims that throughout his career he was cynically indifferent to the proper functioning of the Church.

By midsummer 1473 he had been in Spain for more than a year. He had won assurances of royal support for the war against the Turks, and though that support seemed certain to be modest, there was no prospect that by remaining longer he could achieve more. Meanwhile he was receiving troubling reports about developments back in Rome. The most alarming were being sent by Cardinal Jacopo Ammannati-Piccolomini, bishop of Pavia, an adoptive member of the late Pius II's family and one of the *Pieschi* who had been too opposed to Cardinal della Rovere to allow a declaration of unanimous election. He begged Rodrigo to hurry back to Rome to help counteract the influence of Pope Sixtus's nephews. There is irony in his appeals, because at this same time he was writing to others in ways that have contributed to blackening the Borgia name. Having earlier accused Rodrigo of securing Sixtus's election through "cunning and bribery," he was now complaining—from Rome, it must be noted—that Rodrigo's conduct in Spain was "vain, luxurious, ambitious, [and] greedy." The sad truth appears to be that Ammannati, in many ways an admirable individual, was bitter about the election of Sixtus, about not having been among the legates chosen in December 1471, and about finding himself—not surprisingly, all this considered—out of favor at the papal court. He heaped scorn not only on Rodrigo but on the other legates as well, even the venerable Bessarion, and could be absurdly reckless in his accusations. The credibility of the things he wrote can be measured by his complaint that while in Portugal Rodrigo spent "most of his time with the ladies." In fact, there is no evidence that Rodrigo ever set foot in Portugal. Nor is it irrelevant that while spreading such slanders Ammannati was imploring their object to return to the Vatican to help counteract what was happening there. If it is not impossible that he would turn to a man he regarded as seriously corrupt for help in fighting corruption, it certainly is odd.

From Segovia Rodrigo returned to Madrid, then to Valencia, where he spent time with King Juan's clever son Ferdinand, planting the seeds of what would grow into a long-lasting friendship. Early in August he at last paid a visit to his boyhood home, Játiva, where he was received as a hero, next to his uncle Alonso the greatest personage the town had ever produced. His entourage was joined by a contingent of Spanish dignitaries wanting to accompany him back to Rome, and in September they put to sea in a pair of Venetian galleys. On October 10, almost home, they were caught in a storm off the Italian coast near Pisa. In the course of a terrifying night one of the galleys went down with the loss of approximately two hundred passengers and crew. Among them were seventy-five members of Rodrigo's retinue (the number suggests just how expensive the mission had been), three Spanish bishops, and property and gold (the cardinal's personal baggage included) with a value of at least thirty thousand ducats. Rodrigo survived thanks to the skill of his vessel's captain, who saved all hands by intentionally running aground on a sandy beach.

Though Sixtus must have hoped that Rodrigo would return with more support for his crusade than he was able to—and though some of what he had obtained may have gone to the bottom of the sea with the doomed galley—the mission had accomplished great things all the same. The cardinal received a deservedly warm welcome and learned that he had been the most successful of the legates in terms of mustering resources for the war against the Turks. Bessarion had died after being rebuffed by wily old Louis XI of France. Capranica was in poor health after failing to persuade many of the princes of Italy to join the cause, and the jealousies of the eastern European monarchs had made it impossible for Marco Barbo to accomplish anything. Cardinal Carafa had taken a combined force of papal, Venetian, and Neapolitan galleys into the eastern Mediterranean and had had some early success, including the burning of the Ottoman port of Smyrna. But his fleet had then disintegrated as the Neapolitans and Venetians fell to quarreling and sailed off to their respective homes.

Rodrigo, by contrast, had resolved disputes that had long plagued the Iberian church and launched important reforms. He had shown the way to peace in Aragon and in Castile and had helped lay the foundations for eventual unification of the two kingdoms. No less important was the respect and gratitude of the Spanish royals. A few years later, when Isabella gave birth to a son and heir, she and Ferdinand would ask Rodrigo to serve as godfather. This was but a token of the friendship that would bind the houses of Borgia and Trastámara for the next quarter-century, becoming a factor of real significance in the politics not only of Italy but of Europe.

As he took up once again the management of the chancery, Rodrigo saw that Ammannati had not been exaggerating when he wrote of trouble in Rome. The situation was, if anything, more disturbing than the cardinal had warned. The balance of power on which the peace of Italy depended, always fragile and frequently violated, was in danger of falling apart completely. The reasons were numerous and complex, but few were more important than the far-reaching fear and resentment now being aroused by the pope's lavishing of favors on his relatives. Acceptance of papal nepotism had limits even in Rome, and its beneficiaries were expected to conduct themselves with a measure of restraint, at least early in a reign. Sixtus, however, was conducting himself as though the limits did not exist, his nephews as though restraint was contemptible. They had been feeding ravenously at the pontifical trough almost from the day of their uncle's election, they gave no sign of being satisfied, and indignation was rising to a level not seen in many generations.

The eldest of the cardinal-nephews, the explosively temperamental Giuliano della Rovere, was, though not yet thirty, archbishop of both Avignon and Bologna, bishop of five dioceses, and abbot of two major monasteries. His cousin Girolamo Riario, not so long ago a small-town fruit peddler but now a member of the titled nobility, was papal enforcer in his role as captain-general of the Vatican soldiery and clearly set on rising higher. But even they were eclipsed by their uncle's great favorite, Girolamo's younger brother Cardinal Pietro Riario. Intelligent and cultivated where Girolamo was a Caliban-like bundle of mindless animal energy, Pietro was so loved by Sixtus that the rumor mill declared them to be father and son. Gossip of this kind is understandable, was probably inevitable, and certainly was not uncommon in such circumstances. In the absence of evidence, it can only be noted with interest—and an appropriate measure of skepticism.

Pietro, the pope's most trusted adviser especially but not only where questions of foreign policy were involved, had become the recipient of an avalanche of nepotistic largesse. He was archbishop of Florence as well as bishop of a handful of cities and head of the great abbey of Saint Ambrose in Milan, and he bore the honorary title of patriarch of Constantinople. His income was stupendous—estimated at between sixty and seventy thousand florins per year—but so inadequate to his way of life that he was piling up debts at a rate that should have alarmed Sixtus. He brought the finest artists to Rome and put them to work on an immense new palace, spent without restraint on everything from racehorses to pearl-covered gowns for his mistresses, and was accompanied on his rounds by five hundred attendants all dressed in scarlet silk.

Italy had rarely seen anything to compare with the arrogance and presumption of these upstarts from the hinterlands, and trouble was inevitable. It began in the spring of 1473—Rodrigo was still in Spain—with a clash over territory between Sixtus and a much younger man of equally strong will, Lorenzo de' Medici of Florence. In his fourth year as de facto chief of the Florentine republic in spite of being only twenty-four, Lorenzo was well along in his development into the fabled Lorenzo the Magnificent, one of the supreme personalities of the Renaissance. It is difficult to say whether he or Sixtus was most responsible for their conflict. Lorenzo made the first move, entering into an agreement by which Duke Galeazzo Maria Sforza of Milan was to sell the town of Imola to Florence for a hundred thousand florins. Imola was far from being one of the great urban centers of Italy, but it lay just north and east of the Apennine Mountains and commanded miles of the rich flatlands of the Romagna. It also sat athwart the old Roman highway called the Via Emilia, a lifeline that helped to connect Florence to the Adriatic and the markets of the East. Thus it had a strategic importance out of proportion to its size.

Like the whole of the Romagna Imola owed fealty to Rome, but like much other papal territory it had long ago slipped out of papal control. It was one of the jumble of petty city-states ruled by clans that at best paid lip service to Rome while ruthlessly exploiting their subjects. Sixtus like Paul II had entered upon his reign determined to reestablish control of as much of the Papal States as possible, and again like Paul he gave particular attention to the Romagna. There were good reasons for this: the fertility of its soil made the Romagna an agricultural cornucopia, and many of the region's warlords had no legitimate claim to the towns they ruled and no grounds for complaint if displaced. It had become a centerpiece of papal policy to displace them if possible, and therefore Imola was at least as important to Rome as to Florence. The sale arranged by Lorenzo de' Medici was as unthinkable for the pope as control of the city by Rome—or by any state except Florence—was for the Florentines.

When Sixtus ordered Milan's Duke Galeazzo Maria Sforza to cancel the sale on grounds that he had no right to sell what he did not own even if his troops happened to occupy it, what followed was not obedience but prolonged, multisided, and indescribably complicated negotiations. These ended in a new agreement, this one between Milan and Rome with Florence relegated to the sidelines. Imola was to be handed over not to Florence but to the pope, and for forty thousand florins rather than a hundred. Seller and buyer were to be brought together in harmony via the marriage (which had long been under discussion) of Count Girolamo Riario to Galeazzo Maria's illegitimate daughter Caterina, now all of eleven years old. Such a marriage had become advantageous in a new way: it would allow all parties to pretend that Imola was not being sold at all but was the dowry of the bride-to-be. Florence, neither fooled nor mollified, was soon in an uproar of indignation.

The Vatican treasury did not have forty thousand florins to spare. The Roman branch of the Medici bank having had a monopoly on the papacy's business since a grateful client became Pope Nicholas V back in 1447, Sixtus found himself applying for a loan to none other than Lorenzo de' Medici. If he was less than shocked at being turned down, he definitely was infuriated. He broke off relations with the House of Medici and put in its place a rival Florentine establishment, the bank of Francesco de' Pazzi.

That might have been the end of it, but was only the beginning. When Sixtus sent envoys to assert his authority in the Romagna, hostile local warlords forced them to turn back. The pope then raised the stakes, sending an armed force northward under his nephew Cardinal Giuliano della Rovere. The compulsive determination to dominate everyone and everything, to impose his will upon every situation and accept no setbacks, made Giuliano a throwback to the ferocious warrior-cardinals of the past. He was also an abler soldier than his cousin

Girolamo, the papal captain-general, because he was more intelligent and courageous. He was thwarted all the same, forced into retreat by a superior Florentine force. Predictably, and with considerable justification, Sixtus again seethed with indignation. Eventually, after considerable to-ing and fro-ing, the pope's troops succeeded in reaching Imola, and Girolamo Riario was installed as its lord.

Girolamo's brother Pietro, meanwhile, was occupied with other matters. Still in Milan and on the friendliest of terms with its murderous duke—it was partly because of their friendship that the duke had elected to sell Imola to the pope rather than to Florence—the cardinal and his host were engaged now in hatching a breathtakingly bizarre scheme that if somehow carried to completion might have satisfied the voracious ambitions of both men. Galeazzo Maria was to become king of Lombardy, his coronation performed by the pope. He would then advance on Rome and use his army to install Pietro on the papal throne. (Sixtus would be willing, one must assume, to abdicate in his nephew's favor to make this possible.) That these things could ever have been accomplished is extremely unlikely; the forces in opposition would have been daunting. In any case the question was never put to the test. Upon returning to Rome, presumably to finalize arrangements with his uncle, Pietro was struck down by fever. In January 1474, after weeks of struggle and amid the usual rumors of poisoning, he died aged twenty-eight. Whether or to what extent Sixtus knew of Pietro's plan and the part he was expected to play in it remains a mystery.

Pietro's death left his uncle bereft and a vacuum at the heart of the papal court. With all his excesses the young cardinal had been a comfort to Sixtus, a source of pride and even, at times, of helpful counsel. No greater question faced the pontiff, now in the third year of his reign, than where to look for a new right hand.

There were several satisfactory answers, both in the College of Cardinals and elsewhere.

Sixtus would choose badly.

WAR, ITALIAN STYLE

TO BE A FIFTEENTH-CENTURY POPE WAS TO BE FACED WITH A humiliating and costly form of political impotence: the inability to establish even limited control over those whole provinces of Italy that by law and tradition were the property of the papacy but in fact were in other, rarely friendly, hands.

The resulting conflicts and frustrations are a dark thread running through the reigns of all the century's popes. Time after time succeeding pontiffs found themselves blocked from their own territories by even the pettiest of lordlings, especially when, as commonly happened, those lordlings were under the protection of more powerful neighbors. We saw this in the reign of Paul II, who was able to take control of his fiefdom of Cesena only because its reigning strongman had died without an heir and the other interested powers were momentarily distracted. We saw also that only the help of Federico da Montefeltro enabled Paul to drive the vicious Anguillara clan from the little domain they had carved out of the Papal States, and that when this same Montefeltro changed sides (in spite of being himself a papal vassal), the pope was rendered helpless.

It was much the same for Sixtus IV, who would never have been able to obtain Imola for his nephew Girolamo if the duke of Milan had not been willing to sell it. What had been given to the popes by emperors was taken from them by gangsters during the years of exile and schism, and after the papacy returned to Rome, those families proved impossible to control and all but impossible to uproot.

To understand the Borgia story it is necessary to understand who these families were, and how they had come to matter as much as they did. Most of them were, by the time the first Borgias arrived in Rome, members of a brotherhood called the *condottieri,* which means simply that they signed contracts, *condotta,* to sell their military services in return for hard cash: for gold.

It is appropriate, if less romantic, to call them warlords. Most were lords in a quite literal sense—the rulers, even when they did not bear titles of nobility, of one or more cities or towns. In most cases their rule was brutish and tyrannical, with no basis in law or justice. They spent their lives fighting one another, waging war for pay, or collecting retainers while waiting for the call to battle.

It could be a lucrative line of work, being a *condottiere,* and it was not necessarily all that dangerous. A good *condotta* was a thing to be coveted, so fine a source of honor and income that by the fifteenth century breaking into the business had come to be nearly impossible for anyone lacking the right family connections. For anyone not born, that is, into the increasingly exclusive circle of Italian tyrant families.

The world of these families was Italy's version of the phenomenon that historians refer to as "bastard feudalism." In its unadulterated form, feudalism was an arrangement by which a king granted land to his nobles, the nobles in turn parceled out their land among knights, and the knights used peasants to farm the parcels. Everyone at every level of this pyramid owed service to whoever stood directly above him and ultimately to the man at the apex, the prince. Part of the price for possession of land, and for protection, was an obligation to report for military service when summoned. This was the only dependable way of raising an armed force where not much money was in circulation. But it became a nuisance to everyone involved as economic life became more sophisticated. Gradually it mutated into the debased form that permitted noblemen, rather than fighting the king's wars themselves, to send the king a purseful of gold instead.

Things developed differently in Italy. As we saw earlier, feudalism failed to sink its roots as deeply south of the Alps as in the north, and it began to fade away earlier. The development of manufacturing and trade, the emergence of lively urban centers, and the absence of even a vestige of national government combined to create more opportunities for the freelance fighting man in Italy than elsewhere, and in ways that few ordinary Italians could have welcomed. When German kings began to invade the sunny lands of the south, they did so at the head of armies that seemed to the onlooking locals (no doubt accurately enough) to be not much of an improvement over the barbarian tribes that had overrun their forebears a thousand years before.

Inevitably, amid the disorder created by these invasions, troops of battle-hardened foreigners found themselves at loose ends but unwilling to return to the cold and backward north when the emperors who had brought them to Italy were obliged to go home. Armed and unemployed in a rich and fragmented country, they rather naturally took up the business of pillaging. They came together to form companies that sometimes numbered more than ten thousand men, enough to make them a threat to the largest city-states. By electing their officers and providing opportunities for quick wealth that would have been inconceivable in any other line of work, they achieved surprisingly high levels of cohesion. Of course they left devastation behind them wherever they went. Their opportunism and ruthlessness are illustrated by an episode of 1329, when a force of eight hundred German cavalry deserted from the army of Emperor Ludwig of Bavaria and independently laid siege to the city of Lucca. The man sent by the emperor to order them to return defected himself instead and was rewarded with election as their leader. Upon capturing Lucca they looted it of everything of value, and then sold it to Genoa for thirty thousand florins.

One of the most notorious early captains, Werner von Urslingen, is said to have displayed on his breastplate the motto "Enemy of God, of pity, and of mercy"—and to have earned it in years of savagely pillaging the Romagna, Tuscany, and Umbria. For a while he sold the services of the force he had created, the notorious Great Company, to the pope. When that proved insufficiently lucrative, he switched to ravaging the Papal States.

Another fourteenth-century legend, Ezzelino da Romano (of German extraction despite his name), became so notorious for his atrocities that, two and a half centuries after his death, the poet Ariosto wrote that he was "believed to be the son of a demon." He was not devoid of redeeming qualities, however. He was the only commander to remain loyal to Frederick II as that extraordinary emperor was brought low by the pope, and he was generous in his treatment of vanquished foes. It appears likely that the most horrifying of the stories he inspired—accounts of his monstrous treatment of children, for example—were invented by his enemies. The moral caliber of those enemies, and the standards of conduct prevailing at the time, might fairly be measured by what happened after Ezzelino was captured and subjected to a slow, agonizing death. His brother and partner Alberico, also captured, was forced to watch as his wife and two daughters were burned alive. All six of his sons were then executed, their bodies chopped into pieces and scattered. Finally, ropes were tied to Alberico's extremities and to horses that pulled him apart. If the brothers were monsters, their enemies were no better.

The most successful of the early mercenary chieftains was John Hawkwood, the one Englishman to rise to prominence fighting in Italy for pay. Of humble origins and probably illiterate, Hawkwood fought in France under King Edward III in the early stages of the Hundred Years' War. He is believed to have been about forty when he entered Italy and became a member of the Great Company. In the early 1360s he was elected commander of its successor the White Company, and he spent the next thirty years engaged in almost every significant conflict in Italy. He and his company regularly changed employers, not infrequently signing on with a patron's enemy. They would accept a *condotta* from one city and then take money from that city's enemies in return for not attacking. Hawkwood came to be honored all the same, perhaps in part because he never made the mistake that led to the ruin of Ezzelino and many others: he never tried to carve out a principality for himself. He married into the Visconti dynasty of Milan, and when he died, the city of Florence buried him in state in its cathedral, where his monument can be seen to this day. King Richard II asked for the return of his body to England.

By early in the fifteenth century the *condottieri* were becoming not just freebooting mercenaries but instruments of governance, and were more respectable as a result. It was another time of severe instability, with city-states large and small both threatened by external enemies and weakened from within as rival factions fought for control. Many of the cities had long been organized as communes, with substantial numbers of the citizens having at least some voice in government. Now, however, and with increasing frequency, powerful individuals (men both ambitious and rich, usually) were using the pervasive uncertainty as an excuse to take command, impose order on their own terms, and set themselves up as tyrants. As early as the thirteenth century, Dante had complained that "the cities of Italy are full of tyrants." By the fifteenth century tyranny was the rule.

Typically, upon seizing power a new tyrant would disarm the citizenry. This was not as unpopular a measure as one might suppose; random bloodshed stopped as swords and daggers disappeared, so that the change was not greatly deplored. Still, the need to maintain order and defend against invaders remained, and even leaders as supposedly enlightened as the Medici found it advisable to suppress dissent. The tyrants needed soldiers to do such work but, being usurpers, most found it impossible to trust the people they ruled. And so it became the practice to sign outsiders to *condotta*. This was made easier by Italy's early development of a money economy. The employment of *condottieri* became policy even in such republics as Venice and Florence, partly because the merchants and bankers who dominated these cities had no wish to go soldiering themselves. The papacy too made frequent use of *condotta*. The lure of cash had a further effect, causing many tyrants to become *condottieri* themselves and see to it that their sons were trained to take up military careers. As the warlord families intermarried in an endless and largely futile quest for dependable allies, non-Italians found it impossible to win contracts. *Condotta* became an oblique way of paying tribute to a feared warlord—of buying his neutrality if not his friendship. Many ruling families became dependent on their earnings as mercenaries to cover the costs of running their own little states.

The mid-fifteenth century produced the greatest of the *condottieri*. The most admired was a figure we have already encountered more than once because he was employed in almost every conflict of consequence during his lifetime. This was Federico da Montefeltro, scion of the dynasty that had long ruled the remote hilltop city of Urbino. The eagerness of other cities to hire him generated the fantastic sums with which he turned Urbino into an architectural showplace of international renown, established one of the greatest libraries and most brilliant courts of the century, and raised his family to ducal status.

Even more spectacularly successful, and by a wide margin the most feared, was Francesco Sforza. Though not born into a ruling family, he gained admittance to the brotherhood of *condottieri* while still half-grown by virtue of being the son of one of the leading mercenary commanders of the early 1400s, Muzio Attendolo. In the course of his own impressive career, as a kind of early experiment in branding, this Attendolo had given himself the name Sforza, meaning "force." Francesco, twenty-three when his father drowned crossing a river during one of their campaigns, took charge of the family business and soon showed himself to be a general of immense courage and rare ability. In the manner of his profession he changed sides whenever it was advantageous to do so, first fighting against Pope Eugenius IV and then contracting to work for him. Later, in the service of Venice, he inflicted a painful defeat on Milan, after which he married the sixteen-year-old only child of Milan's ruler, the last Visconti duke. When his father-in-law died, Francesco laid claim to the ducal title. To win it he had to fend off challenges from the German emperor (whose fiefdom Milan was), the French duke of Orléans (whose mother was a Visconti), and the military might of Venice. In succeeding he became the only *condottiere* to found a ruling dynasty.

It might go without saying, in light of all this, that there was nothing remotely demeaning about accepting employment under a *condotta*. The contrary was more often true: demanding a contract could be a kind of blackmail, a levy imposed by the strong upon the less strong. On the other hand, employment as a *condottiere,* even success as one, was no proof of ability or courage. The nature of the system meant that commanders rarely had reason to care passionately about whatever side they had been hired to fight for, or to put themselves in danger. Machiavelli would identify this problem, and the cynical self-interest that it engendered, as one reason for Italy's inability to defend itself against invaders. Warfare in Italy, as long as it was conducted by Italians only, was often a ritual affair in which the risks even to combatants were kept within narrow limits and harm to civilians was often a thing to be avoided. Statistically, the warlords stood in far greater risk of being murdered by their own relatives than of dying in battle.

All this would change when the foreign armies came.

10

Innocent VIII:
Plumbing the Depths

Sixtus IV's priorities were not changed by the death of his nephew Pietro. He was still determined to start bringing the Papal States under control, pledged to oppose the advance of the Turks, and passionately, obsessively, blindly committed to lifting his family into the highest ranks of Italian society.

The clarity of his goals and the strength of his will, however, were not matched by his talents as a strategist. He needed help not just in the execution but in the formulation of policy—in deciding how to get what he wanted. There were also tricky questions having to do with what he wanted *most,* because fighting the Turks and satisfying his young kinsmen proved to be not quite compatible objectives. Among the most obvious possible sources of counsel was Cardinal Rodrigo Borgia. In his early forties now, with nearly two decades of experience as one of the Vatican's top men, he had a deserved reputation as a hard worker and an intelligent, capable manager. His affability and even temperament had made him a well-liked member of the Sacred College, and his achievements in Spain had reinforced the good opinion that Sixtus had always had of him. Since returning to the papal court, however, Rodrigo had found himself eclipsed, first by Pietro Riario and then, after Pietro's death, by his cousin Giuliano della Rovere. Though the pope's nephews were by no means a united force—Giuliano allied himself with the Colonna, for example, while the Riario brothers encouraged Sixtus to make war on them—the conflicts among them served only to increase their visibility and deepen the shadows to which Rodrigo found himself relegated. The death of Pietro improved his situation somewhat, making it impossible for a bereft pope not to increase his reliance on a veteran vice-chancellor whose judgment he respected. Rodrigo remained a power in the great bureaucracy that was the Curia as well as in consistory, but a power of not quite the first rank. The seat at the pope's right hand went not to him, not even to Sixtus's strong-willed and gifted nephew Giuliano, but to the worst choice available, the late Pietro's conspicuously untalented brother Girolamo, now lord of Imola.

Trouble did not follow quickly from the pope's decision, however. Instead there ensued an Indian summer of quiet and stability for Rome and for Italy, the last tranquil interlude of Cardinal Borgia's life. The wars with the Turks raged on, but so far out on the fringes of Europe that the monarchs of the West usually found it possible to ignore them. In Moldavia, at the eastern end of faraway Romania and therefore seemingly in another world, the amazing Stephen III was annually beating back invasions by Mehmed II. In 1476 his neighbor Vlad III Dracula met his death in a last courageous stand in Wallachia, but his passing attracted little notice in Italy. The Italians paid somewhat more attention when the Turks captured the Black Sea port of Caffa, a crucial link in the chain of commercial colonies that Genoa had painstakingly put together in the East over the centuries. But nothing came of Sixtus's call for a counteroffensive, and the Turks met little opposition as they fanned out from Caffa to take control of the whole Crimean coast.

In the spring following the fall of Caffa a flood of unprecedented magnitude buried much of Rome under a blanket of stinking mud and brought on an outbreak of plague that by summer had decimated the population and sent the pope and his court fleeing to Viterbo. Months later Milan was shaken when the cruelties of the psychopathic sadist Duke Galeazzo Maria Sforza caused him to be assassinated by desperate subjects who were destroyed in their turn. Galeazzo Maria's heir was a seven-year-old child, his son Gian Galeazzo, and though the boy's mother Bona of Savoy attempted to take charge, she was pushed aside by her brother-in-law, the murdered duke's brother Ludovico. Proclaiming himself regent, Ludovico restored order so quickly that none of Milan's neighbors had time to exploit the situation.

Sixtus brought Rodrigo out of the background when King Ferrante of Naples announced that he was marrying his first cousin, a daughter of his uncle King Juan of Aragon. Ferrante, one of the most vicious rulers of his violent times, now a fifty-four-year-old widower with three grown sons, was perhaps not the bridegroom of a twenty-two-year-old princess's dreams. But he and his relatives in Spain required careful handling, and the obvious choice to take charge of the marital formalities was the cardinal who already had the friendship of Aragon. In August 1477 Rodrigo traveled to Naples, bearing with him the powers of a plenipotentiary envoy. There he crowned Ferrante's bride, conferred a papal blessing on the marriage, and, as in Spain earlier, attended to various matters of Church business.

Sixtus and Girolamo Riario meanwhile nursed their ambitions for the Romagna, probing for signs of weakness in the neighboring states. In so doing they inflamed the suspicions of the Florentines, fearful as always of allowing the Romagna to fall into unfriendly hands. In 1477 Girolamo was allowed to consummate his marriage to the now fourteen-year-old, and strikingly beautiful, Caterina Sforza. After triumphantly parading her through the streets of Imola, he took her to Rome, so as to have ready access to the pope's ear. He made no secret of wanting to rule more than Imola, and Sixtus encouraged his ambitions. Florence for its part made clear that it would not stand by idly if the two of them tried to expand their Romagna holdings beyond Imola. There was fear on both sides, and fear led as usual to bad decisions.

When Lorenzo de' Medici worked out a defensive alliance with Milan and Venice, the two great powers to his north, Pope Sixtus denounced it as an act of aggression. But in the mind of Girolamo Riario, a mind incapable of subtleties yoked to a spirit incapable of restraint, this was a problem with a simple solution. Florence needed a new regime, one more understanding of the pope's rights and needs. The Medici, specifically the meddlesome Lorenzo and his brother Giuliano, had to be replaced. Then everything would be fine. And so was hatched the Pazzi Conspiracy, in which Girolamo plotted with the banker Jacopo de' Pazzi, the archbishop of Pisa, and others to murder the Medici brothers while they were hearing mass in Florence's great Duomo.

Here again fear was the driving force: Lorenzo's refusal to tolerate challenges to his authority, coupled with his resentment of the loss of the Vatican's banking business, had caused the Pazzi to suspect that he was planning their destruction and to conclude that their only hope of survival was to destroy the Medici first. The archbishop too was spurred by fear mixed with thwarted ambition. For three years Lorenzo, seeing him as an agent of the pope, had been refusing to allow him to enter Pisa and take up his duties there. The archbishop was certain that if he tried, he would pay with his life.

Rodrigo knew nothing of the plot. Girolamo, aware that the vice-chancellor had no respect for him and had long been on friendly terms with Lorenzo, made certain that he knew nothing. Sixtus on the other hand was informed, in delicate terms and strict confidence, that certain steps were being taken to clear the Medici out of Florence; not even his favorite nephew would have dared to keep such a momentous undertaking from him. But when told that it might become necessary to kill Lorenzo and his brother (Girolamo pretended that none of the plotters *wanted* that to happen), Sixtus forbade the shedding of blood. That his problems with the Medici had engendered in him an icy hatred for the entire clan is not to be doubted, and he would have celebrated a change of regimes in Florence. But none of this stopped him from calling Girolamo "fool" when asked if the assassination of Lorenzo would be forgiven, or from repeating what he had said earlier: "I will not have anyone killed."

The plot went forward and became the fiasco of the century. When the assassins attacked, young Giuliano de' Medici was all but cut to bits, but Lorenzo escaped with a knife wound in his neck. Supporters of the murderers ran through the streets of Florence shouting *"libertà! libertà!"* but got nothing like the enthusiastic reception they expected. Within minutes the dead bodies of various members of the Pazzi family, the archbishop of Pisa, and the two priests who had done the stabbing were hanging in the city's central piazza. A general bloodbath would have ensued if Lorenzo had not intervened. Among those saved was the newest of Sixtus's nephew-cardinals, Raffaele Sansoni Riario, whose stop at Florence en route to Rome had been used by the conspirators to lure the Medici to the Duomo. A grandson of one of Sixtus IV's sisters, born into poverty like so many of the pope's relatives and adopting the Riario surname because of its new prestige, this boy, just sixteen, was one of the youngest cardinals in history. He had known nothing of the plot, and stood at the Duomo's altar in a state of stupefaction as the brothers came under attack. Lorenzo took him into protective custody and later provided guards to escort him safely to Rome. It would be said that over the next forty years, which he spent as one of Rome's wealthiest cardinals and greatest patrons of the arts, his face never lost the haunted expression it acquired that Sunday in Florence.

Sixtus's response to the debacle was perhaps the most ignoble episode in what was turning into a deeply disgraceful reign. He denounced the killing not of Giuliano de' Medici but of the archbishop of Pisa, on grounds that even obviously guilty clerics had to be handed over to the Church for judgment. He summoned Lorenzo to Rome, and when his order was not obeyed Lorenzo was excommunicated—a punishment supposed to entail eternal damnation. When Florence's city council refused to hand its leader over, the whole city was put under an interdict, which meant that none of its priests were to make the sacraments available to the citizenry: no weddings or baptisms, no mass or communion, no last rites or burials. When this too had no effect, the Florentines forcing even the most reluctant of their priests to carry on as usual, Sixtus declared that Rome and Florence were at war. He was immediately joined by Naples: Ferrante saw an opportunity to seize some Florentine territory at little cost or risk. He and Sixtus found a third ally in the Tuscan city-state of Siena, which always welcomed a chance to weaken its bigger and much-feared neighbor Florence.

Fear of Sixtus's ambitions brought Venice and Milan in on Florence's side. They were followed by Ferrara, Bologna, and Rimini, all of them papal fiefs and therefore now in rebellion against their overlord. An indignant Sixtus then persuaded Genoa to rebel against Milan and recruited companies of Swiss mercenaries to attack the Sforzas from the north. Thanks to Girolamo Riario and his reckless scheming, the whole of Italy was at war, almost all the northern powers arrayed against Rome. If Sixtus was distressed to learn that summer that the capital of Albania had fallen to the Turks, and that the Turks had also taken possession of the Friuli region at the northern end of the Adriatic and were beginning to encroach on Austria, he no longer had the means even to try to respond.

In Italy, however, alliances were made to be broken, and to be win-ning today was almost an assurance that one would be losing tomor-row. Milan's new strongman, the regent Ludovico Sforza, decided that it would be to his advantage to break with Venice and Florence and join Naples and Rome. When a hard-pressed Venice reacted to this betrayal by abandoning its sixteen-year war with the Turks, signing a treaty by which it surrendered strategic outposts in the eastern Mediterranean and consented to pay Constantinople a hefty annual tribute, the course of Italian history was changed in ways few could have foreseen. Having accepted a position subordinate to the Turks in parts of the world where it had once been supreme, Venice began looking to the Italian main-land as its best—its last—opportunity for an expanding sphere of influ-ence. It became a more volatile, more aggressive element in the age-old contest for primacy among Italy's leading states, because it no longer saw any reason to accept the status quo put in place by the Italian League a generation before. It saw its only choices as expansion or stag-nation, and few ways of expanding except at the expense of its Italian neighbors, the neighbors that were currently its allies included.

Sixtus's war dragged drearily, pointlessly on. He was urged to end it by the College of Cardinals, the Holy Roman emperor, and the kings of France and Hungary, but paid them no heed. He was encouraged to fight on only by his nephew Girolamo and by Ferrante of Naples, both of whom had narrow and purely selfish motives. Lorenzo de' Medici meanwhile was himself under heavy pressure, his support among the people of Florence eroding as the war brought increasing hardship. His position became even more difficult in November 1479, when after a siege of more than half a year the Neapolitans captured the town of Colle di Val d'Elsa just thirty miles from Florence. This cut the Floren-tines off from one of their primary sources of food and put them in danger of famine.

Lorenzo bet everything on a final throw of the dice. He raised sixty thousand florins by mortgaging much of what he owned, boarded a galley at Livorno, and proceeded to Naples. There he delivered himself into the hands of his enemy Ferrante—an act as brave as it was desper-ate. In departing Florence, Lorenzo accepted the very real possibility that the city's exhausted and demoralized citizens might abandon him for the sake of peace. And in going to Naples he was putting himself at the mercy of a truly sinister man. On an earlier and somewhat similar occasion, when visited by a mercenary commander who had long been his partner in crime, Ferrante had entertained his guest lavishly for weeks before abruptly having him strangled. The murder was entirely characteristic of the Neapolitan king.

Lorenzo was no fool, however, and though his courage in going to Naples cannot be disputed, the venture was not a blind leap. He had friends at the Neapolitan court and in fact had been encouraged by Ferrante's son Alfonso to undertake his daring journey. Also, he was a head of state in effect if not quite officially, not some troublemaking soldier of fortune, and so was unlikely to be put to death. Ferrante was, as it turned out, fascinated by his charismatic young visitor. The two talked frequently and at length, and Lorenzo used his borrowed florins to put on flamboyant displays of princely generosity, winning the applause of the Neapolitan public by buying the freedom of a hundred galley slaves and giving each of them ten florins and a new suit of clothes. He appeared to be bringing Ferrante around to the idea that Florence, as a friend of France and Venice, would be a more valuable ally than the pope, but whenever he proposed an alliance, the king became evasive. It was only by pretending to give up and actually setting off for home that Lorenzo was able to extract a treaty from Ferrante at last. When this became known in Florence, Lorenzo was once again a hero.

But Sixtus remained immovable, and his shabby little war dragged on. Nothing was accomplished by either side, though in the summer of 1480 Girolamo Riario was able to use his uncle's army to pry the town of Forlì out of the hands of the squabbling heirs of its last Ordelaffi lord. With this one stroke—barely related to the wider war—he doubled his holdings in the Romagna. That wider war might have gone on indefinitely if reality had not suddenly intruded. It arrived with the news that a seaborne Turkish army, wandering the Mediterranean after unsuccessfully attacking the island of Rhodes, had come ashore on Naples's east coast and captured the city of Otranto. Almost half of Otranto's twenty-two thousand inhabitants had been massacred, many of them after being raped or tortured, and the survivors had been taken away as slaves. Both Otranto's governor and its aged archbishop had been sawed in half alive.

The Turks were in Italy. This shocking development changed everything, and immediately. Ferrante begged the pope for assistance, warning that if it was not forthcoming he was prepared to come to terms with the invaders. Sixtus responded with a shipment of gold, a special tithe on the churches of Naples and the Papal States, and an assessment of one ducat on every household in the territories he controlled. He also extracted pledges totaling 150,000 ducats from the cardinals. The money thus raised financed the recruitment of troops and a new crash program of galley construction, and even the princes of northern Europe promised to send help. Preparations got under way for moving the papal court to France if the Turks advanced on Rome.

Having been brought to his senses, Sixtus removed the interdict from Florence and restored Lorenzo to good standing in the Church. The Turks at Otranto were being brought under siege when, at the start of the summer of 1481, another bolt of stunning news arrived. Mehmed II was dead. The sultan had been only forty-nine years old and brimmed with vitality almost to the end, making this one of the rare instances when rumors of poisoning may have been justified. One suspect, an Italian-born convert to Islam who served as the sultan's physician, was put to death. An equally plausible possibility, Mehmed's son Bayezid, was too powerful to be accused. Whatever its cause, the death was celebrated with the ringing of church bells in Naples and Rome. And it really did change things drastically. The Ottoman Empire found itself caught in a contest between two claimants to the throne, Bayezid and his brother Cem, and when the former quickly prevailed, he showed himself to be both less belligerent than his father and less interested in Italy. The vast territories he already controlled were presenting him with an abundance of headaches, a war with Persia among them, and so he both revised the treaty that his father had imposed upon Venice, making its terms less onerous and the Venetians grateful, and pulled his troops out of Otranto. The withdrawal was hailed as a great victory for the Christians but should be seen as a shift in strategy on the part of the Turks.

Be that as it may, this was without question a moment of weakness and indecision for the Ottoman Empire. A Christian counteroffensive might have achieved great things—might have retaken Albania and Greece, even conceivably Constantinople. But when Sixtus proposed an advance on Albania, no one else was interested. He therefore turned his attention back to Italy and to matters in which he might better have never become involved. Mere months after the death of Mehmed, the Italians were once again at war with one another. And for no better reason than Girolamo's hunger to become lord of the whole of the Romagna, and the pope's desire for revenge.

The great obstacle to the pope's freedom of action in the Romagna and on the Adriatic coast was Venice. It needed to be neutralized if the Romagna was ever to be subdued, but it was far too mighty for this to be accomplished by force. Diplomacy was required—bribery, really—and so Sixtus offered the Venetians a stupendous prize. He said they could have the duchy of Ferrara, which lay just to the southwest of Venice and for centuries had been a papal fief ruled by the House of Este, one of the oldest and proudest families in Europe. The price, of course, was that Venice must become Rome's friend and ally once again. To do so it would have to take on the dirty job of defeating Ferrara's duke, a tough and experienced soldier who had long been making himself a nuisance by supporting Lorenzo de' Medici and refusing to pay the annual tribute that he owed, as a vassal, to Rome. He was certain to put up a hard fight, but if the Venetians were not exactly delighted by the prospect of taking him on, they certainly were willing. This was an opportunity to vastly expand, at a single stroke, their holdings on the mainland. And the expansion would come with a papal blessing, which would cloak it in legitimacy. Venice accepted the pope's offer, its rivals were outraged when they learned of the deal, and Italy again went up in flames. Again the cause lay entirely in Rome.

In the protracted and terrible conflict that would be called the War of Ferrara, Rome and Venice were opposed not only by Ferrara itself but by Naples, Milan, Florence, and smaller city-states including Bologna, Mantua, Roberto Malatesta's Rimini, and Federico da Montefeltro's Urbino. All were convinced that their safety required them to resist what they saw as the pope's unprovoked betrayal of one of his own vassals. The complications that ensued were often bizarre and included even more than the usual number of inexplicable surprises. With the violence at its height Roberto Malatesta and Pope Sixtus were somehow reconciled. Malatesta was given command of Venice's army, inflicted a ruinous defeat on a Neapolitan force that had invaded the

Papal States, and was received in Rome as a hero just days before dying there of malaria. His father-in-law Montefeltro died on the same day, so that two of Italy's best generals simultaneously disappeared from the scene. Most bizarrely of all, Sixtus then broke with Venice and teamed up with Ferrante, probably because he felt endangered by the latter's repeated attacks on the Papal States.

It is a measure of the irresponsibility of nearly all the participants in this lunatic conflict that Ferrante hired fifteen hundred *Turkish* cavalry to fight his fellow Italians on Italian soil. Most irresponsible of all, and also incompetent, was Girolamo Riario. At one crucial point, with enemy troops threatening, he used the main altar of a Roman church as a dicing table on which to gamble away his army's payroll. Eventually, having proved even to himself that he was incapable of accomplishing anything on conventional fields of battle, he launched a gratuitously savage campaign aimed at the destruction of the Colonna and their allies. As this was largely a matter of forcing the Colonna out of their strongholds inside Rome, the streets of the papal capital were engulfed in the general mayhem.

By the summer of 1484 almost everyone understood that what was happening was madness. The exceptions, inevitably, were Sixtus and Girolamo, whose obsession now was to subdue and humiliate Venice. They could not be persuaded to negotiate, and so their weary allies entered into talks with Venice without consulting them. The result, the Peace of Bagnolo, ended the conflict on terms so unfavorable to Rome that the Venetians celebrated it as a victory. Sixtus when he learned of it was horrified—convinced somehow that the defeat of Venice had been near. In fact the settlement was deficient in serious ways, failing to reflect the realities of how power was distributed among the Italian states at the time. It planted seeds that would produce further disorder in years to come. If that outcome was a vindication of Sixtus's disgust, he did not live to see it. Less than a week after the signing of the peace he was dead of fever—or, as was widely said, of rage at the smashing of his dreams. His great error—one is tempted to say his besetting sin—had been to attach those dreams to his nephew Girolamo, a man whose every act had shown him to be unworthy of trust.

Rome exploded in an orgy of fresh violence upon learning of the pontiff's passing. Mobs plundered the palaces of the Riarii, the Colonna came flooding back intent on vengeance, and Girolamo, in company with his Orsini allies, marched toward the city hoping to take control before anyone else could. As he approached, his young wife Caterina Sforza assumed command of the Castel Sant'Angelo in her husband's name. The cardinals, meanwhile, were preparing for the burial of Sixtus and the opening of a conclave. When they issued orders for the Colonna to leave Rome and for Girolamo and the Orsini to stay out, civil war seemed imminent. The situation was defused by Marco Barbo, an able and serious-minded young cardinal who owed his red hat to his uncle Paul II. He persuaded the Orsini, the Colonna, and Girolamo to obey the Sacred College's instructions, averting a bloody showdown.

Caterina Sforza Riario, disgusted to learn that her husband had turned back rather than bringing reinforcements, surrendered the Castel to the College of Cardinals in return for a payment of four thousand ducats. She then returned with Girolamo to Forlì, unofficial capital of their mini-empire in the Romagna. The Orsini and Colonna withdrew to their lairs in the hill country outside Rome. The city became subdued enough for the election to proceed.

This was Rodrigo's fourth conclave. He was in his fifties now, old enough to be taken seriously as a candidate, and though his foreign birth remained a disadvantage, it was increasingly counterbalanced by the accomplishments of his undeniably distinguished career. His credentials could not have been better—he was now both dean of the Sacred College and prior of the cardinal-bishops—and in 1484's first round of balloting he received several votes. Giuliano della Rovere also showed strength in spite of being barely in his forties and having little experience as an administrator or a diplomat; the presence in the college of three cousins gave him a rock-solid base of support. The leader by an impressive margin, however, proved to be Marco Barbo. His strong showing reflected both the respect of his colleagues and their gratitude for his success in preventing a disaster just days before. But the Venetian origins that had helped to elect his uncle Paul II were now a major handicap. Fear of Venice's new hunger for territory, along with resentment of the city's separate peace with the Turks and the benefits that had come to it through the Peace of Bagnolo, ran high enough among the electors to stop him from increasing his vote.

That evening Rodrigo Borgia and Giuliano della Rovere, both of them controlling enough votes to act as power brokers, met to consider their options. They had no interest in helping each other to the throne, which put Rodrigo out of the running. Della Rovere for his part had no chance because he was Sixtus's nephew, too young, and a disagreeable character to boot. After some discussion the pair of them agreed to join in supporting an unobjectionable nonentity named Giovanni Battista Cibo, a tall, handsome, and mildly genial son of Genoa. Cibo's roots contributed importantly to his appeal: Genoa had grown prosperous through seafaring, though never as rich or powerful as Venice, and the long rivalry between the two states had cost the Genoese much and taught them to regard the Venetians as a malignant force. Many cardinals were willing, in 1484, to embrace almost any enemy of Venice as their friend. Cibo was elected without difficulty the next morning and took the throne as Pope Innocent VIII—a name that can sound absurd to modern ears. Those who had hoped for a different result voiced the customary complaints about corruption—Rodrigo was just one of several cardinals accused of having sold their votes—but credible evidence is entirely lacking.

The selection of Cibo turned out to be better for della Rovere than for Rodrigo. The new pope was by no means unfriendly to the vice-chancellor, in the postelection dispersal of benefices appointing him administrator and therefore beneficiary of a major Valencian monastery. Other signs of favor followed: in an early bull Innocent described Rodrigo as "constantly at work and afraid of no kind of labor," praised him for his prudence, acuteness, mature counsel, and loyalty, and stated that he "fills first place in the order of our venerable brethren of the Sacred College." It was obvious nonetheless that in the most important matters Innocent was della Rovere's man. This should have surprised no one, it having been della Rovere who persuaded his uncle to make the compliant Cibo a cardinal back in 1473. For Italy the result was going to be further tragedy, and as before it would be brought about by greed, vindictiveness, and rank stupidity.

The tragedy opened this time in an essentially trivial way, with a visit to Rome by Ferrante's son and heir, Alfonso duke of Calabria. Though approaching forty, an able enough soldier when not in the grip of his occasional fits of panic, Alfonso proved to be an absurdly ham-handed envoy. He so offended the papal court with his boorishness and arrogance that he returned home having accomplished nothing except the alienation of Innocent and Giuliano della Rovere alike. Thus, when Alfonso later persuaded his father to launch an attack on the chronically troublesome barons of Naples, Cardinal della Rovere demanded that the pope weigh in on the side of the barons. Though Rodrigo counseled patience, Innocent followed della Rovere's instructions. Reasons of self-protection once again impelled other powers to let themselves be drawn in, and another bloody mess ensued. Things did not go well for Rome, Innocent quickly lost his enthusiasm for military adventures, and the result was a settlement in which Ferrante received bits and pieces of the southernmost Papal States and in return promised amnesty for his rebellious nobles. Nothing could be more characteristic of Ferrante and his son than the nonchalance with which they violated this promise at the first opportunity, butchering as many of the barons as they could get their hands on and seizing their lands and castles.

The effects of this short war were far-reaching and significant. Cardinal della Rovere, because he had drawn Innocent into an unnecessary conflict that cost much and ended in humiliation for Rome, lost his influence at the papal court. The resentment that he had long directed at Rodrigo Borgia, perhaps because he had been kept on as Sixtus's vice-chancellor in spite of not being a member of the family, turned into a hard and enduring hatred. The surviving barons of Naples, who with good reason had always feared and distrusted Ferrante, began to look far to the north for deliverance. They sent envoys first to Milan, then to Hungary, and finally and most fatefully, as time would show, to France. They told all who would listen that Ferrante had no right to the Neapolitan throne and should be unseated. All these developments would bear toxic fruit.

The rest of Innocent's reign was a sordid affair. He had two grown children (not sixteen as has often been said), both of them illegitimate but born in his youth before he took holy orders, so that their existence was not really a scandal. He did create scandal, however, by putting the Vatican and its treasury at the service of his offspring. The papal palace became the scene of lavish festivities when the pope's granddaughter was married to a grandson of Ferrante, and his son Franceschetto to Lorenzo de' Medici's daughter. This Franceschetto was a singularly worthless character, dissolute, spineless, and evidently somewhat dim.

Once, after losing fourteen thousand ducats gambling with Cardinal Raffaele Riario, he went crying to his father that he had been cheated. It was partly to finance the profligacy of his dependents that Innocent dragged the papacy to new depths of financial corruption, putting more and more offices up for auction—new positions were created solely for the purpose of being sold—and creating a special bank for the sale of pardons. Rulers from Naples to France took advantage of his weakness to encroach on the Church's property and prerogatives.

It was in the year of Franceschetto's marriage that Girolamo Riario came to his fittingly violent end. He and his wife Caterina, after retiring to the Romagna, had imposed on their two little city-states of Imola and Forlì painfully high taxes and the kind of savagely arbitrary rule that was typical of the region. One April evening, while idling with cronies in his newly built Forlì palace, Girolamo was set upon by a gang of assassins led by the captain of his personal guard, Cecco Orsi. While her husband was dying under a flurry of knife blows, his body stripped naked and thrown out a window onto the piazza below, Caterina was warned of the danger. She barricaded herself and her children—in a decade of marriage she had borne six sons and a daughter—in her bedchamber. She was eventually made a prisoner but persuaded Orsi and his brothers and their fellow conspirators that if they allowed her to enter Forlì's *rocca* or fortress, which had refused to surrender to her husband's killers, she could get its commandant to open the gates. Once inside, however, she mounted the battlements and hurled down curses on the Orsi and their comrades. One of the most colorful stories of the Italian Renaissance—not certainly true, but endlessly repeated because so typical of the beautiful and ferocious Caterina—tells of how, when her enemies threatened to kill her children, she retorted that she could make more children and lifted her skirts to display the equipment that gave her the ability to do so.

She was soon rescued by troops dispatched from Milan, where her cousin was duke and her uncle Ludovico was regent, and from Bologna, whose ruling Bentivoglio clan welcomed the opportunity to make clear that in the Romagna there could be no tolerance of rebellion. Caterina, coming into her own now, took personal charge of punishing the conspirators. Those who could be caught were publicly tortured before being executed, their houses leveled, and their wives and children crowded into dungeons. The assassin Cecco Orsi's aged father, who had no involvement in the plot and when he learned of it cursed his sons for failing to kill Caterina and her entire brood when they had the chance, was forced to witness the demolition of his palace before being handed over to the butchers.

Caterina, claiming to act in the name of her eldest son, took up the reins of power in Forlì and Imola and the miles of rich farmland that came with them. She became Italy's only female ruler, so strong of will and so cold-bloodedly ruthless that before long she became legendary as a true *virago*—a woman with all the characteristics of the most formidable males. She did not mourn her husband, who in addition to being a sadist had been fat and lazy and as cowardly as he was stupid. The character of their marriage is suggested, chillingly, in something that Caterina wrote before his murder: "You cannot imagine the life I lead with my husband. It has often caused me to envy those who die." Now she was free and answerable to no one. If it is true as has been alleged that Lorenzo de' Medici was involved in the plot to kill Girolamo— by 1488 the last participant in the Pazzi Conspiracy still living—or if Pope Innocent encouraged the Orsi as has also been suggested, Caterina appears neither to have cared nor to have shown any resentment. The purging of all opposition in Forlì was sufficient to her needs, personally as well as politically.

As Innocent's reign limped to its sorry conclusion, he chose Tomás de Torquemada, nephew of the famed cardinal-theologian encountered earlier, to be inquisitor general in Spain. At about the same time he granted indulgences to all who would contribute to a war of extermination on a puritanical sect known as the Waldensians in central Europe. He went through the motions of urging the powers of Europe to mount a campaign against the Turks but was not heartbroken when the conflicts of the Hapsburgs of Germany with Hungary and France made any such venture impossible. The extent of his commitment to resisting the Turkish threat can be inferred from his willingness, in 1489, to accept Sultan Bayezid II's offer of 120,000 crowns plus an annual stipend of 45,000 ducats to keep his brother Cem in the custody of the Vatican. In effect he was agreeing to run a kind of prison-hotel for displaced Ottoman princes.

Almost the only responsible ruler in all Italy was Lorenzo de' Medici, whose exertions to maintain a stable balance of power had defused one explosive situation after another. By age forty he had been the chief executive in Florence through two difficult decades. He was worn out, had many interests unrelated to governing and a son whom he believed to be capable of taking over for him, and was talking of withdrawing from public life. He was also in financial difficulty, having been not nearly as skillful at the family business of banking as he was in other fields. In late 1491 his health was declining alarmingly, rheumatic fever having aggravated the effects of a disabling affliction that his physicians put under their catchall diagnosis of gout. One doctor prescribed pulverized pearls and precious gems, which must have been approximately as helpful as doses of ground glass. When he died in April 1492, aged only forty-three, his passing sparked intense grief in Florence. Elsewhere the news aroused mixed feelings, but the whole of Italy would have gone into mourning could it have foreseen how badly this greatest of the Medici would be missed in the terrible times that now lay just ahead.

When Innocent followed Lorenzo to the grave three and a half months later, few except his relatives could see any reason to be sorry.

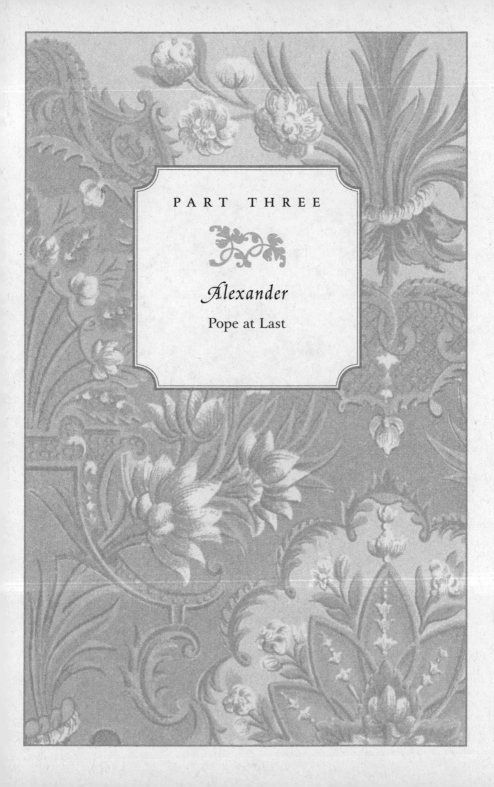

PART THREE

Alexander

Pope at Last

11

The Best Man for the Job

I am Pope! I am Pope!

This is what Rodrigo Borgia is reported to have cried out in jubilation, almost in ecstasy, upon being chosen by his fellow cardinals to succeed Innocent VIII in August 1492. An alternative and more imperious version, translated from the Florentine Italian of five centuries ago, is:

I! I am Pope!

These words have invariably been interpreted as a spontaneous eruption of dark things that supposedly lay concealed under Cardinal Rodrigo's cheerful exterior: pride, arrogance, joy in mastering people and things and bending them to sinister purposes.

But of course his outburst—assuming that it happened—can just as plausibly be seen in an entirely different light. As an expression of surprise—which Rodrigo's election almost certainly was, to himself no less than to others. As an effusion of simple, almost childish joy from a man who had served five successive popes, had been witness to their innumerable failures and misdeeds, their few and dubious triumphs and sometimes gruesome tragedies, and was justified in thinking himself capable of doing better.

To which it is necessary to add that it is not certain—that it is on balance less than probable—that Rodrigo ever said any such thing. The first report of it appeared nine years after his election, in an anonymous pamphlet written for the purpose of showing him to be what its author explicitly called him: "the monster," "this cursed beast" in the course of whose papacy "the bestiality and savagery of Nero and Caligula are surpassed." Suffice it to note, for present purposes, that such a depiction of Rodrigo's performance as pope is dubious at best.

This is the Borgia problem in a nutshell: wildly outlandish accusations accepted as true generation after generation because when taken together they add up to one of the most gloriously lurid stories in all of history. Anecdotes about murder and incest that are especially delicious because their subject is a pope, and that have become so firmly embedded in the consciousness of the whole world that to question them can seem fatuous, to challenge them preposterous.

If the problem begins with a notorious garden party in Siena during the reign of Pius II, it bursts into full bloom with the conclave that raised Rodrigo to the throne as Pope Alexander VI. It is vividly apparent, for example, in the work of the first noteworthy historian of medieval and Renaissance Italy, Francesco Guicciardini. He wrote—and influenced countless later historians by writing—that Cardinal Borgia's election is a tale of how "with money, offices, benefices, promises, and all his powers and resources he suborned and bought the votes of the cardinals and the College." And that the 1492 conclave was "a hideous and abominable thing, and a most apt beginning to [the new pope's] future deplorable proceedings and behavior."

As with so much Borgia history, Guicciardini's allegations require closer examination than they have usually received. At the time of which he is writing, Guicciardini was a nine-year-old schoolboy in Florence. He never met a Borgia, is not known to have set foot in Rome when the Borgias were in power there, and in the course of growing to manhood absorbed his home city's deep-rooted hostility toward Roman and papal power in general and the Borgias specifically. He could be ridiculously credulous, reporting for example that one night early in Alexander's reign three suns appeared overhead and that "huge numbers of armed soldiers riding enormous steeds were seen for many days passing across the sky with a terrible clash of trumpets and drums." He laced his *History of Italy* (written some forty years after Rodrigo became Alexander) with the choicest products of the anti-Borgia pamphleteers who flourished in the opening decades of the sixteenth century. Though a pioneer in the use of documentary evidence, he had no credible documents to work with in writing of the 1492 conclave and little more than gossip to draw upon in dealing with the lives of the Borgias.

That Rodrigo nursed little hope of being elected is suggested by the fact that, during the five months or more during which Innocent VIII was declining toward death, he made no effort to increase the number of votes available to him. He could have asked the two cardinals then resident in Spain, his cousin Luis Juan del Milà (who had been appointed to the College of Cardinals with him back in 1456) and Pedro González de Mendoza (who owed his red hat to Rodrigo's mission to Castile in the early seventies), to travel to Rome in time for the increasingly inevitable election. They would have represented nearly ten percent of the electors present at the conclave, providing a counterweight to the various nephews of Sixtus IV on hand to vote for their cousin Giuliano della Rovere.

If Rodrigo did in fact give himself little chance of being elected, this was in part because, of the twenty-three cardinals able to attend the conclave, only he and Jorge da Costa of Portugal were not Italian. Among the Italians, in addition to the della Rovere-Riario circle, were a Medici, a Sforza, representatives of the Orsini, Colonna, and Savelli families, Paul II's three nephews, nephews of Pius II and Innocent VIII, and several cardinals who, if not so bountifully endowed with family connections, were esteemed for their personal qualities. In terms of talent as well as clout, it was a formidable assortment of plausible candidates, almost all of them preferring to keep the papacy in Italian hands.

In the summer of 1492 the usual intricacies of papal politics were complicated by growing antagonism between Naples and Milan, which threatened the stability of all Italy. The trouble originated this time not with a pope's ambitions but with those of Ferrante of Naples, just a year short of his seventieth birthday, in his thirty-fourth year as king, but still probing restlessly for opportunities to extend his reach. Ferrante, whose political tool kit included everything from torture and cold-blooded murder to the subtlest diplomatic intrigues, had over the preceding three decades used arranged marriages to link his family to the Sforzas of Milan. In 1465 he had married his son and heir, Alfonso duke of Calabria, to Duke Francesco Sforza's daughter. A generation later a daughter of this marriage, Isabella of Aragon, was wed to her nineteen-year-old first cousin Gian Galeazzo Sforza, who had inherited the ducal title at age seven following the assassination of his father. Aware that Gian Galeazzo was physically delicate and weak of will, Ferrante hoped to dominate Milan through Isabella. All such plans crumbled into dust, however, when Gian Galeazzo came of age and the self-appointed regent, his uncle Ludovico Sforza, refused to step aside.

If as tough an old cynic as Ferrante is not likely to have been much moved by the tearful complaints of the Duchess Isabella—who in addition to being a stronger personality than her husband was a great beauty, believed by some historians to be Leonardo da Vinci's Mona Lisa—he did care greatly about the thwarting of his own schemes. His reaction had come at the start of 1492, when he radically changed course, calling a halt to his aggressions in the Papal States and resuming the annual payments that he owed to Rome as the pope's vassal, thereby making peace with Innocent VIII and positioning Naples in opposition to Milan. Thus did Italy's balance of power begin to totter. Because Rome was suddenly no longer at odds with Naples, the Venetians with their fear of Ferrante ceased to regard the pope as a dependable ally. Florence, which had long managed to keep both Milan and Naples as allies, found it difficult to do so now that the two were on such unfriendly terms.

Lorenzo de' Medici's death in April removed the one man who might have saved the situation. It left the leadership of Florence in the hands of his twenty-year-old son Piero. Lorenzo had been the same age when he succeeded his own father, and he had said with fatherly pride that Piero promised to be the greatest of the Medici. About that he was lamentably wrong. Florence's new first citizen would come to be known as Piero the Unfortunate, an inappropriate label insofar as the worst of his misfortunes would be of his own making. His first great mistake was to turn his back on the Sforzas and ally Florence with Naples exclusively. The result, as predictable as it was laden with ill fortune for all of Italy, was a badly frightened Ludovico Sforza. Feeling himself isolated, with a hostile Venice to his east and Florence, Rome, and Naples all seemingly arrayed against him to the south, he could think of only one place to look for help. To the north. To France.

This was how things stood in July, when Innocent VIII expired, and in August, when twenty-three cardinals gathered in the Sistine Chapel (still a good many years from being handed over to Michelangelo for decoration) to elect a new pope. What became most obvious at the start was the bitter opposition of two irreconcilable factions. One, essentially Milanese, was led by Cardinal Ascanio Sforza, who in addition to being an able politician in his own right was a brother of the usurper Ludovico Sforza and therefore had all the resources of Milan at his disposal. Ascanio put himself forward as a candidate, and among his early supporters were Rodrigo Borgia and the cardinals then representing the Orsini and Conti clans. The group opposing him was led by the most relentlessly ambitious ecclesiastical politician then living, Cardinal Giuliano della Rovere, who entered the conclave as the representative of a formidable assortment of interests. Among his supporters were Ferrante, whose aim was to achieve whatever result would be most damaging to Milan; young King Charles VIII of France, who had ambitions of his own where Italy was concerned and was reported to have made two hundred thousand ducats available for della Rovere's use; and the city-state of Genoa, which contributed an additional hundred thousand out of fear of its neighbor Milan. Venice too leaned toward della Rovere for the simple reason that Milan opposed him, and the Colonna and Savelli cardinals were on his side because their rivals the Orsini and Conti supported Milan. In the Sistine Chapel as elsewhere, the enemy of your enemy was your friend.

In the first balloting no favorite emerged. Ascanio Sforza showed no strength at all, a reflection of his age, thirty-seven, and the unwillingness of his colleagues to put the papacy in the hands of a brother of the tyrant of Milan. Through subsequent ballots the feared and disliked della Rovere found himself stuck at five votes—just one more than the total delivered by himself and his cousins. As it became clear that another deadlock was taking shape, Rodrigo Borgia emerged as the only cardinal whose tally was rising, though just barely. It increased to seven while he was still giving his own vote to Ascanio, and a day later it was up to eight. The leader with nine was Oliviero Carafa, who was in an awkward position despite his impeccable reputation and his long record of achievement in diplomacy. He was drawing support from friends of Milan and of his native city of Naples as well. It was obvious to all that, if elected, he could find himself impossibly conflicted.

By the fifth day it was clear that no one closely associated with either

Naples or Milan had a chance of being elected. The Sforzas, with Ascanio pulling every possible string, were prepared to go to any lengths to block della Rovere and his party. Della Rovere for his part would accept schism before a Milanese pope. As so often in the past, compromise was unavoidable. Once accepted as necessary, it was achieved quickly and with surprising ease. August 11 brought not only the election but ultimately the unanimous election of Rodrigo Borgia. And with it the start of rumors, immortalized in the reports of various ambassadors back to their home cities, of how the Spaniard had used his supposedly colossal wealth to buy the crown. According to one particularly colorful story, four stout mules had been needed to transfer a fortune in silver—or was it gold?—from Rodrigo's palace to the residence of Ascanio Sforza.

What actually happened was that Ascanio, knowing his own election to be impossible and fearful that a prolongation of the deadlock might end in a shift to della Rovere, decided to instruct the members of his faction to support Rodrigo. Records of the conclave, lost in the Vatican archives for centuries, show that from the first day Ascanio had himself been voting for Rodrigo, as had two cardinals generally acknowledged to be incorruptible, Carafa and Piccolomini. Getting votes from the other camp was less easy, Rodrigo's relationship with the prickly della Rovere being no better than anyone else's. But that too came to pass, della Rovere himself deciding to align himself with the inevitable and undoubtedly not foreseeing just how bitter the loss of this election was going to make him. No tales of simony—of paying for votes—are needed to explain the outcome. Rodrigo's initial support for Ascanio did not change the fact that, having declined to choose sides in the quarrel between France and Milan on one side and Naples and Venice on the other, he had no bonds of obligation to any of the leading powers. Thus if none of these powers could count on him for special favors, neither did any of them have reason to fear him or regard him as the agent of their enemies. At a dangerous time for all Italy, with the Church in urgent need of competent and responsible leadership, Rodrigo's experience was unequaled. He was also respected and liked on all sides. And one searches in vain, even in the writings and recorded comments of his most intransigent political enemies, for contemporary evidence of immoral behavior. By any reasonable measure, taking into account the general state of affairs in Italy in 1492, he was quite simply the best man for the job.

None of which constitutes proof that the best man did not get the job by buying it, of course. But consider: to whatever extent money may have been a factor in the election, the big money was in the hands of della Rovere and, to a lesser but still impressive extent, of Ascanio Sforza. We have already seen that Rodrigo's wealth was probably never nearly as great as is commonly assumed; if the papacy had in fact been for sale in 1492, he would have found it a challenge to outbid the competition. Nor, if he had attempted to buy it, could he ever have bought the votes of those cardinals who were definitely not for sale. The ambassadors who wrote home complaining of simony had personal agendas of their own. Usually they were attempting to excuse their failure to predict the election's outcome. It is said that when Ferrante of Naples learned of the election's result, he burst into tears. It is even suggested that he did so because it grieved him to see the papacy fall into the hands of such a bad man. That so vicious an old reprobate would be capable of deploring any such thing is preposterous. If anything made Ferrante weep, it was not corruption (almost the least of his own crimes) but the emergence of a pontiff who was likely to be impossible to control. While the conclave was still in process, he had described Rodrigo as "this one who has energy, brains, and resources"—and who should, therefore, be stopped from taking the throne. France, Venice, and Florence were all uneasy for exactly the same reason. Ferdinand and Isabella, on the other hand, were delighted at the election of an old friend and another Spanish pope.

Regardless of what or whether he shouted for joy, a man as well prepared and brimming with vitality as Rodrigo Borgia must have been thrilled to be elected. After a daylong coronation ceremony during which the people of Rome rejoiced at the crowning of a popular figure and the heavily robed object of their celebration fainted more than once in the summertime heat, Pope Alexander VI threw himself into his new role with his customary brio. Required as all new popes were to relinquish his benefices, he ended the month of August with a consistory at which the many bishoprics, abbeys, and other properties that he had accumulated over the decades were passed to other hands. Most of the cardinals benefited to a greater or lesser extent, providing inexhaustible ammunition to those writers who, over the centuries, have pointed to this first consistory of his reign as the mechanism through which Alexander redeemed the pledges that had bought him the throne.

But what is proved, really, by the fact that Alexander made Ascanio Sforza his successor as vice-chancellor? That he saw in the young Sforza not only a political ally but someone to whom he was willing to entrust important responsibilities, obviously. But if that is evidence of corruption, so is the time-honored practice of new U.S. presidents giving top posts not only to members of their own party but to individuals who helped them get elected. As for the fact that Alexander also gave Ascanio the sprawling palace that he had cobbled together out of a collection of derelict buildings, we saw earlier that it had from the start been not only Cardinal Rodrigo's residence but a headquarters for the chancery's great bureaucracy. Ascanio had no property of his own suitable for such purposes. That it was and would remain less a personal residence than a place of business is suggested by its subsequent history. It would pass from Ascanio to the next vice-chancellor after him, and beyond that to three more incumbents before finally being taken over by the papal treasury. That it was ultimately torn down and built over, and that no one ever bothered to make a picture of it or describe it in detail, raises doubts about whether it ever merited comparison with the many grand palaces that were being constructed in Rome at this same time and that continue to draw visitors to the city to the present day.

Alexander also attended to the interests of his family, but to an extent far too modest, in the beginning, to cause concern or even attract attention. At the same consistory at which he distributed his benefices, he appointed a single new cardinal, a Lanzol kinsman known in Rome as Giovanni Borgia. This was in no way shocking, not only because nepotism was taken for granted but because in this case the beneficiary was unquestionably well qualified. The new Cardinal Borgia, whom historians call Giovanni Borgia the Elder to distinguish him from a subsequent appointee of Alexander's of the same name, had been brought to the papal court by his uncle Rodrigo many years before and had carved out an impressive career for himself there. He became a protonotary apostolic and then archbishop of Monreale in Sicily under Sixtus IV, served as governor of Rome under Innocent VIII, and had long been one of his uncle's closest associates. Alexander's transfer of his archbishopric of Valencia to a little-known adolescent named Cesare Borgia at this same time was, if less defensible, by no means a scandal. The see of Valencia had been in the Borgia family for more than sixty years at this point. If passing it along to a third generation was an act of nepotistic excess, it was nonetheless trivial when compared with some of the things that had come before, and the fact that Valencia was in Spain meant that it was a matter of little interest to the Italian cardinals. Beyond that, Alexander limited himself to bestowing the captaincy of the papal guard on a great-nephew and namesake from Spain, Rodrigo Lanzol y de Borja, and giving some minor administrative positions in the Papal States to a few other kinsmen so obscure that we don't know how they were related to him.

The initial distribution of offices completed, Alexander turned to the most pressing of the problems left to him by Innocent VIII. The weakness of the late pope, especially in his final half-year when failing health made him more passive than ever, had allowed Rome and the surrounding territories to fall into even worse disorder than they usually did in the absence of firm leadership. The College of Cardinals had attempted to maintain order, sending crossbowmen into the streets, but this had limited effect. The Orsini and Colonna and other baronial clans got up to their usual black mischief, and criminals of all sorts found themselves free to do their worst with little fear of consequences. From the point at which it became known that Innocent was dying, more than two hundred murders were known to have been committed inside the city walls.

Alexander cracked down hard. On September 3 two notorious murderers, the del Rosso brothers, were publicly hanged and their house was pulled down. Those guilty of lesser crimes found themselves locked in the dungeons of the Castel Sant'Angelo. Not many weeks of this were needed to bring the city under control. A new force of watchmen and constables—twenty-one of them just for the Tiber bridges—made certain that it stayed that way.

Alexander was equally quick to address the abuses of a municipal justice system that had become seriously corrupt. He created new judgeships, appointed doctors of law to fill them, and ordered them to give a hearing to all complaints. He saw to it that they and other officials were paid promptly and well enough not to be tempted by petty bribes at least. This was the start of a series of reforms that culminated in a decree prescribing stern penalties for any officer of justice in any of the Papal States who either solicited or accepted a gift from anyone connected with a criminal or civil case. All decisions issued by judges found to have accepted a gift, or even to have agreed to do so, were declared null and void.

All this was remarkably advanced for its time, and Alexander went further still, initiating a practice without precedent in the history of the papacy. He reserved Tuesday as a day on which, every week, he would be personally available to any Roman, male or female, who came to see him with a complaint or petition. Those who came were allowed to speak for as long as they wished on any subject of their choosing. And he reformed the Vatican's financial administration, imposing new checks on spending and significantly reducing the costs of the papal household. Even as intransigent a hater of popes in general and Borgias in particular as Stefano Infessura (in whose diary we find a weird story of a Jewish doctor bleeding three boys to death in a futile effort to save the life of Innocent VIII) conceded that Alexander's reign "began most admirably."

At the start of the conclave that had ended in his election, like all the other cardinals present, Rodrigo had signed a capitulation pledging, if he became pope, to call a general council of the Church. Even if after his election he had remained free to choose, quite possibly Pope Alexander would have followed the example of his predecessors and ignored this promise. Possibly but not certainly—by 1492 most cardinals wanted a council, not as in the past to undercut the authority of the pope, but to develop a program for raising the standards of the clergy generally. Throughout his life Rodrigo Borgia was not only not opposed to reform but a champion of it, as he had shown in his missions to Spain and Naples. The question is academic in any case; Alexander was not long free to choose. In short order problems arose that made the convening of a council first inadvisable and ultimately impossible.

The first of these problems emerged almost simultaneously with Alexander's coronation. Count Franceschetto Cibo, Innocent VIII's feckless son, had decided as his father's death approached that he had no wish to try to hold on to the various properties of which he had been made lord. This was a sensible decision, Cibo being totally unsuited to the cutthroat struggle for advantage that dominated the lives of Italy's petty tyrants. He was not only a worse weakling than his father but a compulsive and unsuccessful gambler, and in chronic need of cash. As Innocent's reign ended, he prudently left Rome for his wife's home in Florence. There, with the connivance of his brother-in-law Piero de' Medici and the pope's old rival Cardinal Giuliano della Rovere, he set out to sell his property.

An eager buyer turned up in the person of Virginio Orsini, lord of Bracciano and at this time his family's most powerful layman; only his cousin Cardinal Giovanni Battista Orsini possessed comparable influence. Virginio, recognizing a rare opportunity, declared himself willing to pay Cibo upward of forty thousand ducats for an assortment of castles and settlements less than a day's ride north of Rome. There were difficulties, however. They began with the fact that the location of Cibo's properties—at Cerveteri, Anguillara, Canale Monterano, and Rota—gave them strategic value in the eternal contest for control of the Papal States. Nobody distrustful of the Orsini, or of their ally and patron Ferrante of Naples, would be happy to see them fall into Virginio's hands. The Sforza would regard such a development as intolerable. Worse, the properties in question were not actually Cibo's to sell; they were fiefs of the pope. Complicating the situation still further, Virginio Orsini was himself simultaneously a papal vassal by virtue of his lordship of Bracciano and a *condottiere* serving as great constable of the kingdom of Naples—as, that is, commander of the armies of that tormenter of popes King Ferrante. At a time of recurrent friction between Naples and Rome, Virginio's position was so ambiguous, his loyalties so mixed, as to be indecipherable. Such were the ambiguities of Italian life as the Renaissance was coming to full flower.

Not surprisingly, in light of how useful Cibo's castles could prove to Ferrante whenever he next set out to make trouble in the Papal States, Alexander thought he saw the king's hand in the proposed sale. He became convinced, very likely with Ascanio Sforza's encouragement, that Ferrante was lending the purchase price to Virginio as the first step in a plan to turn the castles into outposts from which Naples could threaten Rome. About the financing of the transaction, at least, Alexander was wrong. The money was being supplied by Piero de' Medici, whose mother and wife were both Orsini and whose sister was married to Cibo. But even if he had learned of his error, the pope would have had reason to remain troubled. The proposed sale would weaken papal authority in the Campagna district near Rome whether the castles ended up in Virginio's possession or in Ferrante's, and regardless of where the money came from. And an important principle was at stake: if Cibo and Virginio could close the deal without so much as acknowledging a need for papal approval, all the warlords of the Papal States would be encouraged to forget their obligations to Rome.

Nor would Alexander have been comforted had he known how deeply the Medici were involved. Or if he had been able to see that the driving force behind the crisis, its evil genius, was Giuliano della Rovere, whose continually building anger at having lost the papal election had sent him to Florence in search of ways to make trouble. He found his opportunity in Cibo's eagerness to sell, Virginio's hunger to buy, and Piero's willingness to arrange the financing. The situation must have delighted him, especially the prospect of punishing Alexander and Ascanio for denying him the papal crown. The ramifications reached in every direction, and so many powerful men had a stake in the outcome that the potential consequences were beyond reckoning. Even the College of Cardinals broke once again into factions.

It was from such petty beginnings that the undoing of all Italy proceeded. Cibo had already handed over the castles to Virginio by the time Alexander learned of the sale, and when the pope objected, he was ignored. When word reached Milan of what was happening, Ludovico Sforza's fear of being left isolated turned into something approaching panic. It was undoubtedly his brother Ascanio who, making full use of his insider position as vice-chancellor and papal friend, persuaded Alexander to summon a consistory at which he denounced Ferrante and effectively accused della Rovere of treason. Ferrante, himself alarmed now and in the unfamiliar position of being innocent of the charges against him, sent his son Federico to Rome to smooth things over. Duke Federico's instructions were to offer not just an alliance but marriages between two members of the Neapolitan royal family and a couple of the numerous young Borgias who had been crowding into the papal court since Alexander's election. Nothing came of this; a pact with Naples would have wrecked negotiations that Ascanio Sforza already had in process, on the pope's behalf, to reconcile his brother in

Milan and the government of Venice. Federico had to return to his father with nothing to show for two months at the papal court. Della
Rovere, back in Rome but seeing the tide running strongly against him,
withdrew to Ostia and barricaded himself inside a fortress commanding the Vatican's access to the sea. Alexander responded by moving
troops into the nearby coastal city of Civitavecchia, creating a standoff.
When Ascanio's negotiations bore fruit in the form of a new League of
St. Mark, allying Rome not only with Milan and Venice but with the
smaller city-states of Siena, Mantua, and Ferrara, a shocked Ferrante
assured della Rovere that Naples would come to his aid if Alexander
moved against him. General war seemed just one provocation away.

Everyone was afraid and mistrustful, and therefore everyone had
become dangerously unpredictable. The League of St. Mark, created
largely to assuage Ludovico Sforza's sense of isolation, was inherently
unstable. Though its members pledged themselves to remain allies for
twenty-five years, Venice's hunger for Milanese territory made this almost laughably unrealistic. Nevertheless it spooked Ferrante into preparing for a war that he emphatically did not want, the forces arrayed
against him being now so numerous, and simultaneously launched him
on an almost hysterical campaign to break the bond of trust that had
linked Ferdinand of Spain and Rodrigo Borgia for the past twenty years.
In a flurry of letters to his agents in Spain, to officials at the Spanish
court, and to Ferdinand and Isabella themselves, Ferrante warned that
Rome was now ruled by a monster in human form. In one of these missives, signed on June 7, 1493, and addressed to Ferdinand, he complained
that "the Pope leads such a life that he is abhorred by everyone . . . he is
anxious to be engaged in war, for from the beginning of his papacy he
has done nothing else than seeking or causing trouble [and is] constantly at work with fraudulent machinations."

Ferrante's motives were transparently self-serving, his credibility
nil. Ferdinand of Spain was as far from being credulous as it is possible
for a human being to be, and he knew his Neapolitan cousin far too
well not to see through this invective. Thus Ferrante's word had no effect on Ferdinand's opinion of a pope whom he had good reason to regard as a friend. To the extent that those words have provided rich
fertilizer for the black Borgia myth, they should be measured against
the reply of Juan López, bishop of Perugia, when asked by Spain for his

opinion. "Rest assured," López replied, "that the life, the intentions, and the sagacity of the Pontiff are different from what your letter represents them to be. I tell you, sir, that of the other popes whom you mention, not a one had a mind so exalted nor was one so respected as Pope Alexander, for his long experience, his intelligence, and his activity." López was a native of Valencia who had entered the service of Rodrigo Borgia at an early age and served for a time as his private secretary. He knew whereof he wrote, therefore, and would appear to have had no reason to deceive the Spanish court. Even if one assumes that loyalty caused his opinion of Alexander VI to be excessively high, surely this implies nothing discreditable about the object of his admiration. Nor does it seem likely that loyalty to a onetime patron would have induced him to deceive a monarch as powerful as Ferdinand of Spain.

At the same time that Ferrante was attempting to interest Ferdinand in his problems, Ludovico Sforza of Milan was attempting to interest Charles of France in *his*. In this lay the tragedy of Italy—that its arcane quarrels drove its most important rulers to seek outside help at precisely the moment when the two rising powers of the north, France and Spain, were looking for new worlds to conquer. France, having absorbed the great duchies of Brittany and Burgundy and recovered from its long war with England, was as the 1490s began in the hands of an inexperienced king who nursed fantasies of achieving military glory on an intercontinental scale. Ferdinand and Isabella, having completed the unification of Spain by conquering Granada just seven months before Rodrigo Borgia became pope, were brimming with confidence and looking for uses for their growing power. Though they neither respected nor trusted their cousin in Naples—in fact they believed that their own claim to the Neapolitan crown superseded that of the bastard Ferrante—they were also acutely aware of French claims not only to Naples but to Milan as well. There could be no doubt about which side they would favor if Ferrante found himself in conflict with Milan and, through Milan, with France. And so the ludicrous character of Ferrante's complaints about Pope Alexander did not deter Ferdinand from dispatching one of his most distinguished envoys to Rome to intervene on Ferrante's behalf. Diego López de Haro arrived at the pontifical court with a long list of issues that his master wanted resolved. At the top were the League of St. Mark's hostility to Naples and—another matter with which the Spanish monarchs urgently wanted help— Spain's rights in the uncharted lands that Christopher Columbus had reported finding upon returning from his epic voyage of discovery only a few months earlier.

The timing was good, and things came together nicely. When the pope issued a bull legitimating Spanish claims in what Columbus himself believed was easternmost India or perhaps China, López de Haro was freed to be equally cooperative in return. And when Ferrante offered to press Virginio Orsini to compromise on Franceschetto Cibo's disputed castles—he would have been eager to get that quarrel settled even if he had not been prodded by Ferdinand's ambassador—Alexander too was willing to be responsive. It was known that representatives of Charles of France were in Italy on their way to Rome and that their assignment was to request—to demand, really—that Alexander invest their master with the crown of Naples. Ferrante most desperately of all, but also the pope and López de Haro, wanted to get their business settled before the Frenchmen arrived. Alexander knew as well as anyone that the League of St. Mark was worth little more than the parchment it was written on, and he was quicker than most to see the dangers of the Sforzas' growing entanglement with France. As for Virginio, not even the chief of the Orsini could defy a combination that included his liege lord the pope, his employer the king of Naples, and the distant but fearsome king of Spain.

Thus it was all speedily wrapped up: a multifaceted settlement at the core of which was an end to the quarrel over the Cibo castles. Virginio agreed to pay thirty-five thousand ducats for the properties and to pay them not to Franceschetto Cibo, who was left out in the cold, but to Alexander as overlord. To put some political distance between the castles and Naples, they were sold not to Virginio himself but to his son. Virginio acknowledged that the transaction required the pope's approval, thus resolving a crucial question of principle in Rome's favor. The extent of Ferrante's fear of the French, his determination to get everything settled before Charles VIII's representatives could get to Rome, is evident in the fact that he and not the Medici bank ended up advancing the Orsini the purchase price. When Charles's envoy Peron de Basche arrived just a few days later and demanded that the pope acknowledge the French king's right to Naples, Alexander replied that the issue was legal rather than political and would have to be decided by a panel of lawyers. Basche responded angrily, knowing that he was being finessed, warning that the pope's refusal to cooperate could lead to the calling of a general council. He knew, however, that the answer he had been given was as reasonable as it was adroit. Alexander took pains to be clear about one thing: his willingness to submit Charles's claim to the scrutiny of experts would be contingent on France's refraining from the use of force. If France attacked Naples, its claim would be rejected forthwith. In laying down these terms he foreshadowed the policy that would guide him in the months ahead and make it forever impossible to accuse him of being duplicitous in this matter. His deflection of Basche's demands was masterful. Though it baffled and infuriated the ambassador, it kept Alexander free to offer his friendship to Charles and Ferrante alike.

On the diplomatic front, Alexander was racking up one success after another. He had profited handsomely from the transfer of the castles from Franceschetto Cibo to the Orsini, receiving both an infusion of gold ducats and confirmation of the papacy's feudal rights. He had diverted Ferrante from going to war and had settled his own differences with the Orsini. He had even effected a reconciliation with Giuliano della Rovere, who came out from behind his battlements in Ostia and in company with Virginio journeyed to the Vatican to dine with the pope. The stature that these achievements had conferred upon him, and through him on his family, is reflected in the sudden interest of the kings of Naples and Spain alike in linking themselves to the pope through marriage.

There were difficulties all the same, and if these were unintended, they were nonetheless laden with danger. The return of della Rovere to the papal court was taken as a rebuke by Ascanio Sforza, who repaired to his brother's court in Milan. His arrival, which Ludovico may have interpreted as meaning that Ascanio had been banished, angered and frightened the regent anew. Seeing that Naples was now rich in allies, certain that at the first opportunity Ferrante would gleefully drive him out of Milan and make Gian Galeazzo duke in fact as well as in title, Ludovico can hardly be blamed for thinking that his survival depended on recruiting support wherever it might be found.

He must have been comforted, however, by evidence that the rapprochement between Rome and Naples was quickly beginning to fray. When Alexander tried to demonstrate that he would welcome friendship with Milan and France, Ferrante took this as a betrayal. He resumed his old game of hiring *condottieri* to make trouble in the Papal States. Sensitivities grew so keen that it became impossible for Alexander to strike a balance acceptable to both sides. His nomination in September 1493 of twelve new cardinals sparked angry objections among the Sacred College's sitting members. This happened not for the reason usually given—the youth of two of the pope's choices, Alessandro Farnese and the same Cesare Borgia who had earlier been given the see of Valencia—but mainly because of the sheer number of nominees, and to a lesser extent because so many of them were longtime associates of the pope's and disposed to follow his lead.

The college had always been uneasy about increases in its size, nothing being more obvious than that as the number of members grew, each member declined in importance. And now Alexander was adding a full dozen at once, more than half of them Curia officials likely to side with him in almost any crisis, plus two fellow Spaniards and a scattering of northern Europeans unlikely ever to become much involved in Roman or Vatican politics. The number was not unprecedented, but it was certainly unusual, half a century having passed since Eugenius IV's creation of seventeen new cardinals at a single stroke in 1439. Even those cardinals who were not in sympathy with Alexander's policies would have conceded that it made good sense for an ambitious pontiff to start loading the Sacred College with longtime associates, youthful protégés, and distant foreigners. To do otherwise would have been folly; by appointing cardinals likely to be uncooperative, Alexander would have been impeding the pursuit of his own priorities. His choices confirmed—as though confirmation were needed—that he was no fool and that he was in firm charge of Rome and the Church. He was entrenching himself for the battles he knew to lie ahead.

As for Farnese and Cesare Borgia, there was no real problem. Farnese was of distinguished family and well known at court, having been singled out for advancement in the reign of Innocent VIII. He was also virtually a member of the papal household, his famously beautiful sister Giulia being married to Orsino Orsini, the son of Alexander's cousin and domestic manager Adriana del Milà. Cesare Borgia, if not familiar to many of the cardinals, was certainly a familiar type, and no one could have been astonished by the spectacle of a pope raising an unproven kinsman to the highest level of the hierarchy. The question of exactly how this particular young favorite was related to this particular pope will be addressed in due course.

The real problem with the new cardinals rose out of the grievances of the Italian states. Not one of the appointees was from Naples, Alexander perhaps thinking that he was already seen as excessively friendly to Il Regno. Predictably, Ferrante took this as an affront. The sole Milanese nominee was a protégé of Ascanio Sforza, who in fact had proposed him as a candidate, but by this point Alexander's relations with the Sforza brothers had deteriorated to such an extent that no mere red hat could make a significant difference. Ludovico had become convinced that his fate and those of his wife and children depended upon getting himself invested as duke, and that the only man in Europe with both the ability and the willingness to make this happen was Charles VIII of France.

Charles for his part had ample reasons to want to be helpful: dreams of greatness that he thought it his destiny to fulfill. Barely twenty-three years old in the summer of 1493, he had inherited the crown from his father Louis XI while still a child and spent several years under the tutelage of his canny sister Anne de Beaujeu, who ruled as regent until he came of age. He was an odd little figure, comically ill formed, with a large red nose on a head too big for his spindly body and splayed feet that caused him to walk in a crablike shuffle. Not long after he became king, his sister's government had provided men and ships for the quixotic expedition that led to their cousin Henry Tudor's coronation as Henry VII of England. The improbable success of this adventure undoubtedly contributed to Charles's romantic vision of himself as a future conquering hero. He fixated on a part of his supposed inheritance that his father had been too shrewd to take seriously: the idea that with the extinction of the House of Anjou they had become the rightful kings of Naples, and that Alfonso V and his son Ferrante were interlopers with no legitimate claim. Told that as king of Naples he was also king of Jerusalem, Charles clutched that fantasy to his breast as well.

Ludovico's urgent wish to become duke of Milan fit in nicely with Charles's aspirations. As early as 1491 the young king communicated his willingness to support Ludovico in supplanting his nephew as soon as circumstances permitted. Thereby he won Milan's strongman as his ally and willing agent. In the autumn of 1492 Charles summoned representatives of his kingdom's three estates to the city of Tours to hear his announcement of a crusade against the Turks and his intention to take possession of Naples along the way. When the more experienced of his counselors threw up their hands at the impracticality of all this— among other problems it was impossibly beyond the French crown's financial resources—Charles cheerfully ignored them. It was at about this time that the Venetian diplomat Zaccaria Contarini, in a description of the France of his day, included a revealing sketch of the young king.

"He is small and ill-made," Contarini wrote, "ugly of countenance, with large, colorless eyes; he is short-sighted; his nose is aquiline and both longer and thicker than is natural; he has lips likewise thick, always hanging open; his hands twitch with spasmodic movements very ugly to see, and his speech comes hesitantly. My opinion may be erroneous, but it seems to me certain that physically and morally he does not amount to a great deal."

As king of a nation the power of which had been painstakingly restored by his father's long years of crafty diplomacy, however, Charles amounted to a great deal indeed. He had it within his means to commit great folly, and to that purpose he was willing to give away much of what Louis XI had gained. To make certain that his back and flanks would be secure when he departed France for Italy and perhaps the Ottoman Empire as well, he entered into a series of fantastically costly treaties. With the Treaty of Étaples, his onetime hero Henry VII of England agreed to call home the invasion force that he had sent to Brittany and relinquish his claim to that county (a claim he had never expected to make good), receiving in return a payoff in the colossal amount of £159,000, payable in installments that would double the income of the Tudor court for years. To secure the Treaty of Barcelona, and with it Ferdinand's and Isabella's pledge of neutrality, Charles paid an even higher price, surrendering the Pyrenees regions of Roussillon and

Cerdagne. Finally he signed the Treaty of Senlis, by which he renounced his claims to the counties of Burgundy, Artois, and Charolais in favor of Maximilian of Hapsburg. His counselors were in despair.

Despite everything he was sacrificing, it was going to be impossible for Charles to legitimate his designs on Naples unless he could secure papal approval. He needed to get Alexander VI, who as pope was Naples's suzerain or overlord, to repudiate Ferrante and his dynasty and invest him, Charles, with the crown. At the end of 1493, in a fresh effort to win the pope over, he sent a delegation headed by his chief minister and mentor Guillaume Briçonnet, bishop of St. Malo. This mission, like the one sent earlier in the year for the same purpose, came to nothing. Alexander and Briçonnet had long talks, the pope going so far as to offer his visitor a cardinal's hat in return for making his young master see the dangers, not only to Italy but to France itself, of an attack on Naples. Briçonnet appears to have found the pope's arguments persuasive and his offer tempting, but to the extent that he expressed his concerns upon returning to France, they had no impact.

If Charles cared about the pope's refusal, he did not care enough to be deterred. His court had become home to a large contingent of Neapolitan nobles who had fled northward to escape destruction after the failure of their rebellion against Ferrante. These refugees told the king something he was childishly delighted to hear: that all Naples would rise to support him as soon as he arrived. France's cardinals (not one of whom had been present at the 1492 conclave) were meanwhile telling him that Alexander's opinion was of no importance because he had not been honestly elected and so was not a legitimate pope. In removing Alexander, these cardinals said, Charles would be rescuing Holy Mother Church and making himself all the more a hero. Bankers from various Italian city-states were demonstrating their commitment to the great cause by offering to lend Charles huge sums—so long as he put up the crown jewels as collateral and agreed to pay fourteen percent interest. Hearing such things, monarchs less gullible than Charles VIII might have found it easy to believe that the enterprise he was planning had been ordained by God and could not fail.

Still, Naples was a long way from France, and to reach it Charles would have to take his army first across the Alps, then across the great duchy of Milan, and finally across the Apennines. And even after all the loans and all the pawning of royal treasure, he was seriously short of funds. But then Ludovico Sforza stepped forward with an offer impossible to refuse. He promised not only to do nothing to impede the passage of French troops through Milan, but to facilitate their advance with all the means at his disposal. He would put his warships at the service of the king, along with money and five hundred "men at arms"—mounted and armored knights accompanied by their squires and pages.

Italy had long been a powder keg. Now, in an act that he would live to regret bitterly, Ludovico had lit the fuse.

MADNESS AND MILAN

THE MILAN OF LUDOVICO SFORZA WAS A CLASSIC TYRANNY OF the distinctly Italian type: a city-state ruled by a family that had taken it by force, used force to keep itself in power, and had only the scantiest legitimate claim to its position, its wealth, and its power.

It was also the greatest of the tyrannies, with a capital city that was immense by the standards of the time (as many as a quarter of a million people may have lived within the walls of Milan as the fifteenth century approached its close). It had command of the great Lombard Plain with its thousands of square miles of fertile farmland, and a large middle class that was growing rich in banking and the manufacture of products ranging from silk to weaponry.

Milan was an archetype in another way as well. Its ruling dynasty, which had been in place for 215 years when Rodrigo Borgia became pope, exemplified a phenomenon that was tragically common among both the greatest and pettiest of Italy's warlord families. Power beyond the reach of any rule of law, mixed with the insecurities inherent in having little right to that power and being under chronic threat from jealous and ambitious rivals, had a way of breeding homicidal psychopaths. The Ludovico Sforza who invited Charles VIII of France into Italy in 1493 was a paragon of sanity, decency, and restraint compared with the most memorable of his Visconti and Sforza forebears. This of course raises the question of whether it was precisely *because* he was not as savage as those forebears that his fate would be tragic.

Ludovico and his brother Cardinal Ascanio owed their exalted positions in state and church to half a dozen generations of talented, strong, ruthlessly grasping, and in some cases only marginally sane ancestors. All the Visconti and Sforza were tall and fair with red-blond hair—descended, almost certainly, from the Langobards or Lombards who poured into Italy from Germany in the sixth century and gave their name to the enormous plain on which they settled. The Visconti were already prominent among the Milanese nobility when, in 1277, one of their members, a warlike seventy-year-old archbishop, defeated a rival family, made himself master, *signore,* of the city, and positioned his relatives to retain control after his death. Half a century later the fourth Visconti to serve as Milan's prelate, the "pseudo-cardinal" Giovanni (pseudo because his red hat was conferred by a schismatic antipope), paid half a million florins for papal recognition of himself and his brother Luchino as official co-rulers. The brothers greatly expanded the Milanese state, absorbing many other cities on the Lombard Plain.

Their conquests passed in the next generation to another set of brothers: Matteo, Galeazzo, and Bernabò Visconti, the first members of the family to show symptoms of serious mental (and moral) instability. Matteo was so incompetent and irresponsible, and such a slave to bestial sexual appetites, as to make not only himself but the whole family an object of popular revulsion. He died suddenly one evening after supper, and though there is no proof that he was poisoned by his brothers (their mother insisted that he was), it is not implausible that Galeazzo and Bernabò had resorted to murder to protect their own positions. For the next twenty-three years each of the two surviving brothers had possession of half of the Milanese state, Galeazzo ruling the western portion from a great palace at Pavia while Bernabò ruled the east from the city of Milan. The latter became legendary for his ferocity and bellicosity, in the process getting himself excommunicated by three successive popes and on one occasion forcing envoys to eat the bull of excommunication that they had traveled from Rome to deliver. Chastised by an archbishop of Milan who happened, rather unusually, not to be a Visconti, he replied with a purely rhetorical question: "Do you not know, you fool, that here I am pope and emperor and lord in all my lands and that no one can do anything in my lands save I permit it—no, not even God?"

Even if the most terrible stories about Bernabò were the inventions of his enemies, it does appear to be true that he had a propensity to remove people who offended him by burying them alive, and to inflict gruesomely disproportionate punishments on those accused of crimes. (Anyone daring to hunt on land reserved for his use, for example, would be blinded or hanged.) But he was not entirely monstrous: law and order were strictly maintained during his long, hard rule, and his humblest subjects found that they could expect to be treated justly in the Milanese courts even when challenging the rich and powerful. Bernabò's fatal mistake turned out to be not his excessive willingness to make war on his neighbors, not the licentiousness that made him the admitted father of at least thirty children, but his failure to take the measure of his nephew Gian Galeazzo, who had inherited command of the western half of the duchy upon the death of his father, Galeazzo.

Gian Galeazzo was a refined and cultivated man, exceptionally well educated by the standards of fourteenth-century warlords and free of the rude and brutish arrogance of his uncle. Bernabò interpreted all this as foppish weakness and regarded his nephew (whom he had also forced to become his son-in-law) with undisguised contempt. Told that Gian Galeazzo was plotting against him, he dismissed the warnings as ridiculous and so found himself being tricked, taken captive, and thrown into a prison where he soon died, reportedly of poisoning. At which point the quiet Gian Galeazzo reunited the two halves of the duchy and launched a campaign of conquest more ambitious than anything attempted by his predecessors.

Tall and impressively handsome, Gian Galeazzo was also physically timid. He spent most of his adult life in semiseclusion, protected by phalanxes of armed guards. Though he never commanded an army in the field, he hired capable *condottieri,* instructed them never to engage an enemy except when they had a decisive advantage, and spent lavishly to make sure that they always had such an advantage. Step by step he brought city after city to heel—first Verona and Vicenza, then Padua and Pisa and Siena, and eventually Perugia, Assisi, Nocera, Spoleto, and Lucca. Finally even great Bologna submitted to him. Along the way Gian Galeazzo became the first duke of Milan, paying Holy Roman emperor-elect Wenceslaus of Bohemia one hundred thousand ducats for the title. The flagrant sale of such an exalted rank—the highest after royalty—was such a scandal that it contributed to Wenceslaus's deposition from the imperial throne. But it was not revocable and gave Gian Galeazzo a semblance of legitimacy.

Gian Galeazzo's father, in an earlier effort to purchase respectability, had spent a comparable fortune to secure the marriage of his twelve-year-old son to a daughter of the financially desperate King Jean II of France. The boy became a father at fourteen, but when his wife died after ten years of marriage, only one of her six children, a daughter named Valentina, survived. When this daughter was grown, Gian Galeazzo returned her to the French royal family, marrying her to Louis duke of Orléans, brother of King Charles VI. Two generations later this marriage would have troublesome consequences: when the male line of Viscontis became extinct, Valentina's grandson, another Louis of Orléans, would come forward with a credible claim to the duchy of Milan.

Gian Galeazzo aspired to be no mere duke but monarch of a kingdom of Lombardy encompassing not only his duchy but all of Tuscany and more. When Bologna fell into his hands, this dream appeared to be within reach; only an exhausted and isolated Florence remained to be taken. But Milan was exhausted also, its wealth gone to fund Gian Galeazzo's wars and palaces and other extravagances, its people (called "subjects" rather than citizens now that their master was a duke) taxed to the brink of rebellion. All remained in suspension as Gian Galeazzo, triumphant but without the means for further action, withdrew into deeper seclusion and contracted the fever of which he died aged fifty.

His collection of conquests fell apart with astonishing speed, one city-state after another breaking free from the regency of his widow, Duchess Caterina. She was Gian Galeazzo's first cousin, daughter of the late Bernabò, who had bullied his nephew into marrying her after the death of his French first wife. By her he had two sons, both of whom became exemplars of the dangers of inbreeding, displaying all the worst characteristics of the Visconti bloodline and few if any of its strengths. The elder, Giovanni Maria, was barely in his teens when he became duke, and in short order he had his mother thrown into prison. Like her father before her she soon died, and she too is said to have been poisoned. The new duke was a depraved monster—the word really does apply—best remembered for the delight he took in watching his dogs tear apart the bodies of living men. When he was assassinated at age twenty-three, mercifully before reproducing himself, his brother and successor Filippo Maria proved to be, if less obviously insane, profoundly disturbed. His father Gian Galeazzo's reclusiveness and paranoia were in him carried to extremes. Perhaps because physical ugliness intensified his innate shyness, perhaps just because he became too fat to mount a horse, he sequestered himself behind the high walls of his father's grandiose palace and made himself the center of a network of spies, secret agents, guards, and soldiers responsible for protecting him from his guards. He waged war across northern Italy without himself ever coming within miles of a skirmish, using *condottieri* in a lifelong, sometimes atrociously cruel and only partly successful campaign to restore the duchy to what it had been at the time of Gian Galeazzo's death.

Why he bothered is a mystery, for he never displayed the smallest interest in the future of the dynasty. He had a marriage of convenience with the wealthy widow of one of his father's generals, and a single mistress with whom he sired two daughters only one of whom, Bianca Maria, lived past infancy. When in 1430 he betrothed the six-year-old girl to the greatest *condottiere* of the century, the thirty-year-old widower Francesco Sforza (whose first wife and child had been murdered by his aunt), Filippo Maria offered valuable properties as his daughter's dowry and appears to have been motivated solely by a determination to keep Sforza in his employ. He later made repeated attempts to break off the engagement, with Sforza sometimes on his payroll and at other times leading the armies of Milan's enemies. When the wedding finally took place in 1441 (Bianca being sixteen by then, the bridegroom forty), Filippo Maria was forced to consent to it because of defeats inflicted on him by Venetian forces commanded by none other than his prospective son-in-law.

Filippo Maria anointed no heir, and when he died in 1447, the claimants to Milan included the Holy Roman emperor (because he was Milan's feudal overlord), Valentina Visconti's son Charles duke of Orléans, the Republic of Venice, and Francesco Sforza. All were held off as Milan became a republic, but this proved a doomed enterprise. Sforza made war on the capital, forcing it to surrender after a prolonged siege that reduced the population to eating cats and dogs. Once securely in place as duke, he became less interested in conquest than in protecting what he had won and turned into a force for peace and stability. He forged a close friendship with Cosimo de' Medici of Florence, and the two worked together to put a durable balance of power in place across Italy.

He found himself happily married as well. Bianca Maria Visconti Sforza proved to be a dependable manager, a capable diplomat, and therefore a duchess of real consequence. The pair had eight children, and of these only one, unfortunately their eldest son Galeazzo Maria, gave evidence of having inherited the Visconti tendency to madness. Upon succeeding his father at age twenty-two, Galeazzo Maria set about building a reputation as a rapist, torturer, and murderer (starving to death a priest accused of predicting that his reign would be short). He cast aside his worried mother and inevitably was accused of having her poisoned when she died in exile. We have already seen the calamities that flowed from all this. First Galeazzo Maria was himself murdered, by Milanese nobles he had pushed too far. Then his brother Ludovico seized power, took custody of the seven-year-old heir to the ducal title, Gian Galeazzo, and proclaimed himself regent. Things got mortally serious a decade later, when Gian Galeazzo came of age, his wife Isabella protested to her grandfather Ferrante of Naples that Ludovico was refusing to relinquish control, and Ferrante broke with Milan and left Ludovico feeling so alone and fearful that he not only invited the king of France to invade Italy but offered to pay him to do so.

Anxieties about Naples notwithstanding, by 1493 there was every reason for the Milanese to think themselves fortunate to be ruled by Ludovico. He was as solidly normal a man as the Visconti-Sforza family tree had produced, with the exception of Duke Francesco. Intelligent, energetic, and cultivated, superbly educated under the direction of his mother Bianca, he displayed none of the psychopathic viciousness of his elder brother, his maternal grandfather, his great-uncle, and other ancestors dating back to Matteo and Bernabò Visconti. Since pushing his sister-in-law out of the regency, he had given much attention to the development of Milan's economy. He had come to be known as Il Moro not (as has often been written) because he was dark like a Moor (in fact he was fair with his family's golden hair) but because *moro* is the Italian word for his personal emblem, the mulberry tree. Known since ancient times as "the most prudent of trees," last to put out leaves in the springtime, the mulberry was an essential source of food for the worms on which Milan's lucrative silk-manufacturing industry was based.

Prudent or not—the 1490s would provide reason for doubting that he was—Il Moro had much cause for satisfaction as it became clear that Charles of France was serious about attacking Naples. Now it was Ferrante's turn to be frightened—he and Pope Alexander as well. Il Moro meanwhile had a bride with whom he was delighted, the lovely and vivacious Beatrice d'Este, daughter of the duke of Ferrara. Since her arrival in Milan in 1491, Beatrice had, almost inevitably under the circumstances, developed a poisonously hateful relationship with the frustrated

Duchess Isabella. Still only sixteen, Beatrice became a determined advo-
cate of the use of French power to drive her rival's family out of Naples.

In the year following Il Moro's marriage, the resolution of issues that
had long put the French crown at odds with the Holy Roman Empire
made it possible for him to form a friendship with emperor-elect Maximilian of Hapsburg without offending France. The two worked out a
deal. The cash-strapped Maximilian got, in addition to Duke Gian Galeazzo's sister as his bride, something that probably mattered to him far
more: a dowry in the amount of four hundred thousand ducats. Il Moro
got the prestige of linking the Sforza family to the highest level of European royalty and also (what mattered to *him* far more) the promise that
upon becoming emperor Maximilian would invest him as duke of Milan,
stripping the title from Gian Galeazzo.

Ludovico il Moro was no longer isolated. To the contrary, his position
as de facto French agent in Italy, coupled with the expectation of an imminent French invasion, made him an enemy to be feared and an ally to
be coveted. Thus even his old rival Venice, wanting no trouble with
France, joined with Milan and Rome in the newly formed League of St.
Mark and accepted Ludovico as its head. And Beatrice's family connections now proved their value. Her father Ercole d'Este brought his duchy
of Ferrara into the league, followed by Francesco Gonzaga marquess of
Mantua, who was married to Beatrice's sister Isabella.

To cap it all off, Milan had as its representative in Rome none other
than the vice-chancellor of the Church, Ascanio Sforza, cardinal since
1484 and pivotal figure in the election of Alexander VI. Comfortably
back in his old place at the papal court now that Milan and Rome were
allied in the league, Ascanio was prepared to do everything in his power
to persuade Alexander to support the French claim to Naples. He was
no less willing, if that proved impossible, to join the chorus of voices
urging Charles to depose the pope as he passed through Rome on his
way to Naples.

Of all the princes in Italy, Ludovico Sforza seemed best positioned to
profit from the drama that was beginning to unfold.

12

The Coming of the French

The rush of hungry relatives and hangers-on to Rome whenever a new pope took office appears to have been no less a spectacle in the case of the Borgias than at the start of other pontifical reigns.

This was true in part simply because the family was so large and so fast-growing. At a time when infant mortality rates were heartbreakingly high, the ability to produce healthy babies in abundance and bring them to maturity was one of the Borgia family's gifts. Most of the Borgia couples of whom we have record were survived by impressive numbers of daughters and sons, who were prolific in their turn if they did not go into the Church—and no doubt occasionally even then. They were a vigorous and hearty lot, ready to go wherever opportunity beckoned.

The family tree was not only thick with branches but maddeningly tangled—a trap for genealogists ever since. As happens in many families, baptismal names were handed down from generation to generation: Rodrigos and Jofrès, Juans and Juanas, Pedros and Isabellas appear again and again, sometimes more than once in a single generation. The confusion to which this gave rise was compounded twice over by a practice somewhat more unusual: the tendency of the offspring of Borgia daughters to discard their father's surname beçause their mother's, belonging as it did not merely to a pope but to *two* popes, had come to carry so much more weight.

The confusion spread everywhere and has been long-lasting. Even today one sees it asserted that the Rodrigo Borgia who became Alexander VI was actually not a Borgia at all in the male line but a Lanzol (or Lançol). This particular misunderstanding is not only unnecessary but inexcusable, there being no possible doubt, as we saw in Part One, that Rodrigo's father *and* his mother were de Borjas. It grew out of the marriage of Rodrigo's sister Juana to a Valencian baron named Pedro Guillen Lanzol, and the fact that their children bore, in keeping with Spanish practice, the name Lanzol y de Borja. The first members of this branch of the clan to migrate to Rome created the impression that all Borgias were actually Lanzols, and this assumption—valid with respect to all the Roman Borgias except the two popes and Rodrigo's short-lived brother Pedro Luis—came to be attached, incorrectly, to Rodrigo. It clung to him even as his relatives gradually discarded the Lanzol patronym because being Borgias marked them as people not to be taken lightly.

Some of the Roman Borgias remain mysteries to this day. When Cardinal Scarampo took a fleet of warships off to fight the Turks in 1456, two of his galley captains were named Juan and Miguel Borgia. We have no idea where these two came from, but their name and the fact that both later turn up as administrators in the Papal States make it impossible not to suppose that they were related to Calixtus and Alexander. More strikingly, no one has ever been able to explain the parentage of a certain Francesco Borgia who was a prominent figure at the papal court throughout Alexander's reign, was repeatedly given responsibility for handling important family business, and would become a cardinal in 1500. Speculation that he was Calixtus's illegitimate son is supported by no evidence and has to be considered improbable. Perhaps it needs to be added that he was no more than a decade younger than Alexander VI and therefore was not *his* son. One hypothesis—not implausible considering that he is believed to have been born in Játiva—is that he was Alexander's younger brother.

Young Borgia clerics found themselves rising even higher and faster after Rodrigo became pope than they had before, and the family's laymen too found doors opening for them in delightful ways. Some of the most dazzling opportunities were in the dynastic marriage market. We have already seen the lofty unions arranged by Sixtus IV for his nephews and nieces, and by Innocent VIII for his son and grand-daughter. By the early 1490s, with Italy in turmoil and a French invasion seemingly inevitable, the desperation with which the peninsula's rulers were looking for allies had brought that market to a rolling boil.

Pope Alexander, attractive as an ally himself and as needful of friends as any of his fellow rulers, had four especially fine pieces of merchandise to put on offer in Rome. They were the quartet of Cesare, Juan, Lucrezia, and Jofrè Borgia, siblings who at the time of Alexander's election ranged in age from about ten or eleven to seventeen. They had an older, closer connection to the pope than any of their cousins, having been part of Cardinal Rodrigo's household for at least four or five years, in some cases possibly longer. We have already seen Ferrante, at the end of 1492, send his son to Rome in search of an alliance, offering both a daughter and a granddaughter as brides for Borgias and being turned down. Just weeks later, as part of the agreement by which Rome, Milan, and Venice all came together in the League of St. Mark, Alexander and Ludovico il Moro jointly decided that Lucrezia, still not thirteen years old, was to be married to Ludovico's cousin Giovanni Sforza, lord of Pesaro and a twenty-six-year-old widower.

It was Alexander's policy, from which he never deviated except when circumstances made consistency impossible, to seek friendly relations with all the major powers and try to keep any of them from feeling isolated. Thus the creation of the Italian League, because it excluded Naples, became the pope's cue not only to restore his lines of communication with the excluded Ferrante but to respond, if belatedly, to the latter's proposal that the Borgias and the royal House of Aragon should become linked through matrimony. The result, abetted by Ferdinand of Spain's envoy to Rome Diego López de Haro, was a pair of significant betrothals. Jofrè, who could not have been more than eleven years old, was promised to Ferrante's illegitimate granddaughter Sancia, then about fifteen. Jofrè's elder brother Juan, then in his late teens, was to return to Castile to be married into the Spanish royal family. The youngest of the Borgia brothers would not have been Ferrante's choice as bridegroom for Sancia, his brother Cesare being not only more suitable in age but clearly the brightest, liveliest, and most promising of the young Borgias. But Alexander had long since assigned Cesare to a career in the Church, and though his young ward had not yet taken any clerical vows, the pope had no interest in changing his plans. Jofrè too was in the earliest stages of being groomed for the clergy, but in his case the pope was willing to make adjustments. He certainly understood that Cesare was made of stronger stuff than his younger sibling—that he had far more of what it would take to become a third Borgia pope.

By the end of the summer of 1493, the futures of Cesare, Juan, Lucrezia, and Jofrè seemed to be assured. Juan, who had inherited from a deceased elder brother (more about him later) the Spanish dukedom of Gandía, was married in Barcelona to a young cousin of Ferdinand and Isabella (who were themselves cousins, as we have seen). The monarchical couple attended the wedding, though Isabella was skeptical about the bridegroom—presciently doubtful about the kind of husband and courtier he was likely to be. At almost the same time Cesare became one of the dozen new cardinals appointed by Alexander VI, and in a ceremony at the Vatican, young Jofrè was quietly married by proxy to Sancia of Aragon, becoming thereby prince of Squillace in the kingdom of Naples and lord of extensive Neapolitan estates. Two months later, in a secret ceremony, Lucrezia was married to Giovanni Sforza and became countess of the city-state of Pesaro on the Adriatic coast. The sensitivities of Milan, Venice, and the other northern states made it seem prudent to defer making these arrangements public, and in light of the extreme youth of Lucrezia and Jofrè there was certainly no need to hurry. At Alexander's insistence it was agreed that Lucrezia would remain in Rome and the consummation of her marriage would be deferred even after the performance of a public wedding ceremony.

All too soon it became clear that things were not working out as planned. Juan duke of Gandía, a difficult character under the best of circumstances, had been sent off to Spain in the care of a guardian appointed by Alexander and under a deluge of papal admonitions to behave himself. The first reports to reach Rome showed that he was already out of control. His tactless arrogance had offended the king and queen, and immediately after his wedding he went off on such a wild spree of drinking, gambling, and whoring that it was said to be improbable that he had bothered to consummate the marriage. Sent to Spain to cement the pope's relationship with the dual kingdom's royal family, beautifully positioned to reap the rewards of Ferdinand and Isabella's indebtedness to Alexander, Juan was becoming instead a threat to the survival of the connection.

Though Lucrezia eventually had a grand public wedding, a lavish spectacle used by Alexander to express the importance of the event and indulge his love of ceremony and display (the bride was escorted by 150 daughters of Rome's leading families), it did not appear to be leading her into a happy or even a stable future. In the weeks following, Lucrezia's husband became so dissatisfied with their sexless "white marriage," and so uneasy about the way the pope appeared to be cooling in his friendship with the Sforzas and inching toward Naples instead, that he departed Rome alone and without explanation, sending back an insulting demand for money. He appears to have been an unusually ordinary Sforza, colorless in personality and devoid of ambition, but he was not wrong to be worried. The political landscape had changed considerably since he and Lucrezia were first betrothed, his marriage was losing its political value for the Borgias as a result, and his presence in Rome had become a nuisance for everyone concerned. His departure for Pesaro, by setting the tongues of Rome wagging, accomplished nothing except to create frenzies of speculation and embarrassment. The pope tried to show himself still friendly to the Sforzas of Milan, but his gestures in that direction were thin in substance and impressed no one.

In May 1494, when the Jofrè-Sancia marriage was made public and the youngest Borgia brother was sent off to Naples to take up his new life as a husband and prince, his situation was little less awkward than Giovanni Sforza's. The problem in this case was that Jofrè, physically attractive like his siblings but scarcely out of childhood and already showing himself to be passive and as bland as Lucrezia's husband, had been given as his wife a headstrong and recklessly pleasure-hungry young woman whose character had been shaped in the morally lax court of her grandfather Ferrante. She showed herself to be less than delighted with a spouse significantly younger and less lively than herself. The fact that Jofrè was by all accounts a well-behaved youth did nothing to ease her restlessness; good behavior never had much appeal for her. The marriage, ill conceived from the start, was already troubled and rich in potential for more of the same.

As for the eldest of the four, Cesare, in him there was potential not just for trouble but for calamity. Not yet twenty, he was already high in the Church and had been so from early childhood: appointed an apostolic protonotary at the preposterous age of seven, he became archdeacon in the Borgia hometown of Játiva and rector of Gandía not long afterward. He was bishop of Pamplona at about sixteen (this is not quite as appalling as it sounds, as Cesare got the title and the income that went with it, but was not expected and indeed would not have been allowed to actually *function* as bishop). Only a year after that, upon Rodrigo's election, he was given the see of Valencia, and by the time another year had passed he was a teenage cardinal.

The problem was not just grossly premature advancement but the fact that, though intelligent, ambitious, educated in canon and civil law, and attractive both physically and in personality, Cesare never had and never pretended to have the slightest aptitude for an ecclesiastical career. There survives a unique early description from about this time, written by the duke of Ferrara's ambassador to Rome Giovanandrea Boccaccio, who exclaims that though only about seventeen Cesare "possesses marked genius and a charming personality; he bears himself like a great prince; he is especially lively and merry, and fond of society. Being very modest, he presents much better than his brother, the duke of Gandía, although the latter is also highly endowed." Boccaccio's words make it understandable that Alexander VI could come to dote on a youth of such promise, but even he, astute as he was, must have seen that this high-spirited, strong-willed, and lavishly talented youth, fearing nothing and no one, was not going to be easily kept on the path that had been laid out for him. He was not likely to be even briefly satisfied with the gift of a red hat, or to see in it any reason to moderate his behavior.

For a while things settled down, and the careers of all four young Borgias appeared to be coming right. Alexander rejoiced when word arrived from Spain that Duke Juan's bride was pregnant: not only had the marriage been consummated, but an heir to the duchy of Gandía was possibly on his way. Not long afterward Cesare submitted to taking "minor" orders, first as a subdeacon and then as deacon. These were steps toward priestly ordination but did not involve the taking of permanent vows. It was not at all unusual for cardinals to be deacons only, and it was not unheard of for newly elected popes to be ordained shortly before their coronation. One rationale for this was the demands that ordination put on a man's time and the wish to keep senior Curia officials focused on their bureaucratic responsibilities. Rodrigo Borgia himself had been a cardinal for years before finally being ordained.

Jofrè and Sancia too were giving no great cause for worry. They appeared to be settling contentedly enough into their new life as married Neapolitan royalty—a grandiose life that provided the boy-prince with scores of attendants and his bride with almost as many. As for Lucrezia, she in company with her mother and her best friend and companion Giulia Farnese Orsini, the beautiful daughter-in-law of Pope Alexander's cousin and housekeeper Adriana del Milà, had joined her husband at Pesaro, presumably now sharing with him the conjugal bed. All seemed to be well on the domestic front.

In the wider world things were not at all well. January 1494 brought a momentous event, the death from cancer of Ferrante of Naples. As shrewd as he was cruel, as treacherous as he was skilled in statecraft, through his three and a half decades as king Ferrante had remained always at the center of Italian power politics, constantly in search of opportunities to make trouble for his rivals and frequently succeeding. His last months, however, had been steeped in dread and the expectation of ruin, the fear that everything he had spent his life preserving and everything he had accomplished was soon to be laid waste. He knew of course that Charles of France was preparing an invasion, knew that Naples was Charles's prime objective, and foresaw all too clearly that this meant disaster. At a less troubled time the demise of such a man might have given rise to jubilation, in Naples no less than elsewhere. But not now, and especially not in Rome. With the death of Ferrante it became impossible for Alexander to continue dancing on a diplomatic tightrope between Naples and Milan—and, beyond them, between Spain and France. Suddenly all eyes were on Rome, and the question being asked was who Alexander would recognize as Ferrante's successor. It was a repeat of what had happened in the last days of Calixtus III's reign, with the death of Ferrante's father.

The most obvious choice was Ferrante's eldest son, Alfonso duke of Calabria, whom Innocent VIII had pledged to invest with the crown when Ferrante was gone. On the personal level Alfonso was unpromising material. He was at least as objectionable as his father in moral terms; Renaissance historian Jacob Burckhardt would describe him as "a savage, brutal profligate." But he was already in place as de facto ruler of his father's and grandfather's kingdom, understood the precariousness of his position, and was taking swift action to get himself firmly entrenched.

He knew that, with the king of France preparing to descend upon him, he needed to organize a defense and was going to require help in doing so. Ferrante had attempted to provide him with a lasting source of help by marrying him to the daughter of one Sforza duke and his daughter to another. Thanks to Ludovico Sforza's usurpation, however, that connection was now worse than useless. The late Pope Innocent's pledge to install him as king was likewise useless. Other support was needed, which explains why Alfonso and Ferrante, to secure Pope Alexander's friendship, had already bestowed rich estates, grand titles, and Sancia of Aragon on young Jofrè Borgia, endowed the duke of Gandía with a lifelong income, and granted lucrative benefices to Cardinal Cesare. The benefits of having done these things seemed almost trivial, however, when balanced against the certain knowledge that Charles VIII was preparing to invade and for that purpose was assembling an army bigger than any seen in Italy in living memory.

Alexander's connections to the House of Aragon notwithstanding, the question of whom to anoint as Ferrante's successor had no easy answer. Though at the urging of Cardinal Giuliano della Rovere and others Charles was threatening to depose the pope, nothing could have been more obvious than his readiness to forgive and forget Alexander's refusal to approve his invasion. In return he wanted only one thing, something that would cost the pope nothing in the near term. He wanted an assurance of papal investment as king of Naples once his campaign had succeeded. And he had much to offer in return. If as seemed likely the French army proved to be an irresistible force once it was on the march, it would place in Charles's hands the ability to dispense rewards beyond anything that Alfonso of Naples could ever possibly offer. In any case the time for artful dodging—for positioning himself as the friend of Milan and Naples as well, or at least as the enemy of neither—had ended. Someone was going to become king of Naples, and Alexander had no choice but to place a bet.

He did so on April 18, when gathered with the cardinals in consistory. To the indignation of Ascanio Sforza and the French members of the Sacred College, he declared his intention to send a legate to Naples to crown Alfonso on his behalf without delay. Part of his motive was, almost certainly, to present King Charles with a fait accompli and thereby—with luck—discourage him from invading. Also, by showing his hand he was signaling to the other Italian rulers that the time had come for them to do the same. He underscored the point by assigning the coronation duties to his nephew and confidant Cardinal Giovanni Borgia, and by instructing him to proceed to Ferrara and Venice upon leaving Naples and encourage those cities too to come to Alfonso's support. Cardinal Giuliano della Rovere's response was to depart for the north, first for Milan and then on to the court of the French king. He sensed the opportunity for which he had been waiting. Now that Alexander had in effect declared himself an opponent of France, or if not that at least unwilling to acquiesce in a French conquest of Naples, the gullible Charles was more likely than ever to see the wisdom of replacing him with someone more cooperative. It need hardly be said that della Rovere was confident that the king would not have to look far to find exactly the right replacement.

Wiser men than Charles might have thought success a certainty when so many important Italians were not only encouraging him to invade but offering to join his campaign and help to finance it. Within weeks of Alexander's decision to confer the Neapolitan crown on Alfonso II, therefore, Charles had his war machine in motion, sending all the great and petty powers of Italy scrambling to save themselves from disaster or even, should opportunities arise, to profit from the confusion and mayhem. The jealousies and conflicting ambitions that had always divided the Italian states, worsened now by panic, removed any possibility of their coming together in the common defense. Duke Ercole d'Este of Ferrara, who had done his best to stay clear of war since his conflict with Venice a decade before had brought his dynasty to the edge of ruin, now saw a chance to recover some of what had been lost. He not only allied his duchy with France and Milan—that was no surprise, his family having long looked to Milan for protection against Venice, and his daughter Beatrice being married to Ludovico il Moro— but sent off a son to join the French army. The Venetians, whose resources would have been sufficient to make even Charles think twice about proceeding, withdrew to a position of neutrality. Giovanni Bentivoglio, strongman of Bologna, also had the capacity to make things difficult for Charles but would continue to temporize until it was too late for his decision to matter.

Charles moved with glacial slowness at first, evidently not caring that as the weeks passed the summer was passing too and with it the best months for offensive operations. He was still at Lyons at the beginning of June, when Cardinal della Rovere caught up with him and added his insistent voice to the many urging him to press on and show no more mercy to Pope Alexander than to Alfonso II. Della Rovere, until recently on cordial terms with Naples, was now its implacable enemy thanks solely to Alfonso's recognition by the pope. This was characteristic behavior on della Rovere's part; he had thrown in with Charles for no better reason than that the French king was the only man in Europe able and presumably willing to tear the papal tiara from Alexander's head. When Charles finally got his forces in motion once again, he advanced only as far as Vienne before stopping for three weeks of amusements including dalliance with the gaggle of mistresses that accompanied him wherever he went.

On June 14, at the Orsini fortress of Vicovaro northeast of Rome, a pathetically small assembly of princes and warlords gathered to explore ways of mounting a resistance. The key participants were Alfonso II and his liege lord the pope. The two devoted part of the day to a discussion so private that no one else was admitted. Also in attendance, somewhat improbably, were the chiefs of Rome's two great baronial clans, men more experienced at fighting one another than at tangling with foreigners. Fabrizio Colonna, who shared the leadership of his family with his cousin Prospero, had come to Vicovaro in spite of having recently signed a *condotta* that put him on the payroll of Charles VIII. It was typical of the relaxed view that Italian warlords took of their contractual obligations that Fabrizio saw nothing wrong in exchanging views with his employer's principal opponents, or in participating in a conference hosted by Virginio Orsini, not only chief of the Colonnas' hated rivals but great constable, general-in-chief, of the army of Naples. One wonders what France's romantic young king would have thought had he known that Fabrizio, whom he was paying handsomely with money borrowed on onerous terms, was now promising that neither his clan nor its junior partners the Savelli family would do anything to make trouble for Naples or the Papal States when the French attack came.

A plan of defense was agreed upon that day. Alfonso II's son Ferrandino, who now bore his father's old title of duke of Calabria, would take a Neapolitan army north into the Romagna to block the French from using the Apennine passes. Once in place, Ferrandino would also be positioned to protect the flank of Piero de' Medici's Florentine army as it sealed off the roads leading southward into Tuscany. Alfonso's brother Don Fadrique, meanwhile, was to take Naples's war fleet northward up the coast in an attack on the port of Genoa, to prevent the French from using it to supply and reinforce their army. Virginio Orsini assumed responsibility for keeping the French out of his family's territories north of Rome, while Alexander was to do the same for those parts of the Papal States effectively under his rule.

The army with which Charles VIII entered Italy at the start of September 1494, numbering possibly as many as forty thousand men, was an immense force not only by Italian standards but by the European standards of the time. It was a *hard* army too, made up mainly of Breton and Gascon veterans and Swiss and German mercenaries. Upon crossing the Alps they would find themselves scorned as barbarians, and they would repay the contempt of the Italians with the kind of atrocious savagery that had come to northern Europe in the time of the Hundred Years' War. They brought with them something else that the Italians had never seen: mobile heavy artillery. It was heavy by the standards of the day, at any rate, the biggest barrels being all of eight feet long. Never before in history had it been possible to transport such devastating weaponry at the speed of a walking horse and use it to batter down the high, thick fortress walls that for millennia had been virtually impregnable.

Precisely because it was so big and so awesomely equipped, Charles's army had to do almost no real fighting. Its approach spread panic across the Lombard Plain and on southward, causing the forces mustered to resist its advance to move out of its path instead. This set off a sequence of betrayals, reversals, and defeats that threatened to go on until nothing of Italy's old order remained. Events as they unfolded seemed almost to conspire to confirm Charles VIII's fantasies about himself as an epic hero embarked upon God's work and fulfilling his own magnificent destiny. His troops marched under standards bearing the words *Voluntas Dei* (By the Will of God) and *Missus a Deo* (Sent by God). These slogans were said to have been suggested by Giuliano della Rovere. He, like the king, saw impossible dreams coming true.

That the arrival of the French marked the opening of a tragic new era in Italian history was clear from the beginning. When the fleet commanded by Don Fadrique of Naples arrived too late to keep Genoa's harbor out of the hands of a French force led by Charles VIII's cousin Louis of Orléans, it moved on to the port of Rapallo and linked up with friendly local forces there. Just days later, however, the arrival of 2,500 of Charles's Swiss mercenaries forced Don Fadrique to withdraw, leaving Rapallo's garrison to be massacred and the town itself to be sacked so savagely that news of what had happened spread terror to the farthest reaches of Italy. War Italian style, in which captured towns were more likely to be ransomed than destroyed and *condottieri* tended to be forgiving of defeated foes because they knew that in the next little war the shoe might well turn up on the other foot, was consigned to the past.

On September 9 Charles reached the Lombard city of Asti, which had been a French outpost since being given to Louis of Orléans's grandfather as part of the dowry of his bride Valentina Visconti. After receiving a warm welcome from Ludovico Sforza and his father-in-law Duke Ercole d'Este of Ferrara, Charles fell ill with smallpox. Though his case proved to be not fatal, it brought the offensive to another halt and so alarmed his court as to resurrect the old question of whether it was sensible to proceed all the way to Naples and expect that once there the French would be capable of overcoming Alfonso II's defenses. There was talk of how much easier and more profitable it could be to simply take Milan instead. The duchy already was, after all, virtually in French hands, and every lawyer at the French court eagerly agreed that it belonged by right to Louis of Orléans, who was conveniently on the scene as one of Charles VIII's senior commanders. Though Charles when sufficiently recovered dismissed such talk out of hand—probably he really did expect his campaign to continue until he sat on a throne in Jerusalem—Il Moro inevitably learned of it and was understandably distressed. He began to have belated second thoughts about having enticed the French to come to Italy and solve his problems.

He was given further cause for worry when Charles moved on to Pavia, second only to the city of Milan as a bastion of Visconti-Sforza strength and home of Duke Gian Galeazzo Sforza, his wife Isabella of Aragon, and their young children. The king called on the duke, who as it happened was his first cousin (their mothers were daughters of the duke of Savoy) and in his usual bad health. Duchess Isabella took the initiative, throwing herself on the king's mercy and begging him to assure the succession of her son Francesco if his father died. Charles, who had more than the average man's susceptibility to women as beautiful as Isabella, responded sympathetically. Though he promised nothing before moving on again, this time to Parma, Il Moro was left to brood in solitude about just how dependable a patron the king of France was likely to prove.

Charles resumed his effortless progress, with nothing to worry him except the costs of keeping his immense army paid, fed, and in tolerably good order. As city after city opened its gates without even a pretense of resistance, and in each new place Charles's scouts marked the buildings where troops were to be billeted, it began to be said that the king was conquering Italy with a piece of chalk. The juggernaut rolled on, and as effortless victories followed one after another, the defensive confederation formed at Vicovaro began to crumble. Betrayals of Alexander and Alfonso came almost weekly. As early as September 18, when the French court was still at Asti awaiting the king's recovery from smallpox, the Colonna had broken their chief's promise to remain on the sidelines of the conflict at least where papal and Neapolitan territory were concerned. The cousins Fabrizio and Prospero Colonna launched a surprise attack on the Roman port of Ostia, which they had been forced to hand over to the pope earlier in the year after its governor, their patron Cardinal Giuliano della Rovere, departed for France. By retaking Ostia they gave France's warships control of the Tiber, without which Rome had no easy access to the sea. As they already controlled the main road connecting Rome to Naples, holding it in readiness for the French while blocking communications between Alexander and Alfonso, the Colonna now had the Vatican in a stranglehold.

If it is true as alleged that Ascanio Sforza persuaded the Colonna to commit this act of betrayal, the cardinal deserves credit for a tactical masterstroke. With the Colonna now positioned to do so much mischief so close to his kingdom, Alfonso II decided that he could not reinforce his son Ferrandino's army in the Romagna. This left Ferrandino without the strength to keep the French from outflanking his army and seizing the mountain passes, and when this happened the Neapolitan army was so dangerously exposed that Alfonso ordered a general retreat. Thus the Florentines found themselves unsupported as the French bore down on them. Every setback seemed to lead to further setbacks, and the French flags flying over Ostia seemed to mock a humiliated and defenseless Pope Alexander.

Not even Ludovico Sforza could rejoice in the successes of the invasion he had instigated. When his nephew Duke Gian Galeazzo died on October 22, murder was so widely assumed that he found it necessary to send letters to his fellow princes, protesting his innocence. A supine Milanese parliament decreed that Ludovico and not Gian Galeazzo's son Francesco was now duke, but the dire circumstances must have made this fulfillment of Il Moro's lifelong dream much less sweet than he had expected.

In Florence, weakened by a long and inconclusive war to subdue the neighboring city of Pisa, Piero de' Medici had even more to worry about than Il Moro. His decision to side with Naples in this crisis had been a reversal of long-standing Florentine policy, which traditionally favored France as a rich market for the city's bankers and manufacturers. The new alignment came under increasing criticism as France imposed an embargo on Florence's goods, causing immediate economic distress. As the French army approached, more and more influential Florentines openly questioned Piero's judgment, questioning also the wisdom of leaving the city's destiny in the hands of an inexperienced youth who, it was becoming obvious, was not nearly the equal of his late father Lorenzo. Piero's position became alarming when news arrived that Charles's mercenaries, having used false promises to extract a surrender from the defenders of the Florentine stronghold of Fivizzano, had put the entire garrison to death and subjected the town to the kind of scorched-earth sacking for which Rapallo had first made them notorious. Florence seemed doomed to a similar fate, with Piero responsible.

Perhaps it was sheer desperation, or perhaps the memory of how Lorenzo the Magnificent had once saved Florence by journeying to Naples and putting himself at the mercy of the vicious Ferrante, that prompted Piero to venture forth in search of the French king. He found him at the end of October, at Sarzana near the port of La Spezia. Instead of talking terms as his father surely would have done, however, Piero simply prostrated himself before the misshapen little conqueror. He abjectly declared himself ready not only to ally with the invaders but to hand over to them much more than they would have been likely to demand of a less craven envoy. By the time Piero stopped talking, he had given Charles free access to Florence itself and every one of the city's satellite strongpoints. He had even given Charles the strategic port of Livorno and, more shocking still, the city of Pisa, the control of which was considered economically and militarily essential by many leading Florentines. When the citizens of Florence learned of all this, their festering resentments, the inevitable result of generations of domination by a single family, erupted in communal rage.

Their anger was brought to white heat by the denunciations of an extraordinary figure who, though an outsider who had moved to Florence only five years earlier and had done so at the invitation of Lorenzo de' Medici, had already established himself as the spokesman and de facto leader of the city's numerous anti-Medici factions. This was Friar Girolamo Savonarola, a Dominican priest and preacher whose energy and charisma were fueled by revulsion against the hedonism and materialism of the Italy of his day, a burning hatred of the Medici and the Renaissance papacy alike, and (his most attractive feature) a conviction that Italy's people could and should rid themselves of rule by tyrants.

On the momentous day of November 9, 1494, when Piero de' Medici and his family were expelled from Florence, Savonarola was not present. Instead he was in Pisa, where he had gone to represent the *signoria* of a new Florentine republic in welcoming the French invaders. Charles VIII was received as a liberator when he entered Pisa at the head of his army that day; the Pisans were in ecstasies at having been freed—or so they believed—from Florence's hard rule. Rather oddly, the envoy from Florence figured prominently in the festivities and took the opportunity to heap praise on the conqueror from the north. Charles, Savonarola declared, was the liberator whose arrival he had been predicting in his sermons, a messenger sent by God to cleanse Italy—wicked Florence especially, the papacy above all—of the corruption in which it had long been sunk. Of course he got an affectionate response from king and Pisans alike and upon returning to Florence was himself received as a hero, the man whose prophecies had proved accurate and who had restored both the city's dignity and its old friendship with France.

When on November 17 Charles rode into Florence with Cardinal della Rovere at his side, they received a more mixed reception. Supporters of the Medici, especially those who resented what almost everyone was interpreting as Charles's intervention on behalf of Pisan autonomy, looked on sullenly. But those who regarded the Medici as usurping tyrants, and Piero as a disaster, were jubilant at what they hoped would prove the dawning of a new era. Their joy was tamped down, however, when Charles revealed where his priorities lay. He told the assembled citizens that he had entered their city not as a liberator but as a conqueror, that it was a matter of no interest to him whether they were governed by the Medici or the foes of the Medici, and that what he wanted from them was what Florence had a gift for producing in abundance: money.

Charles's position, however, proved to be not as strong as he had assumed. The sum that he demanded was so outlandish that the Florentine officials all but laughed in his face, and when he threatened to use force ("I shall sound my trumpets!"), they dared him to try ("We will ring our bells!" meaning that they would summon the people to resist). The plain fact was that Charles needed an intact and nonhostile Florence: the city lay athwart the lines of communication connecting him with the coast and with home, and if it took up arms against him, his army could be cut off. If he destroyed Florence, he would destroy with it the banking houses without which his whole enterprise might very well be doomed. And so he backed down, providing a clue as to how easily he might have been stopped if Venice, Ferrara, and Bologna had joined the resistance at the start. He accepted payment of 120,000 florins, recognized the new regime, and moved on.

Now it was the turn of Ludovico Sforza to turn traitor. Early in November, having learned that Louis of Orléans was sporting the title duke of Milan as he advanced with his troops southward toward Naples, Il Moro decided that enough was enough. He quietly dispatched his brother the cardinal to call on Pope Alexander in Rome and offer an alliance. Implicit in this, obviously, was a Milanese abandonment of Charles of France. Unfortunately for himself, however, Il Moro mistakenly believed his own position to be so strong, or the pope's so hopeless, that he could exact an extortionate price for changing sides. On his behalf Ascanio demanded Alexander's pledge that all future appointments to the College of Cardinals would require the duke of Milan's approval. The pope's response was as bold as the demand: he had Ascanio locked up.

Where were Ferdinand and Isabella while all this was transpiring? They were, in spite of the pleas for help from Alfonso of Naples and from the pope as well, in spite of their own horror at the thought of a French conquest of Naples, carefully saying and doing nothing. The only possible explanation is the Treaty of Barcelona by which Charles had bought their neutrality, surrendering two border provinces that his father had struggled mightily to make part of France. The Spanish monarchs had no wish to jeopardize such lovely acquisitions. For the time being they were satisfied to stand by, wait to see what happened, and leave both their old friend the pope and their cousin the king of Naples to manage as best they could.

Alexander expressed his view of the situation on November 9, in words of reproach addressed to Ercole d'Este's ambassador to the papal court. "The triumph of France," he said, "involves nothing less than the destruction of the independence of every state in Italy." Rome itself included, of course. But Ferrara included as well, even if Duke Ercole had put himself unreservedly on France's side. That was what the pope saw: that in this squalid affair there could be no Italian winners. Knowing that even Ludovico Sforza had grasped the truth, he probably knew also that Venice was awakening to how, by electing to remain neutral, it had jeopardized its own future.

Probably the blindest man in Italy was its new master, Charles VIII. His unimpeded progress made it unnecessary for him to see that his own high-handedness, and even more the brutality with which his troops were looting and raping as they worked their way south, were making enemies even of those who at first had welcomed him. Before leaving Florence he had issued a grandiose manifesto, declaring that his purpose was to recapture the Holy Land and end the Ottoman threat to Christendom, and that the conquest of Naples was a necessary and legitimate step in the achievement of those epic goals. Also necessary, he noted, was that the pope "grant us the same courtesy he has granted to our enemies, that is to say free passage through his territories, and the necessary provisioning, to be paid for by us."

The subtext was unmistakable: he, King Charles, was an eminently reasonable man who wanted only what was fair, and if the pope knew what was good for him, he would be reasonable too. The king was finding reasonable people everywhere he went. Viterbo surrendered to him without a murmur of complaint. Siena did the same. Montefeltro of Urbino declared that he too was the king's man, as did, finally, Giovanni Bentivoglio of Bologna. When the pope sent envoys, Charles refused to see them. He saw no need to negotiate with anyone.

Alexander sat alone in Rome, without options. When an opportunity arose to have Prospero Colonna taken into custody and imprisoned, he quickly seized it. It has been speculated that he hoped this act, by sparking an uprising in Ostia, would lead to the recovery of that crucial coastal city. Nothing of the kind happened, however, and the pope remained as isolated and without prospects as before.

At the beginning of December Ludovico Sforza was visited by envoys from Venice, sent to make certain that he understood just how dangerous the situation now was and to urge him to consider his next steps. A report on the meeting includes the Venetians' verbatim account of what Il Moro had to say. It shows him to be deeply disillusioned and resolved to contribute what he can to sending the French back to France. Charles, he says, is "young and of poor judgment; he is not advised as he ought to be . . . The king is haughty and ambitious beyond all imagining; and he has esteem for no one . . . How should we have confidence in him? He has been guilty of so many cruelties and has behaved with such insolence in all those of our territories through which he has passed, that the moment cannot come quickly enough of his leaving our territory. They are evil men, and we must do all possible not to have them in our country." He claims to be encouraging the pope to stand firm, and to be assuring Alfonso II that if he can hold out for two more months, the offensive will collapse for want of funds.

For him and for everyone involved in this fiasco, the worst still lay ahead. On December 17 Alexander was subjected to a fresh betrayal and his worst humiliation yet. It happened at the town of Nepi, not far north of Virginio Orsini's stronghold of Bracciano. As King Charles approached, he was met by Virginio's illegitimate son Carlo, sent to put the whole of the Orsini holdings, Bracciano and other fortresses included, at the disposal of the invaders. Thus the man who at Vicovaro had agreed to stand shoulder to shoulder with the pope so as to seal off the way to Rome was not only abandoning his ally but reinforcing the invader he had pledged to fight. Charles must have been delighted to make Bracciano his latest headquarters. Virginio for his part took off for Naples and—incredibly—continued employment as Alfonso II's grand constable.

Ten days later the French occupied Civitavecchia, Rome's only link to the sea since the fall of Ostia. By December 18 the whole papal court had been packed for flight, the Vatican's treasures locked away in the Castel Sant'Angelo. Almost at the hour of departure, however, Alexander decided not to go. In the days following he was joined by Ferrandino, Alfonso II's resourceful young son, who had an army camped just outside the city walls and was making ready to stand and fight. But on Christmas Day, after formally investing Ferrandino with the dukedom of Calabria as a gesture of gratitude and admiration, Alexander asked him to return to Naples forthwith and take his soldiers with him.

Ferrandino was furious. He thought that the pope too was defecting to the French. But Alexander insisted; there was no possibility of holding off Charles's huge army, now nearly within sight of the hills of Rome, and any effort to do so was likely to result in the destruction of the city.

So Ferrandino grudgingly departed. Alexander opened the doors of his prison, releasing Ascanio Sforza and Prospero Colonna among others. In company with those cardinals who had remained loyal, a cadre of trusted Spanish guards, and the Ottoman prince Cem, he settled down behind the walls of the Castel to await the arrival of the French.

If attacked, he told the departing Prospero, he intended to fight.

FLORENCE: AN ANTI-RENAISSANCE

WHAT THE PHYSICISTS TELL US ABOUT EVERY ACTION HAVING an equal and opposite reaction proved to be relevant to politics in the time of Charles VIII's invasion. It found expression in the uniquely glorious city-state of Florence, which not only expelled the family that had provided its leaders for sixty years but cast aside some of the values of the Renaissance to which it more than any other place had given birth. It did these things in the course of throwing itself at the feet of a charismatic friar whom most people today would regard as not only a fanatic but seriously unbalanced.

That friar, a brilliantly gifted preacher who if not for the extremes to which he finally went might be remembered as one of the heroic figures of his time, was the same Girolamo Savonarola who had represented the new post-Medici government of Florence in welcoming King Charles at Pisa. He was not Florentine or even Tuscan by birth but a native of Ferrara, where life under the Este dukes instilled in him something close to hatred for warlord princes and their ways. He gave early evidence of being unable to accept ordinary human frailty: in 1475, after running off to enter a monastery in Bologna, he wrote to his physician father to explain that he "could not endure the corruption of the Italian people."

After rising to become his friary's novicemaster he was sent out as an itinerant preacher, which proved to be the perfect application of his gifts. Though short and thin and rather ugly with his great beak of a nose, from the pulpit he radiated extraordinary power. His appeal grew out of the passionate conviction with which he spoke, and his use of a direct, colloquial style devoid of the polished and formal rhetoric taught at the universities of the time. His travels took him to Florence in the early 1480s, but whatever his message was at that point, the sophisticated Florentines found little of interest in it. Having fallen flat, he moved on.

When he was thirty-seven, Savonarola was heard speaking by the philosopher Giovanni Pico della Mirandola. Impressed with what the friar had to say about the need for reform of both the Church and civic life, Pico wrote to Lorenzo de' Medici reporting that he had discovered a jewel, a man so electrifying that he should be persuaded to take up residence in Florence. Lorenzo, barely forty years old but in his twentieth year as de facto head of the Florentine state, acted on his friend's suggestion. Thus it became the supreme irony of Lorenzo's life that at his initiative Florence became the home of the man destined to bring the long rule of his family to an end and undo, if temporarily, much of his life's work.

The Florence that welcomed Savonarola back in 1489 was fully formed physically and culturally, already the beautiful place that today draws millions of visitors from around the world and home to an extraordinary assortment of artists and thinkers. Though the Tuscan hills in which the city is set have few natural resources and are not nearly as fruitful as the flatlands of Lombardy to the north, over the centuries the enterprising Florentines had become pioneers in the manufacture of cloth (an industry employing fully a third of the city's population) as well as in banking and trade. Its merchants introduced Arabic numerals to the West, and the innovations of its bankers included international letters of credit and Europe's first gold currency. Florence's little coins, called florins, each contained precisely seventy-two grains of gold and became the preferred medium of exchange throughout Europe. When the Venetians began producing the ducat, they made them identical to the florin in gold content and therefore interchangeable with them. Other states followed suit in introducing their own gold coins.

Experience in commerce taught the Florentines the value of prudence, precision, and a reputation for honesty, and so simple self-interest caused them to become a prudent, precise, and honest people. In the Middle Ages, once they had fought free of the Holy Roman emperors, they established republican institutions in which all members of the various trade and professional guilds had the rights of citizens, guild membership was open to qualified newcomers, and membership in the governing group known as the *signoria* was chosen by lot every two months. Florence's feudal nobility, meanwhile, was denied citizenship and thereby neutered politically. The resulting regime was far from being a utopia; slavery was lawful, only a minority of adult males were guild members and therefore citizens, and bloodshed was all too common as family fought family for advantage or on points of honor. But as the fifteenth century advanced, Florence remained one of the few republics not to fall under the control of tyrannical warlord clans. Instead, as a kind of evolving compromise made necessary by the need for continuity and a strong executive, the city's political institutions gradually subordinated themselves first to a wily banker named Cosimo de' Medici, then to his son Piero from 1464 to 1469, and thereafter to Piero's son Lorenzo.

The wealth, worldliness, and fixation on classical culture that Savonarola encountered upon returning to Florence were all, in his eyes, symptoms of moral rot. The ethical and sexual standards of a pleasure-seeking population he saw as decadence. His call for a purifying of the whole culture, delivered in an earnest and plainspoken style that was a novelty in a time of preachers and orators schooled in classical rhetoric, began to attract large and receptive audiences. Success increased the vehemence of his pronouncements, and his condemnation of the world he saw around him grew more and more extreme. No doubt encouraged by the rivals of the Medici, he blamed Lorenzo for the paganism into which Florence, he said, had fallen. He predicted that not only Lorenzo but also Pope Innocent and Ferrante of Naples would soon be in hell. When the first two expired in 1492 and Ferrante followed in 1494, Savonarola's credibility was vastly enhanced. He prophesied also that God would soon send a great power to purge Italy and the Church, and when Charles VIII's army came down out of the alpine passes, the credulous were convinced that the friar did indeed speak for the Almighty. When Piero de' Medici's abject submission to Charles of France caused him and his family to be sent fleeing from their home, it was Savonarola who got the credit for saving Florence from destruction. His popularity rose to such frenzied heights that the entire state was his to command. The young Michelangelo heard him speak and was as impressed as everyone else. Half a century later he would say that he could still hear Savonarola's words ringing in his ears.

The friar was not a charlatan or a hypocrite and by no means an entirely bad man. He was not an enemy of classical learning to the same extent as, say, the English Puritans of a century later; those zealots would have burned the great Medici library rather than taking pains, as Savonarola did, to save it from the French. They certainly never would have approved his friendship with many of the city's leading artists. Under Savonarola's influence, Florence achieved something much closer to truly democratic government than had ever been possible under the Medici, and his reforms included such things as a cooperative lending society to protect people in need of credit from being exploited.

But perhaps it is in the nature of such men to be drawn by their own success into increasingly extreme positions. Certainly it was in Savonarola's nature. The things he would do in progressing from criticism of Rome to an attack on the legitimacy of the Church's authority, and the way in which the pope responded, provide very nearly the best insight we have into just what kind of man Alexander VI was.

13

The French Depart

The meeting of King Charles VIII and Pope Alexander VI, when it finally took place in Rome in the first week of January 1495, was an encounter in which all the important advantages appeared to lie on one side.

Charles, for all his youth and inexperience and foolishness, was ruler of one of the two mightiest kingdoms in Europe and in the preceding few months had made himself master of half of Italy as well. He commanded an army so fearsome that it had been obliged to fight no real battles as it worked its way down the peninsula; no one could see any point in attempting to stop it.

Alexander by contrast had nothing with which to oppose the invaders except whatever value was to be found in the prestige of his ancient office. He had opened Rome's gates to the French for the most practical of reasons: because in military terms he was powerless, utterly without means of defense. Aside from Ferrandino of Naples, every supposed friend with the capacity to provide help had either defected to the enemy or declared a neutrality that amounted to acceptance of French domination. His decision not to flee as Rome fell into the hands of a king committed to deposing him must have seemed an act less of courage than of madness—or perhaps of abject surrender.

And yet the results of their encounter would demonstrate, as eloquently as anything in history, that brute power is not always everything. That there are times, even in the realm of international power politics, when a strong man can bend a weak man to his will even when he has few resources to draw on beyond the force of his own personality.

Though units of the French army were inside the walls of Rome by December 27, Charles delayed his own entry until New Year's Eve, a day approved by his astrologers. Led by 2,500 nobles on horseback, the great army arrived at the Porta del Popolo at the north end of the city at three in the afternoon and continued to stream through the gates until nine that night. The people of the city looked on in wonder as, hour after hour, they were passed by foot soldiers and cavalry from Switzerland and Germany, from Brittany and Gascony, and by dozens of horse-drawn guns. At the king's side rode Cardinals Ascanio Sforza and Giuliano della Rovere, and immediately behind them came Cardinals Colonna and Savelli, members of two of the baronial clans that had abandoned the pope and entered the service of the French. Crowds that at first had gathered out of simple curiosity were soon swept up by the spectacle, shouting *"Francia! Francia!"* and *"Colonna! Colonna!"* What had to be most bitter to Pope Alexander, if he could hear it from his perch high in the Castel, they also shouted *"Vincoli! Vincoli!"* This was a salute to the man most unalterably committed to the Borgia pope's destruction, Giuliano della Rovere, cardinal of Rome's San Pietro in Vincoli Church. Hearing his companions saluted in this way must have confirmed for Charles that he had allied himself with the right faction of the ecclesiastical hierarchy.

As he commandeered for a headquarters Rome's most magnificent residence, the Palazzo San Marco that had once been the home of Pope Paul II and now belonged to his nephew Cardinal Marco Barbo, Charles released his troops to pillage the part of the city that lay across the river from the Vatican. The palaces of cardinals who had not declared their support of the invasion became prime targets, and the homes of a number of Borgias—Cesare and Lucrezia's mother included—were stripped bare. Alexander meanwhile made no effort to see the king. He sent three cardinals in his place, instructing them to point out to Charles the advantages of doing business with a sitting pope rather than trying to put a new one in his place. He empowered them to agree to any arrangement that left him secure in the Vatican and did not recognize Charles as king of Naples.

Charles at this point saw no need to concede anything and was encouraged to think so by the eight cardinals now attached to his court. With a decree for Alexander's deposition already drawn up and ready for his signature, he gave Alexander's envoys a set of demands to carry back to the Vatican. The pope, if he wanted talks, would first have to surrender the Castel Sant'Angelo, his only defensible stronghold. He would also have to hand over his prisoner Cem, the brother of Ottoman sultan Bayezid II, a valuable hostage and a potent symbol of resistance to the sultan's rule. Finally, Alexander was instructed to assign Cardinal Cesare Borgia as legate to the French court; obviously this meant surrendering Cesare as a hostage. Charles must have been taken aback when the pope, from where he was holed up in the Castel with Cem, a small group of cardinals including Cesare, and a company of troops, rejected every one of his demands out of hand. If the splendor of his entry into Europe's most fabled city had encouraged the king to think that the pope was his to command, he was being disabused.

During the standoff that ensued, Charles amused himself with visits to the principal churches and pilgrimage sites of Rome. Though his commanders set up gallows in public places as a caution to their troops to control themselves, the soldiers largely ignored them, regarding the right to pillage as one of the fringe benefits of their trade. Some of the French cannons were hauled up within range of the Castel but stood ominously quiet. The pope's show of defiance took on a farcical note when, without a shot having been fired, a section of the Castel's massive but decayed outer wall spontaneously collapsed into the Tiber, opening a hole through which the French could almost certainly have forced their way. Instead, however, king and pope began to negotiate through intermediaries and by mid-January came to an understanding. Charles got things that Alexander had no way of denying him: freedom of passage through the Papal States and possession of the papal fortresses at Civitavecchia, Terracina, Viterbo, and Spoleto. Additionally, Alexander agreed to hand over Prince Cem—but only on condition that he and not Charles would continue to receive the forty thousand ducats that the Ottoman sultan paid annually to prevent his brother from being set free. Charles wanted the prince as a trophy, evidently— one whom he could put on display when he set out to conquer Constantinople. Alexander agreed also to send Cesare to Charles as a legate-hostage. More significant were the things that Charles did *not* get: surrender of the Castel, recognition of himself as king of Naples, or a repudiation of the kingship of Alfonso II. The one bitter pill the pope had to swallow was the king's demand that all the cardinals who had supported him in his invasion be granted amnesty, including the restoration of their property and offices. In context, however, this was of limited importance. It was made easier by the fact that Alexander was throughout his life a forgiving rather than a vindictive man.

Charles now abandoned all thought of deposing Alexander or trying to curtail the powers that had come to him with the papal crown. Instead he became intent on showing himself to be the pope's faithful subject. The two met for the first time the day after the terms of their agreement were settled, and they did so in a theatrical fashion that had been carefully choreographed in advance. It was arranged that the pope would be carried in a sedan chair from the Castel to the Vatican gardens, where Charles would come upon him, supposedly deep in prayer. Charles would then fall to one knee not once but repeatedly, his third genuflection serving as Alexander's cue to take notice, raise him to his feet, and greet him as a son. Whereupon, also by prearrangement, Charles would ask that his chief minister Briçonnet be made a cardinal, Alexander would not only agree but invite Charles to come live in the Vatican, and their reconciliation would be complete.

All went according to the script, and with Charles now under his roof the pope had time to apply the full force of his charm to the cementing of their friendship. He was, as usual, successful. When even the king's appearance at consistory and direct appeal failed to win a promise of recognition, he nevertheless remained in thrall to his host. He lowered himself to the floor, kissed Alexander's foot, and said he had come to Rome "to offer obedience and homage to your Holiness, as my predecessors the kings of France had done before me." A member of his entourage, the president of the *parlement* of France, then read out a declaration that Charles acknowledged Alexander to be Christ's vicar on earth and the successor to Saint Peter. The king's reward for thus freeing Alexander from the greatest danger facing him was, by comparison, rather paltry. The only addition to the things that the pope had conceded before their meeting was another French seat in the College of Cardinals, a red hat for Charles's cousin Philip of Luxembourg.

It was enough. In the days following, Alexander and Charles were together almost constantly, touring the city on horseback and giving no evidence of disagreeing about anything. The cardinals who had ridden into Rome as part of the king's entourage, by contrast, were left to absorb the bewildering fact that they had been, if not exactly betrayed, inexplicably denied the great prizes that had seemed within their grasp. An exasperated Ascanio Sforza departed for Milan as soon as he saw that Charles and the pope had settled their differences. Giuliano della Rovere remained in Rome, but only in the hope that something might still be salvaged from the wreckage of his dreams.

When Charles departed for Naples on January 28, taking Prince Cem, Cesare Borgia, and Cardinal della Rovere with him, he had nothing to show for his weeks in Rome except the two hostages and a promise of unimpeded passage through the Papal States that his big army would have been perfectly capable of doing without. The main part of that army had been preceded out of Rome by an advance force under the command of the *condottiere* Fabrizio Colonna, whose path took him first through territories belonging to various branches of his family and then into the Abruzzi region. Now he was on Neapolitan ground, but even here he encountered no significant resistance. The local barons, with their memories of two generations of abuse at the hands of Alfonso II and his father Ferrante, could not have been less interested in fighting to defend the House of Aragon. Any who might have been so inclined were cowed not only by the size of the invasion force but by fast-spreading reports of how, throughout their long advance, King Charles's troops had shown themselves prepared to employ mass murder wherever they met with even the threat of opposition.

The town of L'Aquila, upon learning of the approach of Fabrizio Colonna, opened its gates and hoisted a French flag. Sulmona did the same, and then Popoli. Soon the whole of Il Regno was in turmoil, with the lords of town after town declaring themselves faithful to the French crown. King Alfonso, an experienced soldier and the one man to whom every Neapolitan soldier looked for leadership, went almost catatonic with fear. A legend would arise to the effect that he was haunted at night by visions of the countless people he had destroyed in the course of his ignoble career and sank into a slough of remorse. He roused himself enough not to rally his troops but to have a flotilla of galleys loaded with as many of his treasures as could be crammed aboard, at which point he abdicated in favor of his son Ferrandino and sailed away to Sicily, a safe haven securely in the hands of Spain. His departure came five days before Charles so much as left Rome. The twenty-five-year-old Ferrandino, who gave promise of being a better man and king than his father or grandfather, threw himself into organizing a defense. At every step he found his efforts impeded by the hatred of his subjects for the dynasty he now headed.

Charles, on his second night out of Rome, halted at the town of Velletri in the Alban Hills. Upon awaking the next morning, he and his entourage discovered that Cesare was nowhere to be found. They eventually learned that a local nobleman had shown him a secret passageway out of the *rocca* and that he had slipped away in the middle of the night disguised as a stableboy. The escape, an early expression of Cesare's inability to be submissive to anyone, violated the terms of the pope's agreement with the king. Horsemen carried complaints back to Alexander, who responded with profuse apologies and assurances that he was no less surprised than Charles and had no idea where Cesare might be. (In fact he had gone to Spoleto and would quietly remain there for almost two months.) King Charles's men fell greedily upon the wagons containing the baggage that Cesare had brought with him from Rome. They discovered to their disgust that they had been tricked yet again: under their rich coverings the wagons were heaped with rubbish.

The king was still at Velletri when envoys of Spain rode into his encampment and demanded an audience. Ferdinand by this point was deeply uneasy about the dispatches he was receiving from Italy and had run out of patience. He could never have accepted a restoration of French rule in Naples and had been so taken aback at the ease with which Charles VIII was bringing all Italy to its knees that he was now transferring troops from Spain to Sicily with instructions to make ready for action on the mainland. What his ambassadors delivered at Velletri was a stern warning for Charles: his campaign was in violation of the Treaty of Barcelona, which reserved to Spain the right to protect the Papal States. They demanded that the port of Ostia be restored to Alexander, that Cesare Borgia be released (not knowing that the young cardinal had seen to that himself), and that the advance on Naples be brought to an immediate halt. When Charles made it clear that he took none of this seriously, his visitors tore up their copy of the Barcelona pact and threw it at his feet. The chronicles tell us that "high words" were exchanged before their departure.

And so Charles resumed his southward journey, his army continuing to meet with no serious resistance but spreading devastation everywhere it went. He allowed the Colonna to use the troops for which he was paying to lay waste to the fortresses, homes, and orchards of their old enemies the Conti. His mercenaries continued to take looting and rapine as their right. When the *rocca* at San Giovanni was annoyingly slow to submit, its garrison of almost nine hundred men was put to the sword, the town burned to the ground. The new King Ferrandino, having had no time for a coronation, was attempting to form a line of defense at Capua when reports of a revolt in his capital obliged him to gallop off to the south. As soon as he was out of sight, Capua surrendered to the invaders, and Gaeta did the same three days later. Ferrandino returned on February 21. Finding Capua in enemy hands, and no support anywhere, he accepted the hopelessness of the situation and took ship for the island of Ischia in the Bay of Naples. Soon thereafter he was with his father in Sicily, having taken his half-sister Sancia and her husband Jofrè Borgia with him. Within twenty-four hours of his flight Charles VIII passed in triumph through the gates of Naples, where he was welcomed by cheering crowds. They hailed him for delivering the city from decades of tyranny and terror. And his arrival was, in its way, an extraordinary achievement. He had taken possession of the largest state in Italy, long one of the richest and most powerful in all Europe, without having to fight a single battle worthy of the name, almost without having to fire a round from one of his great brass guns. Italy had collapsed at his feet like a house of cards.

Cem, who had ridden into Naples just behind the king, a living symbol of the crusade against his brother that supposedly lay just ahead, was found dead in his bed three days later. Years later, when the campaign to demolish the reputation of the Borgias was fully under way and no rumor was too outlandish to be set down in print, it would be alleged that the prince, who at the time of his death had been a pampered prisoner for some thirteen years, must have been poisoned. And that the poisoner could of course have been none other than

Alexander VI—who else? If reminded that Cem had died approximately one month after the pope handed him over to the French, the accusers would respond that obviously the Borgias possessed the secret of some delayed-action poison, some concoction capable of suddenly felling its victims weeks after being ingested.

In fact it is not at all unlikely that Cem died of natural causes, having lived a life of relentless self-indulgence throughout his captivity. His death, far from benefiting the pope, deprived the pope not only of an enormous annual stipend but of a powerful diplomatic weapon, one that even in French hands could have been used to threaten the Ottoman sultan and keep his aggressions in check. The only European prince who could possibly have wanted that death was the king who had taken Cem to Naples and in whose custody the prince had spent his last weeks. Cem was to have been the figurehead behind which Charles would lead his assault on the Turks—assuming that Charles still wanted to push on to Jerusalem.

That was not an entirely safe assumption. Cem's corpse was barely cold before Charles announced that the crusade would have to be called off. The pope's response to this change of plans was interesting: he authorized Ferdinand of Spain to impose a special tax on church properties within his domains, in order to build ships to be used against the Turks. This was probably an oblique rebuke to Charles VIII for abandoning the great purpose that supposedly had taken him to Naples. It may also have been a way of helping Ferdinand to muster the resources needed for war with France.

Over the next three months Charles VIII earned the contempt in which he has ever since been held. Having been received as a hero by the people and nobility of Naples, he proceeded in an impressively short time to alienate virtually all of his new subjects. Having brought Italy to its knees, he then conducted himself so atrociously as to provoke the states he had so easily subdued to take up arms. He surrendered to the seductions of a licentious Neapolitan capital and a glorious Neapolitan spring, wallowing in the pleasures of the flesh while his troops preyed on a helpless population and the hundreds of French nobles in his entourage treated themselves to every office, title, and estate they could find an excuse to claim. As outrage followed outrage, Naples's joy at the fall of the House of Aragon turned first to annoyance and then into smoldering rage. In due course it burst into flame as the Neapolitans became determined to rid themselves of the intruders.

Charles, blissfully distracted, remained oblivious. Ferdinand of Spain meanwhile had ambassadors at all the major capitals, and under his instructions they encouraged the various princes to imagine the consequences of a continued French presence in Italy and to understand that such a fate was not inevitable. Milan was receptive, Ludovico Sforza needing no one to tell him that he had blundered, and the Venetians were aware by now that what had happened to Naples could happen to them as well. Even in faraway England, King Henry VII was prepared to contribute to keeping France from growing stronger than it already was, and Maximilian of Hapsburg had not only the Holy Roman Empire to protect from France but a deep personal grudge dating back to the time when Charles had simultaneously jilted his daughter and stolen his fiancée, depriving him of the great duchy of Brittany. As for the pope, his position could not have been clearer; he was the only leader in Italy neither to have thrown himself at Charles's feet nor to have fled at the approach of his army. When in March a congress was convened in Venice, all of the above attended or sent representatives. In short order they formed what they named their Holy League. Its members pledged to remain allied for twenty-five years—not one of them could have thought that possible—and to contribute thousands of troops to the formation of an army the sole purpose of which would be to drive the French back to France.

Charles, convinced by his successes that he was invincible, was slow to awaken to what was happening. His only political interest at this point was the old one of getting the pope to invest him with his new crown. When a new round of appeals proved as futile as the ones he had made personally while in Rome, and when the things he offered in return for investiture grew more and more lavish but still produced no response, the realization finally dawned that his position was not as solid as he had supposed. His initial response was not, however, either to reinforce that position or to prepare for an orderly withdrawal. Instead he staged an elaborate ceremony at the Naples cathedral at which, to the acclaim of nobody except his own hangers-on, he crowned himself as monarch of Il Regno and "Emperor of the East." Even he was beginning to have some sense of the growing dangers of his situation,

however, and to see the absurdity of his self-coronation. He sent ambassadors to Rome with an offer he hoped would be impossible to refuse.
In return for cooperating, Alexander would receive an annual tribute
of fifty thousand ducats, repayment of the hundred thousand ducats
that Naples had owed to the Vatican since the time of Ferrante and Alfonso II, and the promise of a French-led crusade against the Turks.
Alexander's refusal made it impossible to doubt that, with all the Italian
states now rallying against him, Charles was no longer safe so far from
home. Preparations began, in haste, for an escape.

Charles departed Naples on May 20, taking with him half of what
remained of his army after six months of casualties, desertions, and
disease. With him went also the perfect symbol of just what kind of
expedition his foray into Italy had been: a vast procession of mules—
estimates of their number run as high as ten thousand—each laden
with treasure stripped from all the places through which the French
and their mercenaries had passed. In Rome, meanwhile, an annoyed
Alexander was calling the attention of the Holy League to the failure of
every member state except Venice to provide the troops that all had
pledged. Only two of the states of central and northern Italy had no
reason to fear what might happen when Charles returned from Naples.
One was Ferrara, whose Duke Ercole hated Venice far too much to
enter any league to which it belonged. The other was Florence, now
more than ever dominated by Friar Savonarola, who in spite of abun-
dant evidence to the contrary continued to insist that the king of France
was God's own agent in Italy.

The whole peninsula was in turmoil as the French retraced the path
they had taken the previous year. In Rome, the question of whether the
pope and his court should stay or go was debated ad nauseam. The consensus of the cardinals was that all of them should stay in place, and this
opinion was reinforced when Charles wrote suggesting a meeting and
promising to keep his troops under better control this time. Alexander,
however, thought it a mistake to receive the king again, seeing no way
to do so without arousing suspicion among the other members of the
Holy League. He knew that the immense task of keeping the French
troops fed would prevent Charles from halting them at Rome for more
than a few days, so that eluding him would pose no great challenge.
And so when Charles arrived on June 1, he was, in keeping with Alex-

ander's instructions, received with full honors and invited to take up residence in the Vatican once again. But the pope himself was not on hand; he had left for Orvieto. When Charles sent horsemen racing to bring him back, they arrived at Orvieto only to learn that Alexander had moved on again, this time to Perugia, well out of the way of the road back to France. Charles was as good as his word where the conduct of his troops was concerned; the now-infamous Swiss were not allowed near the city walls, and the others were confined to their encampments. And as the pope had foreseen, Charles moved out again less than forty-eight hours after his arrival. He knew that Venetian and Milanese troops were coming together in anticipation of a showdown, and that he would be lucky to get home without a fight.

And so on they went, with speed now the priority and Charles making little effort to maintain the good order that he had imposed upon his troops while in Rome. French marauders all but wiped the town of Toscanella off the map. The Swiss did much the same to Pontremoli. Avoiding Florence and its tiresomely demanding republican government, Charles chose a route that took him first through Siena and then to Pisa, where he was obliged to pause long enough to permit a delegation of the city's womenfolk, all weeping theatrically, to beg him to save them from falling back under Florentine control. He said just enough to give them hope that their appeals would not go unheeded, thereby contradicting his most recent assurances to Florence, and departed with as much haste as decorum allowed. Something worse than wailing ladies was awaiting him at Poggibonsi: the gallingly fearless and obsessed Savonarola, who had traveled from Florence so as not to miss the opportunity to berate Charles for failing to fulfill the mission on which God had sent him from France. Here we see Savonarola at the point when he is beginning to be tinged with madness, proclaiming himself the instrument through which God gives the rest of the human race its marching orders. The king's divine assignment, Savonarola declared, had been not to make himself king of Naples, not to launch a crusade, but to cleanse Italy, the Church, and Rome. "You have incurred the wrath of God," he told Charles, "by neglecting that work of reforming the Church which, by my mouth, he had charged you to undertake, and to which he had called you by so many unmistakable signs. This time you will escape from the danger which threatens you; but if you again disregard the command which he now, through me his unworthy slave, reiterates, and still refuse to take up the work which he commits to you, I warn you that he will punish you with far more terrible misfortunes, and will choose another man in your place."

This is the Savonarola who, back home in Florence, will soon be condemning even the most innocuous forms of petty gambling, not only immodest but costly dress, even racing. Who will be organizing the boys of Florence into vigilante gangs that bring to mind the Red Guards of Mao Zedong's Cultural Revolution, sending them out to disrupt card games, confiscate musical instruments and diversions as innocent as magnifying glasses, and either attack or report whatever forbidden amusement they find. In time he will be advocating the death penalty for anyone who supports tyranny—which means anyone foolish enough to speak favorably of the Medici—and the stoning and burying alive of anyone found guilty of sodomy (for which the penalty had previously been a fine of fifty ducats). The carnival preceding Lent will be cleansed of drinking and revelry, becoming instead an occasion for Savonarola's famous Bonfires of the Vanities—his public burning of great heaps of clothing, books, jewelry, games, and works of art deemed unacceptable. A visiting Venetian merchant will offer 22,000 ducats for the treasures laid on one of Savonarola's pyres and will be scornfully refused.

A noose, meanwhile, was tightening around King Charles's frail neck. One after another the fortresses that had welcomed him on his way south locked their gates against his return, and he could spare neither the time nor the manpower to break down their defenses. The great worry was the high passes through the Apennine Mountains—the danger that his army would not get through them before being set upon by Holy League forces assembling on the Lombard Plain. Once clear of the passes, Charles would be able to make a run for Asti, where by merging his army with that of his cousin Louis of Orléans he would once again be strong enough to repel any attackers. Inexplicably, the league's commander in chief, Francesco Gonzaga of Mantua, held back until the French had put the passes behind them and were able to regroup in open country. Then, when Gonzaga finally attacked, he did so across the River Taro, throwing away all the advantages of having the larger, fresher army.

The ensuing battle of Fornovo was the bloodiest to have taken place on Italian soil in two and a half centuries, but it lasted only a single hour: an initial clash that after only fifteen minutes left the French in command of the field, followed by forty-five minutes during which the victors ran down and butchered all the fleeing Italians they could catch. When it was over, as many as 3,500 Italian troops lay dead, against perhaps two hundred French. Both sides, however, would claim victory. The Italians would point to their capture of Charles's thousands of mule-loads of booty, including the souvenir that King Charles was said to treasure most: an album of pictures of many of the ladies whose intimate favors he had enjoyed before, during, and after his brief reign in Naples. In the end Charles would take back with him to France little more than his own skin, still luckily intact.

The people of Naples, impressed with the courage of their exiled young king and realizing that he could not possibly be worse than Charles of France, welcomed Ferrandino's return with no less approval than they had showered on his enemies four months earlier. The speed of his return was made possible by support from the Holy League, the seasoned troops that Ferdinand of Spain was sending over from Sicily, and even by Fabrizio and Prospero Colonna, who had signed a *condotta* offered by Ferrandino almost immediately after their discharge by the French. The army of occupation that Charles had left behind under the command of the count of Montpensier, meanwhile, was broken up to garrison so many small and scattered strongholds that its doom was all but inevitable.

One final drama remained to be played out. Fittingly, it involved yet another betrayal—another pair of betrayals, to be precise. First, soon after reaching the safety of Asti, Charles worked out a deal by which, in return for a substantial payment in gold, he abandoned Pisa to the Florentines. Next he moved on to Turin, where a surprising pair of guests came to call. These were Ludovico il Moro, his onetime host and ally and currently his enemy, and Ludovico's wife Beatrice d'Este. The result, hastily arrived at, was the Peace of Vercelli. By its terms Charles restored the captured city of Novara to Milan, an essentially trivial concession because the French position there was untenable, and received in return an impressive number of good things. Ludovico abandoned Milan's longstanding claim to Genoa, thereby providing the French with a solid foothold on Italy's northwest coast. He also agreed that Louis of Orléans could keep Asti and pledged to support France in any conflict with Venice. What was most shocking, he promised to assist Charles in any future invasion of Italy.

This separate peace reduced the Holy League to the shambles it had always been fated to become. Soon the Italians were at one another's throats as before, with Florence, for example, sending out troops to attack not only Pisa but Siena as well. The concessions made by Il Moro and his strong-willed young duchess repaired Charles's fortunes to such an extent that, his army replenished with freshly bought Swiss mercenaries and his fleet safe at Genoa, he might have found it possible to remain south of the Alps and begin rebuilding his position there. But he had had enough, at least for the time being. Before the end of the year he was back in France, and the first chapter in the long and tragic story that would come to be known as the Italian Wars had reached its ambiguous end.

It is too easy to heap scorn on Ludovico and Beatrice Sforza for so eagerly coming to terms with a weakened and retreating French king. They could have done otherwise only by trusting that if Charles invaded again, he would not make an unfaithful and demonstrably unfriendly Milan his first target. And that, in the event of such an invasion, their neighbors would come to their aid. They would have had to be deeply foolish to believe that the Venetians would do any such thing, rather than satisfying their hunger for the great breadbasket that was Lombardy. Nor was it reasonable to expect that Ferrandino of Naples, remembering how the Sforzas had abandoned his father, would ever risk anything for the benefit of Milan. With the single exception of the pope, no prince in all Italy had shown himself inclined to risk anything, or for that matter forgo any possible gains, for the sake of a league holy or otherwise.

Charles VIII's great adventure had changed nothing and everything. Naples remained in possession of the House of Aragon and under the protection of Spain. Florence remained a client of France. Alexander had not been deposed, and a council of the Church had not been convened. But in the long run other things would prove to be more important. France had discovered Italy—had discovered the Renaissance—and would never be the same. Its nobles had seen what a treasure house

Italy was and knew now how absurdly incapable it was of defending it-self.

The Italians, who should have learned that their survival depended on cooperation, instead decided that it was folly to trust one another. Alfonso II, a feared military commander, had run away without a fight. Venice had remained on the sidelines until it was safe to do otherwise and had joined the Holy League largely in the hope of poaching the land of its neighbors. The Orsini had changed sides, the Colonna had changed sides, and Florence and Milan had changed sides twice.

One state only had taken a stand early and stood firm even as its situation came to seem hopeless. That state was Rome, the steadiness of which was entirely the work of Alexander VI.

Having survived the first great crisis of his reign, Alexander now found himself able to turn his attention to other matters. That not all such matters would be of his choosing became clear in December, when another of the Tiber's periodic floods transformed much of the city into a filthy lake, leaving hundreds dead and whole districts in ruins. It was a fitting conclusion to a gruesomely eventful year.

THE PATERNITY QUESTION: AN "APOLOGY"

FOR FIVE HUNDRED YEARS IT HAS BEEN PRETTY MUCH UNIVERsally understood—*accepted* is the better word—that Cesare Borgia and his siblings were Alexander VI's children. The story of how the pope fathered these and other offspring during his decades as vice-chancellor of the Roman Catholic Church, schooling them to become moral monsters, has always been the cornerstone of the Borgia legend. More than half a century has passed since the last time anyone questioned it in print, only to be, like those few who had done the same thing earlier, almost completely ignored before being forgotten. It is nonetheless the opinion of the author of the present work, after examination of all the source materials of which he has knowledge:

That although it long ago became impossible to establish the truth beyond possibility of doubt, it appears that Cesare and his siblings were not—indeed almost could not have been—the children of Rodrigo Borgia.

That the familiar story of how over a period of some ten years the vice-chancellor of the Roman Catholic Church maintained an intimate relationship with a shadowy mistress named Vannozza, becoming the proud father of a large family while nobody took notice in even the most gossipy chronicles and diplomatic reports of the time, becomes all but incredible when evidence to the contrary is given its proper weight.

That though there was a Vannozza, and though she was the mother of as many as four Borgia sons and three Borgia daughters (see page 424 for more on her), she was not Rodrigo's mistress but the wife and then the widow of one Guillen Ramón Lanzol y de Borja, eldest son of Rodrigo's sister Juana.

That Vannozza and her children—most and probably all of whom were conceived and born in Spain while Rodrigo was in Italy—were taken into Cardinal Rodrigo's care after Guillen Ramón's death around 1481, and that in the years following all were brought to Rome except the eldest son, Pedro Luis (quite possibly so named in memory of Cardinal Rodrigo's deceased brother), who remained in Spain to pursue a career at the royal court.

And that, although much about Rodrigo's personal life is unknown, it is unproven that at any point either before or after his election as pope he had a mistress, fathered a child, or was involved in even a brief sexual relationship with anyone male or female.

This is not to say that no such thing ever happened, or that it was improbable considering the times, or that our understanding of Rodrigo would be radically altered if we learned that several such things had happened. It is simply to point out that, in connection with this as with so many other questions, where the Borgias are concerned too many things have always been assumed to be true for which satisfactory evidence does not exist. That having been said, it becomes necessary to acknowledge that the opinions expressed above, being so far at variance with what is generally believed of the Borgias, obviously require defense and explanation. The defense begins with the contents of a deeply obscure work with the intriguing title *Material for a History of Pope Alexander VI, His Relatives and His Times,* by a long-forgotten researcher named Peter De Roo.

Anyone who does a good deal of reading in the history of the Borgias is sure to notice, sooner or later, scattered references to De Roo. Such references are uncommon and invariably brief and oblique; where the existence of *Material* is noted, it is almost always *only* noted, without comment. A rare exception is Michael Mallett, who includes in the bibliography of his 1969 book *The Borgias* two references to De Roo, describing his work first as "a vast collection of Vatican documents," then, in a different context, as a "vast apologetic work in which useful material is often almost undetectable under the coat of whitewash."

Mallett's repetition of "vast" is appropriate: at five volumes, three of them well over five hundred pages long, *Material* is a physically substantial achievement, without parallel in the literature of the Borgias. It seems unlikely that De Roo himself would have objected to the use of the word *apologetic,* defined in the traditional sense of a defense of a position and not as an offering of apologies. He says forthrightly that his researches into Alexander's life and career, motivated in the beginning by curiosity about whether there was anything to be said in defense of a man assumed to be "totally depraved," ultimately persuaded him that his subject had in fact been "a man of good moral character and an excellent pope." That is his thesis, and he makes no secret of it.

Mallett is misleading, however, in calling *Material* a collection of Vatican documents—so wrong as to make one wonder if he examined it closely. The hundreds of documents that make *Material* so voluminous were found in archives across Europe, from Spain to Vienna, as well as in a number of Italian depositories. As for the comment about whitewash, it seems a dubious way of characterizing a work in which the author lays out what Mallett himself describes as "useful material" with exhaustive completeness, offering his own understanding of what that material means but also going to sometimes tiresome lengths to provide the reader with every possible means of drawing his own conclusions.

De Roo's conclusions are at odds with one aspect after another of the established Borgia myth. This is most strikingly true with respect to the personal life of Alexander VI, starting with the assumption that he was the father of Cesare and Lucrezia plus five or six or nine or whatever number of additional offspring. An answer to the question of why De Roo published only "material for" a life of Alexander, rather than writing that life himself, is suggested by what little is known of his own story. He was born in 1839, which means that he was eighty-five when *Material* was published in Belgium and the United States in 1924. He writes of spending some thirty years, off and on, gathering his documents. Perhaps he waited too long to begin a biography, finding himself at last unable to do more than organize what he had collected, add his commentary, and send it all off to be printed. In any case he was dead less than two years after publishing the fruit of his labors.

The first volume, at more than six hundred pages, amounts to a radical revision of Pope Alexander's family tree. Borgia genealogy has always been a challenge, and a playground for mischief-makers. Gaps in the surviving records (to be expected in the provincial Spain of more than five centuries ago), the repeated use of the same given names generation after generation, the adoption of the Borgia patronym by the descendants of at least one of Alexander's sisters, and the speculations and intended and unintended distortions of generations of writers combine to make it impossible to know whose children even some fairly prominent Borgias were and how they are related to one another. The author knows of no other researcher who has gone nearly as deeply into these mysteries as Peter De Roo or has uncovered nearly as much original material. His evidence, and the arguments based on that evidence, are not in every case as complete or conclusive as one would wish; this is for example true with respect to exactly where and when the members of Cesare and Lucrezia's generation were born. In the end it becomes necessary, therefore, to consider the case of the Borgias not quite closed. Nevertheless, and in the absence of any real evidence at all for many key aspects of the accepted Borgia myth, the content of *Material* provides a substantial basis upon which to assert that the following points are probably, and in some cases certainly, true.

1) The four young Borgias who came to prominence in Rome with Cardinal Rodrigo's election as pope—Cesare, Juan, Lucrezia, and Jofrè—were what genealogists called "siblings german." That is, all four had the same father and mother; their parents also had at least three other, older children. The eldest was the aforementioned Pedro Luis Lanzol y de Borja, who inherited considerable wealth upon his father's early death, became the first duke of Gandía, and died years before Rodrigo was elected pope. After him came two daughters named Isabella and Girolama or Geronima. *Which means that the threshold for proving all seven to have been Alexander's children is not as high as one might expect. If he can be shown to have fathered just one, he must have been the father of all.*

2) At least five of the children in question, and probably all seven, were born in Spain (see item 3 for additional matter related to this question). Though this is one of the areas in which more documentation is needed, about Pedro Luis there can be no doubt: he is not known ever to have been outside Spain. Nor is there any record of Cesare being in Italy before 1488, when his name appears in the dedication of a book titled *Syllabeca* by one Paolo Pompilio. At the end of the Italian part of his career, in an exchange with the viceroy of Naples, he stated explicitly that he was Spanish by birth and his siblings were also. As for Juan (or Giovanni the second duke of Gandía), even the historian Gregorovius, who somehow never doubted Alexander's paternity, says that he was born in Spain, and the Vatican master of ceremonies, Johann Burchard, goes further and describes him as a native of Valencia. About the youngest two, Lucrezia and Jofrè, there is no comparably credible information. Though Lucrezia is often said to have been born in Spoleto in Italy,

the supporting documentation has (some might say conveniently) disappeared. Gregorovius, interestingly, says he found her date of birth (April 18, 1480) in a *Valencian* document. But as we have seen, the young Rodrigo Borgia left Spain for Rome no later than 1455 (at least five years before Pedro Luis's birth) and returned only once, on the diplomatic mission that kept him there from June 1472 to September 1473. Thus he was too late to have impregnated the mother of Isabella and Girolama, and too soon to be responsible for Cesare or Juan. *Which means that Rodrigo Borgia cannot be the father of the seven young Borgias—unless, of course, their mother was shuttling back and forth between Spain and Italy with a frequency all but inconceivable in the fifteenth century.*

3) The father of the seven, Cardinal Rodrigo's nephew Guillen Ramón Lanzol y de Borja, was the firstborn of the numerous children of Rodrigo's eldest sister Juana de Borja and her husband Pedro Guillen Lanzol, of noble rank as lord of Villalona in Valencia, a wealthy landowner and figure of some distinction (serving as, among other things, Pope Pius II's envoy to the kings of Aragon and Castile). Guillen Ramón does not appear in the most commonly used Borgia genealogies, but De Roo claimed to have found him in Jacob Wilhelm Imhof's exhaustive *Genealogie XX illustrium familiarum in Hispania* of 1712. The author of the present work was able to confirm this claim by inspecting Imhof's great sprawling volume in the rare books archive of Oxford University's All Souls College. Guillen Ramón's wife was, according to De Roo, named Violanta—diminutive Vanotia or Vannozza. He describes her as the daughter of Gerard lord of Castelvert and his wife Damiata del Milà, daughter of Alonso Borgia's sister Catalina and her husband Juan del Milà. *Which means that, although Alexander VI was not the father of the young Borgias, he had a double connection to them by blood. As the grandchildren of his sister Juana, they were his grand-nephews and -nieces. As the great-grandchildren of his aunt Catalina, they were also his first cousins twice removed.*

4) When Guillen Ramón Lanzol died, in or very shortly before 1481, Vannozza was pregnant with their last child, Jofrè. Pedro Luis, as eldest son and heir, remained in Spain, where he was achieving precocious success as a courtier and soldier. By the end of that decade, at some date or dates uncertain, separately or together, Vannozza and the younger

children made their way to Rome and came under the patronage of Cardinal Rodrigo. This was a reprise of what had happened thirty years before, when Rodrigo and his brother Pedro Luis and their cousin Luis Juan del Milà had been brought to Rome by *their* Borgia uncle. Vannozza never lived in Cardinal Rodrigo's palace or the Vatican but before, during, and after Alexander VI's reign maintained her own establishment.

5) Various documents supposedly establishing Rodrigo's paternity are, to put it gently, suspect. A typical example is a supposed papal bull bearing the date October 1, 1480, by which Pope Sixtus IV legitimatizes a child whose name is given both as Cesare de Boria and Cesare de Borja and who is described as the son of a cardinal and a married woman, neither of them identified by name. The use of the Spanish form of the family name rather than the Italian Borgia, along with other usages standard in Spanish but not in Vatican documents, brings the bull's authenticity into question. More damningly, no record of any such bull is to be found in the Curial registry in Rome, into which copies of all official documents were entered before being dispatched. De Roo notes that Cesare would have been about five years old in October 1480 and that as a second son he was in line to inherit nothing and stood in no need of being legitimatized even if a bastard. It is also worth noting that it was established Vatican practice, in documents granting benefices to a person previously legitimatized, to include brief mention of that fact. There exist a number of documents in which Popes Paul II, Sixtus IV, and Innocent VIII granted offices and revenues to the boy Cesare, and in none of them is there any such mention.

De Roo devotes eighty-three pages of his first volume to a close examination of this document and others of its kind, finding in them so many anomalies (incorrect facts, deviations from standard practice, absence of corroboration in the appropriate registers) as to make it seem probable that they are what he calls them: the "fabrication of some criminal ignorant of the habits of the Roman Curia." He notes, correctly, that the forging of papal documents was widespread for many centuries and was not always so clumsily done.

6) Nothing should be deduced, though much often has been, from those many instances in which Alexander VI refers to Vannozza's children as sons or daughters—when, for example, he opens a letter to Lu-

crezia by saluting her as "our beloved daughter." He addressed Queen Isabella of Spain in exactly the same way, and her husband Ferdinand along with Emperor Maximilian as "beloved son," while Louis XII was his "most beloved son." He addressed almost everyone with whom he had correspondence in the same terms, which were standard usage in the personal and official communications of popes (or *papas*), and was himself repeatedly referred to as a "beloved son" in documents of the popes he served. The fact that he commonly refers to Lucrezia as "our daughter *in Christ*" seems little less than an acknowledgment that he is expressing himself figuratively and expects to be understood accordingly. Similarly, when in the 1480s he provided Lucrezia's elder sister Girolama with a dowry of four thousand ducats, the instrument of conveyance described the girl as "the issue of his family and house" and himself as acting as the representative of her brothers "for the honor of this house." The instances in which the young Borgias are referred to as sons and daughters are vastly outnumbered by those in which Alexander's friends and enemies as well as neutral observers write of them as the pontiff's nephews and nieces. Typical are a 1493 ambassador's letter to the marchioness of Mantua in which Cesare is called *nepote de uno fratello di N. Signore* (nephew of a brother of Our Lord), a letter of 1494 in which the duke of Ferrara's agent in Rome writes of Jofrè Borgia as a "nephew son" of the pope, two letters in which the bishop of Modena calls Lucrezia Alexander's "niece," a document in which Ferrante of Naples calls his granddaughter Sancia *illegitimi* but says nothing of the kind about her intended husband Jofrè, and an October 1500 Venetian proclamation that admitted Cesare to the republic's nobility and described him as *nepote di papa Alessandro VI*. Peter Martyr d'Anghiera, an Italian-born historian of Spain, wrote that Cesare was rumored to be Alexander's son—such gossip would have been inevitable—but always denied it. In 1573, long after there could have been any reason for concealment, a grandson of Cesare's referred to Pope Alexander as Cesare's *oncle* in a lawsuit seeking restoration of property confiscated by the French crown.

The above could be expanded into a book of its own and probably should be, but even in severely abbreviated form it demonstrates the legitimacy—the necessity—of questioning what is taken for granted about how Alexander VI was related to Cesare and his siblings. A few other points seem so compelling that not to mention them in this context would be almost irresponsible:

Of fifteenth-century writers whose work has survived, only the credulous and notoriously unreliable scandalmonger Stefano Infessura, keeper of a famous diary and implacable enemy not only of popes but of the institution of the papacy, so much as suggested *during Alexander's lifetime* that he had an intimate relationship with the lady Vannozza— who, by the way, is not known ever to have set foot inside the Vatican. Not even the supporters of Charles VIII's invasion of 1494, not even the bitterly vengeful Cardinal Giuliano della Rovere, not even Savonarola at his most unrestrained, ever accused Alexander of sexual immorality.

It is not true that Cardinal Rodrigo Borgia, either to aggrandize an eldest son or for any other reason, bought the dukedom of Gandía for Pedro Luis Borgia. As the eldest son of Guillen Ramón Lanzol y de Borja, Pedro Luis at the time of his father's death inherited great wealth including the Gandía properties that later became the nucleus of his duchy. Far from being financially dependent on his kinsman Rodrigo, Pedro Luis actually lent the cardinal a substantial sum in 1483.

A Spanish royal brief of the early 1480s, one confirming the noble status of the boy Juan de Borja (later Giovanni Borgia), refers to his "father the late illustrious [name deleted]." This wording is more laden with significance than is at first apparent. It not only states explicitly that Juan's father (and Cesare's and Lucrezia's et cetera) is deceased (*quondam*), which Rodrigo Borgia was many years from being when the brief was issued, but also sheds light on who his father was and was not. The word "illustrious" indicates that the father had been noble *and a layman*; had he been a cardinal, the appropriate modifier would have been "most reverend." The deletion of the name—a sad fact for scholars—suggests tampering for purposes of concealment, possibly for the same reason that papal bulls may have been forged.

Orestes Ferrara, in a biography of Alexander VI that first appeared in English in 1942, offers a persuasive hypothesis as to why so many writers have been misled into believing that Alexander VI's true family name was not Borgia but Lanzol. As noted in the foregoing pages, the future Alexander VI was Rodrigo de Borja y de Borja from birth, both of his parents having the same surname. The sons of his sister Juana and her husband Pedro Guillen Lanzol, on the other hand, began life under the name Lanzol y de Borja, and it was *their* children and grandchildren (including Cesare and his siblings) who introduced that name to Rome before allowing the less prestigious (and utterly unknown in Rome) Lanzol to fall away. They were so numerous, and several became so prominent, that it may have come to be assumed, in Rome, that all Borgias were actually Lanzols.

Questions abound, and at this late date many of them must be considered unanswerable. Be that as it may, so many things weigh against Rodrigo/Alexander's being the father of Vannozza's children that it becomes inexcusable to treat his paternity as settled fact.

One final question: why have De Roo's volumes, which probe the character, career, and family connections of Alexander VI in far greater depth than any other works before or since, had so little impact in the nine decades since their publication? Have later biographers examined them only to conclude that they are not only wrong but unworthy of rebuttal, even of acknowledgment? Or has he simply been ignored?

Something suggestive of an answer lay untouched, deep in the recesses of Oxford's Bodleian Library, until 2010. That was the year in which the author of the present work first requested access to the Bodleian's single copy of *Material*. And began at the beginning, with volume one, the six hundred pages dealing with the Borgia family tree and little else. And found that the pages were uncut—meaning that no one could possibly have ever read them. Other copies exist, of course. The one held by the British Library in London, when examined by the author of the present work, proved to be literally in tatters, the binding having dried and disintegrated, clumps of loose pages held together with strips of knotted ribbon. Is their condition the result of heavy use by researchers over the generations? Or does it indicate so little demand that no one has seen a need to have them rebound? The total absence of detailed attention to De Roo in any work since *Material* itself was published makes the second possibility seem the more plausible of the two.

14

A Shattering Loss

Charles VIII's withdrawal to France did not bring peace to Italy. It did not even mark the end of the French invasion. The thousands of troops that the king left behind were a violation of Neapolitan sovereignty and a threat to Il Regno's neighbors.

The Italians in attendance at Charles's court, meanwhile, reported that he was making no secret of his intention to invade again in the not very distant future. He was even said to be talking openly, now that he was no longer exposed to the force of Alexander VI's personality, of placing Cardinal della Rovere on the papal throne.

Though the Holy League had not disintegrated in the aftermath of Ludovico il Moro's defection, Charles's return to France had deprived it of its reason for existing; few of the Italian powers saw further need for cooperation. Ferrandino of Naples was an exception. With the French holding a number of his strongholds, and the weakness of his once-great kingdom having been revealed to the world, he was in desperate need of friends. Only Venice was both able and willing to help, however, and it did so only after Ferrandino ceded it the seaports of Brindisi, Trani, Gallipoli, and Otranto. Alexander VI was another exception. In all of Italy he was the sole champion of unity and of unqualified opposition to incursions by outside powers. He like Ferrandino looked first to Venice for support, and he too found the Venetians focused on their own affairs. When he looked to Florence, he saw cause for alarm. Savonarola and the city's republican government remained openly loyal to France, an inducement to Charles to return. Finding a way to sever that connection became one of the fundamentals of papal policy.

Despite all the turmoil and uncertainty, Alexander had reason to feel confident. He had won much respect, both in Rome and elsewhere, for the adroitness and persistence of his opposition to Charles VIII. And he was far from isolated; Milan and Venice were with him in supporting Pisa's rejection of Florentine domination. What mattered more, he still had the friendship of Spain—could count on it more surely than ever, because of his refusal to submit to the French king even when at his mercy. This friendship was a sword with more than one edge, however. On the positive side it had become a source of security, because Ferdinand and Isabella were still building up their forces in Sicily and making it known that they would never accept French control of Naples—or for that matter of Rome. Less comfortingly, the growing power of the Spaniards in Italy created the possibility that they might decide to use that power in a campaign of conquest of their own. Ferdinand was ambitious and crafty, and he had never concealed his conviction that Naples was rightfully his.

Against this background, Alexander must have been less than enthusiastic when he learned that Spanish troops were being moved in substantial numbers to the Neapolitan mainland, and that they had been put under the command of one of the most fearsome generals of the age, Gonzalo Hernández de Córdoba, known as Gonsalvo and destined to be immortalized as the Great Captain. He was a veteran of the long, bitter campaign that had ended in 1492 with the expulsion of the Muslims from Granada, and he was formidably smart and tough. As an ally of Ferrandino he was certain to be invaluable. But if ever used to plant the banners of Aragon and Castile in Italy, he would become at least as big a problem as the French. He, and his master and mistress in Spain, needed careful management. Alexander alone was attempting to manage them constructively, in such a way as to maintain the autonomy and integrity of the peninsula.

It is remarkable, in light of his later conduct, how little attention Alexander gave, throughout the invasion crisis and its immediate aftermath, to the fortunes of his young relatives. That whole agenda appears to have been set aside. With the crisis behind him, however, he was

freed to turn his attention to other matters, and the matters that interested him most were those young relatives and conditions in the Papal
States. One thing in particular rankled, and it was an issue with deep
roots: the power, and the troublesome behavior, of the Orsini. Though
the Colonna had accepted employment with Gonsalvo and Ferrandino
after being discharged by the retreating Charles VIII, and though they
had been reconciled with Rome as a result, the old warhorse Virginio
Orsini followed an insultingly different course. First he declined an
offer to take command of the Holy League's armies, possibly because
accepting would have put him on the same side as the Colonna, more
likely because he received a better offer from the count of Montpensier,
the hard-pressed viceroy whom King Charles had left behind in Naples.
Returning to Il Regno at the head of a force drawn from several
branches of his family, Virginio settled in for what he undoubtedly
hoped would be a long and lucrative conflict of the traditional Italian
kind.

What made all this intolerable from Alexander's perspective was
that Virginio, as lord of the great lakeside stronghold of Bracciano north
of Rome, was a papal vassal and therefore—supposedly—subject to
Rome. His flouting of his feudal obligations, if no more than typical of
the high-handed manner in which the Roman barons had been dealing
with their supposed overlords for centuries, served as a galling re-
minder of the disorder in the Papal States and even in the streets of
Rome. Wherever the clans dominated there was thuggery instead
of law, the caprices of autocrats rather than anything deserving to be
called proper government. And Virginio was the whole problem per-
sonified.

The papal army had deteriorated during the reign of Innocent VIII,
and almost from the week of his election Alexander had begun spending to rebuild it. Later, drawing on the lessons of the invasion, he
began investing in artillery. Thus he was prepared to take action when,
early in 1496, he thought he saw an opportunity to break the Orsini
once and for all. Undoubtedly he intended more than this; his ultimate
objective could only have been to subdue all the baronial clans. But it
would have been folly to take on all of them at once, and Virginio's
high-handed insolence made the Orsini the right place to start. Nor was
this pope willing to follow the practice of his predecessors and use one

local clan to subdue another; instead he summoned Guidobaldo da Montefeltro, son and successor of the great Duke Federico of Urbino, to take command of the papal troops. Guidobaldo was a safe choice: the domains he had inherited from his father were far away and separated from Rome by the Apennines, so distant that the thought of augmenting them with the lands of the Orsini could only have seemed absurd.

At the same time Alexander sent word to Juan de Borja, the young duke of Gandía, urging him to hasten back to Italy from Spain, become Giovanni Borgia once again, and accept appointment as the Vatican's captain-general. Alexander saw a double-barreled opportunity: a chance to neutralize the Orsini and raise the status of his own family at a single stroke. By merging the two objectives he put his reign on a momentously new course.

Juan, whose late brother Pedro Luis had become the first duke of Gandía partly on the basis of his achievements as a soldier (his inherited wealth had also been a factor, along with Ferdinand and Isabella's wish to bring him into the royal family by marrying him to their cousin), had no real military credentials of his own. Nevertheless the pope placed him rather than Montefeltro at the head of the campaign against the Orsini, and he can have had no other reason for doing so than the simple fact that Juan was a Borgia. Somebody loyal would be needed to manage the Orsini properties once they had been reclaimed, and Alexander decided to give that job to Juan as well. Who else, in the circus of Italian dynastic politics, could he possibly trust? Even within the family, who but Juan? Jofrè, even if he had been a stronger character, was too young to be a possibility. All the other male Borgias of note, Cesare included, were churchmen. The pope appears to have taken it for granted that the young duke had somehow grown up while in Spain or that, if he remained capable of atrociously immature behavior, that was somehow not going to matter.

We see here the first clear manifestation of Alexander's defining weakness as a man and as pontiff: his growing and soon all-but-unrestrained willingness to subordinate everything else to his favorites. No doubt he remembered how Calixtus III had turned to him and his brother under similar circumstances and had increased his effectiveness as pope by doing so. If the increasing extremes to which he carried his nepotism might to any extent be rationally explained, the explanation must surely have to do with the perception that Juan and his siblings, if empowered, could become Alexander's most effective tools in the pursuit of his policy objectives.

The war on the Orsini began in the south, before Juan's arrival in Italy, and at the start it was impressively successful. This was thanks to the participation of Gonsalvo the Great Captain, who from his new base at Naples set out in pursuit of Virginio and the viceroy Montpensier. With characteristic energy he drove them from one redoubt to another until, by the end of June, he had them bottled up in the town of Atella in the southern province of Basilicata. After a month under siege Montpensier offered a deal: he would surrender if a relief force did not come to his rescue by the time another month had passed, with the understanding that he and his men would then be allowed to return to France. Meanwhile hostilities could cease. Gonsalvo, having provided an early demonstration of his ability to outthink, outmaneuver, and outfight the French as well as Virginio's Italians, confident of his ability to deal with a relief force in the unlikely event that one appeared, was happy to agree. He was wise to do so: Montpensier, his troops ravaged by disease and desperately short of water, gave up halfway through the period of truce. Though Montpensier was set free as agreed (only to die shortly afterward), Pope Alexander sent an urgent appeal to Ferrandino not to let Virginio go. The king did as asked. Virginio, his son Gian Giordano, and a number of their kinsmen were held as prisoners.

In Rome, meanwhile, a separate northern campaign was still being prepared. When Juan landed at Civitavecchia on the coast, he was escorted in state to Rome, where after a formal reception his brother Cardinal Cesare showed him to the apartments that had been prepared for him in the papal palace. Almost three more months passed before all was deemed to be in readiness. During those months Juan appears to have made himself generally despised, not least by his new comrades in arms. One of them would remember him as "a very mean young man, full of false ideas of grandeur and bad thoughts, haughty, cruel and unreasonable." Virginio Orsini remained a prisoner in Naples, but his brother-in-law Bartolomeo d'Alviano managed to escape. He made his way northward to Virginio's main stronghold of Bracciano, where he organized a defense against the assault that everyone knew to be impending.

One wonders if Pope Alexander, usually so circumspect, gave any thought to the risks he was running in entrusting his campaign to the two young dukes—neither of them yet twenty-five, Juan barely twenty—who knelt before him on October 26 to receive his blessing and with it the command of the papal army. Guidobaldo da Montefeltro, heir to one of the greatest military names in Italy, was intelligent, refined, and civilized—an *almost* perfect Renaissance prince. He had limited experience of warfare, however, and time would show him to have few of his late father's gifts. Only the belief that blood will out, that the apple never falls far from the tree, can explain his selection as second in command of the expedition that was about to begin. Juan himself, the newly anointed captain-general, had less experience than Guidobaldo and even less to recommend him. When he rode out of Rome that day at the head of his army, the banners of Church and pope unfurled above his head, he was utterly unprepared for what lay ahead.

The question has to be asked: is it credible that Pope Alexander would have taken such a risk for, bestowed so much favor on, not a son but a nephew only? Yes is the only possible answer—an unqualified yes. And the evidence is as simple as it is undeniable: the fact that so many of Alexander's predecessors had done exactly the same thing. Sometimes the risk paid off handsomely; this was nowhere as true as in the case of Calixtus III and young Rodrigo Borgia. More often the results were catastrophic; for an example it is necessary to look no further back than to one of the popes Rodrigo served—to Sixtus IV and his nephew Girolamo.

As for *why*, we have already considered how difficult it could be for a pope to find trustworthy agents, and how his own early life had been an object lesson in the potential value of papal nephews in consolidating the Vatican's power and extending its reach. Beyond that, it is possible to suspect that even a man as robust as Alexander VI, without wife or children and perhaps susceptible to loneliness as old age descends upon him, might respond gratefully to the presence of four attractive and attentive young relatives at his court and in his life.

In the early going, the two young dukes did well. In short order ten Orsini castles were taken, and the papal army continued to advance. As the end of the year approached, only three strongholds, all of them in the heart of Orsini country at Lake Bracciano, remained to be taken.

Isola then fell, followed by Trevignano, so that only the majestically high-towered Bracciano Castle remained in Orsini hands. Virginio's father Napoleone had strengthened and modernized this fortress in the 1480s, adapting it to withstand artillery. Now its defense was in the capable hands of Virginio's sister Bartolomea d'Alviano and her husband Bartolomeo, an experienced soldier recently escaped from imprisonment in Naples and now acting as the family's de facto military chief. Their ability to hold out was in doubt, however, until in the depths of winter help suddenly arrived in the form of troops led by Virginio's illegitimate son Carlo, his cousin Giulio Orsini, and their henchman Vitellozzo Vitelli, tyrant lord of Città di Castello. The three had been in Provence in the service of Charles VIII when word reached them of the pope's offensive, and the king had given them money with which to ride to the rescue. Giuliano della Rovere had come with them, desperate to make certain that the pope's campaign failed.

Guidobaldo da Montefeltro was away from Bracciano at this time, recuperating from an injury. At the approach of the relief force, Juan Borgia broke off the siege—probably a sensible move—and removed his artillery to safety behind the walls of the town of Anguillara. When Guidobaldo rejoined him, they set out in search of the enemy, coming upon them near Soriano on January 24, 1497. D'Alviano and his Orsini kin, as it happened, were spoiling for a fight, knowing as they did that Virginio had died in Naples nine days before. Perhaps they had already heard the rumor—it is not impossible that they *started* the rumor—that Alexander had ordered him poisoned.

The battle that ensued, though hard-fought on both sides, cost the pope's young dukes everything they had gained over the preceding months and brought their campaign to an ignominious end. Guidobaldo was taken prisoner, Juan Borgia ran for Rome after suffering a slight wound, and their army was scattered. The cause of the disaster was a blunder by the usually competent Fabrizio Colonna, who by advancing too aggressively had left his flank exposed to the savagely aggressive Vitellozzo Vitelli. The result was humiliation for Guidobaldo, who found himself being held for ransom; for Juan, who became a laughingstock because of his flight; and above all for the pope. For the victors, who found themselves back in control of the countryside north of Rome, it was bittersweet revenge.

Alexander reacted by doing what he would have been wise to do in the first place: he sent an appeal to Naples for Gonsalvo to come north and take command. Other developments, however, soon made a resumption of the offensive impossible. On January 17 the latest conflict between France and Spain was suspended by a truce, and in order not to jeopardize it, Ferdinand began pressing Rome to stop making war on King Charles's Orsini minions. Venice meanwhile wanted to avoid French involvement in a dispute it was having with Naples over certain Adriatic ports—a dispute in which Alexander was siding with Ferrandino, urging him to stand firm—and so it too applied what pressure it could to get the pope to desist. Even the Orsini were eager for an end to hostilities, being satisfied with the fruits of their victory at Soriano and having had a taste of what the Spanish were capable of when under Gonsalvo's command. Alexander yielded, if regretfully. He accepted from the Orsini an indemnity of fifty thousand gold ducats along with their promise to refrain from offensive action. In return he released the Orsini still held prisoner in Naples—the deceased Virginio's vengeful son Gian Giordano among them. He handed over the properties the Orsini had earlier lost to Guidobaldo and Juan. On balance, the Orsini had survived Alexander's offensive with their strength undiminished and their freedom of action unimpaired.

Gonsalvo arrived in Rome four days after the signing of the settlement. Rather than allowing his long journey to go for naught and his talents to go unused, Alexander dispatched him and Juan as co-commanders to the port of Ostia, which was now one of France's few outposts south of Genoa and the last bit of Italy still professing loyalty to Giuliano della Rovere. Its capture came within a couple of weeks and was important. It restored the River Tiber to Rome's control, so that for the first time in two years food and other necessities could be imported by ship and barge. Alexander took personal possession of Ostia amid great celebration, using the occasion to declare all of Cardinal della Rovere's benefices forfeit and to remove his brother as prefect of Rome. The cardinal himself was now in permanent exile, serving as archbishop of Avignon under the protection of the French crown, biding his time and dreaming of revenge.

The only difficulties of the Ostia campaign involved Juan Borgia and rose out of the abrasiveness of his personality. He clashed almost vio-

lently with Gonsalvo, who was more than twice his age and an immeasurably more capable and respected soldier. Gonsalvo developed such
hearty contempt for his young co-commander that later, during Easter
observances in Rome, he refused to accept a palm from the pope's
hands because this modest honor had been conferred on Juan first. Lucrezia Borgia's husband, Giovanni Sforza, also was at Ostia, having finally and with a conspicuous lack of enthusiasm consented to leave his
palace at Pesaro and contribute his troops to the pope's wars. He too
was seen to have a heated dispute with the duke of Gandía, the cause of
which is not known. The duke had a talent for giving offense and did
more than all his siblings to make the people of Rome hate the Spaniards among them. If Alexander had any awareness of this, there is no
evidence that he cared.

The recovery of Ostia coincided with the signing of a truce between
the Holy League—which at this point meant, in practical terms, Venice
and Rome only—and France. Military operations thus came to an end
at last, and Italy entered upon a half-year of general tranquillity. Once
again Alexander was free to turn his attention where he wished, and he
began to make his family his first priority to such an extent that in time
he would appear to be almost in the grip of an obsession. He did so
first—it seems fitting almost to the point of inevitability—in connection with the crown of Naples.

It happened that Ferrandino, only twenty-seven years old, had unexpectedly died some months before. This energetic and courageous
young monarch, recently wed to an aunt with whom he was passionately in love (she was a daughter of his grandfather Ferrante but several
years younger than her nephew-husband nonetheless), probably fell
victim to malaria. His passing is easily seen as a tragedy for the House
of Aragon, as by all accounts he was free of the most appalling traits of
his father and grandfather. In fact, however, the uncle who succeeded
him, Alfonso II's younger brother Federico or Don Fadrique, was at
least as impressive and less alarmingly impulsive. The third new king
of Naples in just three years, Fadrique was in firm control of his throne,
thanks largely to the presence of Gonsalvo's Spanish troops. But he
needed to be crowned, this could only be done by his liege lord the
pope or someone deputized by the pope, and his coronation was now
conspicuously overdue. No one was surprised, therefore, when Alexan-

der announced in consistory that the time had come for one of the cardinals to go to Naples and conduct the necessary formalities.

Eyebrows went up, however, when the pope announced his choice: Cardinal Cesare. Twenty-two years old at most, three years a cardinal, Cesare was known for nothing except the dashing figure he cut in his pursuit of pleasure and such boyish exploits as his escape from Charles VIII. The conferring of such a prestigious assignment on a youth who made no pretense at taking his clerical status seriously was almost a provocation. It was resented by his older colleagues, the ambitious as well as the distinguished, those sensitive to the proprieties as well as those thinking mostly of the rich gifts a ruler of Naples could be expected to bestow upon whoever anointed him as king.

A bigger shock followed just days later, when the cardinals were again called together and informed of the pope's newest plans for Juan duke of Gandía. Still only six months from his flight from the battlefield at Soriano, Juan was to be invested with the duchy of Benevento, an ancient papal fief only some fifty miles north of Naples and, with its great palace and fortifications, an anchor of papal strength in the south. He was also made lord of the cities of Terracina and Pontecorvo, and all these places were to be inheritable in perpetuity by his legitimate male descendants. The kingdom of Naples had historical claims to these places and disputed the pope's right to bestow them on anyone, but Alexander's timing was impeccable: Don Fadrique's need for papal investiture was certain to deter him from objecting strongly. Only one cardinal, Pope Pius II's nephew Francesco Piccolomini, spoke openly in opposition to Alexander's alienation of so much papal territory for the benefit not only of an undistinguished lay member of the Borgia family but of Borgias yet unborn. Gandía being a nephew-by-marriage of Spain's ruling monarchs, the Sacred College's Spanish contingent (to which Alexander had added seven members in the five years since his election) were untroubled to see him treated so generously. Though the Italian cardinals were inured to nepotism, the acquiescence of almost all of them makes it impossible not to wonder if Alexander had used bullying tactics to assure their silence.

As for Juan, there is no sure way of deciding how much credence to give to the many contemptuous descriptions that have come down to us in the chronicles of the time. The number and unanimity of these descriptions make it necessary to accept them as accurate reflections, to some considerable extent, of his character and conduct. Without question he was a pleasure-loving young libertine, capable of displaying the Borgia charm but also of making himself insufferable. The clashes with Gonsalvo and with Giovanni Sforza that we noted earlier were far from unique; a dispute with Cardinal Ascanio Sforza flew so completely out of control that before it ended, their retainers were killing one another in the streets. If it is unnecessary to dismiss the duke as irredeemably vicious, in the face of the available evidence it is pointless even to wonder if he might be an innocent victim of partisan slander. Possibly he had been spoiled as a child; fatherless, he inherited his brother's dukedom unexpectedly and at an early age and from that point forward was immensely rich, immensely privileged, and perhaps excessively indulged. His story may be, at least in part, the familiar one of too much too soon.

The many powerful enemies that Juan had made in the year since his return from Spain, and his ability to remain the pope's favorite in spite of his too-obvious faults, provide the background for one of the most intriguing murder mysteries in all of history. On the evening of June 14, 1497, at a vineyard in Rome, Vannozza Borgia held a going-away party for her son Cesare, who was to depart for his great assignment in Naples within a few days. Juan was among those in attendance, and he was accompanied by a figure in whose company he had been seen repeatedly in recent weeks, a man whose face was concealed behind a mask and whose identity appears to have been unknown to the other partygoers. (Going about masked was somehow not as bizarre a practice in the Italy of the Renaissance as it seems today; it would become almost standard practice for Cesare, especially after his good looks were marred by syphilis.) Late in the evening, as everyone was going home, Juan rode off into the dark streets with his masked companion, the two of them mounted on the same mule with a manservant walking beside. When the three came to a square, Juan told the servant to wait there one hour, and then to go home if his master had not returned. The duke and the masked man then went on their way, the latter to remain a mystery forever, the former never to be seen alive again.

The next morning, when it was discovered that Juan had not returned to the papal palace, no one was concerned. He was notorious for his nocturnal, mainly amorous adventures, and as the day advanced

ALONSO BORGIA, a scholarly lawyer but in Roman eyes a Spanish "barbarian," became Pope Calixtus III thanks to men who expected him to do nothing and die soon. But his reign, as eventful as it was short, forever transformed the fortunes of his family.

Sano di Pietro (1406–1481).
Madonna Appearing to
Pope Calixtus III.
Pinacoteca Nazionale,
Siena, Italy.
Scala/Art Resource, NY

RODRIGO BORGIA, by the time this pious fresco was painted on a wall of his Vatican apartments, dominated central Italy as Pope Alexander VI. He also stood at the center of Europe's power politics— and the crises that would destroy Italy's autonomy.

Bernardino Pinturicchio, 1493.
Fresco. Detail of The Resurrection.
Borgia Apartments, Vatican Palace.
Erich Lessing/Art Resource, NY

LUCREZIA BORGIA, whether or not she served as model for this painting of Saint Catherine, was in fact a stunning auburn-haired beauty. She was also, contrary to the dark legend that grew up around her, everything that the ideal Renaissance princess was supposed to be.

Bernardino Pinturicchio (1454–1513). Fresco. Detail of The Disputation of Saint Catherine. *Lucrezia Borgia shown as Saint Catherine. Borgia Apartments, Vatican Palace.*
Scala/Art Resource, NY

JUAN BORGIA, wild young duke and favorite of Pope Alexander VI, made so many dangerous enemies with his arrogant and irresponsible behavior that when he was murdered, there were myriad plausible suspects.

Portrait, early sixteenth century. Presumed to be of Giovanni (Juan) Borgia. Pinacoteca Civica, Forlì, Italy.
Alinari/Art Resource, NY

CESARE BORGIA, the first man ever to resign from the College of Cardinals and said to be the handsomest man in Italy, gambled everything in the attempt to make himself a great secular prince. He might have succeeded—except for the one turn of fate that he failed to foresee.

Anonymous, sixteenth century.
Palazzo Venezia, Rome.
Scala/Art Resource, NY

GIULIANO DELLA ROVERE, brilliant and volcanically hot-tempered, spent much of his life in bitter conflict with the Borgias, and as Pope Julius II devoted himself to destroying their reputation.

Melozzo da Forlì (1438–1494).
Detail of fresco. Pinacoteca,
Vatican Museums.
Erich Lessing/Art Resource, NY

FERDINAND AND ISABELLA, "the Catholic kings," united Spain with Rodrigo Borgia's help and remained his friends until the adventures of the young Borgias intervened.

Anonymous, Spanish school, fifteenth century. Portrait of the Catholic Kings. *Convento de Las Augustinas, Ávila, Spain.* Album/Art Resource, NY

FERRANTE OF NAPLES, illegitimate son of one of the greatest monarchs of the fifteenth century and a skillful if utterly amoral troublemaker, might never have inherited the Neapolitan crown if not for the timely death of the first Borgia pope.

Artist unknown, fifteenth century, Naples. Bust. Musée du Louvre, Paris. Gianni Dagli Orti/The Art Archive at Art Resource, NY

GALEAZZO MARIA SFORZA, sadist, murderer, and tyrannical duke of Milan, drove his subjects to such extremes of fear and humiliation that finally, in desperation, they killed him.

Antonio del Pollaiuolo and Piero del Pollaiuolo, 1471. Uffizi, Florence, Italy.
Alinari/Art Resource, NY

MEHMED II, sultan of the Ottoman Turks and scourge of Europe's Christians, conquered Constantinople the day before his twenty-second birthday and for the rest of his life was a threat to Italy and Rome.

Attributed to Gentile Bellini, 1480. Oil on canvas. National Gallery, London.
© National Gallery, London/Art Resource, NY

LORENZO DE' MEDICI, "the Magnificent," dominated the great republic of Florence for twenty years but still died too young, exiting the stage exactly when his city, and all Italy, needed him most.

School of Agnolo Bronzino. Uffizi, Florence, Italy.
Scala/Art Resource, NY

PIERO DE' MEDICI, described by his proud father, Lorenzo, as the most promising figure their brilliant family had ever produced, failed so quickly and completely as leader of Florence that he came to be called "the Unfortunate."

Agnolo Bronzino. Uffizi, Florence, Italy.
Scala/Art Resource, NY

LUDOVICO SFORZA, "Il Moro," displaced his nephew as ruler of Milan but then made the fatal mistake of turning to the king of France for support against his enemies.

Master of Pala Sforzesca (1490–1520). Detail from the Sforza Altarpiece. Brera Library, Milan, Italy.
Gianni Dagli Orti/The Art Archive at Art Resource, NY

CHARLES VIII of France, young and as deeply foolish as he was physically clownlike, effortlessly conquered the kingdom of Naples but soon found himself fleeing for his life.

From a Book of Hours *ca. 1450–1500.*
Bibliothèque Nationale, Paris.
Scala/White Images/Art Resource, NY

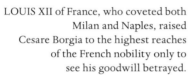

LOUIS XII of France, who coveted both Milan and Naples, raised Cesare Borgia to the highest reaches of the French nobility only to see his goodwill betrayed.

Anonymous, sixteenth century.
Uffizi, Florence, Italy.
Scala/Art Resource, NY

CATERINA SFORZA was a true *virago*, a woman with the bloodthirsty heart of a warlord, but met her match when Cesare Borgia set out to drive her from her strongholds.

Lorenzo di Credi. Portrait of a Lady
(Caterina Sforza).
Pinacoteca Civica, Forlì, Italy.
Scala/Art Resource, NY

ALFONSO D'ESTE, scion of an ancient and proud family and heir to the duchy of Ferrara, resisted a marital alliance with the Borgias until the pressure—and the rewards—became impossible to resist.

Dosso Dossi (1479–1541).
Biblioteca Estense, Modena.
Alfredo Dagli Orti/The Art Archive at Art Resource, NY

GIROLAMO SAVONAROLA, the friar who turned Renaissance Florence into a "bonfire of the vanities," failed to exhaust Pope Alexander's patience but was burned at the stake all the same.

Fra Bartolomeo. Museo di San Marco, Florence, Italy.
Erich Lessing/Art Resource, NY

and he failed to appear, it was assumed that, as had happened before, he was holed up in the room of some paramour, unwilling for the sake of her reputation or perhaps his own to emerge before dark. When night fell and he had still not returned, Alexander became worried. Search parties were sent out. They found the duke's mule, its trappings disarranged. They also found the manservant, gravely wounded but unable to provide any helpful information. At last someone turned up a clue: the statement of a Slovenian watchman to the effect that, in the middle of the night, he had seen five men dump a body into the Tiber and weigh it down with rocks when it floated to the surface. Asked why he had not reported this, he replied that in the course of many nights standing guard over cargo barges he had seen any number of corpses deposited in the river, and that until now no one had ever seemed to care.

Fishermen were deployed to drag the river bottom. One of them hooked the dead body of the duke and pulled it out of the mud. It bore nine deep stab wounds, it was still dressed in the costly garments that Juan had worn to his mother's party, and one of its pockets contained a purse fat with gold. The impossibility of believing that Juan had been killed by robbers added urgency to the question of who had done the deed, and why. As in all the best mysteries, there was an excess of plausible suspects. Ascanio Sforza for one: his recent dispute with Juan had already had fatal consequences. Lucrezia's husband for another: like his cousin Ascanio, Giovanni Sforza had clashed recently and almost violently with Juan, and Ludovico il Moro's reconciliation with Charles of France had made Giovanni's position in Rome so excruciatingly awkward that he believed his life to be in danger. On Good Friday he had fled Rome, first returning to his home base at Pesaro and later proceeding to Milan, where he asked but did not receive help from his cousins Ludovico il Moro and Cardinal Ascanio. The brothers were unwilling to offend Alexander and pressed Giovanni to obey the pope's order to return to Rome. By then, however, there was no point in returning. Lucrezia had gone into seclusion at the San Sisto convent outside Rome, and Alexander had declared his intention to have her marriage annulled. Though neither Ascanio nor Giovanni was in Rome at the time of Juan's disappearance, both certainly had the means to arrange his murder.

Also to be considered was young Guidobaldo duke of Urbino, a gentle, scholarly soul but burning with resentment at being blamed for the defeat at Soriano and left to pay his own ransom in order to win his release. Plus the men of all the families, some of them noble, whose wives and daughters Juan had seduced or targeted for seduction. That line of inquiry brought even the youngest of the Borgia brothers, Jofrè prince of Squillace, into the circle of suspects. He was living in Rome once again, and his wife Sancia was among Juan's numberless paramours (and Cesare's). Finally, most worthy of suspicion of all, were the Orsini. It was Juan who had been sent to destroy them, Juan who was to have been given their lands when his mission was accomplished, and Juan who could be expected to take up arms against them once again whenever Alexander felt ready to make another try. Rome was thick with Orsini who were capable of committing murder.

Alexander was shattered by the discovery of the body. He withdrew into deep seclusion for days, grieving loudly, not eating or drinking or sleeping. When he finally emerged, it was to take control of the search for the killers, though he declared as he did so that he already knew who the culprits were. That he loved the young duke had always been obvious—it is deplorable that we know essentially nothing about the bond that had formed between them, or what exactly about Juan caused the pope to find him so appealing—and the weight of his loss was obvious now. Perhaps too he was tormented by guilt, by the realization that he had given the boy more authority and responsibility than he was capable of handling, thereby exposing him to the wrath of their foes.

Alexander assembled the cardinals and poured out his grief. "The duke of Gandía is dead," he said. "A greater calamity could not have befallen us, for we bore him unbounded affection. Life has lost its interest for us. Indeed, had we seven papacies we would give them all to recall the duke to life. It must be that God thus punishes us for our sins, for the duke has done nothing to deserve so terrible a fate." He then went through an abridged list of the obvious suspects—the Sforzas, Jofrè, Guidobaldo da Montefeltro—and said he knew all of them to be innocent.

Of the Orsini he said nothing. No stretch of the imagination is required to suppose that Alexander had satisfied himself of their guilt and had decided to keep silent. He would have been powerless, in that summer of 1497, to bring the Orsini to justice or to exact other forms of revenge. By keeping his own counsel, he could watch and wait.

Alexander ended his investigation sooner than anyone had expected and forbade further inquiries into Juan's death. In the fullness of time it would be suggested, and repeated in almost everything written about the Borgias, that he did this upon learning that the murderer was in fact Cesare. This is a logical inference—but only if one begins by assuming Cesare's guilt. For at least a century now virtually every responsible student of the Borgias has found it impossible to assume anything of the kind. Scholars have concluded instead that Cesare was almost certainly not guilty (certainty being impossible in a matter of this kind). They finally noticed, if belatedly, that in the aftermath of his brother's death Cesare was never so much as mentioned among the possible suspects, even by the gossips, and that when he began to be mentioned and then declared guilty, this was invariably done by propagandists and sensation-seekers. Cesare had actually stood to gain little or nothing from the murder. Juan was survived by a wife, an infant daughter, and a small son who as third duke of Gandía inherited all of his father's possessions in Italy as well as Spain. Cesare remained exactly what he had been when Juan was alive: a wealthy and restless young cardinal, ridiculously out of place in the vocation in which he found himself.

At that first consistory after the murder, after giving vent to his feelings and doing what he could to clear the Sforzas and others of suspicion, Alexander turned to other matters. He said that during the days and nights when his pain was so intense as to make it impossible to sleep, he had come to a decision. "We are resolved without delay to think of the Church first and foremost," he declared, "and not of ourselves nor of our privileges." He announced that he was creating a commission of six cardinals—men who, when their names were disclosed, proved to be among the most respected members of the Sacred College—and assigning it to set to work immediately on developing a program of ecclesiastical reform. He concluded by saying that "we must begin by reforming ourselves," pledging that he would "submit our own person to the regulations that they [the commissioners] shall make." Obviously it is possible that these words are an admission that Alexander had not been faithful to his priestly vows, that even since his election he had been guilty of serious immorality. It should not be necessary to note also, however, that they are not necessarily anything of the kind. Such things could be said, and at various times have been said, by good men and women of many faiths, including pontiffs known for their humility and virtuous lives.

Three days after the consistory Cesare departed for Naples and the crowning of Don Fadrique. It has often been suggested that he should not have gone so soon after his brother's death, with Alexander in such a depressed state. That he should have asked to be replaced and insisted on going because he was eager to put himself beyond the reach of the men investigating the murder. Eager he may or may not have been, but if he was hoping for anything, it was not necessarily to escape scrutiny. He was young and high-spirited, and it is not implausible that what he wanted to get away from was the deep gloom that had descended upon the papal household and court. Naples offered not only a coronation ceremony in which Cesare was slated to play a central role but all the festivities attendant upon such an event. In any case he departed on schedule, and when his assignment was completed, he decided to remain in Naples, a city with much to interest a vigorous young man with a relaxed moral code

With his departure, none of the young Borgias remained at the papal court. Juan was in his tomb, and in the aftermath of his murder, in the depths of his grief, Alexander had ordered Jofrè to return to his principality of Squillace in Naples and take Sancia with him. He did so possibly for their safety but more likely because he was disgusted with incessant gossip about Sancia's sexual escapades. Jofrè, all of fifteen years old now and in his third year as a married man, is not likely to have regarded his exile as a punishment or a loss. He and Sancia had spent the first two years of their marriage in Squillace and had grown accustomed there to a life of indolent self-indulgence. Alexander must have realized by now that this was one young Borgia of whom not a great deal was to be expected. The boy's tolerance of being repeatedly cuckolded, even by his brothers, bespoke softness of character, a willingness, not characteristic of the Borgias, to settle for a passive if privileged existence.

Lucrezia meanwhile was sequestered at the convent of San Sisto just outside Rome, waiting for an ecclesiastical court to declare that she was not married to Giovanni Sforza and never had been. Their union appears never to have had any substance on the personal level; the available evidence, sparse as it is, suggests that Lucrezia found her new life dreary, her spouse uninteresting. When she refused to end a visit to Rome late in 1496 and return to Pesaro as Sforza naturally expected, he grudgingly joined her, remaining until Easter of the following year. But daily contact with the Borgias served only to worsen matters, showing Sforza that his wife's family had no liking and little use for him, making him increasingly uneasy. It was during his sojourn in Rome that, taking part in the siege of Ostia, he was observed in an angry exchange with Juan Borgia. He was learning too that Cesare, cardinal or not, could be a dangerous acquaintance. He would have heard the story of how, when Charles VIII's army passed through Rome after withdrawing from Naples, Cesare had led an attack on a company of Swiss mercenaries, seeking revenge for the earlier sacking of his mother Vannozza's house. This episode, which ended with sixteen of the Swiss dead and the survivors beaten and stripped of every possession, had become part of a growing body of Roman lore about the Borgia brothers and their reckless ways.

Making everything more frightening still was the painfully obvious fact that the circumstances that had led to Lucrezia's being offered to the Sforzas as a bride no longer obtained. The marriage had seemed important when Alexander and Ferrante of Naples were at odds and Sforza Milan seemed an essential counterweight to Neapolitan power. Now, with not only Ferrante but his heir Alfonso II dead and the pope established as Naples's best friend among the Italian powers, all that was in the past. Shortly after Easter 1497 Sforza left Rome in disguise and returned to Pesaro alone. On an earlier occasion, when he had returned to Pesaro without Lucrezia, he had done so out of simple pique and weariness with a make-believe marriage to a child. This time, however, he was in flight and fearful of his life. Alexander, no doubt pleased to be rid of him, asked the appropriate legal authorities to declare Lucrezia's marriage invalid. She disappeared into the San Sisto convent, and by the time of Juan Borgia's murder the pope and Cesare were already considering where to marry her next.

The murder put all such things in abeyance. In the weeks after Cesare's departure for Naples, little happened at the Vatican beyond the routine performance of the Curial bureaucracy's essential functions. The most conspicuous exception was the pope's newly created reform commission, the members of which began meeting almost daily, filling more and more pages—ultimately more than six hundred—with lists of Church problems and possible remedies. A number of the commission's recommendations were directed at the Sacred College itself: that even when hosting banquets cardinals should not serve more than two meats, that no cardinal should serve as the representative of a secular prince, that when moving about Rome no cardinal should have an entourage of more than twenty horsemen, that there should never be more than twenty-four cardinals, and that among them should be representatives of all the major nations of Europe. Vatican policy came under scrutiny as well: the commission proposed higher qualifications for protonotaries, new ways of dealing with disagreements over how much autonomy the Church should have in various countries, and harsh punishment for the forging of official documents. This last was a problem of real urgency; the rudimentary technology of the time made forgery all too easy, detection exceedingly difficult. This was made freshly apparent in September, when the archbishop who was Pope Alexander's private secretary confessed to having produced and sold large numbers of counterfeit dispensations.

Action, however, was going to require the attention of the pope, and Alexander was only beginning to emerge from seclusion. He was not yet himself, which is perhaps why, after long resistance, he yielded wearily to the demand of the College of Cardinals that Savonarola's excommunication be announced to Florence and the world.

When summer ended Cesare, advised that the pope was no longer in the depths of despair and that life at the papal court was beginning to be tolerable once again, decided to end his holiday in Naples. He was now fully formed, the formidable figure soon to be described by the Venetian diplomat Paolo Capello as "physically most beautiful . . . tall and well-made." He took two things back to Rome with him: "the French disease," syphilis, and a determination to start his life over on an entirely new track.

THE YOUNG ONES

IF THE MOST WIDELY ACCEPTED ESTIMATE OF CESARE BORGIA'S date of birth is correct, he was just reaching his twenty-second birthday when he returned from Naples. He was already, however, a man of obvious and exceptional gifts. Strong, athletic, and restlessly energetic, strikingly good-looking under a mane of dark-reddish hair, he combined the intelligence that had won him distinction as a student of civil and canon law with a winning personality, a steely will, and a degree of self-possession that was quite extraordinary in such a young man.

He was also, as the revenge killing of sixteen Swiss soldiers shows, already capable of utterly ruthless behavior.

The fact that Cesare was a second son explains why his family had set him on the path to a clerical career when he was still a small child. He had a much older brother, Pedro Luis, to pursue success in the lay world and produce heirs. His own assignment was to climb the same ecclesiastical ladder that, two decades before his birth, had taken Alonso Borgia to the papacy and Rodrigo to the vice-chancellorship and brought bounty to the whole family. Inevitably, and for reasons having nothing to do with merit, he was pulled up that ladder at a fabulously (by today's standards, a ridiculously) rapid pace. When all of seven years old, he was made an apostolic protonotary (a coveted position supposedly requiring advanced knowledge of the law), and shortly thereafter he became canon of the cathedral of Valencia, archdeacon of Játiva, and rector of Gandía. Each of these positions brought with it an income that few Spanish clerics could ever hope to achieve. Together they supported Cesare in the style of a young noble and provided him with an elite education without making even small demands on the family's resources.

Everything known about Cesare's eldest brother, Pedro Luis, suggests that he too must have been an impressive young man. Their father died in the early 1480s, possibly while his wife was still pregnant with Jofrè. Pedro Luis, as heir, was taken into the court of Ferdinand and Isabella and became a favorite there, serving while still a boy both as standard-bearer to the king and honorary chamberlain. As a young nobleman in the age of the *conquistadores* he naturally took up soldiering and was quick to win distinction, becoming the first of Ferdinand's men to break into the besieged Muslim stronghold of Ronda. Things turned suddenly bad for him in 1484—he must have been in his early twenties—when a dispute over money caused Pope Innocent VIII to excommunicate Ferdinand and Isabella. The royal couple retaliated by confiscating the revenues of all the Spanish benefices held by the vice-chancellor's family and imprisoning Pedro Luis. It was a petty quarrel and soon patched up, and afterward Pedro Luis was showered with new signs of favor. Ferdinand and Isabella raised him to the status of grandee, conferring the same honor on his younger brothers as they did so. In 1485 they made him duke of Gandía (he having inherited extensive properties in and around the town of Gandía at the time of his father's death). His career reached its zenith when he was betrothed to Doña Maria Enriquez, a royal cousin and a stupendous marital prize. The girl was too young to be wed, but when she came of age, Pedro Luis was to be taken into a royal family as powerful as any in Europe.

It never happened. Pedro Luis died before it became possible, the place, year, and cause of his death being uncertain. Either not long before or not long after his death his mother Vannozza took the rest of her children—three daughters and three sons—to Rome. The two eldest girls, Isabella and Girolama, were married into the minor Roman nobility, their great-uncle Cardinal Rodrigo serving as their sponsor and helping to provide dowries. Juan, as the eldest surviving son not marked for the Church, inherited not only his brother's ducal title and estates but his fiancée, the royal cousin Maria Enriquez de Luna. It can be assumed that he also underwent whatever education and training were deemed appropriate to the highest reaches of the nobility. The child Lucrezia had been remembered in Pedro Luis's will with a bequest of eleven thousand Valencian ducats for her dowry. Cesare, financially independent thanks to his benefices, continued his studies, enrolling at age fourteen in Perugia's prestigious Sapienza and advancing two years later to the university at Pisa. However impressive his talents and attainments may have been at this early stage, nothing but the influence of Vice-Chancellor Rodrigo can explain his appointment to the bishopric of Pamplona in Navarre in 1491.

Cesare's precocious advancement was carried to the furthest possible extreme when Rodrigo became pope: he was immediately given the see of Valencia, which Innocent VIII had raised to archiepiscopal status, so that that prestigious benefice had now been held by three consecutive generations of Borgias. When, a year later, he was named to the College of Cardinals, he was not only not a uniquely youthful appointee but not even the youngest of the dozen men given red hats at that time. The one flaw in all this, and in whatever great plans Pope Alexander had for Cesare's future, was the boy's glaring unfitness for an ecclesiastical career and his refusal to pretend otherwise. He rarely wore ecclesiastical garb and persisted in a way of life that, though it would have been accepted as natural in any lively and highborn young layman of the time, in a prince of the Church was nothing less than scandalous.

Long afterward, when propagandists for enemies of the Borgias began finding it useful to assume that Cesare had murdered his brother, it came to be taken for granted that he must have seethed with jealousy at having been shunted into the Church while the less able Juan was left free to make war, marry royalty, accumulate noble titles and great estates, and indulge in wild behavior without being pointed to as a disgrace to his vocation. But even if it was at about this same time that Cesare decided to reject the future that had been laid out for him, it does not necessarily follow that he had ever seen his brother as an obstacle to his escape. It definitely does not follow that he decided to take his brother's life in order to get him out of the way. It does not follow even though we know him to be capable of murder.

As a cardinal Cesare devoted himself mainly to amusements: racing horses, bullfighting, carousing, and pursuing the fair sex. It was hardly to be expected that he would show any interest in the affairs or the needs of the Church—in the work of Alexander's reform commission least of all. He was drawn to politics, however, and to the winning and using of power. This led him to become deeply involved in the life of his sister Lucrezia. Pope Alexander had already, in spite of his love for Lucrezia, repeatedly used her as an instrument of diplomacy, first betrothing her to two Spanish noblemen when she was still a child, then marrying her to Giovanni Sforza when she was only just barely more than a child. Cesare, in cooperation with his brother Juan while the latter was still alive and then on his own, carried her exploitation a big step further by setting out to undo her marriage. His motives, so far as we can tell, were entirely political and entirely selfish.

This turned into a messy business. What Alexander or Cesare or both wanted—it is unclear who was the strategist in this matter—was a decree of annulment, a ruling that Lucrezia had never been validly married to Sforza and so was free to become someone else's bride. The pope could have accomplished this by papal bull, simply declaring the marriage to be null, but he rejected this approach as insufficiently credible. He turned instead to the canon lawyers, suggesting that they might find it interesting to consider whether one or both of Lucrezia's Spanish betrothals might have been sufficiently binding to leave her unfree to marry Sforza.

When the lawyers replied that this was an unpromising way of approaching the question, the Borgias decided to claim instead that the marriage had never been consummated because Sforza was impotent. The beauty of this approach was that it entailed an official confirmation of Lucrezia's virginity, thereby fully restoring her value on the marriage market. The drawback was that it required Sforza to confess to something that any man would have found humiliating. He reacted in almost hysterical terms, pointing out that his first wife had died in childbirth and complaining that Alexander wanted to end the marriage in order to have Lucrezia for himself.

Thus was born the immortal legend of incest among the Borgias, with Lucrezia at its center. The story would expand over the centuries until Lucrezia was an international institution, a universal symbol of evil, not only a sexual wanton but a serial murderer, a poisoner of the most exquisite skill. In fact she was never anything of the kind. At the time of her final separation from Giovanni Sforza she was nothing more or less than a pretty, normally frivolous girl of about seventeen. She took a natural delight in her life as a princess, her beautiful gowns, and the attentions of the many young gallants who frequented the papal court. She took an equally natural pleasure in sharing center stage at that court with two close friends, her similarly pretty, distinctly less innocent sister-in-law Sancia and the stunningly beautiful Giulia Farnese Orsini, wife of the young lord Orsino Orsini, who was Lucrezia's somewhat distant cousin by virtue of being the son, as noted earlier, of Adriana del Milà. (See page 426 for more on the alleged intimate relationship between Pope

Alexander and Giulia Farnese and an explanation of why that part of the Borgia legend is omitted from the present narrative.)

Though the years ahead would be heavy with dark events, and though she was quite human enough to be changed by the misfortunes that befell her, Lucrezia would mature and improve rather than harden with the years. If by the end of her life not a great deal would remain of the fun-loving child-bride she had been when first married, neither would she bear the slightest resemblance to the monstrous Lucrezia of legend.

Be all that as it may, when Cesare returned from Naples, he had changed radically. He had awakened to a whole new world of possibilities—above all to the possibility, for himself, of an entirely new life. While idling at Don Fadrique's court, he had become aware that the king had a grown but unmarried daughter. This princess, Carlotta by name, was a descendant of French royalty on her mother's side, had been raised in France virtually as a member of the king's family, and was living there still. It had occurred to him that she was a prize worthy of a prince and that whoever married her would become, by doing so, princely. He decided that he wanted this Carlotta. What he had to do first was get himself out of the Church.

15

Valentino

If anything is certain in the story of the Borgias, it is that the man who became Pope Alexander VI was not weak and not a fool. Raised at an improbably early age to the second-highest position in the international Church, left to shift for himself when his uncle died just two years later, he not only survived but went on to flourish through the reigns of four very different, often very difficult popes. Finally winning election himself in the face of powerful and richly financed rivals, he spent his first five years as pontiff dealing with invasion, betrayal, rebellion, heresy, and murder. He emerged from each crisis, even the spirit-crushing death of his favorite nephew, with his vitality and buoyancy unimpaired and his stature enhanced. At age sixty-five, operating effectively at the highest levels of European power politics, he was putting on weight but otherwise remained the same cheerily easygoing, life-loving bundle of energy he had been at twenty-five.

All of which says more than anything else can about the power of *Cesare* Borgia's personality, the force of *his* will. Because from 1498 onward, from the point where he made up his mind that he was not going to stay in the Church but instead was going to transform himself into a great secular prince, Cesare began reshaping the mind and will of Alexander to conform to his own. Ultimately he would be astonishingly successful at this, appearing at crucial junctures to reduce the pontiff to a mere instrument and in the process putting all Rome at the service of his own ambition. It is necessary to remember just how formidable Alexander himself was in order to get some sense of just how much force the younger man projected.

Almost the last significant crisis of Alexander's reign in which Cesare and his interests were not significantly involved was the climax of Savonarola's story. In the aftermath of his confronting of Charles VIII at Poggibonsi in June 1495, even as half the French army withdrew beyond the Alps and the half remaining in Naples was destroyed piecemeal by Gonsalvo's Spaniards, the friar had tirelessly predicted that in due course the king would return and do a proper job of purging Italy of its corruptions, including and even especially its corrupt pope. In this case as always, Alexander was indifferent to criticism of himself personally—it must be noted that even as his condemnations became almost insanely extreme, the friar never accused the pope of having mistresses or children—but the problems created by Savonarola's preaching were more political than personal, and they were political in two ways. First, Savonarola's embrace not only of France but of French ambitions in Italy was alarming to the members of the so-called Holy League, originally formed to force Charles to return home and surviving as an instrument for keeping him there. These members wanted Florence to break with France, join them, and become part of the deterrent to a second French invasion. They began to see Savonarola's removal as the only possible way of making this happen.

Second, as Savonarola escalated his rhetoric, he was no longer merely calling Rome an evil place and the pope a bad man but denying the Church's authority and Alexander's right to the papal crown. He was proclaiming himself to be subject to no institution and to no one except God. This was more than shockingly bold in the Europe of his time. It was a direct challenge to the established order, a renunciation of that order, and easily seen as an invitation to chaos. Alexander found himself under growing pressure to respond. It came from the princes of Italy and the princes of the Church in equal measure.

What is remarkable is the restraint with which Alexander responded to the provocation and the pressure. He began, in July 1495, with a letter that, in unthreatening terms, directed Savonarola to come to Rome and explain his prophecies and preachments. When the friar replied that he was unable to comply because of illness and the mischief that the enemies of Florence might commit in his absence, Alexander allowed matters to rest. In the months following, however, Savonarola not only continued to attack the pope from his pulpit but did so in steadily more extreme terms. In September Alexander wrote again, not to the friar this time but to the Dominican monastery of Santa Croce in Lombardy, informing it of a reorganization in which Savonarola's San Marco convent among others was now under its jurisdiction and that the "certain Fra Girolamo" who was San Marco's prior was to be ordered to stop preaching until he visited Rome to explain himself. Savonarola, when he learned of this, sent Alexander a letter that amounted, behind its verbosity and rather fuzzy diction, to a declaration of defiance. For him to submit to the authority of Santa Croce, he said, would be tantamount to "making our adversary our judge." As for a trip to Rome, that would be pointless because "it is now plain that I have not lapsed into error."

By the final months of 1495 Savonarola was not only mocking the pope in his sermons but explicitly challenging the right of the ecclesiastical authorities to tell him to do anything. He announced that the vows of obedience that he had taken early in his career no longer applied because as God's chosen messenger he was now on a higher plane than other clerics. It is of course legitimate to argue that Savonarola was behaving heroically, that his actions echo the earlier, similar courage of Jan Hus of Bohemia and foreshadow the later, more momentous rebellion of Martin Luther (who was, in 1495, an eleven-year-old schoolboy in Germany). Such arguments do not alter the fact that the nature and virulence of his attacks, especially when coupled with the wild enthusiasm of some of his followers, constituted too radical a challenge to be shrugged off indefinitely. Alexander's forbearance was, under the circumstances, impressive. His attitude becomes all the more remarkable when one considers that states including Venice, Ferrara, and Bologna all regarded the friar's preachments as an incitement to the French to invade and were demanding that he be shut up.

Nevertheless, when on October 16 Alexander next wrote to Savonarola, he withdrew his earlier subordination of the San Marco monastery to Santa Croce, and though he repeated his order that Savonarola stop preaching until he had visited Rome, he promised to receive him "with a father's heart." Savonarola responded with enigmatic silence, neither leaving Florence nor, at least for some weeks, returning to his pulpit. The situation hung in suspense until February 1497, when Florence's ruling council took fright at reports that Piero de' Medici was plotting a coup. Knowing that Savonarola's hatred for the banished Medici was no less intense than his hatred for Rome, the council not merely encouraged but ordered him to resume preaching. He did so with relish, throwing off all inhibition in a round of Lenten sermons that went further than before in denouncing the Church as corrupt. "Oh prostitute Church," he railed, "thou hast displayed thy foulness to the whole world, and stinkest up to heaven."

This went on week after week, the Church decried as "lower than a beast, a monster of abomination," until finally Savonarola was telling his listeners that it was necessary to accept what he was saying in order to be a good Christian. Florence's council, weary now of the kinds of disturbances that it had earlier encouraged and less fearful of a Medici coup than of letting things get out of hand, used an outbreak of plague as an excuse to order not only Savonarola but all members of religious orders to desist from preaching. After all that had transpired, Savonarola's response could have surprised no one: he declared that to oppose him was to oppose God. When his words failed to ignite the kind of public excitement to which he had become accustomed, he pulled back, sending a vaguely conciliatory letter to the pope and lapsing once again into silence. People who had earlier responded sympathetically to his demands for reform—people as respected as Cardinal Oliviero Carafa, who was known to have a good opinion of Savonarola and had been appointed vicar-general of the Dominicans of Tuscany as a gesture of goodwill on Alexander's part—began to turn away in disgust or alarm. From every direction came demands that the pope *do something*.

Once again, Alexander did nothing. By March 1497 the friar was calling for a council to install a new pope. He was also writing to the kings of France, Spain, England, and Hungary and the Holy Roman emperor, informing them that Alexander had usurped the pontifical throne and that his position was "opposed to charity and the law of God." Carnival time brought another Bonfire of the Vanities, followed by a series of Lenten sermons, delivered in Florence's glorious Duomo, that in their extremism surpassed anything that had come before. On May 12, yielding to demands from all sides, Alexander signed a brief of excommunication. It charged Savonarola with having "disseminated pernicious doctrines to the scandal and great grief of simple souls" and forbade all Christians "to assist him, hold intercourse with him, or abet him either by word or deed." He resisted making it known, however, until June 18, at which time, predictably, Savonarola denounced it as invalid. The friar also, however, obeyed the papal brief's order to stop saying mass in public and for some months assumed an ambiguous posture somewhere between quiet obedience and passive resistance.

He burned with too much passion, however, to remain silent forever. On Christmas Day, sweeping aside the prohibitions imposed by his excommunication, he publicly said mass three times and distributed communion. The pope of course learned of this flagrant defiance but yet again did nothing. He continued to do nothing as, early in the new year, Savonarola resumed preaching in Florence's cathedral (anyone opposing him was "supporting the kingdom of Satan"), thereby not only disobeying the pope but violating a municipal order to confine his oratory to his own friary church. Without question Alexander understood that the friar had become a real and present danger not only to him but to the Church and the security of Italy, but his continued passivity had political purpose. Rome was an enemy in the eyes of many Florentines, and aggressive action by the pope might not only have been defied but have cast Savonarola in the role of victim, causing the city to rally to his defense. Savonarola was on a path to self-destruction, and Alexander had no reason to get in his way.

At this point the story rises to tragedy and descends into farce. The head of a Franciscan monastery in Florence, fed up with the successes and presumption of the Dominican Savonarola, challenged him to a trial by fire—a test in which the two of them would be simultaneously burned at the stake, and God would be given the opportunity to intervene and save the life of whichever he favored. The Franciscan was obviously calling Savonarola's bluff; he was said to be prepared for both of them to perish if his challenge was accepted, and to believe that his sacrifice would be worthwhile if it delivered the people of Florence from the grip of a lunatic.

Savonarola disappointed his adherents by not accepting. He then amused the cynics by allowing one of his associates to accept in his place, making it impossible to believe that he had refused on principle and difficult not to wonder if he might be a coward and a fraud. From Rome, Alexander and the College of Cardinals condemned the whole affair as barbaric and superstitious, but it went ahead anyway. When on April 7 thousands of people gathered in Florence's great central piazza to witness what they hoped would be an immolation and perhaps a miracle as well, they found themselves having to listen to a tedious and interminable address in which Savonarola laid down conditions that he insisted must be fulfilled before the ordeal could proceed. He demanded that his surrogate, for example, be allowed to hold in his hands a consecrated communion host. When at length the flames were lit, a spring shower arrived to put them out. That ended it. The dampened crowd dispersed in a mood of surly dissatisfaction. Savonarola returned to his friary with his credibility in tatters.

He was so diminished a figure that Pope Alexander found it possible to leave his fate to the *signoria* in Florence, thereby sparing himself no end of trouble. Three trials ensued, in the course of which the friar was physically tortured and confessed himself guilty of a list of offenses that filled forty-two pages. A number of his most impressive prophecies, he said, had been based on information that his fellow Dominicans acquired in hearing confessions. On one occasion, he said, he had arranged for his prediction of attempted murder to be fulfilled by having a dish of poisoned lampreys fed to a cat (which promptly died) instead of to the man he had identified as the intended victim. Being the fruits of torture, these tales should have been given no weight, but they destroyed what remained of Savonarola's reputation all the same. He and his two closest associates were condemned to death by hanging. They died with dignity, and in his final hour Savonarola denied everything that he had earlier confessed. Afterward his body was burned, the charred remains thrown into the River Arno to prevent the collection of relics. His removal had no impact on Florentine policy, which remained openly friendly to France.

Cesare, meanwhile, was moving to center stage in Rome. This was happening in part as a result of his own actions, starting with his role in the dissolution of Lucrezia's marriage. Just why he was so determined to break the link that Pope Alexander had forged between the Borgias and the Sforzas is not clear—though the marriage had lost its political value, it was not a serious liability—and of Lucrezia's attitude nothing at all is known. In spite of Cesare's willingness to use his sister for his own ends it is impossible to doubt that the two were genuinely close, as we shall see repeatedly. Though there is no evidence that he was doing as Lucrezia wished in ridding her of her husband, there is also no evidence that he was ignoring or overriding her wishes. He certainly shared his late brother's dislike for their brother-in-law, apparently a glum and passive figure with no appetite for the kinds of escapades in which the young Borgias were constantly involved, and it was his failure to conceal his antipathy that had provoked Sforza's flight in disguise from Rome. Possibly Cesare regarded him, though he was a count and ruler of the handsome and prosperous seaside city of Pesaro, as unworthy of the beautiful Lucrezia. What mattered most, however, was Cesare's growing awareness, as his ambition expanded in daring new directions, of just how useful his sister would be if she could be returned to the market as a virginal prospective bride.

This was proving to be difficult, however, because of Sforza's refusal to cooperate. He could not be induced to confess to impotence, the grounds on which an annulment of the marriage was being sought, or to give up either Lucrezia or her dowry of thirty thousand florins. He was acutely aware that, as lord of a papal fief, he would be vastly more secure if he could restore good relations with the pope's family, but in the absence of a way of making that happen he could only keep himself walled up inside his great moated *rocca* at Pesaro. The pressure, however, mounted steadily. Even the head of the Sforza family, Ludovico il Moro of Milan, declined to side with him, sensibly regarding a cousin's marital difficulties as not worth a showdown with Rome. At last, having been promised that he could keep the dowry, Giovanni signed an admission that his marriage had never been consummated. Later he would write to Il Moro complaining that he had been coerced into doing so. The truth of the matter is anyone's guess. On one hand, it is surely significant that in a later marriage Sforza would sire two children. On the other hand, it is at least curious that this was the only one of Lucrezia's marriages that did not result in her rather quickly becoming pregnant.

In any case things worked out well enough from Cesare's perspective. In December 1497 Lucrezia was summoned to the Vatican to hear the nullification of her marriage pronounced—to hear it declared that she had never been married, was at eighteen still *virga intacta,* and so remained entirely worthy of whatever lofty union the pope and her brother might be able to arrange for her. But suddenly new problems loomed—rumors that threatened to plunge her into irreversible disgrace. The gossips of Rome were saying that, in appearing at the Vatican, Lucrezia had been dressed in such a way as to conceal pregnancy. That her pregnancy was the result of a love affair with a young Spaniard named Pedro Calderón, a Vatican chamberlain. And that the two had become involved when Calderón (also referred to in various accounts as Pedro Caldes, and as Perotto or Pierotto) was employed as Pope Alexander's courier, carrying messages to and from Lucrezia when she was living at the convent of San Sisto.

What makes this episode impossible to dismiss out of hand is the macabre fact that in February 1498, two months after the annulment, Calderón's decomposing body, bound hand and foot, was pulled out of the Tiber. In the most colorful account of what had been going on, found in a report by the Venetian ambassador, Calderón had not been drowned but stabbed to death. By none other than Cardinal Cesare Borgia personally. After fleeing in terror to Pope Alexander, who was spattered with blood when the furious Cesare ran Calderón through with his sword. It is not easy to know what to make of this, and the varying opinions of writers across the centuries are so contradictory that they simply compound the uncertainty. Suffice it to say here that, judged against Lucrezia's whole life story, the pregnancy seems highly improbable, the story about how Cesare supposedly murdered her lover in the presence of the pope extremely so. (For more on this question, and on how it has been treated by historians, the reader is directed to page 429.)

The princes of Italy obviously gave little credence to the gossip, because as soon as her marriage was annulled, Alexander and Cesare had an impressive array of eager suitors to choose from. Among them were a young Orsini duke; the Riario who as Caterina Sforza's eldest son was titular lord of Imola and Forlì; a leading member of the baronial Sanseverino clan of Naples; and a member of Naples's royal family. There were expressions of interest from Spain as well. But the matter remained undecided when developments beyond the Alps changed the political status quo and confronted the Borgias with an entirely new set of challenges.

What happened first was that Charles VIII of France and Ferdinand of Spain astonished all Europe by announcing, in November 1497, that they were setting aside their differences and making peace. This was done largely for financial reasons, both kingdoms being nearly insolvent after years of conflict with numerous adversaries including each other, and no one could have expected it to last long. It was significant all the same, and not least for the Borgias: for the first time they found themselves free to deal on friendly terms with France without appearing to betray Spain. Within limits, of course. So long as they did nothing that conflicted directly with Ferdinand's view of his own interests, they could explore possibilities that had been closed to them through all the years when keeping the friendship of Spain required shunning France.

But then, another and far bigger thunderbolt. Word came that Charles VIII was dead. It is appropriate that this incorrigibly foolish young monarch, still only twenty-seven and by all accounts sweet-natured and charming even when dealing face-to-face with enemies, should have perished in an odd, boyish, and distinctly unheroic way. He cracked his skull against the stone lintel of a castle doorway while playing *jeu de paume*—handball—and a short time later fell into a coma from which he never recovered. The ancient and royal House of Valois was at this time in the process of petering out, as one monarch after another either failed to produce heirs (who had to be male under France's Salic law) or watched all his sons die early. Charles himself, sickly and ill formed, had not been born until his father was nearly fifty and was the only one of five brothers to live beyond infancy. Though he himself produced three legitimate sons and a daughter in the last six years of his life, not one of them survived him. Because he had no paternal uncles or male first cousins, his heir was his second cousin Louis, the same duke of Orléans who had joined him on the march to Naples and claimed to be rightful duke of Milan. Now King Louis XII, he was himself thirty-five and childless in spite of having been married for more than twenty years. He was also a seasoned and shrewd politician who had been through some hard times, including three years as a prisoner of his father-in-law King Louis XI, Charles VIII's father. It was obvious from the start that his coronation was likely to have consequences for the Italians. He immediately reasserted his old claim to Milan as well as appropriating to himself Charles's claim to Naples.

While the ruling families of Milan and Naples should have been frightened and undoubtedly were, for Cesare Borgia the new situation was rich in promise. He remained enthralled by the thought of a princess he had never met, Don Fadrique of Naples's daughter Carlotta. What he knew of her made her seem the perfect bride: eldest child of a king whose only son was still a boy; great-granddaughter of a king of France; a lady-in-waiting at the French court, where she had been sent to be brought up when her mother died not long after her birth. The man who married her could be confident of becoming one of the leading lords of Naples and of being accepted into the French royal family. And only one life, that of a very young brother-in-law, would stand between Carlotta herself and the Neapolitan crown.

Soundings were taken in Naples, and the results were not encouraging: Don Fadrique showed no interest in marrying his daughter to Cesare. The fact that Cesare was a cardinal of the Church is itself sufficient to explain the king's wariness, but beyond that the summer that Cesare had spent in Naples had obviously done nothing to enhance his attractiveness as a possible son-in-law. Whatever his opinion of Cesare personally, Don Fadrique probably thought that his father Ferrante and brother Alfonso II had bestowed quite enough Neapolitan riches on various Borgias, especially in connection with Sancia's marriage to Jofrè. But with a new king of France now in the picture, and Carlotta virtually that king's ward, Don Fadrique's feelings would not necessarily decide the issue. If Louis could be won over, Don Fadrique might find it difficult not to go along.

And there were ways of winning Louis over. The pope, as it happened, had the power to grant something that the French king wanted at least as much as he wanted Milan, probably even more: the annulment of his marriage. Alexander for his part, having by this time digested whatever regrets he may have felt over Cesare's determination to abandon his clerical career, made it known to Louis that he wanted essentially nothing for himself but several big things for Cesare. He wanted Carlotta, plus a high place in the French nobility, plus sources of income commensurate with that place. Pope and king alike could see that the ingredients were in place for a thoroughly satisfactory arrangement. Soon they were well along with intricate, and secret, negotiations.

Rather oddly, it was Cesare's determination to make Carlotta his wife, Alexander's acquiescence, and above all Don Fadrique's reluctance that decided Lucrezia's fate. The pope's representatives in Naples reported that, whatever his doubts about Cesare, Don Fadrique was quite open to a marriage of the cardinal's sister to his late brother Alfonso's illegitimate son and namesake, the brother of Sancia Borgia. He was more than just open, actually; to Fadrique such a marriage seemed an opportunity, a necessary gesture of goodwill, a way of tempering his rejection of Cesare and preventing it from spoiling his relations with the papal court. Cesare for his part must have seen it as a step toward winning Carlotta, and the pope was agreeable. In preparation for a wedding young Alfonso was elevated to duke of Bisceglie, and Don Fadrique agreed to Alexander's request that Lucrezia never be required to live in Naples so long as he remained alive. (That the aging pontiff made this request is the most poignant testimony we possess to the neediness in his attachment to Lucrezia.) A simple wedding was performed in Rome in July 1498, with a lack of pomp that was in sharp contrast to the bride's first wedding.

It was fortuitous, considering the cynical calculations that brought it about, that the marriage turned out to be a happy one. Bride and groom were well suited: Alfonso charming, cheerful, handsome, and almost exactly Lucrezia's age, Lucrezia a well-bred, intelligent, beguilingly good-natured beauty. Together they settled into a life of easeful enjoyment at the center of a social set of high-born young Romans in which Alfonso's sister Sancia, who with her husband Jofrè had been allowed to return from Squillace, also figured prominently. The House of Borgia and the House of Aragon were now connected not only through Jofrè's and Lucrezia's marriages but also because, back in Spain, the late Juan's little son the third duke of Gandía was related to Ferdinand and Isabella through his mother. One more such union, of Cesare and Princess Carlotta, must have seemed an entirely realistic objective. It would require nothing more than a single repetition of an established pattern.

What next commanded attention was Louis XII's annulment. He

had an admirable queen—she would be canonized a saint four and a
half centuries after her death—but his wish to be rid of her is not hard
to understand. She was Jeanne of France, so called because her father
was King Louis XI; it was at his direction that she had been married to
her cousin Louis duke of Orléans when both were about twelve years
old. The marriage was amicable enough though childless and devoid
of passion, but the unexpected death of Jeanne's younger brother
Charles VIII had not only made her husband king but given him reason
to question whether the union should continue. At issue was not only
Louis's new status as a monarch without a son and heir but the equally
big question of whether the great duchy of Brittany was going to remain part of France or revert to what it had been for centuries, a separate and sovereign principality.

Brittany had become loosely and not irrevocably united with France
as a result of the 1491 marriage of Charles VIII and Anne of Brittany,
sole living child of Brittany's last duke. That marriage appears to have
been a surprisingly happy one; the dignified, devout, and rather beautiful Anne loved her gnomish little husband despite his physical and
moral deficiencies, and in spite also of his promiscuity and his practice
of sharing their bedchamber with his groomsmen and hunting dogs.
But when all four of their children died in infancy and then Charles met
his end on a handball court, France lost its claim to Brittany, which reverted to being an independent state with Anne as its sovereign. The
only way for Louis XII to recover it, and keep it out of other hands, was
to marry Anne himself. Which was not possible if he already had a
wife. Which is why he wanted something only the Church could grant.

Alexander set out not only to accommodate Louis, but to do so in
accordance with the letter of the law. In July 1498 he established a tribu-
nal to hear the king's case, signaling his eagerness to be helpful by
appointing as one of its two leaders Archbishop Georges d'Amboise
of Rouen, a trusted friend of Louis and for years his chief minister.
The proceedings, however, soon turned unpleasant, a precursor of
what would happen a generation later when Henry VIII of England
demanded that the Church rid him of Ferdinand and Isabella's daughter
Catherine of Aragon. When Louis testified that Jeanne's deformities
had made it impossible to consummate their marriage, the queen tear-
fully denied that this was true.

While the commissioners continued with the tedious business of assembling evidence and hearing arguments in France and Rome, pope and king entered into a secret agreement that shows how much Louis was prepared to pay. With respect to Cesare's matrimonial hopes, he would promise only to encourage Carlotta to consent, insisting that everything must depend, in the end, on her doing so freely. But beyond that, he promised everything the pope had asked and more: for Cesare the title duke of Valentinois; the lordship of two French counties that together would bring him twenty thousand gold ducats per annum; a royal subsidy in the same amount; command of a thousand or more mounted soldiers to be maintained at royal expense; and the lordship of Asti as soon as France won possession of Milan. These were extraordinary benefactions. And Louis capped them by offering to make Cesare a member of his hyperexclusive Order of St. Michel, a kind of French Round Table that he regarded as the highest honor within his power to bestow.

It is improbable that the king disgorged this much bounty simply to get an annulment. His lawyers would have advised him that the strength of his case made such generosity unnecessary. Quite apart from the question of consummation, the extreme youth of both parties and the fact that they had been ordered to marry by the king made it impossible that their union had involved free and responsible commitment on either side. Louis's largesse is likely to have had more to do with his ambitions in Italy and his memory of the difficulties that Alexander's refusal to cooperate had created for Charles VIII. As little as the king was demanding at this stage, Alexander must have been aware that he was likely to demand a good deal more later, when he returned with an army to Italy. The agreement was, not explicitly but by clear implication, a reversal of papal policy, an abandonment of the consistency with which Alexander had refused to acquiesce in Charles VIII's invasion and opposed possible future incursions. Spain's rulers, understandably enough, interpreted the whole arrangement as a betrayal. Though Alexander had not repudiated his decades-old friendship with the Spanish crown, he definitely had put it at risk.

One nagging detail remained to be addressed: Cesare was pursuing a wife and becoming a vassal of the king of France while still a member of the College of Cardinals. He needed to get out from under his red hat. On August 14, 1498, he donned the full regalia of a prince of the Church for the last time—that in itself was a dramatic gesture, Cesare being rarely seen in clerical attire—and appeared before the pope and his fellow prelates. He asked to be allowed to resign from the college and revert to the lay world. Unique though this request was in the centuries-long history of the Sacred College, there was no obstacle in canon law to its being granted, Cesare in his five years as a cardinal never having taken the perpetual vows that priestly ordination entailed. The reasons he gave for requesting release were disarmingly persuasive. He simply told his colleagues what was obviously true: that he had never wanted an ecclesiastical career, had not been consulted before being placed on the path to one while still a child, and knew himself to be so utterly unsuited to life as a churchman that he could only remain in it at the risk of his immortal soul. The only objections came from those few members of the Sacred College who regarded themselves as being under more obligation to Ferdinand and Isabella than to Alexander, and for whom it would have been imprudent to cooperate in the transformation of a Spanish cardinal into a French duke. The college voted to leave the decision with the pope, and so the deed was done. Cesare was permitted to remove himself from a life of total and permanent security, giving up benefices generating an income of some 35,000 ducats annually, and hurl himself into an unforeseeable future.

Consequences followed quickly. Alexander, knowing how angry Ferdinand and Isabella would be when they learned of this, attempted to placate them by granting very nearly the only thing they wanted that he, as pope, had it in his power to grant. He ceded to them increased authority over the Church in Spain and their many other possessions including those in the New World. Most momentously, and with famously tragic consequences, he freed them to use the Spanish Inquisition as they wished and so to intensify their persecution of Muslims, Jews, and whichever Christians they chose to find suspect. Alexander's rapprochement with France also dealt a near-fatal blow to whatever remained of friendship between Rome and Milan, opening up a wide gulf between himself on one side and Ludovico and Ascanio Sforza on the other. The Colonna and Orsini were so alarmed by these developments that they brought an end to a vicious little war in which they had been fighting each other for territory, formed an alliance, and threw in with Milan. Even Naples soon joined them, Lucrezia's marriage to the duke of Bisceglie being not nearly sufficient to overcome Don Fadrique's fear of the impending French invasion. The willingness of four such improbable parties to form an alliance showed just how frightened all of them were by the rapprochement of Rome and Louis XII. Alexander tried to reassure them, insisting that his understanding with France was strictly a personal matter, limited to finding a place in the world for Cesare and changing nothing politically. He cannot have expected to be believed, but his words created just enough uncertainty to buy a little time. Maintaining lines of communication with Milan and Naples, and making certain that the existence of those lines became the worst-kept secret in Europe, enabled him to keep Louis from becoming too complacent as well.

The atmosphere in Rome grew thick with tension. On All Saints' Day, when Alexander said mass in public at St. Peter's Basilica, he did so behind a shield of armed Spanish guards. Days later, in consistory, Ascanio Sforza accused him of risking the destruction of all Italy by connecting himself to France. "Are you aware, monsignor," a scornful Alexander replied to his onetime friend, "that it was your brother who invited the French into Italy?" An even sharper exchange took place three days before Christmas, when envoys freshly arrived from Ferdinand and Isabella warned the pope that if he continued on his present course, he was going to find himself answering to a general council of the Church. Both sides spoke with brutal frankness, and both must have been startled by the things being said. The Spaniards accused Alexander of simony and of nepotism beyond the bounds of reason. Alexander went further, declaring that Ferdinand and Isabella were usurpers with no right to their thrones. Told that God had punished him with the death of the duke of Gandía, the pope retorted that God had punished Ferdinand and Isabella far more severely in taking their only son.

Such intemperate words were so untypical of the usually unflappable Alexander that one shocked observer attributed them to a secret fear that the deal with France had been a colossal mistake. Things escalated from there, with Portugal soon joining Spain in threatening to summon a council and, by implication, elect a new pope. Louis XII sent assurances that there was nothing to fear—that the agreement binding

Spain to France made it impossible for Ferdinand to act on his threats. All the same, the hostility of the Spanish royals must have made Alexander wonder if he had made a perilously wrong turn. That his actions in coming to terms with France had been so widely at variance with his own political instincts is a good measure of just how much influence Cesare now had over him.

Cesare by this time was in France and making himself at home at King Louis's court. He had departed Rome on October 1, at the end of a period of immensely costly preparations. It was said that all the gold, silver, silk, and jewels to be found in the shops of Rome had been bought up for his use. Then, when everything was in readiness, he had refused to go until his face cleared of an eruption of the symptoms of syphilis. When he finally set out, his retinue was so large, its baggage so mountainous, that hundreds of mules were needed for transporting it to the coast. Whole days were required to get everyone and everything aboard a fleet of galleys at Civitavecchia, and the expedition did not reach Marseilles until October 19. Hundreds of thousands of ducats had been raised to pay for all this, and the means by which they were raised were sometimes appalling. No one thought it a coincidence that just at this time the master of the papal household, an aged Spanish bishop, abruptly found himself arrested on charges of heresy and obliged to surrender his riches to secure his release. All this so that a recently (if voluntarily) defrocked clergyman who had just passed his twenty-fourth birthday could show the French that he was a personage of the highest importance and worthy of a royal bride.

Louis saw to it that Cesare was received with all possible honors. His arrival at Marseilles was made a grand event, almost a public holiday, and similar formalities were repeated at every stop along his way. At Touraine he met Louis for the first time, and at the onetime papal capital of Avignon he was given an improbably warm welcome by the city's archbishop—none other than Pope Alexander's old foe Cardinal Giuliano della Rovere. Still in self-imposed exile, della Rovere had resigned himself to the fact that he could hope to gain nothing by remaining hostile to the Borgias if Louis XII was now their friend. From Avignon Cesare moved in stately procession to his ducal seat at Valence, then to Lyons, rejoining Louis at the ancient hilltop palace of Chinon a week before Christmas.

For his entry into Chinon Cesare pulled out all the stops. He had himself dressed in cloth of silver and gold, his horse draped with jewels and pearls and fitted with silver shoes. When he came through the city gates, however, the onlooking crowds found him not so much impressive as ridiculous. They snickered up their sleeves, muttering that ostentation on such a scale might have befitted a Roman emperor but on a Spanish provincial was sheer excess. It is characteristic of Cesare that he noted these japes and took a lesson from them. For the rest of his life he would dress in simple black, his only adornment the emblem of King Louis's Order of St. Michel that hung from a chain around his neck. In matters of attire as in all things, he was a quick learner and rarely made the same mistake twice.

Once inside Chinon castle and quit of his bejeweled horse, Cesare presented Louis with a papal bull freshly arrived from Rome. It was the longed-for *dispensa,* declaring the work of the annulment commission complete, the king's request granted. The nullification was based not on nonconsummation, which could not be proved, but on an eminently legitimate finding that at the time of their wedding both bride and groom had been under royal coercion and too young to bind themselves for life. Having delivered that good news, Cesare further delighted his hosts by unveiling a second bull, this one appointing Archbishop d'Amboise to the College of Cardinals. Both Cesare and Carlotta of Naples were in attendance when, on January 6, 1499, Anne of Brittany was married to Louis XII. Cesare was continuing to press for a betrothal of his own and was continuing to get nonanswers. The king, who by now had secured everything he had hoped for in inviting Cesare to France, nevertheless continued to support his young visitor's cause. Don Fadrique's answer was always the same, an echo of what Louis had said earlier: Carlotta would not be forced into a marriage she did not want. Cesare must have been aware, by this point, that Carlotta was in love with a young count, a member of one of Brittany's most eminent families, and was unwilling to consider any other suitor.

Cesare found himself in a kind of limbo, almost a hostage. To go home unmarried, after all that he and the pope had done to obtain a royal bride, would have been a humiliation. And so he remained at Chinon, waiting for . . . it was no longer quite clear *what* he was waiting for. Weeks passed, and then months, and still he was frozen in place.

Young ladies from the fringes of the royal family were put on display for his consideration, but nothing came of that. One consolation was that Louis, in contrast to Don Fadrique of Naples, had taken a liking to Cesare, giving every appearance of enjoying his company and genuinely wanting to help him. There is nothing surprising in this. Physically so attractive that people spoke of him as the handsomest man in Italy, Cesare also had the same bright good nature as the pope and his sister Lucrezia. He had been given the nickname Valentino when, barely grown, he was made the archbishop of Valencia. It remained appropriate, and in use, now that he was duke of Valentinois. The dashing Valentino would have been a welcome addition to any Renaissance court. Young as he was, though, the pleasures of a courtier's life did not satisfy. He wanted to get on with things. His fate depended entirely on the support of a pope who, though still vital and vibrant, was now approaching seventy. That made Cesare a young man in a hurry.

But winter passed and spring came, and still nothing changed. It must have been maddening, now that he was a duke and supposedly a soldier and no longer constrained by the claims of the Church, to have to remain idle in Chinon as couriers brought news of momentous developments in the outside world. Being at the French court, he would have been among the first to learn, in February 1499, of Louis's entry into an agreement with Venice for the partition of the duchy of Milan. He would have understood immediately what this meant: that with any possibility of Venetian assistance removed, the Sforzas of Milan were doomed. A Milan without major allies was indefensible against France, and the fall of the Sforzas would mean that the road to Naples was open once again. Ferdinand of Spain, when he learned of the agreement, was so furious that he recalled his ambassadors not only from Venice but from Rome. These were portentous developments for Europe, for Italy, for Rome, and of course for Cesare himself.

That the possibility of stopping Louis simply did not exist sheds an intriguing if uncertain light on Cesare's mission to France. It raises the question of whether perhaps there was more to that mission than a quest for a bride, a title, and wealth. It was a quest for those things, without question, but it also created a relationship, a friendship, that had the potential to save both the Borgia papacy and the sovereignty of Rome. Friendship with an invincible invader could mean safety, survival. Surviving could mean continuing to have options—a chance, at least, of controlling one's own destiny. It is difficult to believe that none of this had occurred to Alexander by the time he decided to go to such lengths, financial and otherwise, to help make Cesare's journey a success. In other words, it is not at all certain that Alexander had become incapable of pursuing or even formulating his own policies rather than simply doing whatever Cesare wished. If he was not actively and autonomously attempting to thread his way between the Scylla that was Spain and the Charybdis of France, he was certainly allowing nothing to happen that might close off any of his options.

The most terrible danger remained clear: that by befriending Louis the pope would make enemies of Ferdinand and Isabella. If this came to pass, his options, his freedom to make choices, would be reduced or possibly even destroyed. He urgently needed to repair his old relationship with Spain, therefore, if only to preserve the possibility that eventually he could play off the two great powers against each other and prevent either from taking control of all Italy. How this might be accomplished, however, was by no means obvious. Ferdinand blamed Alexander when it became apparent that French boots would soon be tramping across Italian soil once again and that he had no way of doing anything about it. Isabella for her part was growing sick of the Borgias: the bad behavior of the late Juan, Cesare's wild reputation capped by his departure from the Church, Alexander's move toward France. By springtime it was the declared position of the Spanish government that the election of Alexander VI had been invalid and that a council must be called to put things right. Spain was supported in this not only by Portugal as before but also, now, by that other opponent of French expansion, the Hapsburg emperor Maximilian. The pope's situation was becoming seriously dangerous.

Alexander set out to do what he could to reduce the number of things that the Spanish monarchs had to be angry about without undercutting Cesare's position at Chinon. In response to complaints about how the Church was being stripped bare for the enrichment of the Borgias, he took the Italian duchy of Benevento from the little duke of Gandía and restored direct papal rule. Two months later, to address concerns about the influence of the young Borgias at the papal court, he ordered Lucrezia and Jofrè to once again leave Rome, taking up residence this time in

Spoleto and thus reducing their visibility. Interestingly—we get here an indication of the pope's opinion of the two youngest Borgias—Lucrezia rather than Jofrè was given responsibilities that made her, in effect, governor of Spoleto, in charge of its civil administration. These duties she carried out conscientiously under the watchful eyes of experienced counselors provided for the purpose. She did so in spite of being far along with a second pregnancy (earlier she had suffered a miscarriage, apparently as the result of a fall) and in spite of the embarrassment of having a second husband run away in fear. The duke of Bisceglie, as a new French invasion became a certainty, had understood the implications of Alexander's new relationship with Louis and concluded like Giovanni Sforza before him that he was not safe in Rome. He fled first to refuge in the castles of the Colonna, then home to Naples. He wrote asking Lucrezia to join him, but his letters were intercepted by the pope. Alexander sent an envoy to Don Fadrique with instructions to return Bisceglie to Rome. The king, wanting no trouble, agreed to make this happen—but not quite yet. When Bisceglie finally did rejoin his wife, he did so not at Rome but at her own domain of Spoleto, which promised to be far less dangerous.

And then from France came great news: a letter from Louis informing Alexander that Cesare was married. Not to Carlotta of Naples, but to the beautiful nineteen-year-old Charlotte d'Albret, daughter of an old French family of the highest distinction and sister of the king of Navarre. Louis reported gleefully that the validity of the union was safe from challenge because Cesare had "broken his lance" no fewer than eight times on his wedding night, adding admiringly that this was double the total he himself had achieved on his first night with Anne of Brittany. Thus it mattered not at all that the bride had been less than eager and had agreed to the union only after being urged by the French king, Anne of Brittany, and her own family. The wedding was performed in the queen's apartment at the palace of Blois. It had been arranged in the nick of time; not long thereafter Louis's great army was on the road, marching to Italy. Its lead units were commanded by Gian Giacomo Trivulzio, an experienced and respected *condottiere* who had been born into the Milanese nobility and begun his military career in the service of the Sforzas but defected to France when Ludovico il Moro promoted a rival over him. Trivulzio was a man with something to prove, and in his quest for vindication he pressed forward aggressively. The king and the rest of the army followed at a leisurely pace, accompanied by, among many other dignitaries, Cardinal Giuliano della Rovere and Duke Valentino. Cesare had used some of the wealth he had taken with him to France to hire mercenary troops for Louis XII's use, and Alexander had contributed still others. Behind this generosity lay an understanding: once Milan was secure, Louis would release a portion of his army—a much larger force than the thousand troops put at Cesare's disposal when he was made duke of Valentinois—for the use of the Borgias.

Milan fell with remarkable ease. At the start of September, with Trivulzio bearing down on him, Ludovico Sforza abandoned his capital and joined his brother-in-law Emperor Maximilian in the Tyrolean Alps, taking with him his two small sons, his brother Cardinal Ascanio, and a fortune in gold and jewels. He might not have given up quite so easily if his wife Beatrice d'Este had been on hand to stiffen his spine, but her death two years earlier, still only twenty-one years old, had deprived him of his most trusted source of counsel. When Trivulzio took possession of the city of Milan on September 11, Louis and his retinue were still far behind, crossing the mountains from Grenoble to Turin. The king would not make his own grand entry into Milan until early October, but before that happened his mastery of the whole of the duchy would be complete. All this was capped by expressions of friendship from Ferdinand of Spain, which freed Louis to focus on the consolidation of his gains and ponder his options where his claim to the crown of Naples was concerned.

The conquest of Milan seemed a vindication of Alexander's alliance with France. Louis XII's effortless success, coupled with the commitments he had made to the pope, ensured that the Borgias would now have the resources to pursue their own objectives in the Papal States. As a kind of bonus, Ferdinand's determination to remain at least temporarily on amicable terms with France left him with no option except to put aside his grievances against the pope, Alexander as well as Rome now being in effect under French protection. For the first time in a long time Alexander found himself free not just to react to the actions of others but to take the initiative, and to do so in his own interests.

He did so with as much boldness as he had ever shown in his life, declaring that all the lords of the Romagna had forfeited their right to the cities their families had ruled for generations, in some cases for centuries. The scope of the bull with which he did this was breathtaking. It excommunicated several of the most important families in northern Italy: the Riarii of Imola and Forlì, the Malatesta of Rimini, the Manfredi of Faenza, the Varani of Camerino, and Giovanni Sforza in Pesaro. It even extended to the Montefeltri of Urbino, whose domain was outside the Romagna. All were declared dispossessed. They were to be replaced by one man, a new papal vicar for all the affected states: Cesare Borgia, duke of Valentinois.

The pope's act, if shocking, was entirely lawful, the lords in question being not only without legitimacy in many cases but years behind in paying tribute to Rome. Nor was it unjustified, when one considers the hard methods employed by most of those same lords to maintain control of the places they ruled, and the problems that their lawlessness created for Italy at large.

No words inscribed on a sheet of vellum, however, were going to get them to surrender control. That was going to require force. Force that would be applied by Valentino.

PART FOUR

Cesare

Caesar or Nothing

16

The Landscape Changes

Fourteen ninety-nine changed everything.

It transformed Louis XII's place in the world. His effortless conquest of the great duchy of Milan elevated him, seemingly overnight, from a kind of political abstraction, a fearsome but remote potential threat, into the master of northern Italy. Suddenly he was *the* power that no one north of Naples could dare defy.

His liking for the bold young man he had made duke of Valentinois, and his appreciation of how much trouble Pope Alexander had spared him by not opposing his incursion into Italy, transformed Louis in another way as well. He became—within limits defined by his perception of his own strategic interests—a willing patron of the Borgias. This in turn transformed the pope's position, giving him more freedom of action than he had previously known. That freedom, as things turned out, would be used mainly for Cesare's benefit, as he pursued his dreams of greatness.

For Alexander and Cesare alike, the next step was obvious. The time had come for a new offensive against the warlords of the Papal States, with Cesare in command this time. For Alexander, removing or at least taming the warlords was the only way of achieving control of the Church's domains, a goal that had eluded his predecessors for centuries. Cesare's ultimate objective could scarcely have been more ambitious without bringing his sanity into question. It was to carve out of the Papal States, for himself, a principality substantial enough to place him among the great men of Italy—not just to become a petty tyrant ruling over one or two small cities like Caterina Sforza or Vitellozzo Vitelli, but to assemble a state on an equal level with the Urbino of the Montefeltri and the Ferrara of the Este, conceivably with Florence or even Milan and Venice.

What made this dream feasible was Louis of France's presence in northern Italy and his courting of the Borgias, his willingness to trade his support for theirs. This gave Rome a strength—albeit a largely borrowed strength—that it had barely possessed since the time, seven hundred years before, when Charlemagne and his father had made themselves masters of Italy and shared their conquests with the popes of the time. As for the fact that, to become a *legitimate* ruler in the Papal States, Cesare would have to accept subordinate status as a vassal of the pope, there was so little reason to object that it didn't matter. Even the kings of Naples were papal vassals, and they had rarely been inconvenienced as a result.

Alexander and Cesare made no move until Louis was comfortably settled in the north of Italy and therefore in a relaxed and magnanimous frame of mind, at which point they secured his approval of their plans and were able to start making things happen. They made them happen quickly. In November, barely a month after Louis's triumphal entry into Milan, Alexander made a fast grab at some low-hanging fruit, seizing the lands and castles of the Gaetani, a family considerably less powerful than the Orsini or the Colonna. The Gaetani holdings lay along the frontier where the Papal States abutted Naples and had considerable strategic value because the main highway connecting Rome and Naples ran through them. Though Alexander's grounds for declaring them forfeit were unarguably sound—the Gaetani had allied themselves with Naples when Rome was at odds with Ferrante, thereby failing in a fundamental feudal obligation—such offenses had been routine among the vicars of the Papal States much longer than anyone could remember. Only the support of the French king made it possible for him to proceed. Without that support, without the fact that everyone knew of that support, other and more powerful clans almost certainly would have come to the defense of the Gaetani. Don Fadrique of Naples would likely have intervened as well.

The most surprising aspect of the attack on the Gaetani was not the fact that Alexander attempted it but his way of disposing of the seized properties. He *sold* them, and to, of all people, Lucrezia Borgia. She by this time was reunited with her husband, had just weeks before given birth to a son they named Rodrigo, and in the aftermath of her good performance at Spoleto was now in charge of the papal city of Nepi as well. Where she obtained the purchase price of eighty thousand ducats is unknown; possibly it was given to her out of the pontifical treasury, which if true made the transaction not a sale at all but a swindle. The whole affair is in any case another example of the extent to which restoring the power of the papacy and advancing the fortunes of his family had come to be intertwined not only in the pope's thinking but in his actions. The tangle was probably inherent in the situation. A conquest of the Papal States in the pope's name *would* be an assertion of the authority of Rome, no less if done by Cesare than by anyone else. And, it being necessary to entrust the management of the Papal States to *some* vicar, who *better* than Cesare?

Almost simultaneously with Alexander's move against the Gaetani, Cesare embarked upon his new career as a soldier, bidding farewell to Louis XII and riding out of Milan at the head of a force of eighteen hundred cavalry and four thousand infantry brightly caparisoned in the red and yellow colors of the Borgias. Most of this force was made up of Swiss and Gascon mercenaries on loan from the king, all of them under the direct command of the Frenchman Yves d'Alègre. It was Alexander's reward for his support of the Milan campaign, and it was Cesare's to use—more or less—in whatever way he wished. Thus he found himself with the means to invade the Romagna and begin expelling the rulers of its numerous, mostly small city-states. Strategically the Romagna was a sensible choice: in the shadow of Milan and therefore within easy reach of the French king's protection, far enough from Naples not to heighten the alarm that had been felt there when Alexander attacked the Gaetani.

Alexander had laid the groundwork for Cesare's offensive, his *impresa,* back in July, with his bull excommunicating the Romagna's leading lords. Nothing remained now but to enforce the bull and to do so in a way that was acceptable to the French and did not trigger a countermove by Venice, the only other state both close enough to the

Romagna to have a real stake in its future and strong enough to make trouble. These considerations decided Cesare's selection of his first targets: the little cities of Imola and Forlì on the Via Emilia, the ancient Roman road that runs with scarcely more than an occasional gentle curve from Bologna down to the Adriatic coast. Imola and Forlì were an obvious choice because they were ruled, in the name of her eldest son, by Caterina Sforza, whom the events of 1499 had left utterly isolated. Louis XII had no possible interest in protecting a woman who was not only a Sforza, a niece of Ludovico il Moro, but had helped her uncle to recruit troops in the Romagna as he tried to prepare for the French invasion. When asked to include Caterina in his new alliance with Florence, Louis ingenuously replied that he could not possibly intrude into the pope's affairs in such a way. It was an empty excuse, but the king's position was so strong that he had no need to make himself believable.

Nor would Venice grieve to see Caterina destroyed. A year earlier, when Venetian troops set out to cross the Romagna at the start of a campaign aimed at making Florence a satellite of Venice, Caterina had been alone in offering resistance. She did so with such ferocious determination that the invaders, hampered by their war with the Turks, were obliged to return home. Now, in 1500, she was not only Venice's enemy in her own right but also the chosen enemy of Venice's sole important friend, Rome. Because of the Turkish threat, the Venetians could hardly have considered trying to save Caterina even had they been inclined to do so, which they emphatically were not. They had earlier annoyed Alexander by warning him that they would brook no interference with their near neighbor Ercole d'Este, whose duchy of Ferrara could have been a rich prize and potentially an ideal base for Cesare. They could not have been less interested in offending him further by interfering with Cesare's plans.

Even a friendless *virago* was a dangerous enemy, however. Since the last time we encountered her—in 1488, the year she outwitted and annihilated the murderers of her husband Girolamo Riario—Caterina had made herself as hated and feared as any warlord in Italy. She was violent, ruthless, and capable of almost insane cruelty. At age thirty-six she was still blond and beautiful, though not as slim as she had been in her youth, had been widowed three times, and was the mother of five sons and a daughter by Riario, a sixth son by her second husband Giacomo Feo, and a seventh by her third husband, an obscure member of the Medici family. Feo like Riario had been murdered, again deservedly so, and this time in taking revenge Caterina had not only wiped out the killers but had had their wives and children—including small children—tortured and executed. Though she had added considerably to Pope Alexander's troubles at the time of the first French invasion by allying herself with her cousins in Milan and thus with Charles VIII, this had not prevented the pontiff from later proposing a marriage of her eldest son and heir, Ottaviano Riario, to Lucrezia. Caterina had declined; such a union could have made it difficult for her to continue ruling Imola and Forlì in the ineffectual Ottaviano's name.

Caterina's great problem, as Cesare's assault force approached, was that there was only one of her and she had two cities to defend. She barricaded herself inside the *rocca* at Forlì, leaving Imola under the command of a *condottiere* named Dionigi di Naldi. In Caterina's absence Imola proved impossible to hold, its inhabitants having suffered far too much at the hands of Caterina and her husbands to be willing to sacrifice anything on her behalf. Di Naldi and his troops withdrew into Imola's *rocca,* but when Cesare and d'Alègre arrived and put on a demonstration of what their artillery could do to brickwork battlements, the fight was over. Di Naldi not only opened the fortress's gates but joined Cesare's army. It was agreed, as part of the surrender terms, that d'Alègre's mercenaries would not be allowed inside the town walls of Imola. This proved to be unenforceable, assuming that the French commander made any attempt to enforce it, and the consequences were horrific: pillaging and rapine of the kind that the soldiers of northern Europe regarded as their right but that few Italians then living had ever experienced.

At Forlì, in the beginning, things unfolded much as they had at Imola. The townsfolk, evidently unaware of what had happened to their neighbors, welcomed the invaders while Caterina watched from the ramparts of her fortress. This time, however, Cesare made certain that the French troops were kept away from the civilians. And this time, Caterina Sforza being in personal command of the defenses, there would be no surrender. Having sent her children off to the safety of Florence, Caterina settled in for a fight to the finish, showing her contempt for the people who had been her subjects for the previous twenty years by bombarding their homes with stone cannonballs. "Should I have to perish," she is supposed to have said, "I want to perish like a man." Any doubts about whether it was going to be a long, hard siege were laid to rest when Caterina, to spread the general misery, broke open Forlì's irrigation dams. The Romagna landscape being little less flat than a billiard table, she thereby succeeded in flooding both the town and the countryside surrounding and caused Cesare's siege machinery to bog down in mud. At about this same time, Caterina or someone associated with her attempted to assassinate the pope at long distance, with an early experiment in chemical warfare. A message was sent to him wrapped either in poison or (depending on which version of the story is preferred) in fabric worn by a victim of the plague. The experiment failed and no harm was done aside from a further heightening, if such a thing was possible, of the general hostility.

Caterina hung on doggedly through three brutal weeks as ball after ball smashed into the walls of her *rocca*, which finally began to develop large cracks. Her spirits must have soared at reports that her uncle Ludovico il Moro was coming down out of the Alps at the head of an army, intent upon retaking Milan. The reports were true; the gold with which he had earlier fled Milan had provided Ludovico with ample funds with which to hire and equip a substantial body of Swiss mercenaries. If he moved quickly enough and was at all successful, Louis XII would be forced to recall his troops from the Romagna. Cesare would have no choice but to break off his siege.

Things did not work out that way. On January 12 Cesare's bombardment finally bore fruit, opening a sizable hole in one of the walls of Caterina's stronghold and allowing d'Alègre's infantry to pour through. The hand-to-hand combat that followed ended with Caterina, seeing that defeat had become inevitable, attempting to commit suicide by blowing up her gunpowder magazine. A defective fuse foiled that effort, and she was taken prisoner by the French, her fortress falling into Cesare's hands. He had to pay d'Alègre to hand Caterina herself over, regarding her as far too dangerous to be left in anyone's custody but his own. Soon after, when he set off with his troops for his next objective, Giovanni Sforza's city of Pesaro, he took his captive with him. By not only defeating the famed *virago* but stripping her of her cities, he had catapulted himself into first place among the soldiers of Italy. Stories circulated of how he repeatedly raped Caterina after she was in his custody, and though they enhanced his reputation as an enemy to be feared, they are of dubious provenance. It is just as plausible that Caterina, who in the course of her career had more lovers than husbands, made her person available to Cesare in hopes of gaining an advantage. It is no less possible that the two did not become intimately involved at all.

Cesare was en route to Pesaro, which had already been abandoned by a frightened Giovanni Sforza, when a courier came galloping in with instructions for Yves d'Alègre to quick-march his troops back to Milan. Il Moro had reentered his old capital to the welcoming shouts of his former subjects, who after a taste of French occupation had decided— much like the Neapolitans in the time of Charles VIII—that the Sforzas were not so intolerable after all. D'Alègre's men were to become part of the force that Louis XII was assembling in hope of saving his position. The speed of this reversal made Louis's invasion seem as empty an achievement as his predecessor's had been. It resurrected old questions about how wise the pope had been in allying Rome with France.

The Sforza resurgence, however, was short-lived. In March, with a decisive battle apparently impending, Il Moro found himself abandoned to the mercy of his enemies. The Swiss mercenaries who had made possible his return to Italy, called upon to attack the Swiss in the employ of King Louis, declared that doing so was out of the question. They turned on their heels and departed, leaving Ludovico face-to-face with his enemies without an army at his back. He became a prisoner, as did his brother Cardinal Ascanio. Together they were taken away to France, where Ludovico would remain in confinement for the rest of his life. Louis XII took custody of the child who would have been duke of Milan if not for Ludovico's usurpation: the still only nine-year-old Francesco Sforza, grandson of Il Moro's late brother the psychopath Galeazzo Maria. No doubt to keep him from producing more claimants to the ducal title, the boy was consigned to the Church and to a comfortable future as abbot of a French monastery of no particular importance.

The withdrawal of d'Alègre's troops had brought Cesare's first *impresa* to an unexpected, and from his perspective a deplorably prema-

ture, end. He had to abandon the march on Pesaro. Leaving Imola and
Forlì in the firm hands of a longtime associate, a ruthlessly tough veteran of the Spanish *reconquista* named Ramiro de Lorqua, he set out for
Rome. Pope Alexander, who had ordered bonfires lit all around Rome
upon learning of the capture of Forlì, now outdid himself, arranging an
extravagant public celebration of Cesare's arrival and modeling it on
the "triumphs" with which the emperors of old had marked the return
of conquerors. On February 25 the whole city was turned out: cardinals, bishops, ambassadors, and Rome's noble families stood waiting to
cheer as Cesare passed through the Porta del Popolo at the head of his
shrunken and weary army. With him, a trophy on display, was Caterina
Sforza. After refusing to sign away her son's rights to Forlì and Imola,
she was locked up in the Castel Sant'Angelo, where, so the story goes,
her hair quickly turned white.

The pope conferred on Cesare the Golden Rose, an ancient honor
usually reserved for royalty, and the coveted title *gonfaloniere* or
standard-bearer of the Church, previously held by such masters of the
military arts as Francesco Sforza and Federico da Montefeltro as well as
by Cesare's distinctly less deserving brother Juan.

Louis XII being now back in control of Milan and eager to demonstrate his generosity to faithful friends, Cesare was almost immediately
able to begin planning a second Romagna campaign. Though still dependent on the king's assistance, he was growing wary of it, having
experienced at first hand how viciously uncontrollable France's mercenaries could be and how quickly they could be withdrawn when Louis
decided that he needed them elsewhere. Cesare began looking to the
Vatican for more of the money he needed. With Alexander's skeptical
acquiescence—though the pope definitely wanted control of the Papal
States, he was less confident than Cesare that the Romagna was the
place to start and less certain that trading friendship with Spain for
friendship with France made strategic sense—Cesare began drawing
from the pontifical treasury sums that in time would become nearly
insupportable.

For the moment, fortunately for Cesare, the papal coffers were exceptionally full, the reforms introduced by Alexander having by this
time begun to produce both increased revenues and substantial sav-
ings. The revenues of the alum mines at Tolfa were continuing to ac-

cumulate also, and Alexander had created a cash bonanza by declaring 1500 a jubilee year and promising special indulgences that were drawing pilgrims to Rome by the tens of thousands. Though he cannot be accused of neglecting other needs—in response to the Turkish threat Alexander was sending forty thousand ducats a year to the king of Hungary and paying for the construction and equipping of fifteen warships at Venice—good management and good luck were providing him with the means to help Cesare as well.

For Cesare especially, but for all the young Borgias, the early summer of 1500 was a time for basking in good fortune. Alexander issued a bull appointing Cesare vicar—lord in the pope's name—of Imola and Forlì. News arrived from France that Cesare's bride, Charlotte d'Albret, was expecting his child. There is no explanation of why Charlotte failed to join her husband in Italy. Louis XII may have found it advisable to keep her in his custody, if not quite as a hostage then at least as an enhancement of his leverage over the Borgias. As for Cesare himself, it was not in his nature to pine for any woman; the most famously beautiful courtesan in Rome, a Florentine named Fiammetta, had by this time become his principal mistress. On June 24, as part of the Vatican's celebration of the Feast of St. John the Baptist, he put on a display of his bullfighting skills in the piazza of St. Peter's Basilica, killing five bulls from horseback and a sixth on foot, severing the head of the last with a single blow of his sword. It should not be forgotten that even at this point, recognized though he already was as the most fearsome Italian alive and a rising political force in his own right, Cesare was not yet twenty-five years old. His most colorful and extravagant actions are generally best understood as expressions of sheer animal exuberance—the overflowing vitality of a gifted, ambitious, energetic, and burningly impatient young man.

The summer idyll of 1500 came to an abrupt and frightening end on the night of July 15, a date that marks the beginning of another of the darkest Borgia mysteries. Lucrezia and the duke of Bisceglie had returned to Rome from Nepi, and that night, upon departing the papal palace after dinner, Bisceglie was set upon by a gang of armed men. Whether they intended to kill him or carry him away is not known, but Bisceglie resisted at sword's point and was gravely injured in the ensuing fight. The attackers fled when palace guards heard the commotion

and opened the gates. At Alexander's instructions Bisceglie was carried
to a room on the top floor of the new part of the papal palace known
today as the Borgia Tower, and a round-the-clock guard was posted.
Over the next five weeks, under the care of the pope's own physicians
and with Lucrezia and Sancia serving as nurses and guardians, he gradually regained his strength.

Rome boiled with speculation about whose work the attack had
been, and why. This time Cesare came under suspicion almost immediately. Apparently there had been bad blood between him and Bisceglie; this would have been nearly unavoidable as Cesare and Alexander
allowed their old friendship with Naples and Spain to cool and drew
close to France instead. The grapevine continued to hum with whis-
pers about how, with Louis XII's army likely to be moving on Naples
soon, Bisceglie's connection to the Borgias had become tiresomely in-
convenient. Learning of this talk, Cesare declared cryptically that "I
did not wound the duke, but if I had it would have been no more than
he deserved." Evidently Bisceglie himself believed Cesare to be guilty,
though suspicion also focused, as at the time of Juan Borgia's murder,
on the Orsini. It was said that Bisceglie, in league with his family's longtime allies the Colonna, had been plotting against the Orsini. This is no
less plausible than any number of rival theories, including the one that
had Cesare ordering the attack out of fear that Lucrezia's happy marriage, and Alexander's devotion to Lucrezia, would deter the pontiff
from breaking with Naples. Or the suggestion that it was Bisceglie who
had blocked Cesare from making Carlotta of Naples his wife, thereby
incurring his hatred.

What happened next was even more shocking but considerably less
mysterious. On August 18 Lucrezia, Sancia, and Bisceglie's visiting
mother briefly left the convalescing duke alone, either to attend to
some matter of household business or because someone—possibly
Cesare—had called them away. Upon returning and finding the door
blocked by armed men, the women ran to the pope for help. When at
last they were admitted to Bisceglie's bedchamber, they found him
dead, strangled, it would be said, by a Spanish soldier named Miguel de
Corella—Michelotto to the Italians, a longtime friend of Cesare's but
just now coming to prominence as his most trusted and devoted lieutenant. No reason has ever emerged for thinking this account of the

crime to be untrue. Questions, however, remain. *Why* would Cesare have been so open in arranging the murder, in broad daylight and without any attempt at secrecy, of the husband of the sister whom, as his subsequent conduct would make it impossible to doubt, he loved more than anyone else? And does his responsibility for the murder mean that he must also have been responsible for the night attack on Bisceglie more than a month earlier?

The search for answers has always been impeded by rumor and uncertainty—by reports, for example, that not long before the murder Bisceglie had gone for a walk in the papal gardens, seen the brother-in-law who he believed had tried to have him butchered, fired off a bolt from a crossbow in an impulsive attempt at revenge, and sent Cesare into a murderous rage by doing so. Among students of the Borgia story are some who find it impossible to believe that Cesare had anything to do with the first attempt on Bisceglie's life, others who find it impossible to believe that he did not. As for the strangling, here it is depicted as a cold-blooded act of political calculation, there as a crime of blind passion. When everything known about Cesare is taken into account, it would appear more characteristic of him to have killed for a purpose than to have been carried away by a momentary surge of wrath. Still, as noted earlier, he *was* young and capable of impulsive behavior.

The deepest mystery of all, assuming as we must that Cesare did have Bisceglie killed, is how his relationship with Lucrezia was not destroyed. If we could find the answer to that, it would take us to the heart of a connection that bound brother tightly to sister as long as both remained alive. The intensity of that connection was undoubtedly obvious to all who observed the two together and helps to explain why the allegations of incest that a bitter Giovanni Sforza first muttered when his marriage to Lucrezia was being dissolved took root and grew into a centuries-old legend of international reach.

Whatever the answers to these questions, regardless of whether Cesare at any point had second thoughts or felt a pang of remorse (neither thing is easily imagined), the murder and the furor that followed did nothing to diminish his impatience to return to action. He was poised to respond when, just days after Bisceglie's body was laid to rest, it became known that preparations for Louis XII's move on Naples were under way at last. This put a whole new train of events in motion. Alexander and Cesare alike were quick to see that the situation was ripe for exploitation. It was Cesare, mainly, who set out to do the exploiting, pulling an uncertain pope along in his wake.

He had two great advantages in this situation. The first was the papal soldiery, which if added to King Louis's own troops would increase the size of the French army by at least a third. If used to resist Louis's advance, on the other hand, it could be a serious problem. The other was the power of the pope to approve, or withhold approval of, Louis's claim to the Neapolitan crown. Without this, even if he succeeded in taking Naples by force, Louis like Charles before him would be a usurper with no proper grounds for demanding the loyalty of the people of Naples or recognition by the other Italian states.

The king's need for the Borgias was therefore obvious enough, and his personal attachment to Cesare sufficiently well known, to have immediate impact. It caused the Venetians, eager to demonstrate their willingness to be cooperative, to confer on Cesare the honorary title *gentiluomo di Venezi*. In doing this they signaled that they had no intention of defending Pesaro, Rimini, or Faenza—all of them longtime Venetian protectorates—if Cesare moved against them. Just twelve days later, less than a week after the Bisceglie murder, a team of French commissioners arrived in Rome to lay out the terms on which Cesare could launch his next *impresa* and again receive French support. Louis was generous, offering Cesare the use of 7,700 fighting men and approving his plan to expand his signory, his lordship, across much or possibly all of the Romagna.

The campaign that Cesare was preparing was going to be hellishly expensive—all the more so because he had made it his policy, from the point at which he first became a commander of troops, not only to pay and equip his men well but also—what was most unusual—always to pay them on time. Pope Alexander's main role was simply to cover the costs—to funnel from the papal treasury the sums required to keep Cesare supplied with thousands of well-trained, well-equipped, and satisfied professional fighters. It is commonly said that in late September the pope gave his income a onetime boost of 120,000 ducats by selling, with the terms negotiated by Cesare, twelve seats in the College of Cardinals. In fact only ten cardinals were appointed at that time, and their identities make it doubtful that fund-raising was the primary reason for their promotion. Three of the ten were Spaniards, among them one of the Borgia Lanzols and a former teacher of Cesare's. Among the six Italians were Alexander's physician and a brother of the Gian Giacomo Trivulzio who as commander of Louis XII's attack force had driven Ludovico Sforza out of Milan. Like the three appointments of six months earlier, which had conferred red hats on two Spaniards and a brother of Cesare's wife, most of these men were more capable of tightening Borgia control over the Sacred College and winning favor with the kings of France and Spain than of paying great sums for their new rank. It is clear in any case that Cesare was left free to select the new cardinals, and that his choices, even if not made for cash, had more to do with politics than with the merits of the individuals so favored. He was, not to put too fine a point on it, packing the college with cronies.

The ease with which Cesare's slate of nominees was approved by the College of Cardinals, normally so opposed to attempts to increase its membership, shows how powerful he now was politically, and perhaps how feared. The same thing was shown again when emissaries arrived from the Romagnese city of Cesena and two of its neighboring towns and meekly begged Cesare to condescend to become their lord, their *signore*. The populations of these places were in effect giving themselves to him, seeking to spare themselves unpleasantness or worse by saving him the trouble of having to use force. In granting their petitions, Cesare substantially strengthened his position in the region between Bologna and the Adriatic coast without so much as leaving Rome.

Further gains came quickly and with almost equal ease. When on October 2 Cesare embarked on his second *impresa,* he marched out of Rome at the head of an army of some ten thousand men. Waiting to join him in the Romagna was a force three-quarters that size provided by Louis XII. This was a terrifyingly large number of troops by the standards of the time, and Cesare made himself all the more frightening by telling no one what he intended to do. Florence felt threatened, all the more so because a delegation it had sent to Louis XII's court—one of its members was a young civil servant named Niccolò Macchiavelli—had thus far not succeeded in securing either an alliance or assurances of protection. Even Bologna with all its wealth and power felt threatened, as did such comparatively minor states as Siena and

Mantua. Those even smaller were engaged in a desperate search for potent allies and finding distressingly few. The great duchy of Milan, which under the Sforzas would have been happy to bring its neighbors under its protection in hope of turning them into dependencies, was now an instrument of France and therefore part of the threat. Venice, still mired in its war with the Turks, could not afford to offend, never mind resist, France and Rome combined.

Cesare moved quickly and had startling success. His despised former brother-in-law Giovanni Sforza, alone since the fall of his cousins Ludovico il Moro and Caterina and mindful that nothing could induce his resentful subjects to risk themselves on his behalf, fled Pesaro again. He offered to sell the city to Venice and learned that Venice was not interested at any price. It was much the same with Rimini, twenty miles farther up the coast: Roberto Malatesta's son Pandolfo departed in haste after finding it impossible to rally a defense. When a bishop sent by Cesare arrived to demand Rimini's submission, its citizens hurried to welcome him.

The only place to offer resistance was Faenza, a small but thriving city midway between Caterina Sforza's former strongholds of Imola and Forlì. Its location made it a prize that Cesare needed to complete his control of the Via Emilia. Long the domain of the Manfredi family, Faenza in 1500 had as its lord the eighteen-year-old Astorre Manfredi, a charismatic figure who spurned the demands of Cesare's envoys and was supported by the people of the town. Cesare, whose capture of Pesaro had added twenty cannons to his already considerable strength in artillery, brought Faenza under siege on November 10. A long, hard struggle appeared to be in the offing, but Cesare had sufficient resources to attack other targets while proceeding with the tedious business of reducing Faenza's *rocca* to rubble.

On November 11, however, another stunning development rearranged the political landscape yet again. Those two old rivals Ferdinand of Spain and Louis of France, already bound together in a fragile truce of convenience, now agreed via the Treaty of Granada to divide the kingdom of Naples between them. Louis was to get Il Regno's northern provinces including the capital city and with it the Neapolitan crown. Ferdinand's share for turning on his cousin Don Fadrique and recognizing Louis's right to Milan would be the southern provinces of

Apulia and Calabria. It was a sensible enough arrangement as far as it went. Louis could march his troops down the peninsula from Milan without having to set foot on territory claimed by Spain. Ferdinand would be able to move troops into his part of the sundered kingdom from nearby Sicily, again without risking collision with his new partner in crime. Each got the satisfaction of knowing that he would soon be master of half of Naples without having to fight the other.

Much like the earlier arrangement by which France and Venice agreed to share Milan's holdings on the Lombard Plain but on a larger scale, this deal created a combination so overwhelmingly powerful that all the states of Italy could have no hope of resisting it even if they some-how managed to unite. It removed any possibility that Naples—and Italy—might be saved by playing the two great powers off against each other. Thus it stripped Alexander of any lingering hope of impeding Louis as he had earlier helped to undo Charles VIII. Under these new circumstances a refusal to recognize Louis as king of Naples would have been not only an empty gesture but a potentially suicidal one. The only hope for an autonomous Italy lay in the inherent instability of the alliance. It required two proud, ambitious, and shrewd monarchs, hardened cynics who had never trusted each other and were obviously not going to begin doing so now, to share a great prize that neither really thought he should have to share with anyone. But all this was going to take time to play itself out. In the near term Naples as an inde-pendent state was doomed, and no one could do anything to save it.

The certainty that he would soon be on his way to Naples focused Louis XII's attention on central Italy with new intensity. It brought home to him the importance of securing the hundreds of miles separat-ing Milan from Naples—miles over which he was going to have to move his troops. Obviously he wanted the states that lay along his path to be incapable of opposing him if not positively friendly, and the surest way to achieve that was to make them dependent. This required keep-ing any of them from becoming strong enough to act independently, and all of them divided against one another. From this point forward, these were the considerations that shaped the French king's dealings with the Borgias. He wanted the use of the papal army, and he wanted no trouble from the Vatican, but from now on there would be strict limits to how much he was willing to pay. And if he found Cesare more appealing than the other princes of Italy, he also understood that allowing Cesare to grow too strong could be a painfully costly mistake.

The king's next actions followed from these premises. After months of ignoring Machiavelli and his fellow Florentine envoys, Louis suddenly announced not only that he was putting Florence under his protection but that he would assist it in bringing rebellious Pisa back under its control. Cesare is not likely to have been terribly disheartened to be told that Florence was now off limits. The city had never been more than a distantly long-term possibility for him, and the French king's prohibition gave him an unarguable reason to refuse the demands of some of the *condottieri* he had hired for the Romagna campaign, especially the cousins Paolo and Giulio Orsini and Paolo's son-in-law Vitellozzo Vitelli, lord of Città di Castello. These men had blood connections to the Medici and profound contempt for the republican government that had sent the Medici into exile, and they had been pressing Cesare to begin his new *impresa* with an attack on Florence. They accepted this new proscription grudgingly, having no real interest in Cesare's plans for the Romagna and feeling absolutely no loyalty to Cesare himself. Vitelli in particular was a worrisome character. Even more murderous than most warlords, but also one of the most skillful and experienced soldiers in Italy, he was consumed with hatred for the Florentine republic. He had made its destruction practically the central purpose of his life, and in pursuit of that goal he was constantly making trouble. He was not likely to stop doing so regardless of what the king of France had to say.

The great city of Bologna was more relevant to Cesare's plans than Florence. Unlike Florence it was not separated from his possessions in the Romagna by the Apennine Mountains, with their dauntingly high passes, and its size and wealth and position at the northwestern terminus of the Via Emilia made it a perfect prospective capital for the principality he was in process of creating. He had in fact coveted Bologna since stopping there at the start of his first *impresa* in 1499 and seeing for the first time what an impressive place it was. Its resident tyrant, Giovanni Bentivoglio, saw the danger immediately. Louis XII and Cesare between them had broken one branch after another of his extended family. His wife was a Sforza, a cousin of Ludovico il Moro, Caterina the *virago,* and Giovanni the displaced lord of Pesaro. One of his daughters was married to the Pandolfo Malatesta from whom Cesare had taken Rimini, and another was the mother of young Astorre Manfredi, still besieged at Faenza. Bentivoglio would have gone to his grandson's assistance if not forbidden to do so by Louis XII.

Whatever plans Cesare may have had for advancing on Bologna had to be abandoned when Louis declared that he was taking it, like Florence, under his protection. This was another astute move by the French king. He turned not only Florence but now Bologna as well into client states, narrowing the options of the Borgias by doing so. Venice, if not nearly as dependent as Florence and Bologna, was also not a problem: it remained in no position to risk offending France. The Venetian *signoria* considered itself fortunate to have been allowed a share of the spoils from Louis's conquest of Milan in spite of having contributed little to the success of his campaign. It knew that the king could strip it of its winnings whenever he chose. Fear of France had obliged Venice to yield without complaint when Cesare moved against Pesaro and Rimini, though it had long regarded both cities as within its rightful sphere of influence, Louis having made it known that he would not be pleased by an attempt to defend either place.

Milan, Florence, Bologna, Venice: four of the most important entities in northern Italy, and all now either belonging to Louis or obliged to do his bidding. And all, in consequence, were now closed to the Borgias, as was Naples as well. Alexander and Cesare, unless they resigned themselves to settling for the status quo, were going to have to work around them.

VENICE, SERENE NO MORE

IT IS A MARK OF HOW GREATLY THE REPUBLIC OF VENICE DIF-
fered from Italy's other major city-states that it alone produced neither
a legendary dynasty—scarcely a dynasty of any kind, actually—nor a
single leader whose name anyone not a specialist in Italian history would
be likely to recognize.

Florence had its Medici, Milan its Visconti and Sforza dukes, Naples
the improbably varied monarchs of the House of Aragon, and Rome the
immortally notorious Renaissance popes—fabled figures all. But these
epic figures had no counterparts in Venice, which nevertheless, in the
course of centuries of practically anonymous collective leadership,
turned itself into a power as important as any in Europe or the Mediterranean world.

What makes this all the more remarkable is that whereas Naples and
Milan—never mind Rome—had histories reaching back millennia, and
Florence was a creation of the Roman Empire, Venice didn't even come
into existence until after the empire collapsed. The fall of Rome in fact
led almost directly to the founding of Venice—to its profoundly unpromising beginnings in a place where, under ordinary circumstances, no one
could ever have wanted to live. It was in the fifth century, with Vandals
and Goths and Huns bringing mayhem down out of the north, that a
scattering of refugees found themselves driven by desperation to settle
on a cluster of tiny islands and barren mudflats in a remote lagoon near
the northwesternmost corner of Italy's Adriatic coast.

Against all odds, this turned out to be a brilliant choice, one that
would not only make those first settlers safe but bring their descendants
fabulous wealth and power. The first Venetians, in sole possession of the
secret of how to thread through the shallows of the lagoon and reach
their islands, found themselves to be untouchable as new waves of
invaders—Ostrogoths, Lombards—took their turns at pillaging Italy. The
islanders supported themselves first with fishing, then with trade on a
petty scale. They increased their security by putting themselves under

the protection of nearby Ravenna, then the principal Italian outpost of the Eastern Roman Empire.

Venice remained obscure for centuries, but its improbable location kept it free of the most destructive conflicts of the time. Meanwhile its seafaring traders were growing in experience, expanding their markets and becoming rich. They avoided entanglement with either Constantinople or the new western empire of Charlemagne, who gave up on capturing Venice after two failed attempts. Later they were able to stay clear of the long, debilitating fight between the popes and German emperors. By early in the eleventh century Venice was emerging as what it would remain for centuries, the hub of a commercial network the spokes of which reached not only into the Greek Christian Empire but into the lands of the Slavs, Turks, and Arabs. Its galleys became the means by which the peoples of the Mediterranean traded such staples as grain, wine, salt, wool, and cloth. By venturing to Egypt, Syria, and the ports of the Black Sea, they procured for Europe the exotic (and stunningly profitable) produce of India, China, and Southeast Asia. The soldiers they carried made Venice mistress of the east coast of the Adriatic, less out of any hunger for conquest than because territory so close to the city's shipping lanes could not be allowed to fall into unfriendly hands.

Constantinople, simultaneously a trading partner and a rival, was crucial to Venice's development. In the 1080s, as a reward for using its fleet to save the Eastern emperor from an invasion by the Normans of Sicily, Venice was granted an exemption from Constantinople's excise tax. This gave it a much-resented advantage over its competitors Pisa and Genoa. At the start of the thirteenth century, by providing the transportation that made it possible for the knights of the Fourth Crusade to fall upon Constantinople and sack it without mercy, Venice helped weaken the Eastern emperors so gravely that they never entirely recovered. This would prove, eventually, to have been a terrible mistake, removing the prime obstacle to expansion by far more dangerous rivals. The worst of its consequences, however, would not become clear until the Turkish capture of Constantinople in 1453. In the interim the Venetians were masters of world trade, using their immense profits to raise up a city as beautiful as anything ever created by the hand of man. As for the price ultimately paid for the ruin of Constantinople, perhaps it is unfair to blame merchants for failing to see two and half centuries into the future.

From the beginning, the Venetians had embraced collective—republican—government, giving authority more often to committees and boards than to individuals. The leader or doge came to be elected, generally for life and by a process almost indescribably complex, and his freedom of action was so limited—he could not engage in trade, accept gifts, own property outside Venice, or even leave the city without permission—that the kind of autocracy that became the rule elsewhere in Italy remained impossible. Dynastic ambitions were cut off at their roots by rules prohibiting the sons of doges from holding office or even voting.

In the century following the Fourth Crusade's sack of Constantinople, Venice's government narrowed and hardened into an oligarchy. The city's Great Council came to be restricted to elite families, and only council members could become magistrates or hold other important offices. Executive power passed from the doge, now little more than a ceremonial figurehead, to a central committee known as the Ten, or the Signoria. What resulted has often been depicted as oppressive and stultifying. If it was those things, it was also efficient, effective, and acceptable to the population, strikingly so in comparison with what was happening elsewhere.

The Venetians were a uniquely homogenous people, virtually everyone being either in business or dependent on business, and therefore their city was remarkably cohesive. Its hundred thousand residents remained placid across the generations, thanks to the general prosperity, the availability of "institutions of public utility" such as hospitals, and the absence of the kind of feudal nobility that in other places clashed with and tried to dominate the commercial classes. Even the satellite cities of Venice's growing empire were dealt with generously and gave every evidence of being satisfied; this contrasts sharply with the experience of Florence, which was harsh in its treatment of the cities that came under its rule and was hated and occasionally rebelled against as a result. Not for nothing did Venice style itself La Serenissima—the Most Serene Republic. It saw itself as superior to other states, and in significant ways it was.

Neutrality came naturally to the Venetians; it was the sensible policy for a state whose prosperity depended on doing business with the whole world. It became progressively less feasible, however, as the fifteenth century advanced. First the aggression of the Visconti of Milan so alarmed the Venetians that they felt compelled to enter into an alliance with Florence, thereby being drawn into mainland politics as never before. Then the advance of the Ottoman Turks became a threat to the very survival of Venice's overseas empire. The year 1463 brought a war with the Turks that would drag on for sixteen years and end on terms so unfavorable as to amount to an acknowledgment that the city was no longer capable of checking Ottoman expansion. The Most Serene Republic was serene no more. Thinking now that the only way of maintaining its security was to expand on the mainland, it launched the attack on the Este of Ferrara that turned into two more years of vicious warfare and produced no gains commensurate with the costs. The years following brought scattered successes, the annexation of Cyprus being the most noteworthy, but these were not sufficient to allay the Venetians' pervasive sense that everything their forebears had built was in mortal peril. In the Europe beyond Italy, the unification of Spain and the resurgence of France were giving rise to two more powers that Venice could never hope to compete with. The world was beginning to pass it by.

This was the situation when Rodrigo Borgia became pope in 1492. It explains the Venetians' quiet encouragement of Charles VIII's invasion: they hoped he would help them expand into the Romagna. It also explains why, after joining the league that forced Charles to beat a retreat back to France, the Venetians struck out on their own once again, trying now to subdue Florence but finding themselves foiled by the stubborn resistance of Caterina Sforza in the Romagna and the outbreak of fresh fighting with the Turks. And why they next welcomed Louis XII into Italy, hoping that he could be maneuvered into pulling them out of their predicament.

17

Conqueror

The winter of 1500–1501, like most winters before the industrial revolution brought mechanized all-weather warfare, was a peaceful interval between the close of one fighting season and the opening of another. Lucrezia Borgia, now a twenty-year-old dowager duchess with a baby son, passed the cold months sequestered in the papal stronghold of Nepi, adapting to life without her husband. Her brother Cesare and their patron the pope remained in Rome, where they occupied themselves with, among other matters of state, deciding where to marry her next. Barely five months after the duke of Bisceglie's murder, Pope Alexander had announced Lucrezia's betrothal to the young Francesco Orsini, duke of Gravina. That plan had come to nothing, perhaps because such a union could not be reconciled with Alexander's determination to break the Orsini, perhaps because it became obvious that Lucrezia could be used to bag bigger game.

As in the period after the annulment of Lucrezia's first marriage, there was no shortage of suitors. By January 1501, however, Alexander and Cesare were focusing their aspirations on a prospect who not only had no wish to make Lucrezia his wife but was grimly hostile to the idea. This was Alfonso d'Este, who as eldest son of Duke Ercole d'Este of Ferrara was a scion of one of the oldest noble families in Europe and heir to a city-state that, if not as brilliant as Florence or as mighty as Venice, did not fall far short of ranking among Italy's leading powers.

The Este married in only the loftiest of circles: Alfonso was a grandson of Ferrante of Naples, his sisters had wed Ludovico il Moro of Milan and Francesco Gonzaga, marquess of Mantua, and his own short-lived first wife had been a daughter and sister of Sforza dukes. It was no less desirable for Lucrezia to become one of them than it had been to connect Cesare to the French royal family.

More than prestige was at stake. Because Ferrara lay just north of the Romagna, it could serve as a valuable ally, a northern shield, for the state that Cesare was assembling for himself there. Conversely, it had the potential to become a threat to the achievement of Cesare's plans. A basis for friendship between the two families existed in the person of Louis XII: the Este had traditionally found it advantageous to be attentive to the wishes of the French crown, and in 1501 that history put them, ipso facto, on friendly terms with the Borgias as well. On the other hand the Este had lately been on bloodily bad terms with their mighty neighbors the Venetians. Fear of Venice kept them chronically in search of allies.

Negotiation of a possible marriage began that January. Longtime Borgia retainer Ramiro de Lorqua, the grimly tough veteran of the wars of Spanish unification whom Cesare had left in charge of Imola and Forlì, served as go-between. In the early going the Borgias did all the proposing, the Este merely listening with an air of detachment, and there seemed little likelihood of success. The fact that the Borgias had produced two popes in forty years was not nearly sufficient to impress the proud House of Este, which had a history as rich in betrayal and murder as any warlord family in Italy but was of such antiquity that its roots disappeared among the higher nobility of Germany in the murky depths of the Dark Ages. Like all leading families, the Este took pains to keep themselves informed of events at the papal court, and through their agents they had heard enough stories to make some of them think it inconceivable that Lucrezia could possibly be a suitable bride for the duke's heir. Duke Ercole's daughter Isabella d'Este Gonzaga, marquessa of Mantua and one of the most cultivated women that Renaissance Italy would produce, became almost shrill in her opposition. She was echoed by her husband's sister, the wife of Duke Guidobaldo da Montefeltro of Urbino, who though not an Este herself was offended by the thought of even an indirect connection with the parvenu Spaniards. The pro-

spective bridegroom Alfonso, not unintelligent but coarse-natured, interested less in arts and letters and the niceties of court life than in the
smoky foundry where he spent his days conducting experiments in
the manufacture of artillery, was characteristically blunt in declaring
that no such marriage was going to take place. Faced with all this, and
with Duke Ercole's refusal to be impressed with the pope's explanations of why an alliance with Rome would be good for Ferrara and a
refusal of the marriage would be bad, Alexander and Cesare turned to
Louis of France for help.

Meanwhile there was much else to be done. With the arrival of
spring Cesare was able to bring his troops out of winter quarters and
increase the pressure on Faenza, which he had kept under siege for half
a year now. Toward the end of April the city's stout-hearted young lord,
Astorre Manfredi, yielded to the inevitable and agreed to hand his city
over on condition that it would not be plundered and its population not
mistreated. Cesare was scrupulous in honoring his pledge; he was making it his practice to deal generously with people and places whose lord
he intended to remain, thereby winning the loyalty of cities accustomed to the random cruelties of sadists. When he moved on from
Faenza, Astorre went with him, whether as a prisoner or a volunteer
addition to the papal army is not clear.

In the first great bluff of his military career, Cesare moved his troops
toward Bologna. Though an attack on the city was politically impossible, Louis XII having taken it under his protection, this was not something on which Bolognese strongman Giovanni Bentivoglio could bet
his future. He had no way of being confident either that the French
king would honor his promises or that his young adversary would be
deterred by those promises. Therefore he was frightened and scrambled to prepare his defenses while sending appeals to Louis for help. In
fact Cesare appreciated the risks of flouting the French king's instructions and was far too canny to incur those risks. His target was not
Bologna but its satellite town of Castel Bolognese, the last strongpoint
on the Via Emilia between Imola and Rimini not yet in his possession

As it happened, Louis had disliked Bentivoglio at least since the latter
had been one of the few warlords to support Ludovico il Moro's futile
attempt to fend off the invasion of Milan. He could, however, see no
advantage in allowing Cesare to add a prize as important as Bologna to

his fast-growing list of conquests. He split the difference, forbidding Cesare to attack Bologna but ordering Bentivoglio to give up Castel Bolognese. In the settlement worked out by Cesare's representatives and an angry Bentivoglio, Bologna not only ceded Castel Bolognese but pledged to provide the papal army with hundreds of troops for the next three years and to cooperate with its future incursions into the Romagna. Back in Rome, Alexander celebrated this success by bestowing on Cesare the title duke of Romagna—*Duca Valentino di Romagna*. With Imola, Castel Bolognese, Faenza, Forlì, Cesena, Rimini, and Pesaro all now firmly in his hands, Duke Valentino was master of more of the Romagna than anyone had been in centuries and was the region's duke. Louis XII thought he should be satisfied.

Pope Alexander evidently thought the same thing. Though summer had barely begun, he sent instructions for Cesare to post garrisons at his latest conquests and return to Rome. Cesare did as he was told—or nearly so. He marched his army out of the Romagna, but instead of taking the direct route to Rome, he headed westward into Tuscany, onto Florence's home ground. This was a bold move, easily interpreted as an act of defiance of the French, and it delighted Cesare's *condottiere* Vitellozzo Vitelli and his Orsini colleagues, who had not stopped hoping for a chance to assault Florence. Cesare, however, cannot have planned any such attack—the risks would have been too great. He must have been pleased, even relieved, to be still ten miles from the city when a delegation sent by the Florentine *signori* came riding up to greet him. Talks ensued, and a battle of nerves. The leaders of the republic were able to take small comfort, under these circumstances, from Louis XII's promise of protection. The only French troops in the neighborhood were under Cesare's command, and he was obviously using them for his own purposes, as usual telling no one what he intended to do.

His objective, obvious in hindsight, was to frighten the Florentines and extract whatever concessions he could while the city was helpless. He knew that the French had more pressing concerns than the protection of Florence—Louis was on the verge of beginning his advance on Naples—and would hesitate to take a hard line with Rome at the exact point where their need for the papal army was greatest. Assuming of course that Cesare did not go so far as to attack the city of Florence itself, which the French could never have accepted.

What Florence's envoys wanted was simple: their instructions were to get Cesare out of Tuscany as quickly, and at as little cost, as possible. To this end they offered him a three-year *condotta* paying 36,000 ducats annually. It would have been a stiff price if accompanied by any intention to actually pay, but the Florentines appear to have had no such intention. It was their turn to be relieved when Cesare, eager to be on his way before King Louis got word of what he was doing and had an opportunity to object, accepted their offer and put his army back on the road. Moving down the Arno valley toward the sea, he freed his mercenaries to pillage at their pleasure. This was customary, a way of keeping mercenary troops satisfied, and Cesare saw no reason to care what the people of the area thought of him. He had no expectation of ever needing their loyalty.

On June 4 he reached the little city-state of Piombino on the west coast and brought it under siege. It lay on the northwest frontier of Tuscany, so that if he could take it, he would have Florence virtually encircled. He was unable to tarry, however; word came that Louis XII was marching southward, wanted his troops back, and expected Cesare to join him. Cesare had no choice but to obey, but he detached enough troops to maintain the siege. Some of Piombino's most valuable possessions, including the island of Elba with its iron mines, had already surrendered. The job of taking the city itself was assigned to Vitellozzo Vitelli, one of Italy's first experts in the use of artillery. He could be relied upon to press the siege hard, not because he was trustworthy but because he was driven. He regarded the reduction of Piombino as a step toward the goal that obsessed him: the defeat of the Florentine Republic and the destruction of the men responsible for what in his eyes had been an unforgivable wrong. To the rulers of Florence, who were all too aware of his obsession, he seemed a kind of archfiend, an implacable and malignant force, and a traitor as well.

They had good reasons for thinking so. Though at age forty-four Vitelli was as effective a soldier as was to be found in Italy, an innovator in the employment of artillery and infantry, he was also something very like a homicidal psychopath. He and his brother and partner Paolo, sons of the family that had held the little city-state of Città di Castello in a tight grip for generations, had in the late 1490s been hired by Florence to take command of the war on Pisa. They were an improbable choice, being related by marriage to the Orsini and therefore to the exiled Medici, but their military reputations must have made the risk seem acceptable. Their personal reputations were a very different matter. Paolo was a murderous brute of the classic warlord type, notorious for such acts as chopping off the hands and putting out the eyes of captured enemy musketeers because he thought it outrageous that common foot soldiers suddenly possessed the means of bringing down armored and mounted knights. Vitellozzo was not much better, taking undisguised pleasure in unleashing his troops on defenseless civilians, but as they brought Pisa under siege, all seemed well enough from the Florentine perspective.

At the climax of that siege, in 1499, something occurred that was bizarre even by *condottieri* standards. When their men broke through Pisa's defenses, the Vitelli brothers not only didn't urge them on or lead them into the city but instead intervened bodily to force them back, enabling the defenders to regroup and seal the hole. The authorities in Florence, baffled and infuriated, decided that the Vitelli either had been bribed or had decided to keep the war from being won in order to continue being paid. Paolo was seized and taken to Florence for beheading. Vitellozzo escaped and from that point forward was sunk in bitterness and consumed by his hunger for revenge. His disposition was not improved—neither was his judgment—by a case of syphilis so debilitating that often he had to be carried about on a litter. He was a good enough fighting man to be a useful lieutenant when kept on a short leash, but devoid of scruples and dangerously unpredictable.

Having given Vitelli his orders, Cesare postponed his rendezvous with the French army long enough to make a flying visit to Rome. He found Pope Alexander in a state of uncharacteristic agitation, upset by Venetian complaints about Cesare's actions in the Romagna. The centuries-old fragmentation of the Romagna into a patchwork of quarrelsome petty fiefdoms had kept it too weak to be a problem even for neighbors as near as Venice. Those fiefdoms had been able to remain at least quasi-autonomous because neither Milan nor Venice would allow the other to seize them outright. But now, with Cesare pulling its pieces together, the Romagna had the potential to become a serious problem indeed—not least for Venice, and *especially* for Venice if a Borgia-Este marriage led to an alliance between Cesare's new duchy and Venice's old foe Ferrara. Such worries were making a mess of Alexander's efforts to work with Venice in resisting the advance of the Turks. In May 1501 he had brought Rome, Venice, and Hungary together in a new anti-Ottoman league, but already the Venetians were threatening to pull out. It was becoming all too clear that Cesare's ambitions might not always be compatible with the priorities of the pope from whom he drew his strength.

Cesare was in Rome when Alexander issued a bull that approved the Franco-Spanish agreement to partition Naples and excommunicated Don Fadrique, declaring that he had forfeited his crown by attempting to ally himself with the Turks. The charge was true, but it was far from unheard-of for European and even Italian rulers to look to the Muslim world for help when finding themselves in difficulty, and such renegade behavior had never drawn such a harsh response. At about the same time, probably as a way of returning the favor and possibly as the result of an explicit quid pro quo arrangement, Louis XII began pressuring Duke Ercole d'Este to agree to the Borgia marriage. When Alfonso d'Este persisted in refusing, his widower father threatened to marry Lucrezia himself. Ercole was prepared to accept the marriage if doing so would keep Ferrara in the good graces of France *and* if the price was right. With one additional proviso: it had to be established that Lucrezia's personal history and conduct were not of such a nature as to disgrace the Este name. As negotiations proceeded and the pope remained almost foolishly eager, tough old Ercole focused on two things: learning as much as he could about Lucrezia's character, and seeing how far he could raise his demands without mortally offending Alexander.

Suddenly everything seemed to be happening at once. By the time Cesare and his troops joined up with the French army as it passed near Rome—for reasons unknown, he imprisoned Astorre Manfredi in the Castel Sant'Angelo before departing—Piombino was surrendering. A grimly triumphant Vitellozzo Vitelli was thus able to add most of his men to Louis XII's invasion force. Yet another new league was formed, this one for the purpose of arranging the affairs of Naples once it had been taken. The members were France, Spain, and Rome, the two kings having included the pope in hopes of casting a veil of legitimacy over what was in fact a shamelessly cynical land grab. On June 24 the invaders stormed the city of Capua, which was under the command of

Don Fadrique's *condottiere* Fabrizio Colonna. Capua's people were subjected to a sacking so savage that it has remained infamous ever since, and Cesare has often been blamed. It is fair to recall, however, that the army that took Capua was commanded not by him but by the French general Bernard Stewart d'Aubigny and that Cesare himself had charge of only some four hundred of d'Aubigny's thousands of troops.

Fabrizio Colonna fell into the hands of Gian Giordano Orsini, the late Virginio's son and onetime fellow prisoner, now in the pay of the French. Cesare offered to pay Orsini handsomely if he would either hand Colonna over or do away with him. It is to Orsini's credit that he permitted Fabrizio to buy his freedom and make his escape; it seems likely that he was motivated less by any wish to save a Colonna than by dislike of his own ally Cesare and the chance to turn a quick profit. Fabrizio, no doubt astounded by his good fortune, fled south to join his cousin Prospero, in charge of defending the city of Naples.

Don Fadrique, meanwhile, was repeating the mistakes his brother Alfonso II had made in facing the invasion of Charles VIII almost a decade earlier: he was making a stand in scattered stone fortresses rendered obsolete by the invaders' new artillery. The fate of Capua having showed that he, his tactics, and his kingdom were all doomed, Fadrique sent emissaries to the French in hopes of obtaining tolerable terms. The king and d'Aubigny were prepared to be generous. In return for his abdication, Fadrique was offered a comfortable retirement as duke of Anjou in France. He accepted on August 1 and two days later sailed from Naples to the island of Ischia, from which he was taken to Anjou, where he would live undisturbed for the three final years of his life. His son and heir, named Ferrante after the grandfather who had ruled Naples through three and a half turbulent decades, fell into the hands of the Spanish, now in possession of the southern half of the kingdom. Regarded as a rival claimant to the Neapolitan crown, he would be held a prisoner for fifty-four years, one of history's numberless forgotten victims.

With Il Regno now broken into halves and occupied by the troops of France and Spain, the Borgias were once again free to look to their own interests, Lucrezia's marriage included. At this time as in most periods of her life, Lucrezia remains a distant and somewhat enigmatic figure. There is essentially no evidence of what she was thinking as her life

entered another time of radical transformation, but it is safe to conclude that she had no objection to the proposed union. Whenever the
negotiations seemed in danger of breaking down (usually because of
Duke Ercole's escalating demands), Lucrezia intervened to help smooth
things over and persuade Alexander not to give up. She had obvious
reasons to be attracted to a new life in the north—the prospect, which
would have appealed to almost any lively young woman in a world in
which all power was in the hands of men, of becoming the consort of a
powerful duke and the mistress of a rich and beautiful city. It is impossible not to wonder if she also welcomed this way of escaping from the
intrigues of her brother and the pope.

We would have to conclude, if the most vicious gossip were to be
believed, that this was the point in her life when Lucrezia's conduct was
sinking to the lowest depths of degradation. According to one famous
story, she participated in a Vatican party to which Pope Alexander invited fifty prostitutes who stripped naked and entertained their hosts
with lewd gymnastics involving chestnuts, all of this followed by a rol-
licking orgy. According to another, she and the pope amused themselves one evening by laughingly watching from a Vatican balcony as
mares were led into St. Peter's Square for the purpose of being mounted
by a brace of excited stallions.

Some of the stories did not find their way into print (and may not
have existed) until Alexander, Cesare, and Lucrezia herself were all
dead. Some, however, were in circulation not only during her lifetime
but while Alexander was negotiating with Ferrara's duke. They were
retailed when not originated by the Borgias' political enemies, among
whom were some of the most influential men of the time, and they
spread to every city in Italy. Even when the things being said did not
provoke horror or disgust, as the ones alleging incest inevitably did,
they raised questions about whether Lucrezia was better than a common whore. Duke Ercole found them troubling, understandably. But
he had Lucrezia under close and sustained scrutiny and was receiving
regular reports on her from his agents in Rome. That he ultimately not
only assented to the marriage but bullied his son into it is rather persuasive evidence that his mind had been put at rest by what he learned.

Which is hardly surprising. Believing the stories required believing
other things as well. It required believing that Pope Alexander would

participate in the corruption of a young woman to whom he had become little less than a father and whom he loved as a daughter. This is not impossible, of course. But neither is it consistent with what we know—what we actually *know*—about Rodrigo Borgia the man.

Foremost among Duke Ercole's agents in Rome was Gian Luca Castellini da Pontremoli, long one of his principal counselors, by 1501 an old and intimate friend. At a point when the negotiation of a marriage contract was nearly complete, Castellini advised Ercole that Lucrezia "is of an incontestable beauty and her manners add to her charm. In a word, she seems so gifted that we cannot and should not suspect her of unseemly behavior but presume, believe and hope that she will always behave well. . . . Your Highness and Lord Don Alfonso will be well satisfied because, quite apart from her perfect grace in all things, her modesty, affability and propriety, she is a Catholic and shows that she fears God." Castellini could have had no reason to mislead the duke and would have put much at risk by doing so. And he was in Rome, where he would have had little difficulty in learning the truth if Lucrezia were merely pretending to be modest, affable, and proper et cetera and the rumors about her had a basis in fact.

On August 6 a contract was signed at the Vatican. Its terms, when they became known, raised eyebrows across Italy and sparked indignation in the streets and palaces of Rome. Lucrezia's dowry, greater than the one paid by the House of Sforza to marry one of its daughters to a Holy Roman emperor, included a round one hundred thousand gold ducats; an additional fortune in jewels; a sharp and perpetual reduction in the annual tribute that the duchy of Ferrara owed the papacy as a vassal state; the towns of Cento and Pieve (both of them actually the property of the archdiocese of Bologna, whose prelate was not consulted); and a number of valuable ecclesiastical benefices. Duke Ercole's patience and cunning, the discipline with which he had maintained an air of indifference as to whether a wedding took place or not, had paid rich dividends. It had driven the pope, urged on by Cesare and encouraged by Lucrezia, to increase what he was offering and increase it again until finally more was on the table than the proudest duke in Europe would have been able to refuse, especially now that the prospective bride had been examined and not found wanting.

The invasion of Naples, meanwhile, was turning out to have been a costly affair for the Colonna and their junior partners the Savelli. Both clans, traditionally affiliated with the House of Aragon, had signed on to fight for Don Fadrique, and both had seen one after another of their estates and strongholds fall to Louis XII's army as it plundered its way southward. When Fadrique departed for France, he left behind his generals Fabrizio and Prospero Colonna, who thus found themselves unemployed and vulnerable. Fearing the French, they moved south until they were in territory that now belonged to Spain. There they offered their services to Gonsalvo, Ferdinand and Isabella's newly appointed viceroy, who promptly hired them. Their kinsmen up in the Papal States, meanwhile, were left to fend for themselves. Alexander reaped the benefits, sending units of the papal army to probe the Colonna defenses and seize whatever they could. By contrast the Orsini, having given good service both to Cesare in the Romagna and to Louis XII during the descent upon Naples, ascended to new heights of wealth, power, and prestige. A move against them was out of the question, especially as they continued to have France as an employer and patron.

On September 17, upon returning to Rome from a visit to the south during which he had personally seen to the garrisoning and structural reinforcement of newly captured strongholds, Alexander issued a pair of breathtakingly ambitious bulls. The Colonna and Savelli were declared enemies of the Holy See and excommunicated, and the properties of the Savelli were given to the *condottieri* Paolo and Giulio Orsini in unavoidable—if regrettable, from the perspective of the Borgias—recognition of their contributions to the recent campaigns and their growing importance. The lands and castles of the Colonna were combined with the estates that had been "sold" to Lucrezia after being taken from the Gaetani in 1500 and that she now relinquished, having no need, as a future duchess of Ferrara, for papal territory. The districts thus made available became the basis for a papal revival of two ancient dukedoms. Lucrezia's son Rodrigo, not yet two, was made duke of Sermoneta. A mysterious little character who had been christened Giovanni Borgia but would be known ever after as the Infant of Rome became duke of Nepi. Perhaps three years old at the time of his elevation to the highest noble rank, recently legitimatized by papal decree, this child was variously rumored to be Alexander's, or Lucrezia's, or Alexander *and* Lucrezia's, even Alexander and Lucrezia *and Cesare's*. It is not absolutely impossible that he was the illegitimate child that Lucrezia was rumored to have given birth to after the end of her marriage to Giovanni Sforza. His origins have never been uncovered, but the most reasonable guess is that he was a bastard of Cesare's by a woman whose name is lost to history.

With the bestowal of grand titles and vast holdings on a pair of Borgia infants, one of them of distinctly dubious parentage, Alexander carried nepotism to an extreme that few of his predecessors had dared to approach. In doing so he made it at last impossible for anyone to believe, or to credibly argue, that his real purpose in conferring so much wealth and so many lofty positions on members of his family was to protect the interests of the Church. If that claim had always been questionable, now it was simply laughable. The situation that the pope had created was without precedent: almost the whole of the Papal States had been made the hereditary property of his relatives. It was not defensible, and inevitably it aroused widespread resentment.

Lucrezia's wedding became the event of the year—of the century, at least as far as Italy was concerned. And again everything was at the expense of the Church. The preparations consumed the attention of the Borgias and everyone closely connected with them throughout midwinter 1501–1502. Alexander, who continued to enjoy robust good health as he entered his seventies—"nothing worries him, he seems to grow younger every day," Venice's ambassador reported in an almost complaining tone—continued no less than in his youth to revel in magnificent display. He knew that the people of Rome would judge him by the magnificence with which he marked this grand occasion, and so he poured out the contents of the papal treasury with almost mad abandon, spending even more freely on preparations for the wedding than he had in preparing for Cesare's visit to France in 1498. Ercole d'Este, having won a jackpot of a wedding settlement, felt free to match the pope's outlays ducat for ducat, so that the months preceding Lucrezia's return to married life became an exercise in extravagance on a scale no Roman then living had ever witnessed. A single piece of jewelry that Ercole sent to his future daughter-in-law was said to have a value of seventy thousand ducats.

The party sent from Ferrara to claim the bride and escort her to her husband and new home arrived in Rome on December 23. It included some fifteen hundred persons, many of them high nobles and church-men and other notables, and was headed by the bridegroom's three younger brothers, one of whom, the cleric Ippolito, had been appointed to the College of Cardinals in 1493 in spite of being only fourteen years old. On hand to receive it were all the nobles and officials of the city and nineteen cardinals, each accompanied by two hundred horsemen. Ce-sare's personal entourage included scores of Roman nobles and four thousand mounted troops, all wearing his red and yellow livery, and the stallion he rode was adorned with jewels and precious metals. The welcoming ceremony went on through hours of orations, with the pope not participating but looking on contentedly from the upper reaches of the Vatican.

There followed, after a week during which the whole capital was given over to an unending round of games, tournaments, sporting events, theatrical performances, and other entertainments, a proxy wedding presided over by thirteen cardinals. Another carnival-like week passed before, on January 6, Lucrezia at last bade the pope farewell and rode out of Rome at the center of a retinue of hundreds of sundry dignitaries and a guard of six hundred uniformed horsemen. Her trousseau—trunk after trunk filled with gowns made of the costliest materials to be found in Italy, plus jewels and gold and silver and fine linen and works of art—was strapped to the backs of 150 mules.

Her departure was a true goodbye, a real change of life. Lucrezia and Alexander would never meet again. Nor would Lucrezia ever again see her little son Rodrigo, who in keeping with custom was not permitted to join his mother as she entered a new marriage. He remained behind, like the Infant of Rome now a permanent member of the papal house-hold.

Lucrezia was on the road for just a day short of four weeks, making formal visits to all the places of note along the way. At every stop, local lords and ladies eager to curry favor spent more than they could afford on new rounds of entertainment and display. It was exhausting, and disagreeable in other ways as well; forced jollity and manufactured dis-plays of affection were required of everyone involved, and of Lucrezia most particularly, everywhere she went. One of the stops had deeply unpleasant associations: Pesaro, where Lucrezia had once spent tedious months as the wife of Giovanni Sforza. Bologna too must have been excruciating; there the bride was received by Ginevra Bentivoglio, who in addition to being wife of the city's lord was Giovanni Sforza's aunt and the grandmother of Astorre Manfredi, now a prisoner in Rome.

Arrival in Ferrara brought Lucrezia's first exposure to Isabella d'Este Gonzaga, who had been placed in charge of hospitality by her father Duke Ercole. Lucrezia of course knew that Isabella had opposed the marriage from the beginning and that she remained deeply suspicious of her and doubtful of her moral character. Making things still worse was Isabella's status as a proud and famous beauty, accustomed to being the center of attention at her father's court and her husband's at Mantua and Modena. She saw Lucrezia as a rival, a threat to her preeminence. The effusions of false joy and devotion at this first encounter must have been wonderful to behold.

At last Lucrezia came face-to-face with her husband, the stolid Alfonso, who is not likely to have troubled himself to bring whatever charm he was capable of mustering to bear upon his new mate. She, in consequence, is not likely to have been overly delighted by what she first saw of him. The marriage was consummated with dispatch all the same, and the festivities went on and on until Duke Ercole was hinting sourly and in increasingly loud tones that perhaps it was time for people to be returning to their own homes. Gradually Ferrara returned to normal. It remained for the truth about Lucrezia's character to be revealed by the test that now lay before her: the need to go on with life under the cold gaze of a hardheaded father-in-law, a distinctly uninfatuated husband, a hostile sister-in-law, and platoons of other in-laws and courtiers all looking for reasons to find fault.

An uneasy quiet prevailed across Italy through the first four months of Lucrezia's new life. There was no war anywhere, aside from the minor clashes that broke out from time to time as Florence continued its harassment of Pisa. Signs of impending trouble, however, were not hard to find. Predictably, the division of Naples between France and Spain had proved satisfactory to neither party, leading almost immediately to skirmishes along the frontier separating the kingdom's two halves and making a showdown seem not only inevitable but likely to occur soon. In Rome, Cesare was preparing to set forth on a third *impresa*. His prospects could hardly have been more favorable. He could depend upon France and Spain to be tolerant if not actively supportive;

neither would want to alienate him or the pope with a new war for Naples looming. Florence could put no obstacles in his path; what remained of its strength was being drained away by the struggle to retake Pisa. Venice too was otherwise engaged (with the Turks, as usual), Ferrara was now more or less an ally thanks to Lucrezia's marriage, and the Romagna was his to command. The Colonna had been weakened to the point of irrelevance, and though the Orsini remained strong, Cesare had co-opted them by signing their leading men to *condotta*.

Cesare, who with one more successful campaign could make himself supreme in north-central Italy, was almost ready to move. By letting no one know what he intended to do, where he was going to take his army once it was on the march, he spread anxiety from the canals of Venice to the hills of Tuscany. He already had troops stationed at far-flung strategic points. Some were at Cesena, in the hills bordering the far eastern edge of the Lombard Plain, under the toughest of his Spanish lieutenants, Ramiro de Lorqua. Michelotto Corella, almost certainly guilty of strangling the duke of Bisceglie on Cesare's behalf, was in the Romagna recruiting and training a militia. Other troops waited on the Romagna-Tuscany frontier under Vitellozzo Vitelli and his equally thuggish crony Gian Paolo Baglioni of Perugia. If any of them knew what Cesare was planning, they too were keeping silent.

The fates, however, proved as capricious as ever and plucked the initiative out of Cesare's hands. On June 4 the Tuscan city of Arezzo, fed up with the taxes imposed by Florence to finance its war on Pisa, suddenly rebelled. It expelled its Florentine governors and called for a restoration of the Medici. Cesare's man Vitelli, presumably acting without his knowledge, immediately moved in, and he and his 3,500 soldiers were welcomed as liberators by the Arezzans. Vitelli and Baglioni also took possession of the fertile Chiana valley, west of Arezzo and even closer to Florence. All this was a mortal challenge to the Florentines, a flagrant occupation of their home territory. It was made all the more threatening by the appearance, with Vitelli and Baglioni, of the hapless Piero de' Medici, perpetually in search of an opportunity to become master of Florence once again. These developments immediately brought to the fore the question of where the real power now resided in central Italy. In doing so they left the king of France with no choice but to become involved.

Vitelli, so consumed by hatred of the Florentines as to be nearly incapable of behaving responsibly, was the worst possible man to be in the middle of this situation. One historian has suggested that, being no friend of the Borgias in spite of being in Cesare's pay, he had encouraged the Arezzans to rebel, hoping to put the blame on Cesare and thereby turn the French against him. An alternative hypothesis is that Cesare, upon learning of the rebellion, ordered Vitelli to occupy Arezzo in order to gauge just how determined the French king was to protect Florence. It quickly became clear that he was very determined indeed: he sent unequivocal orders for Vitelli and Baglioni to pull out of Arezzo immediately. When the two of them ignored this edict, Cesare as their employer was put in a severely awkward position. He decided not to be deflected, however, from the execution of his own plans.

The Arezzo crisis accelerated everything. Just two days after the start of the rebellion two corpses, their hands and feet bound, were found in the Tiber River. One was the body of Astorre Manfredi, late lord of Faenza, the other of the illegitimate half-brother who had been his comrade in arms through the long winter when Cesare had them and their city under siege. Both youths, following their negotiated surrender, had become members of Cesare's entourage, then prisoners in the Castel Sant'Angelo. And now they were dead. No one but Cesare could have been responsible. His motive is not hard to guess: to remove a popular young leader in support of whom the people of Faenza might themselves have rebelled. Four days after the discovery of the bodies, having cleared the decks, Cesare was on the move. He led his army out of Rome and headed north and east. As before, no one appeared to have any idea of where he was going or what he intended to do.

Word spread that his objective was Camerino, a city-state of some thirty thousand inhabitants ninety miles north of Rome. It was in a sense an improbable target. Being well to the south of Cesare's Romagna conquests, it could never be easily integrated into the state he was assembling. But it was also a rich little city ruled by a particularly unpopular tyrant. The seventy-year-old Giulio Cesare Varano, who as a young man had seized power by murdering his brother (fratricide having been an almost regular occurrence among the Varani from early in the thirteenth century), had been declared an outlaw for failing to pay the annual tribute owed to the Vatican. He was also, along with his four arrogant sons, hated by his subjects. If brought under attack, the Varani would inspire none of the loyalty that had made it so difficult to take Faenza from the Manfredi.

All such speculation turned out to be irrelevant when, in a lightning stroke that stunned the whole of northern Italy, Cesare abruptly changed direction and, moving his army through sixty miles of rugged mountain country in an astonishing forty-eight hours, fell not upon Camerino but upon the far greater prize of Urbino fifty miles to its north. Urbino was then what it remains today: one of the jewels of northwestern Italy. A beautiful little city on a high hill, it was towered over by the magnificent palace made possible by the colossal earnings of the duke who built it, Federico da Montefeltro, second only to Francesco Sforza of Milan among the great *condottieri* of the fifteenth century. His son and successor, the same Guidobaldo da Montefeltro who had been Juan Borgia's co-commander in the failed attack on the Orsini with which Alexander VI opened his reign, was urged by the townsfolk to organize a defense as soon as they understood that Cesare's army was coming down on them.

The refined Guidobaldo, more scholar than soldier, saw no point in doing anything of the kind. He sensibly concluded that the likely result of resistance would be the destruction of everything his father had built and catastrophe for Urbino's people. He therefore departed with his wife Elisabetta, who as a Gonzaga of Mantua was now related by marriage to Lucrezia Borgia and therefore to Cesare himself. (In an all-too-typical example of the arcane ways in which all the leading families of Italy had come to be interconnected, Lucrezia's third marriage had made Cesare the brother of the bride of Elisabetta's brother Francesco Gonzaga's wife's brother Alfonso d'Este. Diagrams are required to make such things understandable.)

When Cesare reached Urbino on June 21, he met with no resistance and was able to take possession of the city without a blow being struck or a drop of blood shed. He found the ducal palace filled with treasures of every description, everything the Montefeltri family had accumulated over the generations, the magnificent library that Duke Federico had devoted much of his life to assembling included. He ordered all of it packed up for transfer to Cesena, now a base of Borgia operations in the north and under the command of the fierce and faithful Lorqua.

The conquest of Urbino was, depending on one's point of view, either a stroke of tactical brilliance or the cynical betrayal of a blameless duke. Possibly it was both, but it is less than certain that Guidobaldo was entirely innocent. Cesare, who rarely troubled to explain himself, chose to do so in this case, claiming that he had decided to move against Urbino only after learning that Guidobaldo was secretly sending assistance to the outlawed Giulio Cesare Varano in Camerino. This is not necessarily untrue. It would have been prudent of Guidobaldo to surmise that if Camerino were allowed to fall into Cesare's hands, Urbino would become a convenient and logical next target. Nor would he have been wrong in supposing that, by helping Varano and his sons to hold off Cesare at Camerino, he might save Urbino from attack. What mattered, however, was Cesare's capture of an extraordinary prize at almost no cost. This enhanced his stature as the most dangerous man in Italy after Louis XII.

Two questions were on every mind. What was Cesare going to do next, and what was his ultimate objective? When he sent word to Florence that he had important matters to discuss, the city's *signoria* hastened to respond. They assigned one of the republic's leading diplomats, Bishop Francesco Soderini, to hurry to Urbino. There he was to do everything possible to keep Cesare out of Tuscany and get Vitelli and Baglioni out of Arezzo and the Val di Chiana.

Soderini was a capable man, experienced, sophisticated, and clever. He was also a member of one of Florence's most distinguished families; in this same year, his brother Piero would be appointed to the new and immensely prestigious position of gonfalonier for life. It was unthinkable to send such a high dignitary on such a sensitive mission without a private secretary, and a worthy one at that. So when the bishop rode out of Florence en route to Urbino, at his side was a rising young diplomat and civil servant named Niccolò Machiavelli.

THE ANGEL'S CASTLE

ONE THING AT LEAST REMAINED CONSTANT THROUGH ALL THE transformations the city of Rome underwent during the thousand years preceding the arrival of the Borgias. The massive bulk of the Castel Sant'Angelo, the Castle of the Holy Angel, continued to loom over the Tiber River where it passes closest to the Vatican. The Castel was already hundreds of years old when the Roman Empire fell. It was approaching its seven-hundredth birthday when Charlemagne was crowned Holy Roman emperor, and it would be midway through its second millennium when work began on the great basilica that dominates St. Peter's Square today.

The Borgias, once they were on the scene, soon learned what everyone learned who was involved in the politics of Rome: that the Castel was the city's sole impregnable fortress, the place that no ruler seeking to be safe could afford to be without.

There is irony in this. When built, the Castel was not intended for any military purpose—or even for the use of living human beings. It was a mausoleum, a crypt, the creation of the Emperor Hadrian, the second-century Spaniard who also built the famous wall across the north of Britain. When he came to the throne in 117 AD, Rome already had a grand mausoleum for the ashes of deceased emperors and their families, a massive affair built by Augustus in 28 BC. But its last available niche had been filled with the remains of the Emperor Nerva in 98 AD. Nerva's successor and Hadrian's immediate predecessor, Trajan, finessed the problem by arranging to have himself interred beneath the immense column that bears his name and has been one of Rome's landmarks ever since. Hadrian, however, found this an unsatisfactory expedient. In the early 130s he ordered work begun on a structure so ambitious that it would not be completed in his lifetime. His contemporaries, finding nothing to compare it with even in the imperial capital, described it in terms that evoked the gigantic monuments of ancient Egypt.

Hadrian's Tomb, as it was called almost from the start, was an enormous squat cylinder resting on an even bigger boxlike base of four equal sides, all of it sheathed in fine Parian marble and faced with Ionic and Corinthian colonnades. The outer wall of the upper cylinder provided the base for a ring of statues that encircled a garden-in-the-sky, and at the elevated center of this garden, towering over the entire neighborhood, was a kind of cupola sheltering an almost preposterously outsize statue of Hadrian, the head of which can be seen today in one of Rome's museums. The burial chamber was at the center of the basement level. Persons granted admission to the interior could ascend to the garden through a spiral passageway that was eleven feet wide with a thirty-foot ceiling.

Hadrian, one of the empire's more capable rulers, was not the first person to be buried in his tomb. He was preceded in death by his adopted son and intended successor, just as two centuries before Augustus had lost a stepson and two grandsons before expiring himself. Hadrian was joined in due course by generations of later emperors, including such famous figures as Marcus Aurelius, his son Commodus, and Septimus Severus. The last burial was that of the Emperor Caracalla, assassinated in 217, after which the structure was incorporated into a new city wall and stood dormant until, two centuries later, Rome came under threat from Germanic invaders. At that point the city's desperate defenders awoke to the fact that Hadrian's Tomb was by far the most formidable stronghold available to them. Its conversion to military use probably occurred early in the fifth century, during the dismal years when the Emperor Honorius presided over the accelerating disintegration of the empire. Though it gradually lost much of its original grandeur— in 537 Hadrian's magnificent statues were hurled down on attacking Ostrogoths—unlike the Tomb of Augustus it was never reduced to a heap of crumbling ruins.

The year 530 was memorable for a terrible Tiber flood, a consequent outbreak of plague, and a resulting change of name for the tomb. This happened because Pope Gregory the Great, in leading a procession of penitents across the bridge that Hadrian had constructed adjacent to his mausoleum, happened to look up and saw the majestic figure of Saint Michael the Archangel returning to its sheath a bloody sword. This was a sign, as Gregory explained to the faithful, that the epidemic was at an end. It did abate in any case, and Hadrian's Tomb became the Castel Sant'Angelo.

Visitors from the spirit world notwithstanding, the Castel became the setting for nightmarish dramas. The imprisonment, torture, and murder of successive popes that punctuated the so-called pornocracy of the tenth century all took place in the Castel, which subsequently was fought over by the baronial clans and by popes and antipopes. The Colonna had possession for a time, but lost it in a nasty little war that ended with their banishment from Rome. A century and a half later, in order to save it from demolition, the pope of the time had to cede it to the Orsini. It was an Orsini pope, Nicholas III, who in 1277 built a fortified passageway to the Castel as a means of escape from the Vatican. By the early fifteenth century the Castel was permanently in the custody of the Church, and a stout and ugly square tower had been installed atop the cylinder, high up where Hadrian's garden had once been. The marble facade had been stripped away for use in paving the streets.

The Castel had become the key to Rome, or at least to avoiding expulsion. Like the Tower of London in distant England it served a multitude of purposes: stronghold, part-time residence for rulers, prison, symbol of power, refuge in time of danger. Alexander invested heavily in strengthening it and in making it a comfortable retreat.

He also fortified the Passetto di Borgo, the passageway connecting the Vatican to the Castel. It would be the saving of a number of his relatives, at least for a while.

18

"Longing for
Greatness and Renown"

" S plendid."
    "Magnificent."
These are the first two adjectives employed by Niccolò Machiavelli
in the description of Cesare Borgia that he writes as the two are getting
to know each other in Urbino in the hair-raising summer of 1502.

This lord is truly splendid and magnificent, he reports to his masters in
Florence. *In the pursuit of glory and territory he is unceasing and knows
neither danger nor fatigue.*

Such words are remarkable, coming as they do from Machiavelli of
all people. Few men in history have been less easy to impress. He will
be famous forever for the wryness of his observations, the cool detachment with which he arrives at his sometimes stunning insights, and
above all the fathomless cynicism that pervades his classic work *The
Prince.* His writings drip with contempt for some of the greatest figures
of his day. To see him lavishing praise on someone he has just met, an
adversary five years his junior, is not only unexpected but little short of
astonishing.

Despite all the reasons he has to despise Cesare and depict him in the
ugliest possible terms—he is, after all, a mortal danger to the Republic
of Florence—Machiavelli's description reads like a hymn of praise, a
rapture, almost a love song. Cesare is *loved by his soldiers,* he writes. Cesare is *victorious and formidable,* and enjoys *constant good fortune.* As the

words pile up, one begins to wonder if Machiavelli has lost the ability to think critically, if he is in the grip of something akin to infatuation. Once again, as with Cesare's domination of Pope Alexander, we catch a reflection of the power, the raw charisma, of his personality. Of the almost preternaturally magnetic force felt by almost everyone who ever came near him, and of the physical appeal that came with being what he was repeatedly called: "the handsomest man of his time." The historian Pandolfo Collenuccio wrote of the grown-up Cesare in 1500 that he was "accounted valiant, joyous, and open-handed, and it is believed that he holds honest men in high esteem." In a flash of almost Machiavellian insight, Collenuccio further described Cesare as "filled with aspiration" and having "a longing for greatness and renown."

Machiavelli himself looked deeper and saw more. He decided that Cesare, more than anyone else then living, had the vision, the boldness, and the strength of character needed to rescue Italy from the divisions that had made it so vulnerable to invaders.

In company with Francesco Soderini, Machiavelli had arrived in Urbino around sundown on June 24 at the end of a hard ride over the Apennines. The two were given accommodations in the city's episcopal palace, Soderini being a bishop, and shortly before midnight were taken to see Cesare. Rarely are historians given a greater gift than this: that as acute an observer as has ever lived should visit and report upon one of the most strikingly memorable figures of the Renaissance. And that they should continue to meet as Cesare's story unfolds, the result being a kind of three-dimensional portrait extended, and evolving, over time.

It is irresistibly fascinating, the image of these two young men, each destined in his own way and on his own schedule for failure and eternal fame, facing each other for the first time. They have been brought together not just by great events but by need. Cesare needing Florence— needing something *from* Florence, certainly, in spite of the city's weakness and the conquests that have made him so feared. Machiavelli and the bishop, in their turn, needing something from Cesare—needing above all to find some way of keeping him as far from Florence as possible. Reduced to a single word, that is their mission: to keep Cesare *away*.

They meet in one of the numerous vast and high-ceilinged chambers of Urbino's glorious ducal palace, still unfinished in 1502 but already comprising more than 250 rooms. On one side, alone behind an expanse of polished tabletop, sits Cesare, master of the situation no less than of the sleeping city of Urbino. Cesare the crafty, the self-dramatizing, playing his little trick of meeting with callers in the middle of the night, a single burning candle placed behind him so that he can see the faces of his visitors while his own remains in shadow. Dressed as always in a simple black tunic that sets off his ivory skin and is adorned with nothing except the emblem of the Order of St. Michel that the king of France first placed around his neck. Cesare the conqueror. Valentino.

Opposite, alongside the bishop he serves, sits Machiavelli the mere secretary, the civil servant, the promising junior diplomat. He is nobody's idea of handsome, with his close-set eyes in a long ovoid face that narrows down to a sharp chin. If there is not much strength in that face, there is mischief in the eyes, the trace of a smile flickering about the thin lips. Cesare will learn to enjoy Machiavelli's company, and it is not hard to see why. In addition to their shared fascination with power— Cesare the practitioner, Machiavelli one of the most original students the subject has ever had—they have in common a lively wit and a kind of intelligence that can be hard and cold as ice. If Machiavelli is perhaps not capable of rising to Cesare's level of ruthlessness—life will give him no opportunity to find out—he is certainly capable of appreciating Cesare's attainments in that regard. They have been brought together by matters vital to both of them, under circumstances that make it impossible for either to be entirely forthright. Each has to look for hidden meanings in whatever the other says. Something clicks between them all the same. They are more than shrewd enough, both of them, to take each other's measure quickly, and to see how well they are matched.

At this first meeting, which continues into the small hours of a new day, Cesare and his visitors spar cordially, engaging in oblique attempted bluffs. Cesare complains, accurately enough, that Florence has failed to carry out the terms of the previous year's agreement, which was, boiled down to its implicit essence, a promise to pay him not to attack. Soderini counters by suggesting, not implausibly though the truth of the matter cannot be known to him and remains unknown to the present day, that Cesare colluded in the seizure of Arezzo and the

Val de Chiana by Vitellozzo Vitelli and Gian Paolo Baglioni. The two try to trump each other in laying claim to the support of Louis XII, whom they know to be quite powerful enough to obliterate not only Florence and the Borgias but their enemies and friends as well.

The king of France, as it happens, is a subject of which Cesare and Machiavelli share exceptional personal knowledge. Both have spent long anxious months at Louis XII's court. Both went there—at separate times—in search of favors. And both, after much frustration, were ultimately successful: Cesare in obtaining a dukedom, a bride, and adoption as one of the king's favorites, Machiavelli in winning a promise of protection for Florence. What Cesare now hints—that Louis will raise no objection if he simply seizes Florence and installs there a government that can be depended upon to do his bidding—would have seemed plausible to many listeners. It may even have frightened Soderini. Machiavelli, however, knows better and is less impressed than amused. He knows that Louis, in addition to being in real need of Borgia support, is also seriously short of money, is going to need Florence's banks, and can have no interest in allowing Cesare to take control of the Florentine territories through which French troops will soon have to pass on their way to Naples.

Still, not even Machiavelli can find anything amusing about the note on which Cesare ends the meeting. He is not, he declares, going to put up with procrastination or prevarication. Florence has to decide: it is his friend or his enemy, and there is no middle ground. If it chooses to be his friend, it has nothing to fear; it possesses nothing that he wants. If the *signoria* is worried about a possible restoration of the Medici, nothing could be more obvious than that Cesare is in the business of removing, not installing, tyrants. If on the other hand Florence rejects his friendship, he will have no choice but to respond as he thinks best. Thus does the threat of invasion hang in the night air as Cesare dismisses his visitors, advising them to stand by for further talk on the morrow.

The next morning, finding themselves unsummoned, Soderini and Machiavelli left their quarters and went exploring, no doubt doing their best to imitate casual sightseers while in fact on the hunt for information. Even as sons of Florence, that city of splendor, they must have been impressed by what the Montefeltri family had done with the mountaintop redoubt of Urbino. At a time when a common laborer could expect to earn perhaps fifteen ducats in a year, when 2,500 ducats was sufficient to set up an aristocratic family in a respectable home, Federico da Montefeltro had spent two hundred thousand on the expansion and perfection of his ancestral base. He had spent scores more thousands on acquiring exquisite works of art and on assembling a collection of manuscripts said to surpass the library of Oxford University. And now palace and library alike were being stripped bare, paintings and statues and all the rest being loaded onto carts to be hauled a hundred miles north to Cesare's *rocca* at Cesena.

At some point in their tour, presumably to their surprise and undoubtedly to their delight, the two Florentines came upon, or found themselves intercepted by, Paolo Orsini and his cousin Giulio. This pair, well known as soldiers and leading members of their clan, had come to Urbino with Cesare's army as two of his *condottieri*. Their encounter with Soderini and Machiavelli may have been awkward, at least at first. Like almost all members of their family, Paolo and Giulio were Medici partisans and enemies of Florence's current regime. But that morning in Urbino, Soderini and Machiavelli had far less interest in ancient blood feuds than in trying to learn whatever they could, especially about what Cesare was thinking and what he intended to do. And so they gave themselves over to a friendly chat. The Orsini did likewise, and the talk turned inexorably to what had been discussed in Cesare's chamber the night before: the question of how Louis of France was likely to react if Cesare moved against Florence. The Orsini spoke carefully, obliquely. Acknowledging that the king was unlikely ever to explicitly withdraw his promise to protect Florence—by doing so he would make himself look dishonorable and weak—they nevertheless gave the visitors to understand that Louis was willing to advance southward out of Milan slowly enough to give Cesare time to do as he wished without interference. Preparations for an offensive against Florence, they suggested, were already under way. They spoke of how fast Cesare was capable of moving—meaning how little time he would need.

Much of this was the opposite of the truth. Machiavelli was right in surmising that Louis would never let Cesare, or anyone else, seize control of Florence and Tuscany. On that very morning, though no one in Urbino had any way of knowing it, part of the king's army was de-

parting Milan with two related assignments: to see to it that Florence
was left alone, and to force Vitelli and Baglioni out of Tuscany. Ignorant though he was of these developments, Machiavelli must have seen
through the Orsinis' pose. He knew Paolo's reputation—knew that,
though capable of talking tough, he was an unstable character, so un-
steady under pressure that his own troops called him "Madonna" Orsini and not because of any maternal concern for their well-being. And
that Giulio, though a more impressive fighting man than his cousin—
the Borgias would learn to their cost just how relentless a foe he could
be—had a reputation for deviousness second only to that of his brother,
the fork-tongued Cardinal Giovanni Battista Orsini. Machiavelli and
the bishop would have suspected from the start that this encounter was
no accident, and that Cesare had instructed the cousins in what to say
in order to frighten the *signori* of Florence and prompt them to come to
terms.

That night, hours after sundown, Soderini and Machiavelli were escorted back to the ducal palace to meet again with Cesare. This eccentric scheduling, if partly tactical on Cesare's part, was also a reflection
of his youth: he still had a young man's inclination, which he indulged
with an insouciance that could infuriate even the pope, to stay up all
night and sleep the morning away. This time, his visitors soon saw,
there were to be no more amusing preliminaries, no verbal sparring,
no subtleties to be interpreted at leisure. Cesare began where he had
ended the night before, with an ultimatum. Florence had to decide
whether it was with him or against him. And now there was a deadline:
he would give the *signoria* four days to reach its decision and not an
hour more. If he had received no answer after four days, Cesare would,
as he vaguely but ominously put it, act in accord with his own interests.
His insistence that everything be settled quickly seemed to Machiavelli
a confirmation of his suspicions. The duke, he felt sure, hoped to be
able to present Louis of France with a fait accompli in which king, republic, and Borgias were all allies but Florence was in a distinctly submissive role.

Soderini and Machiavelli spent the rest of the night drafting a report
that, immediately upon completion, they handed to a mounted courier
for delivery to Florence with all possible speed. A few hours later, after
snatching a bit of sleep, Machiavelli too set out on the seventy-mile

ride home. He and the bishop had agreed that one of them had better return home to explain some of the subtleties barely touched on in their report. Soderini, as senior member of the delegation, would remain in Urbino, doing what he could to keep Cesare's impatience under control while being careful to promise him nothing.

Ironically, the whole drama came to nothing. The Florentine authorities, benefiting from Machiavelli's account of what he had witnessed in Urbino and his interpretation of the situation, found excuses to delay their response. They sent word back to Cesare that, eager though they were to cooperate, it seemed advisable to commit to nothing until the pope and King Louis had been consulted. This was so unanswerable, so impossible to object to, that it sent Cesare into a white-hot rage and Soderini racing out of Urbino in fear for his life. When French couriers reached Cesare with orders not to disturb Florence but instead to dislodge Vitelli and Baglioni from Arezzo, the game was up, his bluff called.

Unwilling to settle for doing nothing with the army he had mustered at such cost, Cesare sent a body of troops hurrying south in an attack on Camerino. There, at least, things went well. When the old warlord Giulio Cesare Varano tried to organize a defense, his subjects pushed him aside and insisted on immediate surrender. They opened their gates to the invaders, becoming the latest city to fall into Cesare's hands without a fight. Compared to Florence and Bologna, however, Camerino was a small prize of little strategic value. Though Varano had been promised his freedom in return for surrender, he was thrown into a cell. He would die there after a few months, and the three of his sons who had been captured with him would then be done away with.

Vitelli and Baglioni, meanwhile, persisted in refusing to pull out of Arezzo and the Val di Chiana. They continued to do so even when a body of Louis XII's troops arrived on the scene, yielding only—and angrily—when Cesare warned that if they did not withdraw, he would attack their home cities of Città di Castello and Perugia. Quite apart from their wish to hurt Florence, both found this an excruciating reverse. As they saw the situation, they had taken Arezzo and the Val da Chiana fair and square, Florence had proved incapable of taking either place back, and had they been allowed to maintain possession, their domains would have been wonderfully enhanced and their place in the hierarchy of Italian tyrants raised correspondingly. Baglioni, however, knew what it was to lose everything and had no wish to repeat the experience. Early in his bloody career he had been driven out of Perugia by cousins who slaughtered his immediate family and barely missed killing him as well. It was Vitelli who had helped him to retake the city in 1500 and had joined him in butchering as many of the enemy Baglioni, women and children included, as could be stopped from escaping. That had cemented the relationship between the two men, making Baglioni a substitute for Vitelli's executed brother, but it had put a limit on Baglioni's appetite for risk. He was ready to go home, and his decision left Vitelli with no choice but to do likewise.

All the tyrants of north Italy were afraid of Cesare at this point, and all were looking for help. The men he had displaced but not captured or killed—Guidobaldo da Montefeltro, for example, and the sole surviving son of Giulio Cesare Varano—had migrated to Louis XII's court in Milan, the one place they could take their grievances and at least hope to produce a result. They were being joined by men who had not yet lost their places but feared that they soon would: Giovanni Bentivoglio of Bologna, Francesco Gonzaga of Mantua, and others. Louis found himself under a barrage of warnings about the dangers posed by Borgia ambition and the need to understand that Cesare was the enemy even of France. These entreaties were echoed by some of the regulars at the court, most emphatically by Cardinal Giuliano della Rovere. He had returned to his old refrain about how Alexander VI had no right to the pontifical throne and removing him would be a blessed act.

Cesare was aware of all this—he had a keen appreciation of the value of information and always spent freely to keep himself current—and he needed no one to tell him how worthless all his conquests would be if Louis turned against him. Early on the morning of July 27, disguised as a knight of the Order of St. John and accompanied by only three companions, he rode out of Urbino with his destination, as usual, unstated. The next day he showed up in Ferrara, where he found an epidemic of some kind ravaging the city and his sister Lucrezia both pregnant and dangerously ill. The two talked all night, using the Valencian dialect that had been the language of their childhood and that prevented eavesdroppers from understanding what they said. The next day, after summoning papal physicians to come and attend to Lucrezia, accompanied now by his brother-in-law Alfonso d'Este, Cesare mounted up again and started for Milan.

We have no certain knowledge of why Alfonso left his bride, expecting his child and so ill that her life was believed to be in danger, in order to join Cesare on the ride from Ferrara to Milan. Obviously he was not restrained from doing so by any great affection for Lucrezia. He and his father the duke probably thought it advisable, with a new war for Naples in the offing, to provide Louis XII with fresh and direct assurances that they remained his faithful friends. It is equally probable that Cesare had urged upon the Este the importance of demonstrating to the king that they and he were united in his support. It would have been natural for him to want to create the impression that Ferrara was now his to command.

On August 5, when Cesare came pounding into Milan and presented himself at an astonished French court, his enemies were appalled to observe the enthusiasm with which Louis received him. The king found it touching, apparently, that the young Valentino had undertaken such an arduous and risky journey in order to see him, and his old affection was immediately rekindled. A retainer of Francesco Gonzaga observed that "His Most Christian Majesty welcomed and embraced [Cesare] with great joy and led him to the castle, where he had him lodged in the chamber nearest him, and he himself ordered the supper, choosing diverse dishes, and that evening three or four times he went to his room dressed in shirt sleeves. . . . He could not have done more for a son or a brother." Thus encouraged, Cesare spent long hours in conversation not only with the king but also with his chief minister Cardinal d'Amboise, whose hopes of becoming the next pope provided all the encouragement he needed to stay on the friendliest possible terms with the Borgias and their minions in the College of Cardinals.

Cesare remained at court for almost a month, accomplishing everything he could have hoped when setting out. The extent of his success is evident in the transformation that his time in Milan wrought in his relationship with Francesco Gonzaga, marquess (a noble rank lower only than duke) of the city-state of Mantua and lord of Modena as well. Gonzaga had reacted angrily to Cesare's unexpected appearance in

Milan. He treated him with contempt, hurling insults until Cesare challenged him to a duel. The king intervened, demanding that the two find a way to become friends.

They were helped to do so by Gonzaga's wife Isabella, the daughter of Duke Ercole of Ferrara who had objected so bitterly to her brother's marriage to Lucrezia. Like her late sister Beatrice, wife of Ludovico Sforza of Milan, Isabella was more intelligent, more sophisticated, and politically a good deal shrewder than her husband. When, at home in Mantua, she heard about Francesco's clash with Cesare, she sent a letter of rebuke. "I cannot conceal my fears for your person and state," she told her husband. "It is generally understood that His Most Christian Majesty has some understanding with Valentino, so I beg you to be careful not to use words which may be repeated to him, because in these days we do not know who is to be trusted. There is a report here—whether it has come from Milan by letter or mouth, I do not know—that Your Excellency has spoken angry words against Valentino before the Most Christian King and the Pope's servants, and whether this is true or not, they will doubtless reach the ears of Valentino, who, having already shown that he does not scruple to conspire against those of his own blood, will, I am certain, not hesitate to plot against your person."

In saying that Cesare had conspired against his own blood, she was referring of course to the murder of his brother Juan. About that, as we have seen, she was almost certainly wrong. She was right, however, in warning her husband that if he valued his life, he would change his behavior. No one could yet know, in September 1502, just how right she was, but Francesco was sensible enough to take her advice. Isabella also intervened with Cesare directly, writing to him in fawning terms and sending him a hundred carnival masks—a perfectly chosen gift in light of his predilection for going about masked when in Rome. The rift was healed so completely—clearly neither side wanted further trouble—that before Cesare's departure a betrothal was arranged between the three-year-old daughter he had never seen and the Gonzagas' two-year-old son and heir. It is difficult to believe that anyone expected this arrangement ever to lead to an actual marriage, but in the near term there was something in it for everyone. It put Cesare on a newly friendly footing with Mantua, which lay just to the north of Bologna and was closely connected to Ferrara. It spared Louis XII from having to add Mantua to the list of states he was committed to shielding from Cesare.

Isabella was right about something else too. There was indeed "some understanding" with Louis, one that from Cesare's perspective could hardly have been more welcome. The king, betraying his new ally Giovanni Bentivoglio in much the same way that he had already betrayed the people of Pisa, promised not only not to interfere if Cesare chose to attack Bologna—which helps to explain Cesare's eagerness for a rapprochement with Bologna's neighbor, the gratuitously insulting Gonzaga of Mantua—but to continue making troops available for Cesare's use. He further agreed that Cesare should be free to deal with his own *condottieri*—Vitelli, Baglioni, and various Orsini—in whatever way he thought best. In return the king required only that Cesare acknowledge the status of Florence as a French protectorate and join his army with France's when the war with Spain began. On September 2, in bidding the king farewell, Cesare offered profuse thanks and a written pledge that "when the time comes I will present myself to you at the head of ten thousand men." He then started back to the Romagna. Again he detoured to Ferrara, arriving to discover that Lucrezia had suffered a miscarriage and was now so ill that she was not expected to recover. He helped to hold her down while the physicians summoned from Rome bled her, and witnesses would report that the two days he spent at her side "cheered her greatly." Though Lucrezia was given the last rites the day after the bleeding, she went on to make a full recovery. She would, however, never see her brother again. That he had twice added a hundred miles to a hard journey at least partly to see his sister— solely for that purpose the second time, so far as we know—shows the strength of the bond between the two.

Cesare established a headquarters at Imola and, employing some of his clergymen relatives as administrators, set about organizing his new duchy of Romagna. In doing so he demonstrated that he had learned from the example of Pope Alexander, who from the reign of Calixtus III had displayed a good understanding of the problems of the Papal States and a keen appreciation of the value of firm and honest administration in maintaining order and creating loyalty. Cesare replaced the capricious and often savagely cruel rule of the likes of Caterina Sforza with something the Romagnese people had not experienced since ancient times: governmental machinery that functioned fairly and efficiently and delivered real justice. One of his first acts in this connection was to dismiss his vicar-general, the Spaniard Ramiro de Lorqua. Lorqua's hard methods, growing interest in enriching himself, and sneering contempt for the farmers and merchants of the Romagna had made him hated. His demotion to the governorship of Rimini was cheered everywhere except in that suddenly fearful city. Cesare created a new office, *presidente,* and appointed to it a distinguished jurist and humanist scholar named Antonio di Monte Sansovino, not just personally honest but devoted to rooting out official corruption. The administration that Sansovino put in place marked the opening of a new era for the Romagna. It made Cesare a popular figure, a ruler for whom many of the region's people would be willing to fight.

The understanding that Cesare had come to with Louis XII in Milan was supposedly secret, but word of it leaked out soon enough. Possibly Pope Alexander let it slip in the course of talking, as he was increasingly inclined to do as he grew older, too much and too freely. He would alternate happy effusions about Cesare's conquests with complaints about how much he was draining from the papal treasury—no less than a thousand ducats a day at this point. It would not be surprising if he let what he knew of Cesare's plans slip out in the course of one of his monologues. However it happened, the Orsini learned that Louis had given Cesare license to do with them as he wished. Their compeers Vitelli and Baglioni inferred, sensibly enough, that they too were marked for destruction.

Giovanni Bentivoglio of Bologna could feel a Borgia noose tightening around his neck as well. On September 17 he received orders to come to Rome to answer charges of having failed to fulfill his responsibilities as a papal vicar and, even more ominously, to bring his sons with him. Six days later Louis XII sent an even more shocking instruction: Bentivoglio was to surrender Bologna to the pope. Thoroughly alarmed, Bentivoglio assembled the leading men of the city and invited them to vote on whether he should do as the king demanded. The balloting was to be secret, with each participant putting into a box either a white bean indicating that Bentivoglio should stay or a black bean indicating that he should go. Any doubts about the outcome disappeared when the electors discovered that they had been given white beans only. It was all futile in any case; Bentivoglio obviously was doomed, and just as obviously he was not alone. The threatened lords began to meet and talk, and their discussions turned inevitably into the hatching of plans for striking at Cesare while there was still time. Among the plotters were the leading Orsini, the Bentivoglii, the Baglioni, Pandolfo Petrucci of Siena, Vitellozzo Vitelli, the exiled Guidobaldo of Urbino, and the lords of several smaller states. All were soldiers, many were seasoned killers, and almost all commanded substantial territories and significant numbers of men. Together they were likely to be strong enough to defy the pope, escape the wrath of the French king, and perhaps eliminate Cesare as a political force.

Events began to unfold more rapidly than the conspirators expected, but to do so in encouraging ways. On October 7 the people of San Leo, a town some ten miles from Urbino and fiercely loyal to the Montefeltro dukes, learned of the conspiracy against Cesare and spontaneously rose up against the troops he had garrisoned there. This sparked other risings elsewhere, at Urbino itself and its satellite city of Gubbio as well as several smaller places. Some of the Borgia garrisons were not only overwhelmed but annihilated. Suddenly Cesare found himself on the defensive, and the conspirators hastened to press their advantage. They reconvened in Magione, a town far to the south of the Romagna that became their regular meeting place. They agreed to launch two simultaneous offensives. Vitelli and the Orsini would advance together on Urbino, their objective to restore Guidobaldo as duke. Giovanni Bentivoglio's son Ermes, meanwhile, was to attack Cesare directly at his Imola headquarters.

Word came to Imola of setback after setback, disaster after disaster. Seeing that he was overextended, Cesare sent instructions for the two Spaniards he had left in command at Urbino, his friend Michelotto Corella and Ugo de Moncada, to pull back to Imola. They obeyed reluctantly, hating to surrender such a prize. Almost as soon as they were gone, Duke Guidobaldo returned, offering his palace to his fellow conspirators as their new base. To the south, Oliverotto Euffreducci of Fermo helped the last surviving son of Giulio Cesare Varano to retake Camerino. News of Guidobaldo's restoration caused two more towns loyal to the Montefeltri, Fossombrone and Pergola, to rise against Cesare's troops, almost all of whom were Spanish, and kill them to the last man. Virtually all this trouble was south of the Romagna, in Umbria and the March. The Romagna itself remained quiet, its garrisons un- threatened; Cesare's care to win the support of the population was showing its value.

Michelotto and Moncada were on the march when they learned of the loss of Camerino, Fossombrone, and Pergola and the slaughter of their Spanish comrades. Furious, they cast aside Cesare's instructions and changed direction. Their troops, veteran Spaniards hungry for revenge, were unleashed to pillage without restraint. They reduced Fossombrone and Pergola to smoldering rubble, subjecting their popu- lations to every imaginable outrage before essentially wiping them out. When news of these horrors reached Vitelli and Baglioni, they joined forces with Paolo and Francesco Orsini and set out in pursuit of the marauders. The two sides met near the village of Calmazzo, and the battle that followed was another disaster for Cesare. Moncada was taken prisoner, Michelotto barely managed to escape, and the remains of their army were driven in disorder back down the coast.

Ermes Bentivoglio, at about this same time, captured a fortress just seven miles from Imola. Cesare was nearly surrounded, virtually under siege, and his enemies had the initiative. A momentum was building that seemed almost certain to sweep him away.

THE NEWEST PROFESSION

HISTORIANS OF ITALY IN THE TIME OF THE RENAISSANCE ARE ABLE to draw on a rich (if by no means always reliable) source of information that did not exist in earlier periods, or even in other parts of Europe at the same time.

The source in question consists of the reports of ambassadors—of *permanent* ambassadors, a breed not previously seen—stationed first at Rome and later at other capitals by the leading Italian states. Like all source materials, these reports require careful handling, diplomats being as susceptible as anyone else to not knowing as much as they think they know, seeing what they want or expect to see, and allowing their prejudices to contaminate their judgment. When such factors are taken into account, however, the dispatches of the ambassadors add a new dimension to our understanding. And in the time of the Borgias their contribution really *was* new. Routine diplomacy as we understand it today, diplomacy conducted by professionals sent to take up residence in foreign capitals and represent the interests of their home states for extended periods of time, began at about the time Rodrigo Borgia was born. By the time he was pope, it had evolved into something very like its twenty-first-century form.

That it first emerged in Italy was no accident. Its immediate antecedents lay in the Church, which as the only international institution to survive the fall of the Roman Empire was for a long time almost the sole means by which Europeans were able to maintain a sense of shared identity, of belonging to a common civilization. That the Church like the old empire was centered on Rome added to its credibility, its usefulness, in this regard.

Canon law, essential to the Church's cohesion and coherence, kept alive the old imperial notion that some rules were important enough to apply to every part of the community. The sending out of cardinals as papal legates to all parts of Europe, though these envoys were generally expected to achieve some specific purpose and return to Rome when they had done so, put in place the first rudiments of diplomatic representation to be seen since classical times. A special vocabulary came into general use: *legatus* became the name for anyone sent to represent someone else, a *nuncio* was a person authorized to deliver messages only, a *procurator* (later *plenipotentiary*) was a senior emissary empowered to negotiate on behalf of his master.

Systematic diplomacy ceased to be the exclusive province of the Church early in the fifteenth century, as a direct result of what was happening in Italy. Beyond the Alps the German empire had become a shambles, and France and Spain had not yet pulled themselves together into the dominating powers that they would soon become. But in Italy the expulsion of the Holy Roman emperors had left a vacuum that was being filled, as we saw earlier, by a multitude of more or less new, more or less autonomous city-states. The leaders among these states—Milan, Florence, Venice—were not only the most advanced in the Western world economically and culturally, they were also secular, lacking a religion-based legitimacy in a way that was quite novel. Asked to justify the power that they possessed, those leaders could have pointed to little more than the naked force with which they kept domestic rivals in submission and external enemies out.

Being geographically small, the new Italian states existed in close proximity to one another. This, and the insecurities arising out of their lack of legitimacy, contributed to their being often at war. Much more than in the north of Europe, where the distances between the capitals of the greatest kingdoms were so great as to make regime-threatening surprise attacks difficult if not impossible, in Italy the warlords needed to be constantly on guard, ready to react on short notice. They needed to know not only what their neighbors were doing but what they were thinking. This gave rise to the idea of sending representatives, in due course to be called ambassadors, to take up permanent residence in the capitals of states deemed sufficiently significant to warrant the attendant costs. A prime purpose of these representatives was to send home a more or less continuous stream of whatever information—or gossip—they were able to pick up.

Milan was first. Under the Visconti it grew rich enough to invest in new channels of communication, and the ambitions of its dukes stirred up so much trouble that staying informed became essential. As early as the 1420s Milan had a kind of vestigial foreign office managing a small stable of emissaries to some of the more important Italian capitals, and as the usefulness of this arrangement became apparent, it attracted imitators. Europe's first treatise on diplomatic practice appeared in 1436, just a year after what is sometimes called the first international peace conference of the modern era succeeded in resolving, via the Treaty of Arras, a long-standing conflict between France and Burgundy. Before another two decades passed, Milan, Naples, Venice, and Florence all had permanent embassies in one another's capitals as well as in Rome.

The papal court remained central, the hub of the West's farthest-reaching and most sophisticated diplomatic network, the place that the other states could least afford to ignore. Rome became therefore the center of diplomatic scheming and counterscheming, the best information exchange in Europe, the place where every ambitious young diplomat wanted to be sent. Somewhat curiously—perhaps, with foreign agents clustering around them, they saw no need—no pope before Alexander VI sent permanent ambassadors to other courts. Alexander began doing so in the mid-1490s under pressure of the French invasion. He first posted a nuncio at the court of the German emperor, then established permanent representation in Spain, and finally in 1500 did the same in France and Venice.

The start of the Italian Wars, especially the creation of the Holy League of 1495 and its success in driving Charles VIII out of Italy, showed the outside powers the value of the new system. Ferdinand of Spain, though never easily separated from a gold ducat, nevertheless was early to see the light. In short order he found it worthwhile to establish embassies at Rome, Venice, London, Brussels, and the German emperor's court. Before the end of Alexander's reign all the major powers were doing the same.

19

Settling Scores

O n October 7, with the rebellion of a number of Cesare's conquered towns in full flower and the extent of the conspiracy against him just coming into focus, Machiavelli arrived at Imola. He had been sent, as before, in response to a message from Cesare saying that he had important matters to discuss. The fact that he traveled alone this time, as a "special envoy" rather than as part of a full-fledged embassy headed by a senior official, reflected the confidence of Florence's government that now it really was under the protection of France, and that it had little to fear from someone as beset with troubles as the young Borgia upstart.

The Ten, the council that managed Florence's relations with other states, had instructed Machiavelli not to offer Cesare assistance of any kind or do anything that might even suggest an alliance. He was to request safe passage through the Romagna for Florentine merchants—an important issue, but not of the highest urgency under current circumstances—and offer Cesare asylum. This last may have been intended as a subtle insult, implying as it did that Cesare was or soon might be in need of refuge and that Florence, the tables having turned, was strong enough to provide it. Machiavelli's real purpose, in any case, was obvious. It was to stay as close to Cesare as possible and gather as much information as he could. It was not a mission that he welcomed—he wanted to be in Florence, at home—and almost as soon as he was settled in Imola, he began asking for permission to return. His requests were ignored, and almost his only consolation was the surprising amount of access he was granted to the similarly idle Cesare. Though nothing in the way of business was accomplished, Machiavelli having no authority to do or propose anything, with each new encounter he was impressed afresh. What struck him above all was Cesare's cool self-confidence, his ability to remain clearheaded and at ease even as his political and military situation appeared to be collapsing. He was not only calm but in high spirits. The offer of asylum he shrugged aside, without taking offense and nearly without comment.

Machiavelli might have been less surprised by his host's sangfroid if he had been as well informed as Cesare was about the general state of affairs. He didn't know, when he arrived at Imola, that Cesare was aware that his disloyal *condottieri* had recently asked the Ten for help and been refused. This soon became clear, however: without disclosing anything of his own plans, Cesare revealed his understanding that the Florentine government could never have supported the plotters—would have found it impossible to do so even if the conspiracy had not been dominated by such deadly enemies of the republic as Vitellozzo Vitelli and the Orsini. Any move in that direction would have risked alienating Louis of France, Florence's sole and indispensable protector.

Cesare knew that Venice too had been asked to assist the conspirators and had likewise turned them away. And he understood its reasons for doing so. La Serenissima, trapped in its life-or-death struggle with the Turks, was in far too much need of papal and French help—or of their neutrality, at an absolute minimum—to consider taking sides against the Borgias. Its leading merchants, focused as always on protecting the Mediterranean trading routes that were the wellspring of their wealth, had little experience of the *condottieri* who had turned on Cesare and no reason to loathe them as the Florentines did. But they also could see no reason to want them to succeed. If the fragmentation of the Romagna had for centuries helped the Venetians to feel secure on their mainland frontier, and if the consolidation of the region under Cesare was no cause for celebration, nevertheless it would have been folly to throw in with an unstable coalition of rogues formed for the sole purpose of destroying Cesare Borgia. Such a step could only make an implacable enemy of the pope, stir up trouble with France, and secure the futures of some of the worst men in Italy. These things were unthinkable.

And a roguish lot the conspirators definitely were. That would be their damning weakness: the fact that they were, many and even most of them, of such repellent character as to be incapable not only of winning outside support but even of trusting one another. Throughout the generations when fratricide was almost commonplace among tyrant families, the Baglioni of Perugia had murdered one another with a frequency that was startling even to their contemporaries. Dubious paternity was so commonplace in the family as to make it uncertain that the Baglioni of 1502, current clan leader Gian Paolo included, were in fact descended from the ones who had first made themselves masters of Perugia a century before.

Tall and blond with striking good looks, at age thirty-two Gian Paolo was as practiced as any of his forebears in using force and terror to keep his subjects subdued. While it is unlikely that he could have been guilty of all the outrages of which his enemies accused him, he was undoubtedly capable of cruelty on an epic scale. On several occasions he had men whom he had decided were his foes, more than a few of them clearly innocent of any offense, hanged en masse because doing so suited either his political purposes or his whim at the moment. Machiavelli, who described him as "a man who cohabited with his sister, and had massacred his cousins and his nephews," would in later years condemn him not for his crimes but for lacking the resolve to murder a sixteenth-century pope when he had him, briefly, in his power.

Even worse—improbable as that may seem—was Oliverotto Euffreducci. At twenty-seven he was lord of the unfortunate city of Fermo by virtue of having murdered the uncle who raised him and always treated him generously. He had started his career soldiering in the service of Gian Paolo Baglioni, attaching himself to Vitellozzo Vitelli after the former's execution. Like the Vitelli and Baglioni he richly deserved the label tyrant, having terrorized the people of Fermo into dumb submission. Alone among his henchmen he has never had a single defender, anyone willing to suggest that he had redeeming qualities of any kind, even physical courage. Cesare Borgia's best biographer, W. H. Woodward, described Oliverotto as a "harebrained adventurer" who was not so much feared or even distrusted by his associates as simply despised. Machiavelli, in writing about him, plumbed the same depths of cynicism reached in his description of Baglioni, scorning him not for murdering women and children but for lacking the cunning required for survival.

Then there was Pandolfo Petrucci, lord of Siena, at fifty the oldest of the conspirators. He was sufficiently superior in cunning and intelligence to emerge as perhaps the closest thing they had to a leader, but he was also a vicious sadist. He had achieved supreme power in Siena by murdering his father-in-law (who was probably, it must in fairness be noted, plotting to murder him first) and is best remembered for one of his favorite forms of amusement. He loved to roll boulders down on low-lying parts of Siena from the heights above, howling with delight at the resulting devastation.

The weak and gullible Paolo Orsini was among the conspirators as well. And the devious Cardinal Orsini, he of the thousand tricks, along with his slippery brother Giulio. And Gian Giordano Orsini, who had been thrown into a Neapolitan prison with his father Virginio at the time of Charles VIII's withdrawal and was quietly awaiting his chance to avenge the old man's miserable death. Such was the vipers' tangle that was in league against Cesare: an assortment of sociopaths and psychopaths famous not just for ruthlessness, not just for a readiness to torture and murder the innocent, but for a willingness to betray their own blood. The one conspicuous exception was the recently deposed, even more recently restored Guidobaldo da Montefeltro. Adoring son of a majestic father, loved by the people of Urbino for his gentleness and kindness and admired by artists and scholars for his refinement, he was badly out of place in this affair and not taken seriously even by his partners. His prestige among such savages was not enhanced by rumors—almost certainly true—that he was sexually impotent, a fact that adds poignancy to his loving relationship with his wife, Francesco Gonzaga's sister Elisabetta.

Repulsive as they were on the whole, the confederates almost certainly could have overcome Cesare if they had moved quickly, firmly, and in concert. They proved to be incapable of doing any such thing. No real leader emerged to keep them together and focused. It would be said later that Cardinal Orsini had been the driving force behind the conspiracy, and Petrucci of Siena is sometimes described as its brains, but neither demonstrated the kind of mastery that the situation required. Not one of them had an objective loftier than his own survival and perhaps that of his family; almost all would cheerfully have sacrificed the others for his own sake, and they knew one another well enough to understand this. Such things might have been manageable if they had faced a less formidable adversary. But Cesare understood them and their vulnerabilities at least as well as they understood themselves, and he was both clever enough to outwit them and tough enough to undo them.

From his base at Imola, almost certainly drawing on a secret source of intelligence inside the enemy camp, Cesare played on the conspirators' divisions and aggravated their fears. Early on he had identified Paolo Orsini as the weakest and most seducible of his adversaries. He surreptitiously got word to Paolo of his willingness to forgive and forget, to allow the *condottieri* to return to his payroll while demanding nothing of consequence in return. When Paolo shared this offer with his fellow plotters at one of their gatherings at Magione, they showed more interest than was wise in a group of men who had already thrown down the gauntlet to a dangerous enemy, and Paolo was authorized to explore the matter further. In Rome, Pope Alexander opened parallel negotiations with the city's leading Orsini and found that they too were receptive. From Siena, meanwhile, Pandolfo Petrucci sent Cesare an almost craven message, earnestly assuring him that he had never intended to displease. Wherever the Borgias tested the resolve of the men plotting against them, they found weakness and a readiness to cut deals—even separate deals, when that seemed feasible. They could be confident that in a showdown each of the conspirators would look to his own immediate interests regardless of the fate of the others.

They had reason to be worried all the same. The risings south of the Romagna, and the fact that Cesare was all but trapped at Imola, left Alexander feeling deeply insecure. He feared that everything the two of them had achieved and were planning to achieve, the whole grand enterprise into which he was pouring the wealth of the papacy, was suddenly on the verge of collapse. He complained of Cesare's incessant demands for money and of the meager results his own generosity appeared to be producing. Carried on the grapevine, his lamentations must have boosted the confidence of the rebels.

Cesare by contrast waited and watched in silence, using his own inscrutability to unnerve his enemies. When Ermes Bentivoglio moved his troops near the outskirts of Imola but failed to provoke the expected countermove by Cesare, failed even to get an acknowledgment of his presence, he lost heart and withdrew in befuddlement. When it became certain that the plotters could expect no help from Venice or Florence, and that when Louis XII's army arrived on the scene it would come as Cesare's friend, their resolve disintegrated. Cesare meanwhile was continuing to receive infusions of gold from a pope too worried to tighten his purse strings, and he was using them to hire new *condottieri* and send agents into Lombardy to recruit fighters. He was able to keep his troops well paid, well provisioned, and loyal. Week by week, quietly, he was rebuilding his strength.

He and Machiavelli filled their idle hours with each other's company. Though Cesare persisted in revealing little of what he knew and nothing of what he intended, his reticence only increased Machiavelli's admiration of what he called, in explaining to his exasperated superiors why he had so little of value to report, his host's "most commendable secrecy." More impressed than ever with Cesare's perceptiveness and ability to make difficult decisions quickly, he advised the Ten that as things stood, it would be folly for Florence to put itself openly at odds with such a resourceful political player.

Late in October, with the unraveling of the conspiracy too far advanced to remain secret, a nervous Paolo Orsini showed up in Imola in disguise. He was eager to cut a deal, Cesare was happy to oblige him so long as the terms put him in a commanding position, and so a conditional agreement was worked out. When Paolo carried it back to Magione, however, it drew a mixed response. Cesare's sole hard demand was that the two cities of Urbino and Camerino—the homes of the Montefeltri and the Varani—must be returned to him. By and large, the conspirators who were not lords of either of those two cities, though no doubt less than delighted, found this a small enough price for their own deliverance. Though Vitelli and Baglioni at first poured scorn on the idea of trusting Cesare after having been so obviously bent on his destruction, and though their reptilian protégé Oliverotto lined up with them as usual, nobody else agreed, and the three gradually abandoned their objections.

Bentivoglio of Bologna, however, refused to be won over. As did Guidobaldo of Urbino—understandably so, as the terms on offer made him the principal sacrificial lamb. But the deal was accepted, the plotters took up once again their *condotta* with Cesare, and Guidobaldo was ordered to depart. Soon after, in making his second forced departure from the city his father had devoted his life to transforming, he would be heard to cry out to God, asking why such a fate had been visited upon him. As for whether Cesare's demand for possession of Urbino and Camerino was in any way justified, it should be remembered that, in hostile hands, the two cities would have been ideal platforms from which to threaten the Romagna. As soon as the Varani were gone from Camerino, the pope declared it a duchy and bestowed it upon the same mysterious little Giovanni Borgia, the so-called Infant of Rome, who was already duke of Nepi. Further evidence that he was—perhaps—Cesare's son.

In the end, thanks to the intervention of Louis XII, even Bentivoglio was persuaded to make peace. The king, wanting no disputes that might complicate the pursuit of his own goals, wanting also to retain the friendship of the pope and the use of his army without alienating a city as strategically situated as Bologna, arranged a settlement aimed at giving something to everyone. Bologna once again joined Florence in being under French protection and off limits to Cesare. In return, Bentivoglio was obliged once again to pledge a substantial payment in gold to Cesare and provide him with troops.

The conspiracy having been brought to an unsuccessful conclusion, its target and its instigators presumably reconciled, Cesare was once again eager to take the field. Machiavelli, however, came down with a fever as winter tightened its grip on the Romagnese plain, and found himself living in wretchedly constrained circumstances because Florence was neglecting to send his pay while Imola and the surrounding countryside were being picked clean by Cesare's troops and camp followers. He sent letter after letter begging to be allowed to return home, where obligations including children, a young wife, and a widowed mother required his attention. The *signori* replied that he was needed where he was.

On December 10, when Cesare led his army of twelve thousand men out of Imola through a driving snowstorm, several of the former plot-

ters were once again with him, commanding his troops. The disheartened Machiavelli, however, reported himself too ill to go along. He
followed a few days later, and on December 14 caught up with the
others at Cesena after a ride of thirty miles down the Via Emilia. They
were still at Cesena six days later when Cesare sprang his latest surprise, suddenly ordering the French cavalry that formed the core of his
force to depart for Milan and rejoin Louis XII. At a stroke he thus radically reduced the size of his army and stripped it of its best troops, and
as usual he declined to explain himself. One plausible explanation is
that France's men-at-arms were simply too expensive to maintain—
that in dismissing them Cesare was responding to the pope's complaints about costs. Another is that he had seen enough of the brutish
behavior of the foreigners and had decided that if he didn't bring it to an
end, he could never hope to be accepted by the populations whose lord
he intended to remain. A third hypothesis, no less credible and much
more intriguing in light of the events of the next three weeks, is that by
sending away so many of the troops most likely to remain loyal to him,
he was showing Vitelli, the Orsini, and the others that he trusted them
and that they had nothing to fear.

He was still at Cesena on Christmas morning, when the townsfolk
awoke to find a decapitated body on display in their central piazza. It
was the corpse of the hated Ramiro de Lorqua, long one of Cesare's
most important henchmen. Its head was impaled on an upright lance,
an executioner's ax on the ground beside it. There was no need for speculation about whose work this was. Just three days before, Lorqua had
been summoned to Cesena from his post at Rimini, and when he arrived, Cesare had had him placed under arrest. Thereafter he had been
under interrogation, and almost certainly under torture, and evidently
had revealed some dark things indeed.

Lorqua (known variously to the Italians as Lorca, de Orca, and
d'Orco) had always been excessively zealous, not to say bloodthirsty, in
the execution of his duties. His status as a Borgia insider is apparent
in the role he had played in the negotiation of Lucrezia's marriage to
Alfonso d'Este. There had been signs of trouble even then, however:
vague tales of how he had angered Cesare by somehow behaving inap-
propriately while escorting Lucrezia to her new life in Ferrara. More
recently his rough methods as vicar-general of the Romagna had caused

Cesare to demote him to Rimini, where he was now said to be enriching himself through extortion and pillage. His execution, though never
explained, sent unmistakable messages. In the most forceful terms
imaginable, it demonstrated to the inhabitants of the Romagna that
their new duke regarded Lorqua's misconduct as intolerable. It reinforced the signal that Cesare had sent his subjects when he placed the
honest and conscientious Antonio di Monte Sansovino in charge, first
in the Romagna and then elsewhere as well. Even before Lorqua's
death, Sansovino had been sent to Urbino to announce a general pardon of all who had opposed Cesare and the restoration of all the rights
the population had enjoyed under the Montefeltri. Such acts were calm-
ing the conquered territories. In the Romagna especially, with its long
history of misrule, they were giving the population more reasons than
ever to be grateful for Cesare's invasion.

The killing of Lorqua also helped to assuage whatever fears the former conspirators might still have felt. In part simply because he was a
Spaniard, but more because of his undisguised contempt for all things
Italian, Lorqua had been hated by Cesare's Italian *condottieri*. That he
had known Cesare far longer than any of the warlords, and appeared to
be closer to him than any of his other fellow Spaniards except Michelotto, made him greatly feared as well. His dramatic elimination, like
the dismissal of the French troops, was a vivid demonstration of just
how ruthless Cesare was capable of being. But it also gave Vitelli and
the others reason to believe that Cesare had cast his lot irrevocably
with them rather than with the French or even his old comrades from
Spain.

As always, Cesare kept his secrets. Among those secrets were the
things that Lorqua had revealed after his arrest—things of which
Cesare may have already been informed by his secret agent inside the
Orsini camp but that now could be taken as certain. Lorqua, resentful
of his demotion, aware that he was out of favor and fearful of what that
might portend, had entered into an improbable alliance with the members of the anti-Cesare conspiracy. Together they had begun hatching
new schemes for preemptively ridding themselves of Cesare. The
knowledge that he was again being plotted against explains everything
that Cesare would do over the next six days. It also explains why, at

exactly this point and for the first time, he began wearing a shirt of chain mail night and day.

Nevertheless, when Cesare left Cesena on December 26, he took with him only a single company of personal guards, dividing the bulk of his remaining army into units that were spread out across the landscape and ordered to proceed separately. Again he was showing his captains that he trusted them, that he was comfortable enough not to require strong protection and posed no threat to them. When Oliverotto volunteered to go on ahead with enough men to secure the coastal town of Senigallia, Cesare gave his consent. Senigallia, a papal vicariate, was held in defiance of Alexander VI by the widow of Giovanni della Rovere, Cardinal Giuliano della Rovere's brother, on behalf of her young son. Machiavelli was again traveling with Cesare, sensing as everyone did that something momentous was in the air. After a march of some forty miles southward along the coast they paused at Lucrezia's old home of Pesaro, where they received word that Oliverotto had taken Senigallia and was preparing it for Cesare's arrival. Two easy marches more, one of just six miles and another of a dozen, found them passing through Senigallia's gates on the afternoon of New Year's Eve. On hand to welcome them were Oliverotto, Vitelli, and Paolo and Francesco Orsini. They did what they could to make it a triumphal occasion.

Which is how it came to pass that Machiavelli was in Senigallia when, an hour or two after midnight on the first day of 1503, Vitellozzo and Oliverotto were strangled by Cesare's constant companion, Michelotto Corella. He used a violin string. Vitelli, it was said, begged to be allowed to live long enough to ask the pope for an indulgence that would spare him from divine punishment for his sins. Oliverotto whined and wept and blamed Vitelli for everything.

Later that same short winter day, when Cesare marched his troops out of Senigallia once again heading south, Machiavelli was as before part of the procession. So were three Orsini—Paolo, the young Francesco duke of Gravina, and a kinsman of theirs named Roberto, a member of the family's Pitigliano branch. But they were Cesare's prisoners now, not commanders of his troops, and they were manacled and under close guard. Back in Rome, having been advised by Cesare that aggressive action would be called for starting on New Year's Day, Alexander was filling his prisons with as many Orsini as could be rounded up. Cardinal Orsini was in the cell where he would soon die, his palace stripped and his aged mother left to wander the streets alone, unable to find anyone not too frightened to offer her food or shelter. What was in process was not just war against the Orsini but a war of extermination.

At last, in the second week of January, Machiavelli received permission to return home. He would not see Cesare again until nine months had passed. They would meet next in Rome, in October, by which time Cesare would be once more in crisis, beset by dangers far beyond anything encountered in Imola or elsewhere, in 1502 or at any other point in his young life.

THE GREAT DISCOVERIES

EVENTS THAT TRULY CHANGE THE WORLD—THAT CHANGE IT IN fundamental ways—don't come along every year. In Europe, before the Industrial Revolution, they didn't often happen once a century.

It is therefore more than remarkable that two such events happened within a span of five and a half years in the middle of the reign of Pope Alexander VI. The first came in March 1493, when Christopher Columbus returned to Spain after an absence of seven months to report that he had just succeeded in sailing to Asia (which is where he thought he had been). Then, in September 1499, Vasco da Gama dropped anchor at Lisbon and announced that in the course of a voyage that had taken twenty-six months he had done what no one could have imagined doing not many years before. He had rounded the Cape of Good Hope at the southern tip of Africa, crossed the Indian Ocean, reached the west coast of India with its limitless supplies of spices and other precious goods, and returned alive to tell the tale.

Also remarkable is how interconnected these two events were—so much so that they nearly brought Spain and Portugal to war with each other. And how it was Alexander, more than anyone in Spain or Portugal, who did what was needed to keep the peace.

Though ultimately the less momentous of the two voyages—it didn't lead to the discovery of two vast and previously unsuspected continents—da Gama's was the more impressive achievement. And in the near term its results were more dramatic. It was the culmination of almost a hundred years of effort by the Portuguese royal family to promote and underwrite exploration of the unknown parts of the world. The persistence with which this program of exploration was pursued generation after generation, and the financial risks and sacrifices that it entailed, would make the global network of colonies that came to Portugal as a result about as close to being *earned* as it is possible for an empire to be.

It began with a son and brother of Portuguese kings who, though he personally rarely traveled and never explored anything, is rightly known to history as Prince Henry the Navigator. In 1415, a time when in all Europe there was little knowledge of astronomy or mathematics and seafarers tried to stay within sight of shore because otherwise they had dangerously little way of knowing their location or even their direction of travel, he founded a school dedicated to the development of sailors more skilled than any in Europe. By the time of his death in 1460 Portugal had such sailors in abundance. The boldest of them had journeyed far down the west coast of Africa, establishing trading stations along the way and bases on the Canary Islands, the Azores, and Madeira in the Atlantic. They had done so in ships developed under Henry's sponsorship, the fast and nimble little caravels. He had gone to extraordinary lengths to encourage his explorers, providing and outfitting their ships, giving them an equal share in any profits from trade or plunder while making good any losses out of his own pocket.

Magnificent as these achievements were, they had a tragically dark side. The Portuguese captains, always on the lookout for financial gain, found that even the poorest sections of the African coast offered a nearly unlimited supply of human beings who could be transported to the north and profitably sold. Thus traffic in slaves, a feature of the European and Mediterranean worlds from time immemorial, became almost from the beginning a central characteristic of the Great Age of Discovery.

Henry's work was carried on by his nephew King Afonso V, who introduced a licensing arrangement under which a Lisbon merchant was given exclusive trading rights from Guinea southward in return for exploring another four hundred miles of coastline every year. In such ways the Portuguese continued to push on into the unknown, and the late 1480s brought the greatest triumph yet: ships out of Lisbon reached what they named the Cape of Storms (the king, not wishing to discourage the less bold, changed it to the Cape of Good Hope) and entered the Indian Ocean. News of this, when it reached Portugal, electrified the royal court. It was for the first time certain that Ptolemy had been wrong, in the second century AD, when he wrote that a bridge of land blocked access to the Indian Ocean from the Atlantic. It was *not* impossible to sail from the Iberian peninsula to India.

This was a stunning prospect. An increasingly wealthy Europe had for generations been developing an insatiable appetite for the exotic products of India, China, and other points east—especially for the spices grown in these places. But it was able to procure them in severely limited quantities only and at exorbitant prices. These prices were the result of rarity and monopoly control: all the produce of the Orient, after it reached the bustling ports of India's west coast, was in the hands of Arab traders who transported it by ship through the Persian Gulf or the Red Sea and then overland by caravan to the ports of the eastern Mediterranean. These merchants took big slices of profit at every stage, and at Alexandria and other ports they sold their merchandise to the Venetians and Genoese, who marked it up again in carrying it to Italy and other European markets.

There was a bonanza to be reaped by sailing from Lisbon directly to India, thereby eliminating all the middlemen. And so the Portuguese government, having established that it could be done, hurried to organize the expedition that set sail under Vasco da Gama's command in July 1497 and reached the Indian city of Calicut in May 1498. When it returned home in September 1499, it was laden with pepper, cloves, nutmeg, ginger, and cinnamon—things nearly as precious as gold. Another, much bigger expedition was readied with all possible speed, and thus was Portugal's global empire born. It undermined the advantages long enjoyed by Venice and the Arabs and began what gradually became a prodigious redistribution of wealth and national power.

By the time da Gama completed his great voyage, Columbus was midway through his third visit to what he would die thinking was the eastern edge of Asia. His exploits could have been another great triumph for Portugal, but in the 1480s, after hearing Columbus out, a council of experts decided that his plan to reach the Far East by sailing west was impossible. They therefore refused his request for the financing of an expedition. (The council was right and Columbus was wrong, by the way. Its members knew, as did all educated people of the time, that the world was a sphere, and they knew also that it was a much bigger sphere than Columbus believed. He argued that Asia was four thousand miles west of the Canary Islands. His judges found that ridiculous. They judged correctly, but without knowing that between the Canaries and Asia lay North and South America. No ship of the time could cover the required distance before all hands had died on board.)

Columbus, Genoese by birth, then spent years trying to sell his idea to Ferdinand and Isabella of Spain. He had no success until 1492, when their conquest of Granada put the royal couple in an expansive frame of mind, prompting them to provide him with three ships and crews made up largely of convicted criminals. He departed Spain on August 3 of that year, launched into the unknown on September 6 after a stop in the Canaries, and by early October was cruising among the islands of the Caribbean.

King John of Portugal was so offended by Spain's apparent success in finding a new route to the quasi-mythic lands known to Europe as Cathay (China), Cipango (Japan), and India, so certain that the Spanish had no right to impinge upon his kingdom's hard-earned monopoly, that he began preparations to send a Portuguese fleet across the Atlantic to lay claim to what was rightfully his. Learning of this, Ferdinand and Isabella began assembling a war fleet of their own, simultaneously appealing to Rome for a vindication of their rights. The result was a series of four papal bulls, the third of which, *Inter Caetera* of May 4, 1493, granted to the kingdom of Castile all discoveries more than one hundred leagues west of the Atlantic's Cape Verde Islands. Everything east of that point went to the Portuguese. It was a stopgap solution, "league" being an ambiguous unit of measure and no one really knowing how to measure great stretches of longitude, but it averted war. A year later, by the Treaty of Tordesillas, Spain sought to assuage continuing Portuguese anger by agreeing to move the line of demarcation another 250 leagues to the west. This would lead to further momentous consequences when, in 1500, a fleet of Portuguese merchant ships en route to the Cape of Good Hope swung far to the west and happened upon the coast of Brazil. Because of the settlement that Alexander had negotiated, this vast rich land, though part of the South American continent, would for the next three centuries belong to Portugal and not Spain.

20

Man of Destiny

On January 18, 1503, moving slowly as he entered the hills of eastern Tuscany so as to give his troops time to ravage the towns and farmsteads that had the misfortune to lie in their path, Cesare finally had his prisoners Paolo and Francesco Orsini strangled. As at Senigallia the deed was done by Michelotto, quietly, and it reflected the hard fact that the war on the Orsini had passed the point of no return—the point at which too much damage had been done for reconciliation to be conceivable. What provoked comment was not so much the killings themselves—they were colorless events compared with what was happening in and around Rome—as Cesare's mysterious release of his third Orsini prisoner, an obscure figure known as Roberto of Pitigliano. This answered the question, people said, of how Cesare had kept himself so well informed throughout the conspiracy that had nearly undone him. Obviously, they said, this Roberto had been Cesare's secret agent, his prime source of intelligence. And now he had his reward.

Following as they did on the heels of the murders at Senigallia, these latest killings consolidated Cesare's reputation as not only the most feared man in Italy but, at least among the ruling and fighting classes, the most respected as well. Machiavelli, freshly restored to home and family by the time of this second round of stranglings, was typical in his approval. Like everyone associated with Florence's post-Medici republic, he celebrated the liquidation of men as dedicated to the restoration of the old regime as Vitellozzo Vitelli and his henchmen. For him, however, the meaning of what Cesare had done went further. The murders removed any doubt, as far as he was concerned, about Valentino being a man of destiny—about whether his talents, ambition, strength of will, and sheer ruthless courage made him the leader for which all Italy was unconsciously yearning, the one capable of freeing the peninsula from the barbarians. Machiavelli began to invest in Cesare all his hopes for the deliverance of his homeland.

It was said—probably without encouragement from Cesare, who was little more inclined to explain his conduct than to reveal his plans— that the killings had been committed in self-defense. Many believed them a necessary countermove against men whom Cesare knew with certainty to be once again planning to kill him. This is in no way implausible. Vitelli, Oliverotto, and the others were not only murderers but vicious murderers, and endlessly treacherous. If Lucrezia's onetime almost-fiancé Francesco duke of Gravina was made of better stuff, he was an Orsini all the same and could hardly have been allowed to survive after seeing so many of his kinsmen cut down. Regardless of whether the killings were, strictly speaking, necessary or at least defensible, they were widely regarded as sensible and appropriate. Every tyrant still in power in Italy, and every city and town south of Venice and Milan and north of Naples, learned that the only available alternatives were to cooperate with Cesare or prepare to fight him to the death.

Place after place therefore prostrated itself at Cesare's feet. Within a week after leaving Senigallia, he was master of the Vitelli family's stronghold of Città di Castello and of Oliverotto's Fermo, both of which sent out welcoming parties as soon as Borgia troops appeared on the horizon. Gian Paolo Baglioni, whose refusal to trust Cesare or join his *impresa* had saved him from sharing the fate of his cronies at Senigallia, found it prudent to flee his home base of Perugia, so that it too fell peaceably. Cesare stayed on the move, sweeping up everything in his path, and by the time of the second strangling he was at the walls of Siena. He demanded that the city expel its tyrant Pandolfo Petrucci, who like Baglioni had been too wary to join in the rendezvous at Senigallia. Cesare promised Petrucci safe passage out of the city and went through the motions of preparing an attack that he had no intention of carrying out because Siena was now among the places under Louis XII's protection. The city's elders wanted no trouble—were making it clear that they wanted Petrucci to go—but he was in no hurry to give up the rich and beautiful city of which he had been master for much of his life.

The Orsini too were unwilling to go quietly. They knew that Alexander and Cesare were now intent upon their utter destruction, and that their only options were to fight or perish. Led by Virginio Orsini's son Gian Giordano and Niccolò Orsini, count of Pitigliano, joined by the Savelli clan and even some of the surviving but imperiled elements of the Colonna, they used their remaining strongholds near Rome as bases from which to launch a surprise counteroffensive against Rome. The troops that Cesare had left behind turned them back at the Ponte Nomentano at the north end of the city, but not before the attack put such a scare into the pope that he demanded the return of Cesare's army. Learning of this, and assuming that Cesare must now be hurrying toward Rome, the Orsini withdrew to their hilltop castles. With them fled Cardinal Ippolito d'Este, who though the brother of Lucrezia's husband Alfonso had reason to be afraid: to his long list of sexual conquests he had recently added Cesare's favorite mistress, the celebrated Fiammetta, and Jofrè Borgia's wife Sancia. The pope in disgust had Sancia confined to the Castel Sant'Angelo and demanded that Jofrè bestir himself to take a hand in dealing with those Orsini who had not run away.

On January 28 Pandolfo Petrucci finally departed Siena. Cesare, in spite of his promise of safe passage, dispatched cavalry to find him and take him prisoner. Once again, however, Petrucci was saved by the skepticism that life among killers had ingrained in him. Guessing correctly that Cesare had no intention of keeping his word, he took to the back roads and managed to slip away to refuge in Lucca. Two days later, in an absurdly belated effort to ingratiate itself with Cesare, the *signoria* of Siena issued a decree expelling the already absent Petrucci. Whatever temptation Cesare may have felt to sack the city was overridden by his unwillingness to antagonize the French. Instead he started southward toward Rome, allowing his soldiers to plunder until they entered the Papal States, then stopping to regroup at Viterbo.

A breach was opening between him and the pope, one so serious that it threatened to alter the whole strategic situation. The immediate issue at this point was where to send the papal army and how to use it.

Alexander, faced with continuing disturbances and sensitive to the Vatican's vulnerability, insisted that the army return to Rome. He wanted to use it first to control and defend the city, then to go on the offensive and drive the Orsini out of their remaining strongpoints. His prime targets were Ceri, Cerveteri, Bracciano, and Pitigliano, because if they could be taken, the clan would be stripped of the means to defend itself. Cesare, an adventurer to the marrow of his bones but rarely a reckless one, took a different view of what was possible. He could see nothing but trouble rising out of even a successful campaign against Bracciano and Pitigliano; the former belonged to the late Virginio's sons, regarded as friends by Louis XII, while the lord of Pitigliano, Count Niccolò Orsini, held a *condotta* as commander in chief of Venice's armies. And so Cesare dragged his heels, letting more than a week go by without moving out of Viterbo. Alexander fumed.

Not that the pope's anger was unreasonable. The Orsini were playing their old game, creating so much disorder in and around Rome that it amounted to guerrilla warfare, and meanwhile the imprisoned Cardinal Orsini's brother Giulio, from his base at Ceri, was disrupting the operations of the alum mines at Tolfa. On February 7 the pope declared the Orsini to be rebels against the Church (a transparently self-serving charge, but not exactly false under the circumstances) and therefore excommunicated. Without consulting Cesare he dispatched artillery for use in a siege of Bracciano. When Cesare objected, the pope, in an outburst that revealed how unhappy he was with the situation, threatened him with the loss of all his fiefs. Cesare at last responded, but with a conspicuous lack of enthusiasm. He sent his siege equipment not to Bracciano but to the less defensible Ceri. Barely a week after getting his troops into position there, in company with his cousin Cardinal Ludovico Borgia and his wife's brother Cardinal Amanieu d'Albret, he returned to Rome. Once there he showed less interest in conferring with Alexander than in indulging in the pleasures of the pre-Lenten carnival. He was seen coming and going at all hours, his habit of wearing a mask drawing little attention in streets crowded with drunken and masked revelers. For a brief period Cesare the pleasure-seeking youth eclipsed Cesare the calculating empire builder. And the tension between him and the pope threatened to become a rupture.

The situation was fraught with difficulty for all the rulers of Italy.

Even Louis XII had constantly to balance shifting and sometimes conflicting priorities: his need for papal endorsement of his claim to Naples, and for the papal army, against the need to keep the Borgias from becoming unmanageable. The need to keep Cesare under control against the need not to drive Alexander back into the arms of Spain. When in late February the city of Pisa offered to make itself subject to Cesare in hope of getting desperately needed assistance in its long fight for independence from Florence, Louis decided that the pendulum was swinging too far in favor of the Borgias. He pulled Florence, Bologna, Lucca, and Siena together in a new league, making all these cities (some of which he had previously betrayed) not only his allies but his wards and therefore safe from Cesare. This exacerbated the pope's uneasiness and worsened his differences with Cesare.

All these troubles were deepened by what was happening in Naples, where the inevitable breakdown of the accord by which France and Spain had divided the conquered kingdom was proceeding apace. As clashes along the border between the French and Spanish sectors grew more intense, the two powers found themselves sliding into a winner-take-all war. The Spanish had two great advantages: the proximity of Naples's southern provinces to their island kingdom of Sicily, a secure base from which troops and supplies could be sent without difficulty, and the command of their forces by the best soldier then living. Gonsalvo the Great Captain had continued to display the gifts for which he had originally become famous in Spain and at the time of Charles VIII's invasion. Fifty years old at the start of the war with Louis XII, he was at the height of his powers, always able, somehow, to find unexpected ways of dealing with whatever his enemies threw at him.

His opponent in 1503, Bernard Stewart d'Aubigny, was yet another remarkable figure. Descended from Scottish nobles who had entered the service of the French crown and been rewarded with titles and land, he had over the years been commander of the royal bodyguard, leader of the French troops that accompanied Henry Tudor on the invasion of England that ended in his becoming King Henry VII, and French governor first of Milan and then of the city of Naples. At the start of his confrontation with Gonsalvo's Spaniards he had a numerical advantage so substantial that it was generally expected to be decisive, but step by step he found himself being outwitted, outmaneuvered, and finally, humiliatingly, outfought. By springtime Gonsalvo was on the offensive, and as his troops swept forward, some sixty-five fortified towns surrendered without so much as pretending to resist. April 1503 decided the matter: on the twenty-first day of that month a Spanish force freshly arrived from Sicily defeated d'Aubigny and took him prisoner. One week later, at Cerignola, Gonsalvo used explosives in a way never previously attempted to crush the main French army. Among the heroes of the hour were Fabrizio and Prospero Colonna, the same cousins and partners who had narrowly escaped falling into the hands of the Borgias after the fall of Don Fadrique and who soon thereafter had signed on with Gonsalvo. Their contribution at Cerignola was an impressive one: the breaking of the usually impregnable formations of d'Aubigny's Swiss mercenaries.

Cesare had remained in Rome after the end of carnival, still resisting the pope's demands that he prosecute the war on the Orsini. Finally, and only in response to Alexander's mounting threats and imprecations, he had set off on April 6 to resume command of the siege at Ceri. En route, however, he was met by a Rome-bound messenger carrying news that Giulio Orsini had surrendered Ceri, his *rocca* having been broken to bits by Cesare's artillery and all hope of rescue ended by a message from Louis XII urging him to give up. Louis, though unhappy about the Borgia attack on Ceri, had found himself obliged to abandon the city by the deteriorating position of his forces in Naples and his increasingly urgent need for Cesare's army. Cesare hastened to work out a formal settlement with the now-helpless Giulio Orsini, and the agreement that followed was of course heavily in favor of the Borgias. Its central provision was a gift to the pope, the realization of a lifelong dream: Giulio agreed to renounce his family's claim to its possessions nearest Rome. In return he accepted scattered estates in faraway places and safe passage for himself and his family to Niccolò Orsini's base at Pitigliano. Alexander, still intent on the absolute elimination of the Orsini, cannot have been pleased when he learned of Cesare's most important concession. He had promised to attack neither Pitigliano nor the only bastion of importance remaining to the Orsini within striking distance of Rome, the late Virginio's great castle at Bracciano, now the lair of his sons. Cesare, however, was not being cowardly or foolishly generous. Pitigliano was all but untouchable because implicitly under

Venetian protection, and Louis of France had declared Bracciano to be under his umbrella—porous though that umbrella had often proved to be.

The war against the Orsini was thus over, and on terms that Cesare at least found altogether satisfactory. To the extent that Alexander was not as pleased, he too had his reasons. So long as Bracciano remained in Orsini hands, the clan would have a base from which to challenge papal authority in the region. And it was not certain that an attack on it could not have been successful. The straits in which King Louis found himself would have made him hesitate before deciding to take military action against the Borgias and would have limited his ability to bring sufficient force to bear had he overcome his hesitation. The situation was too complicated, the variables too numerous, to judge conclusively that Cesare was right and Alexander wrong or vice versa. Cesare, in any case, was having things his way.

He was by this point convinced that he could never be his own man, that his conquests could never be secure, so long as he was dependent on either France or Spain. The chronic tension between him and the pope over where to position themselves in the Franco-Spanish rivalry simply underscored the seriousness of the problem. His solution was to cut himself off from Louis XII and the alliance that had been the cornerstone of Borgia policy since his first visit to the French court. This was an understandable move in light of Louis XII's financial, military, and political difficulties and his growing skepticism about Borgia power. Its effects on the Vatican, however, proved to be morally corrosive. Alexander, hard-pressed to satisfy Cesare's demands but unwilling to deny him and so risk the loss of what had already been gained at such great cost, created eighty new positions in the Curial bureaucracy and sold them at average price of 760 ducats per job. Two weeks later a respected veteran of the Sacred College, Pope Paul II's nephew Cardinal Giovanni Michiel, died a prisoner in the Castel Sant'Angelo at the end of two days of violent vomiting. His personal fortune, believed to exceed 150,000 ducats, was seized for the papal treasury. As invariably happened in such cases, poisoning was rumored, and this is one instance in which the rumors cannot be dismissed out of hand.

The faithful Michelotto Corella, the strangler of Senigallia, began using his new position as governor of Rome to extort money from the population. Among his methods were accusing members of the city's growing Spanish community of being "Marani"—Muslims pretending to be Christian—and forcing Jews to buy exemption from harassment. This last was a surprising departure for the pope, who up to this point had been a friend to Rome's Jews, welcoming refugees from the Spanish Inquisition. It indicates the degree to which his better nature was shriveling under the pressure of Cesare's ceaseless demands.

The capture of d'Aubigny and the defeat at Cerignola had done nothing to diminish Louis XII's hunger for Naples—a hunger sharpened by the knowledge that Ferdinand, his only competitor for the Neapolitan crown, was also his sole rival for first place among the monarchs of Europe. The survivors of Cerignola were still limping homeward when Louis undertook the creation, at Parma, of a replacement army under Louis de La Trémoille, a commander whose war record in Brittany and impressive performance following Charles VIII's retreat from Naples made him seem a possible match for Gonsalvo. The do-or-die character of the campaign that La Trémoille was about to launch, the knowledge that failure this time could put Naples out of reach for the foreseeable future, made it imperative that the troops of the Borgias become involved on the French side.

After all he had done for Cesare, Louis must have been appalled to find the Borgias driving a hard bargain. In return for full support they demanded the surrender of Bracciano and a free hand to do as they wished in Tuscany—to do as they wished, that is, with Florence and Siena and all the territories traditionally ruled by those cities. These things were out of the question, not only because La Trémoille's army in advancing on Naples was going to have to pass through Tuscany, but because there were no circumstances under which King Louis could have accepted such a further expansion of Roman, or Borgia, power. Thus ended the alliance with France. It was replaced by an uneasy neutrality that left Alexander and Cesare hanging somewhere between a failing and resentful Louis XII and a Spain that was becoming so powerful as to have little need for Italian friends in Rome or elsewhere. When Gonsalvo took possession of the city of Naples in mid-May, his triumph signaled that Spain had replaced France as Europe's dominant power. It did nothing, however, to resolve the nagging question of how

the Borgias should relate to the two powers, or to settle the rift between Alexander and Cesare. Predictably, Alexander wanted to repair
his old friendship with Ferdinand. Cesare's position was probably
shrewder, if little less predictable. He argued that, while Ferdinand
could if he chose treat Rome with cold indifference and had no reason
to care if the Borgias succeeded or failed, Louis XII's need was greater
than ever. If he retrieved his position in Naples, this king whose marriage to Anne of Brittany was producing only daughters and stillborn
sons would be in a position to reward his friends extravagantly. Even if
he failed in Naples, he would continue to dominate northern Italy and
have the power to decide Cesare's fate in the Romagna and elsewhere.

Strange things were happening, symptoms of a deeply unsettled time
and impenetrable intrigues. In May Cesare issued orders for the arrest,
wherever he might be found, of a Monsignor Francesco Troches, one of
the pope's secretaries. After being pursued from Rome to Civitavecchia
and then to Genoa and Sardinia, Troches was finally apprehended in
Corsica. He then either committed suicide by throwing himself off the
galley returning him to Italy or, depending on which story is believed,
was brought back to Rome and quietly executed. What this was all
about has never been entirely explained, but the most persuasive
hypothesis is that he had been discovered spying for France—providing
information about the pope's surreptitious attempts to revive his long-
dead lines of communication with Ferdinand and Spain.

The body of another of Alexander's close associates, Jacopo da Santa
Croce, was found one morning on one of the Tiber bridges. People
were reminded of the discovery, on a morning in the Romagna many
months before, of the body of Cesare's man Lorqua. Was this too a message of some kind? If so, what *was* the message? And who was it *for*?
Who, for that matter, was sending it? Could Cesare possibly be sending
anonymous signals to the pope? None of the proffered answers was
particularly convincing. The atmosphere in Rome was growing dark
and ominous.

Word circulated—supposedly leaked out of the Vatican—that the
pope was negotiating with Maximilian of Hapsburg, the Holy Roman
emperor-elect, to have Pisa, Siena, and Lucca all bestowed on Cesare as
imperial fiefs. Which would have been interesting, even meaningful, if

the emperor were in a position to do anything in Italy. But he had little enough power north of the Alps, thanks to the political fragmentation of Germany, and absolutely none farther south.

It was said too that Louis XII was offering to give all of Naples to Cesare in trade for the Romagna and Bologna. Which might have made sense if the king were in possession of Naples, which he no longer was. Or if Cesare had any voice at all in the status of Bologna, which of course he didn't.

At the furthest extreme of absurdity, it was said finally that Alexander was talking with Venice about having Cesare elected pope. The variety and increasing improbability of these stories is less reflective of anything actually happening than of the prevailing confusion and fear.

Behind all the nonsense, however, lay one monumental reality. Circumstances and his own actions had converged to raise Cesare above every other prince in Italy, kings from the outside of course excluded. As the summer of 1503 began, everything seemed to be—and in fact almost everything was—working in his favor. The city of Rome and its nobles, the papal bureaucracy, the College of Cardinals—all had been subdued and were under Cesare's control either directly or through the pope. The baronial clans that for centuries had been the bane of every pope had been beaten, scattered, slaughtered. The tyrants who until recently had ruled city after city across the Papal States were mostly dead or in exile; only the Ferrara of the Este and the Bologna of the Bentivoglio were not yet under Borgia rule. Ferdinand of Spain had no need to interfere with Cesare, Louis of France no wish to offend him or the pope. Cesare had an army under Michelotto encamped at Perugia awaiting orders, and he was at liberty to do with it almost anything he wished.

Cesare spent most of July in the Romagna, making preparations for whatever it was he intended to do next. Early in the month he had assembled his cavalry, including newly hired units of Albanian light horse for which he clearly had big plans, for a grand review in which he himself rode proudly at the head of the lead squadron and Michelotto led the second. Three days later Alexander appointed him vicar in perpetuity of the late Vitellozzo Vitelli's old home base of Città di Castello. This made Cesare lord of a substantial city at the very edge of Florentine territory, a good platform for a move against Florence itself. It seemed yet another provocation, deliberate if oblique, of Louis XII.

At the start of August, with all in readiness but his intentions as secret as ever, Cesare made a visit to Rome. He found the city in the grip of one of the stifling midsummer heat waves for which it has always been notorious. The pope was in residence, having found it impossible to withdraw to the cool of the hills with so much going on, but Cesare found him in robust good health and his old high spirits. All Rome was electric with expectation; La Trémoille's troops were known to be in Tuscany and on their way south, which meant that the next showdown between France and Spain was imminent. Fever was rampant in the city and indeed in the Vatican, as was to be expected in Rome at this time of year. Among its victims was one of Alexander's oldest friends, the elder of the two cardinals named Giovanni Lanzol Borgia. "It is a bad month for us fat people," the pope ruefully observed as a procession took his cousin's body to its grave.

On August 5 a Vatican regular named Adriano Castelli da Corneto, a onetime secretary to the pope and one of the latest crop of new cardinals, gave a party at his hillside vineyard in Rome. Alexander attended, as did Cesare; probably it was a going-away party organized in the latter's honor.

No doubt it was an afternoon of good food, good wine, the jollity with which the Borgias always spiced social occasions, and—especially as the sun began to set— swarms of river-bred mosquitoes. It certainly was among the most fateful parties ever to take place in Europe. It is possible that the whole subsequent history of Italy, and certain that the remaining chapters in the story of the Borgias, would have turned out very differently if it had never been given. Or if Cesare, at least, had not been in Rome to attend.

SUPERSTITIONS: ANOTHER SIDE
OF THE RENAISSANCE

SEARCHING FOR RATIONAL EXPLANATIONS OF WHY EVEN SOME
of the most powerful figures in Renaissance Italy did the things they did
when they did them can be a fool's errand. With improbable frequency
such people acted less on the basis of a cool analysis of whatever predicament they happened to be in, or a careful weighing of their options,
or even what they were feeling, than in accordance with what their astrologers told them.

This is part of a dark, or at least a singularly unimpressive, side of the
world that produced the Borgias. Fact-based knowledge of the inner
workings of the physical universe being as limited as it was in that world,
superstition was rampant. People at all levels of society turned for understanding and guidance not only to astrology but to its sister disci-
plines of alchemy and necromancy and various schools of magic. If this
is not often mentioned, the reason may be that it does not easily fit in
with what we like to think about the Renaissance. We want to think of it
as a period of glorious achievements in arts and letters, not as a time
when it was generally taken for granted that someone as hardheaded as
Cesare Borgia could rely on someone else's interpretation of what the
stars were saying to arrive at decisions on which his future and his very
life might depend.

Astrology's roots were deep, reaching back to the beginnings of recorded history in Egypt, Babylon, Persia, China, and the Greco-Roman
world. This is understandable; as people began to observe the patterns
and movements of the heavens, it is hardly surprising that they should
have searched for meaning in what they saw. Astrology was widely followed in the Roman Empire until Constantine the Great, having converted to Christianity, launched a persecution of its practitioners that
would keep it underground for half a millennium. In conjunction with
astronomy it flourished in the Arab world, however, and as contacts

between Arabs and Christians became more common and intense, especially in Spain, astrology resurfaced and was soon again widespread.

The greatest of the thirteenth century's Holy Roman emperors, Frederick II, went nowhere without his astrologers. The Gian Galeazzo Visconti who in the fourteenth century became Milan's first duke acknowledged that "I observe astrology in all my affairs," his fifteenth-century successor Ludovico Sforza saw to the appointment of four professors of astrology at the University of Pavia, and an acquaintance of Duke Ercole d'Este complained that he "fills up his time with astrology and necromancy." By Ercole's time there was almost no such thing as an Italian court that did not employ astrologers; this was no less true of the Medici of Florence and the equally cultivated Montefeltri of Urbino than of the most brutish warlords. Alone or in conjunction with such other practices as geomancy (deciphering the patterns formed by a handful of thrown earth) and chiromancy (palm reading), astrology was used to foretell the future and decide what should be done, or when, or where. The secrets of the stars were applied in the practice of medicine and had an accepted place in the administration of justice.

Not surprisingly, considering the challenge that the fatalistic determinism implicit in astrology posed for orthodox Christianity, astrology was opposed by the Church from its earliest days. In the fourteenth century the great humanist scholar Petrarch ridiculed it with icy contempt. A hundred years after him the philosopher Pico della Mirandola attacked it with such devastating effect, pointing to its incompatibility with Christian notions of free will and divine providence, as to reduce its popularity noticeably. It persisted all the same. Though Pope Pius II was stern in his condemnation, Sixtus IV was a devoted believer, and so was his nephew Cardinal Giuliano della Rovere. Much later, in the sixteenth century, there would be periods when ambassadors were not admitted to the papal court or that of the Holy Roman emperor until they had the approval of the official astronomers. One of Savonarola's persistent criticisms of leading clerics of his day was their reliance on astrological readings. He never attacked Alexander VI on those grounds, however, and there is scant reason to think that Alexander, onetime protégé of the skeptical Pius II, took astrology at all seriously.

Wherever astrology was popular, alchemy was usually popular as well. Easily ridiculed for the attempts of practitioners to discover the so-called philosopher's stone and to use it to turn base metals into silver and gold, alchemy too had ancient roots and was not as childish as is generally believed. In its loftier forms it was a pursuit of purity and perfection: alchemists believed that if they could discover how to turn lead into the purest and most perfect of metals, gold, they would then be able to do something analogous with people, turning them not into gold but into superior beings, healthy, wise, and immensely long-lived.

There was nothing that admirable about necromancy, the use of ritual and formula to make contact with the dead and enlist their help in putting curses on enemies, acquiring some desired possession, or learning such secrets as who committed a crime or where a lost object might be found. It was at least as old as astrology, but it had always been less respectable. Moses in his law code made it a capital offense, and millennia later Leonardo da Vinci scornfully observed that "of all human opinions that is to be reputed the most foolish which deals with the belief in necromancy."

Astrology appears to have been far more widely embraced in Italy than elsewhere in Europe. (The University of Paris condemned it in 1494, by which date it was being taught at universities across Italy.) Paradoxically, the difference may have stemmed from Italy's unique status as the birthplace of the Renaissance and from the work of its scholars in rediscovering the literature of the distant past. Astrology's credibility was enhanced by the many ancient texts on the subject that the Italian humanists were unearthing and translating. The cryptic character of such texts helped to make astrology seem both mysterious and a legitimate subject of study, worthy of close attention. It offered the same things it had offered thousands of years before: a way of drawing meaning from the night sky and making sense of a baffling world.

Astrology's failure to get such a firm grip on imaginations outside Italy did not mean that the Italians were more credulous than people elsewhere. For whatever reason, north of the Alps there was less interest in astrology than in magic, which involved the belief that one could achieve even the most ignoble of ends by entering into relations with spirits from other worlds, and which came in "black" and "white" varieties. Thus the appeal of witchcraft, and the fears of the orthodox that witches existed in great numbers and possessed secret spells and concoctions that could make people love or hate one another, visit terrible afflictions upon them, and work all manner of mischief. In 1484 an antiwitchcraft bull of Pope Innocent VIII sparked witch hunts on a terrifying scale—in a single year forty-one accused individuals were burned at the stake in the town of Como—with reverberations echoing down to Salem, Massachusetts, two-plus centuries later.

It was all part of the environment in which the people of fifteenth-century Europe lived their lives, and it would remain a central part of that environment until the first real scientists appeared on the scene with their demands for bona fide evidence and their emphasis on repeatable experiments. In the interim, ironically, superstition contributed in important ways to the birth of science. The work of astrologers in studying the heavens did more than anything else to expand the knowledge of astronomy, just as alchemy turned out to be the parent of chemistry. Ultimately, inevitably, astrology and its sister superstitions were reduced to the marginal things they are today, sources of harmless amusement for many, of income for others, and of irrational obsessions for an unfortunate few.

21

Alone

Cesare, when his luck appeared to have pretty much run out, would tell Machiavelli that at the great crisis of his life, when everything was at stake, he had been prepared for everything except what actually happened.

That climactic crisis, which not only followed Cardinal Castelli's garden party but was a direct consequence of it, was presaged by an event so odd that it has been remembered ever since in spite of being essentially meaningless. On the day after the party, an owl flew into the papal apartments through an open window, fell dead, and was declared by Alexander to be an "evil omen."

An omen of what? First came other harbingers, followed in short order by the thing itself. On August 7, the day after the episode of the owl, the Venetian ambassador paid a routine call on the pope and found him wrapped in a shawl in spite of the punishing heat and in uncharacteristically low spirits. He fretted not only about official business—especially the imponderable consequences of the new war for Naples—but also about such things as the growing number of lives being claimed by that year's summer fevers. All this was unusual enough for the ambassador to make note of it in his report. He made no mention, however, of Cesare; presumably Valentino was not present, occupied with preparations for his return to the north.

On August 11, the eleventh anniversary of Alexander's election, Cardinal Castelli fell seriously ill. On Saturday the twelfth, exactly a week after the party, the pope rose as usual, said mass, breakfasted, vomited, and returned in distress to his bed. Cesare, on the verge of departing the city, was struck down by the same symptoms at almost exactly the same time. He managed to make his way to his quarters directly above Alexander's apartment before collapsing. He appeared to be the more dangerously afflicted of the two. The pope lay in silence after ordering the Vatican barricaded, feeling well enough, after a few days, to sit up and watch some of the cardinals attending him play cards at his bedside. Cesare, by contrast, became so alarmingly feverish that he was stripped naked and lowered into a huge oil jar filled with cold water; his skin was reported to have peeled as a result. He was in a state of delirium when, on the seventeenth, Alexander took such a severe turn for the worse that his physicians were soon declaring him to be beyond hope. After receiving the last rites, he died a solitary death on the night of August 18. The servants attending him, terrified, stripped the pontifical apartments of everything of value (even the throne disappeared) and vanished into the dark streets. Long before sunrise the people of the city knew what had happened and were coming together in rowdy clusters, looking for Spaniards to attack and rob.

Cesare's patron, the man who had made everything possible, was gone. It was a blow, obviously, and it called for an immediate response. But Cesare had long anticipated that such a thing not only could happen but was certain to happen sooner or later. And he had long been prepared—not for the pope's fall from hearty good health into his grave in less than two weeks in August 1503, specifically, but certainly for his removal at some unforeseeable point, and so for the day when he, Cesare, would be entirely on his own. Everything he had done since casting aside the red hat can be seen as preparation for that day: the hurry to carve a principality out of the Papal States; the destruction of the warlords of the Romagna and elsewhere; the building up of an army superior to any the other Italian princes could put in the field; the uprooting and scattering of the Roman barons; and the loading of the College of Cardinals with Borgia loyalists.

The vigor and thoroughness with which Cesare pursued all these objectives was one of the things that Machiavelli found admirable about him. By achieving all of them, he had positioned himself to act swiftly whenever the pope did finally die or become incapacitated, and to deal decisively with whatever obstacles might rise up in his path. What undid all these preparations—what he didn't foresee and could hardly have prepared for had he somehow foreseen it—was that when Alexander exited the stage, he himself, Cesare, would be in a state of total helplessness.

His one great stroke of luck on the night of the pope's death was the presence in the Vatican of the most ferociously loyal of his Spanish companions, Michelotto Corella, who had raced from his base at Perugia upon learning of Cesare's illness. Without Michelotto, all might have been lost. Alexander had been dead only minutes when, accompanied by armed retainers, Michelotto burst into the papal apartments and demanded access to the locked inner chamber that had served as Alexander's strongbox. When the cardinal responsible for the security of that chamber refused, Michelotto put a dagger to his throat and offered a simple choice: hand over the key or die. Chests that must have contained no less than a hundred thousand ducats, possibly much more, were then hauled upstairs to Cesare's sickroom. Guards were posted under the alternating supervision of Michelotto and Jofrè Borgia, and all settled in to wait for Cesare to recover or die.

He recovered, but at a maddeningly slow pace, and while he was doing so Rome descended into madness. The remnants of the old baronial clans came rushing back to reclaim the properties that the Borgias had taken from them, and to settle scores. Twelve hundred men led by Fabio Orsini, vengeful son of the strangled Paolo, fanned out through the streets on the other side of the Tiber from the Vatican, setting fire to the homes and places of business of the city's Spaniards, assaulting any "Catalans" they could lay hands on and killing several. Fabio— whose wife was a Lanzol Borgia—declared that he would not be satisfied until he had washed his hands and face in Borgia blood. Outside the city it was much the same: displaced Orsini and Colonna and Savelli with murder in their hearts jostled with one another to take back what they had thought lost forever and bring ruin to their foes.

In the midst of these horrors it was necessary to get the dead pope buried, and the funeral obsequies were themselves tinged with horror. A fight over silver candlesticks broke out between monks carrying Alexander's body from the palace to St. Peter's Basilica and the guards assigned to protect them, so that the corpse was dumped on the ground and for a time abandoned. By the time it was laid out for public viewing, it had swelled up grotesquely and turned dark, a black distended tongue protruding from the mouth. In the end brute force had to be used to cram it into its coffin like an overstuffed sack of rotting potatoes.

From the start and as usual there was much talk of poisoning. Because whenever the Borgias figured in gossip of this kind they were cast as the villains, this time it was necessary to explain how Alexander and Cesare were murderers and victims at the same time. As the most popular account had it, the two of them had intended to murder their host Cardinal Castelli but had somehow lost track of which goblets of wine were safe and ended up inadvertently poisoning themselves. Why had a full week passed before they fell ill? We have encountered this question before, and the answer that has come to be accepted by the whole world. The Borgias not only knew how to brew a poison unavailable to the rest of the world, they could administer it in such ways as to take effect immediately or weeks later.

The truth of the matter is obvious and simple. Cardinal Castelli, Pope Alexander, and Cesare were all infected, and the pontiff was killed, by the malaria-bearing mosquitoes of the Tiber valley. It happened in a city notorious for its midsummer epidemics, during an August when even more people than usual were dying. As a priest at the Vatican wrote four days before Alexander's death, "It is not surprising that His Holiness and His Excellency should be ill, because every single outstanding man in this court is either ill or else sickening, especially those of the palace, owing to the bad condition of the air." All the recorded symptoms of the two Borgias are consistent with a diagnosis of tertian malarial fever. As for that Borgia poison with its quasi-magical properties, five centuries later the world is still waiting for someone to rediscover it.

As Cesare recovered consciousness, he was made aware that the armies of France and Spain now loomed over Rome like a pair of watchful vultures. A French force commanded by one of La Trémoille's *condottieri*, Francesco Gonzaga, marquess of Mantua (Lucrezia's brother-in-law by virtue of his marriage to her husband's sister), had broken off its march toward Naples upon learning of Alexander's

death. It was camped at Viterbo north of Rome, awaiting developments; the sudden prospect of a papal election, and the hope of installing his chief minister Cardinal d'Amboise on the pontifical throne, had
altered Louis XII's priorities considerably. The Spaniard Gonsalvo,
meanwhile, was shifting his forces northward after securing the city of
Naples. Some of those forces were laying siege to the port city of Gaeta,
essential to the ability of the French army to resupply itself in southern
Italy, while others prepared to meet La Trémoille's offensive. With that
offensive now in abeyance, Gonsalvo too shifted his focus to Rome and
to the question of the papal succession.

Cesare, from his bed in the Vatican, sent messages to the commanders on both sides, keeping his options open by giving each the impression that the writer was his special friend. His communications with
Gonsalvo were entrusted to his private secretary, Agapito Geraldini,
whom he authorized to enter into any agreement that seemed sufficiently advantageous. It happened that Geraldini reached the Spanish
headquarters at almost the same time that two of Gonsalvo's most valued *condottieri,* the same Fabrizio and Prospero Colonna who had
helped him win the Battle of Cerignola four months earlier, requested
permission to pull their troops out of the siege of Gaeta and take them
temporarily to Rome. They knew of the disorder there, and they
wanted to reclaim the palaces and estates that the Borgias had taken
from them while the opportunity was open. Their request could hardly
have been more timely from Gonsalvo's perspective, and it set the
wheels of intrigue turning. He not only consented but gave the Colonna some of his own troops to augment theirs, instructing them
to attend to several matters on his behalf while in Rome. They were to
offer protection to the city's Spanish residents and make a sufficient
show of force to keep the cardinals from feeling intimidated by the
proximity of the French army as they undertook the business of electing a new pope. Also—Gonsalvo got Geraldini's assent to this—as soon
as Cesare was strong enough to travel, the Colonna were to escort him
southward to Naples. All this having been agreed, Gonsalvo dispatched
twelve galleys northward to secure the port of Ostia at the mouth of
the Tiber, to keep it from falling into French hands.

Adding to Cesare's torments, news was reaching the Vatican of the
accelerating disintegration of his little empire. Like ravenous wolves

moving in on crippled prey, the *signori* of Venice were helping Guidobaldo da Montefeltro to make yet another happy return to his ancestral seat at Urbino, Giovanni Sforza to reclaim the lordship of Pesaro, and Pandolfo Malatesta to take possession of his family seat at Rimini. Florence for its part was abetting the restoration of the Varani in Camerino and Jacopo d'Appiano in Piombino, and the Baglioni had returned to Perugia. Imola was fighting off an attempted return of the Riarii— a result of the loyalty to Cesare that had taken root in the heart of the Romagna. Cesena too was standing firm, along with several smaller strongholds. Elsewhere, for example at Faenza and Forlì, the Borgias' Spanish captains had been forced to withdraw into their *rocca* and defy demands for their surrender.

Cesare once again seemed doomed. In far-off Ferrara, where she was reported to have gone half-mad with grief upon learning of Alexander's death, Lucrezia was trying to muster help for her brother. But her father-in-law, Duke Ercole d'Este, wanted nothing to do with the problems of his son's wife's brother, especially as becoming involved could have put him once again at odds with Venice. His son Alfonso likewise took no interest.

In the absence of a pope, the College of Cardinals was responsible for governing Rome. Though its members also had to organize a conclave, they were unwilling to do any such thing with Cesare ensconced in the Vatican, much of the city in the hands of thugs, and two foreign armies looking on threateningly from the sidelines. The cardinals refused even to enter the Vatican so long as Cesare remained there, using as their base the Church of Santa Maria Sopra Minerva on the other side of the Tiber. To break the impasse it was going to be necessary to get Cesare out of the city. Only then might Gonzaga be persuaded to withdraw his French forces, Gonsalvo to do the same with the Spaniards, and the baronial gangs to disband. The Venetian ambassador took the lead, calling on Cesare and probing for a basis on which to negotiate his departure. As the days passed, the ambassador was joined by the Italian cardinals—the Spanish contingent was too loyal to Cesare to be of any use—and by the ambassadors of France, Spain, and the Holy Roman Empire. Finally the pressure became irresistible, and at the end of August Cesare promised that he would depart within three days and swear loyalty to the Sacred College. But only if certain conditions were met. He insisted on retaining his position as captain-general of the papal army until the election of the next pope, and on receiving a pledge from Venice to remove its troops from the Romagna. Once this was agreed, it became possible to get commitments from the French and Spanish to keep not only their own troops but the Orsini and Colonna far enough from Rome for the cardinals to gather in conclave without feeling under duress. Cesare, forced to accept that he could not be in Rome when Alexander's successor was elected, did what he could to ensure that the deadliest of his enemies would be absent as well: he sent riders northward with instructions to intercept Cardinal Giuliano della Rovere as he came southward from Avignon and keep him from proceeding farther.

It was a diminished Cesare Borgia who, on September 2, rode out of the Vatican surrounded by two hundred mounted knights dispatched by Michelotto to serve as his personal guard. No longer astride a prancing charger as in the past, this time he traveled as an invalid concealed behind the curtains of a litter borne on the shoulders of eight stout retainers. He had lost much weight, his feet were grossly swollen, and three weeks after first falling ill he continued to be racked with headaches. A bizarre assortment of his relatives—his mother Vannozza, a couple of his bastard daughters with their mothers, his sister-in-law and onetime mistress Sancia, Lucrezia's little son Rodrigo, the even littler Infant of Rome, and an equally mysterious newborn called Rodrigo Borgia who was inevitably rumored to be the late pope's bastard but was more likely another of Cesare's—had been sent on ahead. They awaited him, under guard, at the papal town of Civita Castellana, the *rocca* of which Alexander had recently expanded and reinforced.

As Cesare set out from the Vatican, Prospero Colonna with a body of his soldiers waited for him on the other side of the Tiber. In the days preceding, communicating through intermediaries, the two had arrived at an understanding: they would combine forces and attack the Orsini who had been ravaging Rome, destroying them if possible and at a minimum driving them from the city. They would then go south, joining Gonsalvo and his Spanish army. The properties that Pope Alexander had taken from the Colonna and given to Lucrezia's son Rodrigo would be restored to them, and the boy would be betrothed to a Colonna girl. But Cesare had been negotiating with the French as well, trying to maintain his options. Before crossing the river he managed to slip away, litter and bearers and all. Instead of joining Colonna, he made his way northward to Nepi, near an encampment of French troops.

There is some evidence that, in going north instead of south, Cesare was following the advice of his astrologers. Be that as it may, the decision was understandable in pragmatic terms. The French rather than the Spanish had it within their power to help him with his most pressing problems—especially the disintegration of his new duchy of Romagna. And Louis XII showed himself willing to be helpful. He ordered the rebellious cities to submit to their Borgia governors, and they quickly began to comply. Venice, seeing that the game it had been playing was up, withdrew and left its Romagnese clients to fend for themselves. Florence, in an almost comically hasty reversal of its recent boldness, declared its allegiance to the duke of Romagna. With numbing speed, Cesare's situation became no longer hopeless. The Colonna, understandably, felt that Cesare had betrayed them, and Gonsalvo had reason to feel the same.

All eyes turned now to Rome and the business of choosing a pope. Cardinal Giuliano della Rovere succeeded in reaching the Vatican in spite of the efforts of Cesare's agents to intercept him on his way south. Immediately he set about recruiting support. Cardinal Georges d'Amboise arrived as well and began campaigning on his own behalf. He was accompanied, to general astonishment, by Cardinal Ascanio Sforza, who had persuaded Louis XII to release him from prison by promising to use his experience and connections on Amboise's behalf. Once free and in Rome, however, Sforza showed himself to be interested in no one's candidacy except his own. The result was one of the most impenetrably complicated conclaves in generations, one that all the powers of Europe tried to turn to their own benefit but in which no one had more at stake than Cesare Borgia. The outcome would determine whether he would, at this decisive point, be able to draw upon enough papal support to save himself from ruin.

Ferdinand of Spain had entertained hopes of getting another of his countrymen elected. When it became clear that the Italian cardinals would never allow this, he settled for using his influence to block the candidacy of Cardinal della Rovere, whom he regarded, understandably if not quite correctly, as an agent of France. This freed the eleven

Spanish cardinals present to do as they wished, so long as they continued to shun della Rovere. To a man they now took their direction from Cesare, to whom a number of them were related and several others owed their red hats. With only four French cardinals voting, Louis XII had to forget about winning the throne for d'Amboise. The power to decide should have rested with the conclave's twenty-two Italian members but, as had happened before, they were too divided to form an effective bloc. The result was reminiscent of the election of Alonso Borgia almost half a century before. Deadlocked, the cardinals finally cobbled together a two-thirds majority by turning to the darkest of dark-horse candidates, an innocuous figure in such markedly feeble health that there was no possibility of his living more than a few years.

This was Francesco Todeschini Piccolomini, only sixty-four years old but so decrepit as to be incapable even of kneeling. Son of a sister of Pope Pius II, who had given him his red hat and whose surname he had taken, in forty-three years as a cardinal he had shown himself to be honest, well intentioned, and kindly, free of scandal and devoid of political ambition. He had also always been on good terms with the Borgias, which turned out to be a decisive factor: the Spanish bloc provided the votes that gave him the election. There could scarcely have been a better outcome for Cesare. Pope Pius III took office knowing that he could not have been elected without the support of his Spanish colleagues and, behind them, of Cesare himself.

News of the election of an Italian was received with joy in the streets of Rome. But it disgusted the French, who sullenly broke camp and resumed their advance on Naples, taking with them soldiers Cesare had hoped to use in the Romagna. Gonsalvo recalled Fabrizio and Prospero Colonna from Rome and, partly out of need but also partly in retaliation, sent orders for Cesare's Spanish troops to detach themselves from his service and come south. Most of the Spaniards obeyed, Gonsalvo's position as viceroy and Cesare's reconnection with the French making it virtually treasonous to do otherwise. Cesare thereby lost at a stroke most of his army including all of its heavy cavalry. The ever-faithful Michelotto, however, chose to remain. Cesare found himself almost alone at Nepi and without the means to make war on anyone. Exposed and vulnerable, fearful of an attack by the resurgent Orsini, he sent a message to Pius III asking permission to return to Rome.

The pope, who in response to complaints from Cardinal della Rovere would later claim to have believed that Cesare was dying, agreed to his return after receiving Louis XII's approval and Cesare's promise to keep the peace in the Romagna and elsewhere. Further demonstrations of papal favor followed. Pius sent an exhortation to the people of the Romagna, urging them to accept Cesare's lordship. He echoed the French king's warning to Venice not to meddle in Cesare's domains, and declared his intention to keep Cesare as gonfalonier of Rome.

There were now more claims on Cesare's time and attention than he would have been able to respond to if he had been in good health, which he was not. He badly needed to visit the Romagna, to reassert his authority there and see to it that his garrisons were properly deployed and his administration still functioning. But he no less urgently needed to be in Rome, where enemies in abundance were doing their best to poison the pope's mind against him, and he had nothing to counterbalance their slanders except the force of his own personality and—he had to hope—Pius's friendship and sense of obligation. He was burning through his reserves of cash at an unsustainable rate, many of his remaining troops were Romagnese amateurs who wanted to go home, and it was largely out of hatred for him that the Orsini chose this most awkward of moments to sever their connections to the French court and join forces with the Colonna and Gonsalvo.

Taking his menagerie of a family with him, Cesare left Nepi in time to be on hand for Pius III's coronation on October 8. It was, for him, an event worthy of celebration: the pontiff confirmed him in all his vicariates and as gonfalonier and installed him in the palace of his brother-in-law, Cardinal Ippolito d'Este, absent from Rome since making himself a target of Borgia anger by becoming sexually involved both with Sancia and with Cesare's favorite mistress. But the streets were still out of control, and neither Pius nor Cesare had nearly enough troops to restore order. Clearly the city was no safer than Nepi had been—much less safe, actually, with Orsini, Colonna, and Savelli gangs roaming the streets unrestrained. Cesare decided that it was necessary to move on again. And so he gathered up his dependents and his soldiers and set out for the north. Their immediate destination was Soriano, a hilltop town east of Viterbo that Michelotto had been sent ahead to secure and where he was now waiting with his troops. Before they could get out of Rome, however, they were headed off by a superior force of Orsini and obliged to turn back. They scrambled to the safety of the Castel Sant'Angelo through the covered passageway that Pope Alexander had improved for just such a purpose. Upon learning that his palace in the Borgo district was being pillaged and put to the torch, Cesare dispatched a messenger with orders for Michelotto to bring his men back to Rome with all possible speed.

Cesare was for all practical purposes a prisoner in the Castel when, on October 18, the world was informed of the death of Pius III. Eighteen days had passed since Pius's election, only ten since his coronation. This time the usual rumors of poisoning could not plausibly be focused on Cesare, the death being so obviously a devastating setback for him, so suspicion settled on della Rovere instead. The cardinal could not have cared less. He had been hungering for the papacy since long before losing the election of 1492 to Rodrigo Borgia, and the passing of the years had done nothing to dull his appetite. Now, after long years of exile, he was at the Vatican as the politicking that always preceded a conclave got under way, determined that this time the prize would not slip out of his grasp.

The troubles that invariably erupted with the death of a pope were rarely more alarming than at this juncture. The descent of Rome into lawlessness could have surprised no one, but the speed with which all Italy seemed suddenly to be veering toward war was truly extraordinary. On one side were Louis XII's France along with his duchy of Milan, Florence and an assortment of minor warlords, and Cesare. Opposing them were Naples under Gonsalvo, supported by the Orsini and the Colonna. Venice was formally unattached but a source of trouble all the same. Its obvious eagerness to seize the Romagna made it in every practical sense the adversary of France, Milan—and Cesare.

The Florentine authorities, justifiably worried, dispatched Machiavelli to Rome to observe, report, and seek opportunities to advance their interests. Upon arrival, on October 27, he found himself in a city in such disorder that when an envoy from Cardinal Giuliano della Rovere paid him a welcoming call, he arrived with a guard of twenty armed men. In the midst of the general mayhem, della Rovere was deploying all the resources at his disposal to ensure that when the papal conclave opened, he would enter it as an irresistible force.

For this to happen he needed the Spanish cardinals, which meant that he needed Cesare. Using the Venetian ambassador as an intermediary, he therefore promised to have all the forces of the Orsini removed from Rome if Cesare would come out of the Castel Sant'Angelo long enough to meet with him at the Vatican. Cesare agreed, the meeting took place, and a deal was struck. Della Rovere pledged that, in return for the votes of the Spanish cardinals, he would confirm Cesare as vicar of all the places bestowed on him by Alexander VI and later by Pius III. He would also reappoint him as gonfalonier, and the daughter Cesare had never seen, the now-three-year-old Louisa, would be betrothed to the thirteen-year-old Francesco della Rovere, son of the cardinal's deceased brother and, as nephew of the childless Guidobaldo da Montefeltro, designated heir to the duchy of Urbino.

This settled the papal election. Two days after his meeting with Cesare, della Rovere was chosen to succeed Pius III in the shortest conclave in history. He had left nothing to chance, bringing into play all the political and financial weapons at his disposal including a willingness to threaten every cardinal susceptible to intimidation and to buy the votes of the greedy. Having achieved the dream of his life, as Pope Julius II he continued to brim over with ambitions unfulfilled. In a decade on the throne, this violent, irascible character would turn himself into one of the epic figures of the Renaissance and one of history's legendary popes. He would be remembered as a reformer in spite of systematically selling offices and benefices and allowing his courts to be corrupted, and would be honored for a restrained use of nepotism that was made easier by the things his uncle Sixtus IV had already done to enrich their kinsmen—and the fact that only one of his illegitimate children, a daughter, lived to adulthood.

Machiavelli, learning of the bargain by which Cesare had ensured della Rovere's election, expressed astonishment at Cesare's willingness to trust the promises of a man whose relationship with the Borgias had always been laced with disappointment and resentment, hatred and deceit. And who, as pope, now held most of the cards. He concluded that Cesare somehow did not understand that in the new pope he was faced with someone whose intelligence, strength, and ruthlessness were at least the equal of his own—and who hated him.

When Cesare and Machiavelli had what appears to have been their first Rome meeting, five days after the pope's election, news had just arrived that the city of Imola was in revolt against its Borgia governor and that Venice was preparing to attack Faenza. Cesare was in a rage. He blamed the Florentines for allowing Venice freedom of movement in the Romagna, warning that Venetian domination of the region would end in Florence's ruin. "He spoke with words full of poison and anger," Machiavelli reported. "I could easily have argued with him, and replied to his charges, but I thought it best to try and calm him down, before managing as best I could to break off the interview, which felt as if it had gone on for a thousand years." This episode marks a change in Machiavelli's attitude toward Cesare—the point where he ceases to be as admiring as he had been before. It also, not coincidentally, shows Cesare losing the self-possession that had long been one of his most striking traits. Perhaps it marks the beginning of his psychological disintegration. From this point forward his moods will swing violently and unpredictably, to the alarm of his friends and the satisfaction of his enemies.

Two things were becoming clear. First, that Julius had no priority more urgent than that of making himself master of the Papal States, starting with the Romagna because of Venice's encroachments there. Second, that he possessed neither the money nor the manpower to do what he wished. In this lay Cesare's hope: that the pope would use him as the means to accomplish this objective. If in such a role Cesare could not hope for the independence and importance that he had enjoyed under Alexander and that he might have recovered if Pius III had lived, it would enable him to remain one of Italy's leading soldiers and give him continued access to money and power. In the long term, Julius being more than twice his age, Cesare could expect to outlive him and possibly his successor and even his successor's successor, perhaps rising to the kinds of heights achieved in the previous century by those master *condottieri* Francesco Sforza and Federico da Montefeltro. Julius encouraged him to think so, going so far as to invite him to return to his apartments in the Vatican.

That the pope's friendship was without substance soon became clear. Just nine days after the election, Cesare attended an open consistory in the expectation of being reappointed gonfalonier. When nothing of the kind happened and no explanation was forthcoming, he decided that the time had come to return to the Romagna and see to the security of Cesena, Faenza, Forlì, and the other strongholds that his captains still held there. With the troops he still had in and near Rome and those waiting for him in the north, he could hope to hold off the Venetians and possibly drive them out. He and Machiavelli met just hours after the consistory, and Cesare proved to be in such good spirits that Machiavelli was surprised. The duke had a plan now: to move the southern parts of his army, reportedly consisting at this point of only three hundred light cavalry and four hundred foot, into Tuscany and from there on to the Romagna, where he would link up with Michelotto and his men. To cross Tuscany safely with such a modest force, however, he would need a guarantee of safe conduct from Florence. Some of his restored confidence is explained by the fact that the pope had promised to write to Florence, demanding that it agree. Cesare's aim, as Machiavelli understood and reported it, was simple and clear. He intended to "prevent the Venetians from becoming masters of the Romagna," something that he was now capable of accomplishing because "the pope is ready to assist him."

All this was going to require money. Cesare needed what remained of the treasure that had been confiscated the night Alexander died—it was now with Michelotto at Cesena—as well as the sums on deposit with banking houses in Genoa. The Genoa funds probably amounted to something on the order of two hundred thousand ducats, enough to finance military operations on a large scale for half a year or more, a time period in which almost anything might be accomplished. To get access to them, however, Cesare needed to go to Genoa in person, and doing so speedily was going to require travel on horseback—through Tuscany.

Thus the shock that Cesare experienced, and failed to conceal, upon learning on November 14 that the Florentine council had voted overwhelmingly to deny him the safe conduct. It had good reasons for doing so, starting with memories of Cesare's past conduct in Tuscany and fear of what he might do if given a second chance, but it probably also acted with the oblique encouragement of the pope. In all likelihood Julius had let it be known in Florence that he did not expect Cesare's request to be taken seriously.

People who saw Cesare at this time wrote of encountering a changed man. His cousin Francisco Lloris y de Borja, a lifelong friend and one of the last cardinals created by Alexander VI, reported that he seemed "out of his mind, for he knew not himself what he desired to do, so involved and irresolute did he seem." Another newly minted cardinal, the same Francesco Soderini whose secretary Machiavelli had been when the two called on Cesare after his capture of Urbino, described him now as "changeable, irresolute, and suspicious." Cesare was not, however, entirely without hope or incapable of making plans. He sent instructions to Michelotto to move his part of the Borgia treasure from Cesena to Ferrara, where Lucrezia, presumably, would be able to keep it safe.

Cesare's claims on the Romagna, Venice's interference in the region after Alexander's death, the return of some of the warlords earlier expelled by Cesare—together these things presented Pope Julius with the first great crisis of what was going to be another extraordinarily eventful reign. The question was whether the pope should make Cesare a junior partner or cast him aside along with his money, his troops, and his connections. It came down to a judgment as to whether Cesare could be depended upon to serve the pope's interests at least as assiduously as he was sure to pursue his own.

Probably Julius would have decided to get along without Cesare; he would show repeatedly, throughout his reign, that he had no interest in sharing what he regarded as rightfully belonging to the Church with anyone. In any case he didn't have to decide; Cesare resolved the matter for him by abruptly leaving Rome and galloping downriver to Ostia, where he boarded one of the papal galleys and ordered its captain to take him up the coast to Genoa. The captain in question, unfortunately for Cesare, was a della Rovere loyalist and a suspicious one. Instead of putting to sea, he took Cesare into custody and sent a messenger racing back to Rome to inform the pope. Again everything was suddenly going wrong: the same developments in the Romagna that had driven Cesare to depart for Genoa—resumed aggressiveness by Venice above all—were emboldening Julius to take a firmer line. He dispatched a delegation of trusted cardinals to Ostia, where they presented Cesare with a list of demands. Julius insisted that Cesare surrender all his vicariates, returning them to direct rule by the Church. He was to reveal the secret passwords, the countersigns, that the Spaniards commanding his remaining Romagna *rocca* were insisting on hearing as proof that Cesare really did want them to surrender. Cesare refused and by doing so sealed his fate.

Julius sent the entire papal guard to Ostia to bring Cesare back to the Vatican, where he was given comfortable rooms ordinarily reserved for visiting cardinals. Gian Giordano Orsini urged the pope to have him killed, but Julius was in no hurry to do away with someone in possession of so many valuable secrets. Shortly after his return to Rome, Cesare learned that Michelotto had been attacked while transferring his hoard of Vatican gold to Ferrara and was now a prisoner. Almost simultaneously a smaller caravan of Borgia treasure, this one bound for Ferrara from Rome, was seized in Tuscany by Giovanni Bentivoglio. Instead of returning it to the Vatican, Bentivoglio locked it up in his own palace at Bologna. Cesare offered ten thousand ducats for the release of Michelotto and was refused.

Cesare by this point was giving evidence of falling apart under the weight of failure and fear. His sending of representatives to Florence to negotiate a *condotta*—Cesare's agents were told to inform the *signoria* that he would soon be in Tuscany at the head of an army—struck Machiavelli as not just pathetic but evidence that the duke he had once admired so deeply was losing touch with reality. Julius intensified the pressure by announcing his intention to conduct investigations into the deaths not only of Lucrezia's husband the duke of Bisceglie but of Cesare's brother Juan, Giulio Cesare Varano of Camerino and his three sons, Astorre Manfredi of Faenza, the last Gaetani lord of Sermoneta, and others. His zeal for incriminating evidence caused him to have Michelotto brought to Rome and, along with other Borgia retainers, put under torture. Cardinal Lloris again visited Cesare and found him so "confused" and "irresolute" that he appeared to have "lost his wits."

The last weeks of 1503 and the first of 1504 were marked by Julius II's relentless but unsuccessful efforts to get the passwords out of Cesare and the stubborn refusal of Cesare's Romagna lieutenants to surrender their *rocca*. The loyalty of those lieutenants almost defies belief. At one point, having somehow learned the password for Cesena, the pope gave them to a Borgia attendant named Pedro d'Oviedo and sent him off with instructions to induce the two men in command there, the brothers Pedro and Diego Ramires, to open their gates. The brothers' response was to seize Oviedo, torture and kill him, and put his body on display. They would never surrender, they declared, until they knew that Cesare was free. Julius, when he learned of this, was convinced that the Ramires were acting on secret instructions from Cesare himself. The Spanish cardinals had a hard time dissuading the pontiff from throwing Cesare into a dungeon in the Castel Sant'Angelo. He consented to having the prisoner moved instead to the Borgia Tower, to the chamber in which Bisceglie had been strangled years before. The torture of Michelotto and others, meanwhile, was adding to the pope's frustration by producing nothing of use.

After many weeks of fruitless discussion, the leader of the Spanish cardinals in Rome, a onetime protégé of Alexander VI named Juan de Vera, managed to broker an agreement that ended the deadlock. Vera had intervened on behalf of Ferdinand of Spain, who had just become undisputed master of the entire kingdom of Naples thanks to a fresh round of victories by Gonsalvo and wanted papal approval of his conquests. Julius for his part was now focused on driving the Venetians out of the Romagna, where they were eagerly gobbling up territory, and to accomplish that he needed possession of Cesare's remaining strongholds. Cesare was driven to deal not by any strategic considerations— he no longer possessed the means to play that game—but by a simple, desperate wish to be released. He agreed to order all his commanders in the Romagna to surrender in return for his freedom and the right to keep his movable property—particularly the gold still held for him in Genoa.

In mid-February, in the custody of Spanish cardinal Bernardino López de Carvajal, Cesare was taken from the Vatican to the Tiber for transportation to Ostia. There is a poignant description of him, while awaiting the galley that was to take him away, mounting a horse and galloping up and down the riverbank: it is the picture of a young man brimming with vitality, half-mad with frustration, and overjoyed to be released from confinement, treating himself to a few minutes of wild freedom.

Upon arriving at Ostia, he was once again locked up, remaining a prisoner for another two months while the agonizingly slow process of getting his Romagna commanders to give up their fortresses was finally brought to completion. Lucrezia's father-in-law Duke Ercole, asked to offer Cesare asylum in Ferrara, refused.

It somehow came to pass that, when Cesare's men at Cesena and the little town of Bertinoro at last gave up and marched out of their strong-holds with music playing and flags unfurled, news of their surrender reached Ostia before Rome. Cardinal Carvajal, satisfied that Cesare had fulfilled the terms of his deal with the pope, told him he was free to go. Whether the Spaniard Carvajal acted so hastily in order to save Cesare's life we do not know, but it is not hard to believe that Julius, given a choice, would have locked Cesare away forever, or killed him, rather than granting him his freedom. Yet it was not he but Cesare who now faced a monumental decision: whether to again go north, to the court of Louis XII, or instead go south to Gonsalvo, Naples, and Spain.

Perhaps it is going too far to say that in opting to go south he made the one truly ruinous decision of his life, but not by a wide margin. In France he was still duke of Valentinois, with a royal wife and child, and it must have seemed possible that the king who had given him both title and bride could be won over once again. Certainly Louis XII had little enough reason to think of Cesare as an enemy. He might very well have found his old friend and protégé Valentino useful in consolidating France's position in the north in the aftermath of his generals' disas-trous failures.

Why then did Cesare turn his back on France and go to Naples in-stead? Not only, surely, because one of his numerous cardinal cousins, another Pedro Luis Lanzol Borgia, was now in Naples himself after fleeing Rome and had sent a galley to Ostia to pick him up. Perhaps because so many other members of his family were already in Naples: not only the cardinal but Jofrè Borgia as well and his wife Sancia, now the mistress of Prospero Colonna. Perhaps too because Gonsalvo's vic-tories over the French made the Spanish seem the more sensible choice. Perhaps the astrologers had a hand in it. Whatever the reason, Cesare boarded the cardinal's galley and allowed it to take him south. In doing so he extinguished whatever affection Louis XII might still have felt for him.

Cesare spent three happy weeks in Naples, enthusiastically making preparations for a return to the Romagna, asking Gonsalvo for financial help and evidently expecting to get it. Unbeknown to him, however, Pope Julius was in communication both with Gonsalvo and with the Roman agents of Ferdinand and Isabella, asking that Cesare be kept under close watch and prevented from making trouble. From Spain, Gonsalvo received instructions that under no circumstances was he to allow Cesare to slip out of his hands.

On the night of May 26, having completed preparations to leave Naples by galley, Cesare visited Gonsalvo to say farewell and was stunned to find himself placed under arrest. He was taken to the island of Ischia in the Bay of Naples and confined there under increasingly harsh circumstances, consigned at last to a chamber so diabolically uncomfortable that it was known as "the oven." Lucrezia, knowing of his plans to return to the Romagna but not of his arrest, had managed to raise enough money to hire a thousand soldiers, put them under the command of the Borgia loyalist Pedro Ramires, and send them off to join him. Ramires did not get far before learning that Cesare was not to be expected. Seeing that there was nothing to be done, he turned back. That other Cesare loyalist, Michelotto, was meanwhile still a prisoner in Rome, Pope Julius continuing without success to attempt to extract from him dark Borgia secrets that might or might not have existed. Eventually he would be released, find employment in Florence with Machiavelli's help, and be murdered under circumstances that have never been explained.

On August 20, Cesare was put aboard a galley that joined a flotilla commanded by the same Prospero Colonna whom he had tricked in departing Rome after Alexander's death. They were bound for Spain, and upon arrival Cesare was confined in a remote castle at Chinchilla in the mountainous backcountry of his native Valencia. Though in no way mistreated—he was allowed a cadre of personal servants and even a mistress—he is not likely to have had much opportunity to keep abreast of what was happening far away. To the great questions of the hour he had become irrelevant, and his chances of being set free were reduced to zero by Isabella of Spain's hostility—she wanted him tried for the murders of the dukes of Gandía and Bisceglie—and by Pope Julius II's refusal to have him back in Italy. Lucrezia and his brother-in-law Juan king of Navarre sent appeals for clemency but achieved nothing. It was entirely possible that Cesare, like Ludovico Sforza of

Milan and the heir to the last Aragonese king of Naples, would spend the rest of his days a prisoner.

Though he evidently still had substantial funds in banks in northern Italy, any effort to retrieve them would have attracted the attention of the agents of the pope, who was himself in financial straits and bent on seizing Cesare's assets wherever he could find them. In the spring of 1505, acting on Cesare's behalf, Juan of Navarre appealed to Louis XII for payment of the dowry that the new Duke Valentino had been promised at the time of his betrothal to Charlotte d'Albret. He was curtly refused. Frustration at this rebuff may help to explain a bizarre event that shortly followed. One day during a conversation atop the ramparts at Chinchilla, Cesare suddenly hurled himself upon the castle's governor, apparently intending to throw him to his death. Instead Cesare was overpowered and injured in the course of being subdued. Not long thereafter he was moved to the great fortress of La Mota at Medina del Campo northwest of Madrid. This was one of the favorite residences of Ferdinand and Isabella, high-walled, stoutly built, and always heavily guarded. There he was confined under far more austere circumstances than at Chinchilla.

This move is likely to have been partly the result of the death, late in the previous year, of Queen Isabella. Her passing had left Cesare's fate in the hands—or so it seemed, for the time being—of her husband Ferdinand. This opened a whole range of new possibilities: the Spanish king was far too cynical and self-serving to attach any importance to his wife's righteous view of Cesare as a moral lost cause, too monstrous ever to be set free. For Ferdinand, by contrast, the only question was whether Cesare might in some way be made useful. Being himself without scruples—a decade hence he would be gulling his young son-in-law Henry VIII of England, drawing him into an unnecessary war with France and then deserting him as soon as his own aims had been accomplished—Ferdinand was incapable of trusting anyone. In 1505 his suspicions were focused on his viceroy in Naples, Gonsalvo the Great Captain. Gonsalvo was as loyal an agent as any king had ever had, and his achievements first in Granada and then in Italy should have made Ferdinand grateful for his existence. The opposite was true, however; the death of Isabella removed the only restraint on Ferdinand's dark imaginings, and in short order he became convinced that Gonsalvo was scheming to seize Naples for himself. He began to consider not only releasing Cesare but sending him to Naples at the head of an army, and the transfer from Chinchilla to Medina del Campo may have been a first step in that direction. Cesare's assignment would be to replace Gonsalvo—or to subdue him if he declined to stand aside.

Cesare, if he learned of this possibility, must have been ecstatic; such an assignment would at a stroke have returned him to prominence in Italy. But it was not to be; the complications were too numerous and too imposing. Ferdinand wanted the friendship of Pope Julius and knew that gaining it would be impossible if he injected Cesare back into Italian affairs. Also, Ferdinand was at this time looking for ways to improve his relations with France. His gestures in that direction would have no chance of success if he freed the onetime protégé whom Louis XII now despised as a traitor.

And it soon developed that Cesare was not Ferdinand's to do with as he wished after all. He belonged, instead, to Ferdinand's son-in-law Philip of Hapsburg, Philip the Handsome so called, with whom the king had a poisonously bad relationship. Philip was the husband of Ferdinand's eldest surviving daughter, Juana, who as a result of her mother Isabella's death was now queen of Castile, and the couple had two small sons. It was a bitter fact, for Ferdinand, that his and Isabella's son Juan had died at nineteen, leaving a pregnant bride whose child was later stillborn, and that the daughter who now wore the crown of Castile and was heir to that of Aragon was producing healthy male offspring for the German House of Hapsburg. It meant that everything Ferdinand and Isabella had built together in three decades of scheming and danger and hard toil would pass after his death from their ancient House of Trastámara to a tribe of grasping Germans.

Philip deepened Ferdinand's chagrin by demanding to be recognized as king of Castile, not just its new queen's consort. Thus it proved to matter a great deal that Medina del Campo and its castle were in Castile rather than Aragon, so that Cesare was no longer in Ferdinand's custody but in that of Juana and Philip, neither of whom had any wish to put him at the old king's disposal. Less than a year after Isabella's death, Ferdinand would attempt to foil Philip by marrying a seventeen-year-old French princess for the purpose of providing himself with a new male heir; any such son would have been first in Aragon's line of succession, ahead of Juana and her brood. And after three years of trying, presumably with the help of the virility potions concocted by his physicians, Ferdinand would succeed in getting his queen with child. In May 1509 she gave birth to the hoped-for son, but the child lived only hours. That was still in the future, however, when in September 1506 Philip suddenly died at Burgos, probably of typhoid. His death left Cesare at the mercy of Queen Juana, who had been taught by her late mother to regard him as the devil incarnate and was beginning to behave in the ways that would cause her to be remembered as Juana the Mad. The first thing that raised questions about her sanity was her refusal to have her husband buried and her insistence on taking his corpse with her wherever she traveled. Possibly with the encouragement of Cesare's sister-in-law the dowager duchess of Gandía, widow of the Juan Borgia who had been murdered in Rome in 1497, she carried out her late mother's wish by having Cesare indicted for the murders of his brother and his brother-in-law the duke of Bisceglie. A trial would presumably follow.

All was not lost, however. With Philip the Handsome and Queen Isabella both dead, Juana losing her wits, and Ferdinand setting out to confront Gonsalvo in Naples personally, discipline at La Mota began to go slack. Cesare's keepers evidently saw him as a man who still had a future, who might eventually be powerful once again and was therefore worth cultivating. Certainly they were open to suasion and bribery. With the help of the governor at La Mota, one Cárdenas, Cesare was able to secure a length of strong rope and make arrangements for an escape.

On the night of October 25, with a small party of mounted confederates waiting below, he climbed out the window of his chamber high in La Mota's walls and began lowering himself down the rope. A watchman saw what was happening and sounded the alarm, a guard entered the chamber and cut the rope, and Cesare was injured as he fell to the ground. He was put on a horse all the same and taken to a remote property belonging to Governor Cárdenas. He remained there a month, a hunted fugitive, and when able to travel was moved in secret to the port of Castres and put aboard a ship bound for Navarre. Evidently he remained a semi-invalid at this point: someone whose path he crossed described him as "a man doubled up, with an ugly face, a big nose, dark."

When storms forced his ship into a fishing port, Cesare was obliged to continue on muleback. Finally, however, he made his way to Navarre's capital of Pamplona, a city he had never seen in spite of having had its bishopric conferred upon him as a sixteen-year-old schoolboy. He was described as descending on the little city "like the devil." Presumably this was a reference to his appearance after weeks on the run and much hardship.

Once settled in Pamplona, he wasted no time before setting out to recover at least some of his old importance. He dispatched envoys to Italy, sending with them letters to various individuals whom he thought might be inclined to help—for example Francesco Gonzaga, marquess of Mantua, who was deeply infatuated with his sister-in-law Lucrezia Borgia d'Este, now duchess of Ferrara following the death of her husband's father. In these letters Cesare signed himself duke of Romagna, signaling that the Romagna was where he hoped to reestablish himself. The lack of response showed that he could expect no assistance in that regard. Gonzaga at this time was employed as captain-general of the forces with which Pope Julius II—following Cesare's example—had recently driven the Baglioni out of Perugia and the Bentivoglii out of Bologna. That he would break with an imperious and increasingly powerful pope for the sake of the penniless Cesare in his distant refuge was inconceivable even if his young son and heir was, supposedly, still betrothed to Cesare's daughter Louisa.

As for Pope Julius himself, sensitive to Cesare's popularity in the Romagna and mindful of the difficulties that his return could stir up, he saw no reason to be friendly or even neutral. When a representative sent by Cesare called on him at Bologna, of which he was taking personal possession after the expulsion of the Bentivoglii, Julius had the unfortunate man thrown into prison. Lucrezia appears to have been alone in daring to request his release, and as before her appeals were politely denied.

At about this same time Louis XII refused a request for restoration of the revenues to which Cesare had once been entitled as duke of Valentinois. Cesare therefore was left without prospects in Italy, France, or Spain—without any friends at all among the crowned heads of Europe, aside from his brother-in-law Juan of Navarre. Juan, being not only short of funds but faced with a rebellion in which Ferdinand of Spain,

Louis of France, and Maximilian of Hapsburg were all meddling, could offer Cesare one thing only: command of the Navarrese army. Now recovered from his injuries—he was described at about this time as "a big man, strong, handsome, and in the full flight of his manhood"—he was soon directing the siege of a rebel fortress at Viana.

Awakened early on the morning of March 12, 1507, when a relief force of rebels attempted to break the siege, he donned his armor, mounted his charger, and led a party of his soldiers in hot pursuit of fleeing enemy horsemen. He chased them into a ravine, where he was ambushed and cut to pieces at the conclusion of a bitter fight in which he killed several men. His body was stripped naked and abandoned. Perhaps he had not realized that he was alone as he entered the ravine— that his own men were either not following or had been outrun. It is not impossible that he committed a kind of suicide, intentionally throwing himself into a situation that made a swift death inevitable, preferring early oblivion to long years as the aging dependent of a poor and insignificant king.

The body when recovered was placed in the church of Saint Mary of the Assumption in Viana. Over it was constructed the ornate tomb that an indignant bishop of Calahorra would later order destroyed.

Aftermath

The end of Cesare left Lucrezia exposed and solitary. Though now duchess of Ferrara, her father-in-law having died in 1505, she was in a cold union with a dour duke who would never have married her if he had not been bullied into it and showed no interest in her except as a body upon which to generate an heir. Married five years now, repeatedly pregnant, Lucrezia had yet to give Alfonso a living child. For this reason and others she remained an isolated figure at the Ferrara court, an outsider.

Anyone wishing to persuade Alfonso that association with the Borgias could lead only to grief needed only to point to what his family had already suffered as a consequence of his marriage. Lucrezia, in moving to Ferrara, had brought along as part of her entourage a young cousin named Angela. A great beauty (painted later in life by Leonardo da Vinci), this Angela was like Lucrezia herself a Lanzol, but like all the Roman Lanzols she used Borgia as her surname. Soon after arriving in Ferrara, she found herself pursued both by Alfonso d'Este's priapic brother Cardinal Ippolito and their illegitimate half-brother Giulio. This led to the cardinal's sending thugs to waylay Giulio and (because Angela had driven Ippolito half-mad with jealousy by rhapsodizing upon the beauty of his rival's eyes) blind him. Giulio escaped with his fine face disfigured but only one eye lost. Outraged to learn that the cardinal's only punishment was to be ordered to leave Ferrara, he began to plot revenge. Soon he was at the center of a conspiracy not only to poison the cardinal but to murder Alfonso as well and replace him as duke with the youngest of the legitimate Este brothers, Ferrante, named for his maternal grandfather King Ferrante of Naples. The scheme was discovered, the conspirators were convicted of treason, and all were beheaded except Giulio and Ferrante, who were literally at the chopping block when reprieved and sent off to confinement.

Ferrante would die in his dungeon in Ferrara's great palace thirty-four years later. Giulio would be released after fifty-four years, a piece of human wreckage in his ninth decade and an object of mirth as he stumbled into the daylight in his tattered, antique clothes. Angela Borgia, untouched by the tragedy she had innocently set in motion, became the bride of an Italian count six months after the brothers' arrest. She later gave birth to a son who would grow up to marry Cardinal Ippolito's illegitimate daughter.

Louis of France encouraged Alfonso to rid himself of his Borgia wife. Such a move would certainly have been approved, and probably abetted, by Julius II, whose hatred of all the Borgias remained so intense that he refused to set foot in the Vatican apartments that had been their private quarters. The duke, however, politely ignored the suggestion. Shedding a wife of several years could be a messy affair. An annulment would be required, and establishing grounds could lead to the kind of unpleasantness that the end of Lucrezia's first marriage had brought down on Giovanni Sforza. What probably mattered more, the financial consequences would have been painful. Lucrezia, if sent packing, would be entitled to take her dowry with her. With northern Italy in turmoil and the relationship between Spain and France unsettled at best, Ferrara was likely soon to be once again at war. Alfonso could ill afford to give up the hundred thousand ducats and other treasure that had come to him with his bride.

Alfonso appears to have been content with his life and eventually with his wife as well. He was a blunt character of simple tastes, dividing much of his time between the workshop and foundry where he tinkered with the production of guns, and his retinue of prostitutes. Her failure to produce children aside, Lucrezia had done nothing with which any sane husband could have found fault. In almost all ways she was an exemplary consort: not only strikingly beautiful and so graceful that witnesses wrote of her seeming to walk on air, but unfailingly sweet-natured, brimming with "laughing good humor and gaiety." She was fluent in Valencian Spanish, Italian, and French, had considerable knowledge of Latin and some of Greek, and was a sophisticated patron of the arts. Finally she was modest in conduct, devout in religion, and, thanks both to her own abilities and to the responsibilities that Alexander VI had given her at an early age, a capable and conscientious administrator. Writers unable to square Lucrezia's terrible reputation with her admirable behavior after the move to Ferrara have sometimes claimed that she underwent an astonishing transformation upon marrying Alfonso d'Este, the murdering libertine somehow turning into a grande dame of the highest quality. But as the Borgia biographer Michael Mallett observed almost half a century ago, this notion is "implausible and unhistorical." There was no transformation because the vicious young Lucrezia of legend never existed.

In 1508 she gave birth to a healthy son, named Ercole in honor of his late grandfather. In 1509 she had a second healthy son, this one named Ippolito after his uncle the cardinal and himself a future cardinal. As the mother of an heir and a spare she was at last relatively secure. By this time a new stage in the so-called Italian Wars had broken out as expected, the focus on northern Italy rather than Naples, and Ferrara was unavoidably involved. This fresh round of fighting, which would go on for eight years, was the work of Pope Julius. First he allied himself with France and Spain to drive Venice out of its recently conquered mainland territories, then later switched sides and joined Venice in making war on France. Alfonso d'Este and the duchy of Ferrara became prime targets of the pope's inexhaustible reserves of wrath; Julius excommunicated the duke, placed Ferrara under an interdict, and declared that the House of Este's right to rule had become null and void. The Este would be saved by Alfonso's skill as a soldier and his mastery of the art and science of artillery, by the fact that when off at the war he was able to leave Ferrara under the regency of his capable wife, and finally, in 1513, by a stroke of immense good fortune. In that year Pope Julius, in the midst of preparations for an invasion of Ferrara, suddenly died. The invasion was called off, and the danger to Ferrara passed. The war years had tightened the bond between Lucrezia and the duke, giving each new respect for and trust in the other.

Lucrezia was in her mid-thirties when peace returned, and had barely a handful of years to live. Those years would be as eventful as the ones that had come before. In 1512 her son by the duke of Bisceglie,

Rodrigo of Aragon, died at age twelve. She had not seen him since being obliged to leave him behind when she departed Rome for Ferrara but had always been devoted to his well-being, and she was deeply wounded by the loss. After another series of failed pregnancies she gave birth to a son named Alessandro in 1514, a daughter named Leonora in 1515, and a boy named Francesco in 1516, the year when little Alessandro died. In the meantime, and originally at Cesare's request, she had assumed responsibility for some of the young Borgias who without her might have been cut adrift, among them the Infant of Rome (endlessly rumored to be her child) and the mysterious Rodrigo Borgia who had been born at about the time of Pope Alexander's death. The diligence with which she enlisted her husband's help in trying to find a place for these children, and Alfonso's efforts to get the unpleasant young Infant an appointment at France's royal court, make it highly improbable that the duke could have thought it even possible that any of them might be her children.

Gradually, Lucrezia became a revered figure in Ferrara, loved for her kindness—she had pawned her jewels to help the city's poor when the war with Rome brought hard times—and admired for her piety. She made romantic conquests of some of the most remarkable figures of her time. Among them were the humanists and poets Pietro Bembo, Ercole Strozzi, and Ariosto, leading literary figures all and deep in her thrall. Other admirers—so devoted that there have always been suspicions of affairs—included Lucrezia's brother-in-law Francesco Gonzaga, a brilliant young French general named Gaston de Foix, and Gaston's commander and friend Pierre Terrail LeVieux, known as the seigneur de Bayard, who left a description of her as "beautiful and good, gentle and amiable to everyone." It is possible to interpret some of the letters that Lucrezia and these men exchanged as evidence of infidelity—but only by ignoring the conventions of courtly love that governed such relationships in those days.

Lucrezia died at age thirty-nine in 1519, shortly after giving birth to a daughter who also did not survive. She was mourned by her husband, her three sons and daughter, a wide circle of admirers, and virtually the whole population of Ferrara. Alfonso lived for another fifteen years, his son and heir Ercole II then ruled as duke of Ferrara until 1559 and was succeeded by his son Alfonso II, who lived until 1597 and centuries later would provide Robert Browning with the model for the monstrous narrator of his poem "My Last Duchess." The legitimate male line having become extinct with his passing, Ferrara was absorbed into the Papal States in 1598. An illegitimate cousin of Alfonso II's, Cesare d'Este, established a line of dukes that would rule the city-state of Modena into the time of Napoleon. Among the descendants of Lucrezia living today are the kings of Spain and Belgium, the grand duke of Luxembourg, France's House of Bourbon, and the descendants of the last royal rulers of Bavaria, Brazil, Saxony, and the so-called Two Sicilies.

Young though she was at the time of her death, Lucrezia had outlived by years Cesare's widow Charlotte d'Albret, who was exactly her age. Because Charlotte had lived as Cesare's wife for only a few months, and because what little has been reported about the relationship between the two is often self-contradictory—it is said both that she refused to rejoin her husband after he left France and that she was prevented from doing so either by Louis XII or by Cesare himself—her behavior during her years of widowhood seems distinctly weird. She withdrew into a state of perpetual mourning, draping her home in black crepe, trimming the harnesses of her mules with black, sleeping between black sheets, eating from black dishware, and requiring her daughter to do the same. The girl Louisa married into an illegitimate branch of the royal Bourbons. Her descendants, like Lucrezia's, are today among the highest of Europe's titled nobility.

Lucrezia was, so far as we know, the last of Vannozza's children to die. Her younger brother Jofrè had predeceased her by two years, leaving four small children and a widow of whom nothing is known except that her name was Maria del Milà and therefore she presumably was a member of that branch of the Borgia family tree. Jofrè had been freed to marry by the death in 1505 of his estranged wife Sancia, who at one time or another, it must have seemed to him, had been the mistress of almost every man of importance in Italy. Jofrè's son by his second marriage, and then his grandson and great-grandson, succeeded to his title and estates as princes of Squillace. When the male line ended, the last prince's only daughter was married to a Spanish descendant of Juan Borgia the murdered duke of Gandía. Her inheritance was thus merged into that of the family's senior line.

The Borgia dukes of Gandía, immensely wealthy, remained important in the public life of Spain and its empire for more than a hundred years. The fourth duke, Francisco, whose mother was the illegitimate daughter of an archbishop who was an illegitimate son of King Ferdinand, was a favorite at the court of the Holy Roman emperor Charles V (the son of Ferdinand and Isabella's daughter Juana the Mad and Philip the Handsome). Francisco served as viceroy of Catalonia before being widowed for a second time and entering the priesthood. This led to his becoming the third head of the young Society of Jesus, the Jesuits, and eventually to his being canonized a saint. Among his eighteen children (only one of them illegitimate) were two cardinals, an archbishop, a viceroy of Peru, a general, an ambassador, and five of the twenty-six Borgia maidens who in the course of two centuries became nuns (and often mothers superior) of the convent at Gandía. Later members of the family included viceroys in Aragon and Sicily, a "patriarch of the Indies," and confidants of kings. By the time the last duke of Gandía died childless in 1740 and all the Borgia family's male lines were extinct in Europe, various offspring of the duke-saint Francisco Borgia had established themselves permanently in the New World. Their descendants are said to be found today in Colombia and Peru.

What, finally, are we to make of this family?

First and most obviously, that the extraordinary durability of its fame is rooted less in its achievements, which though remarkable were in no way unique, than in an unequaled reputation for wickedness: for incest, fratricide, betrayal, and the ruthless pursuit of ignoble goals.

Second, that the darkest parts of this reputation turn out, when tested, to be nonsense pure and simple. Consider one example of which much was made from the sixteenth century onward: the deathbed scene described by Francesco Gonzaga in a letter to his wife just weeks after Alexander VI's passing.

> When he fell sick, [Alexander] began to talk in such a way that anyone who did not know what was in his mind would have thought that he was wandering, although he was perfectly conscious of what he said; his words were, "I come; it is right; wait a moment." Those who know the secret say that in the conclave following the death of Innocent he made a compact with the devil, and purchased the papacy from him at the price of his soul. Among the other provisions of the agreement was

*one which said that he should be allowed to occupy the Holy See twelve
years, and this he did with the addition of four days. There are some who
affirm that at the moment he gave up his spirit seven devils were seen in
his chamber. As soon as he was dead his body began to putrefy and his
mouth to foam like a kettle over the fire, which continued as long as it
was on the earth.*

Et cetera. That the worldly lord of Mantua could write such things
makes it unsurprising that the most fantastically improbable tales won
wide acceptance in the Italy of his time. When Alexander died, the
reader may recall, Gonzaga was not only not at the Vatican but not
in Rome, being in command of French troops on their way to attack
Naples. He notes in his letter that "scandalous epigrams [about Alexan-
der] are every day published," which is hardly surprising when one considers the number and importance of the pope's political adversaries
and the eagerness of the Italian public to believe a Spanish pontiff capable of every imaginable evil.

A third fact deserving notice is that the black myth of the Borgias is
largely a manufactured thing, produced for a purpose, and that the process of manufacturing it was fully under way even before Alexander's
death. It got off to an impressively fast start thanks to the pope's blithe
indifference not only to personal criticism but to gross slander, and his
consistent failure to respond. It accelerated further when he was in his
grave, with Julius II not only encouraging fresh slanders but actually
having onetime Borgia associates tortured in an almost Stalinist campaign of terror aimed at generating damaging material. That nothing
of substance was turned up in this way mattered hardly at all; the
rumors and fabrications were quite colorful and numerous enough to
satisfy every need, and the retailing of them was encouraged and rewarded by Julius and others. Memories of what a formidable character
Cesare had been, and of how potent a combination he and Alexander
had formed, encouraged the generation that followed them to believe
the worst. As the stories accumulated, and then as the Reformation
threw the Catholic Church on the defensive and used Alexander and
his family as prime examples of the decadence of Rome, it came to be
assumed on all sides that the Borgias were indefensible, and that to
question the established view was a pastime for fools.

As soon as that established view is put to the test, it becomes clear that a reconsideration is not only possible but needed. Authoritative contemporary descriptions of Rodrigo Borgia, Pope Alexander, bring to mind what Oliver Wendell Holmes said of President Franklin Roosevelt: a second-class intellect, but a first-class temperament. Alexander has never been described as a genius, political or otherwise, but neither is it possible to doubt that he was a keenly intelligent man. Nor is it possible to dispute that he was hardworking, conscientious, and courageous. As for temperament, virtually everyone who recorded an impression of him testifies to his serene good humor, his friendliness, and his ability to project warmth and sympathy without compromising the dignity of his position. He stands unconvicted of sexual immorality, and whoever wishes to argue that he was as cynical about religion as has generally been assumed carries a weighty burden of proof. He took the lead in saving Italy from one French invasion, and struggled under impossibly difficult conditions to manage another and limit the damage it caused. If in the last decade of his life he went to unacceptable lengths to advance his policies and especially his young relations—and obviously he did—his actions in that regard were nonetheless not totally incompatible with the interests of the papacy and the Church he had been elected to lead. As J. H. Whitfield observed more than half a century ago, in important ways—reclaiming the Papal States for Rome, for example, and resisting foreign interference in Italy—Alexander deserves credit that usually goes to the man who hated him most bitterly and was almost fanatically bent on destroying his reputation, Pope Julius II. Alexander was far from guiltless, as we have seen, but it is not even necessary to consider the historical context to find more in him to admire than to deplore. In context—and especially in comparison with many of his predecessors and successors—he can seem, in some ways, an almost heroic figure.

As for Cesare, the ruthlessness for which he has always been famous is explained if not excused by the milieu in which he operated, and the character of the enemies with whom he was obliged to contend. If he had been less hard and less relentless, he would not have survived long enough to be remembered, and his place would have been filled by men far worse than himself. That he insisted on surrendering a secure place at the top of the ecclesiastical hierarchy is as plausibly interpreted as testament to his integrity as to anything else, and that he transformed himself into such an important figure at such a young age is proof of his immense gifts. And it is fair to ask: if he had achieved his ambitions, establishing himself securely as ruler of a powerful state, in what way would that have been worse for the people of Italy than what they experienced over the centuries after his death? In what way would it have been worse for Europe?

The last of the three notorious Borgias, Lucrezia, is in her limited way even more of an archetype than Alexander or her brother. She became the subject of gutter talk when little more than a child, precociously notorious thanks to the circumstances into which life and family had cast her. Considered by many to be unworthy of marriage into the Este family, distrusted and even despised, she lived long enough to be recognized by her husband, his family, and the citizens of her adoptive home as what in fact she was: "a pattern of womanly virtue."

Surely, these three deserve more serious—more *careful*—attention than they have hitherto commonly received. Not only are they and their stories intrinsically fascinating, but to follow those stories is to reach deep into the world of the Renaissance and shed light on it from innumerable new directions. It is a thing eminently worth doing. To bring to it a burden of demonstrably unwarranted assumptions is a shame and a waste.

Examining Old Assumptions

About the Character of Alexander VI

There is nothing, apparently, that somebody somewhere won't say about the Borgias. About any Borgia, even the blameless Alonso, who by becoming pope in old age unwittingly put his family on the road to infamy.

There is even a website—among the first to appear when one Googles "Pope Calixtus III"—that places Alonso Borgia among the twenty-five most evil people of the fifteenth century. It accuses him of "unprecedented depravity, torture, and inhumanity for the purpose of satanic worship," of turning "the major churches of Rome and Europe into fully operating torture chambers and fully operating satanic temples involving the daily ritualistic sacrifice of innocent men, women, and children," of "depraved sexual acts with victims prior to slaughter and after slaughter," and finally (a rather feeble anticlimax) of mere cannibalism.

We have seen how preposterous this is, and there is no reason to suppose that it is taken seriously by sensible grown-ups anywhere. Alonso is saved from notoriety less by what is actually known of the man and his life than by his profound obscurity—the fact that not many people even know he existed.

It is different with his nephew Rodrigo, Pope Alexander VI. He could hardly be more notorious or less obscure, at least by the standards of long-dead popes. The accepted version of his life story provides the world with something it apparently needs: *the* perfect example of papal decadence. Even today, five centuries on, he is considered sufficiently fascinating—sufficiently lurid—to serve as the centerpiece of a major multiseason television production. Everyone knows or thinks he knows that Alexander was devoid of moral principles, and that his story is laced with murder, lust that did not stop at incest, and unbridled greed. That Alexander belongs in the same corner of hell as the likes of Caligula, say, or Nero—of Mussolini if not quite of Hitler.

The only question worth asking, at this point, is the one that never gets asked: Is the story true? Was Alexander VI in fact a monster? To take that question seriously, rather than putting it aside as settled, is to discover why it remains untouched. Because to let go of the assumptions, preconceptions, and distortions that are universally accepted as the answer is to find oneself adrift on what a French biographer of the Borgias, Jean Lucas-Dubreton, deplored six decades ago as a "sea of uncertainty." It is to enter a place where things previously taken as self-evident can suddenly cease to make sense and where, as Lucas-Dubreton warned, "there is danger of being drowned."

Uncertainty begins with the realization that, with the exception of a salacious Roman gossip named Stefano Infessura and the absurdly sensational anonymous pamphlet that appeared in Rome at the start of the sixteenth century, the most terrible stories about the Borgias did not begin to surface until after Alexander was dead and Cesare's career had come to ruin. These stories appeared when they did in part because there was a voracious one-man market for them: Alexander's successor Julius II, Giuliano della Rovere, who had been blocked by the Borgias from winning the papal throne first in 1492 and again in September 1503 and who had spent most of the intervening years in seethingly bitter exile. Upon bullying and bribing his way to the throne at last, this towering but evil-tempered man, a great hater as well as a great patron of Michelangelo, made it one of the purposes of his existence to blacken the Borgia name. He had former associates of the Borgias tortured in his quest for blacking material. Though the results must have disappointed him keenly—employment by the Borgias turned out to be no guarantee that one had witnessed unspeakable things—the supply of gossip grew steadily all the same, at a pace that accelerated over time. The Borgias were easy to hate in the Rome of the early sixteenth century because they were Spaniards, foreigners, just at the time when Italy was falling under foreign, largely Spanish, domination. Italians high and low, in Rome and elsewhere, were happy to be told that allowing the Vatican to fall into the hands of foreigners could lead to nothing good.

The dark legend of the Borgias, having taken root in Italy, found a much wider audience when religious reformers went forth in search of evidence not just that non-Italian popes were a bad idea but that the papacy was an evil institution, illegitimate and inherently corrupt. As for the Roman Catholic Church, with much of northern Europe breaking away and the loyalty of France in question and the Ottoman Turks reaching the gates of Vienna, it had bigger things to worry about than the lost cause that the reputation of Alexander VI had become. Especially when someone as eminent as the Venetian statesman Francesco Guicciardini was describing Alexander as "mightily lustful of both sexes, publicly keeping girls and boys, but more girls." Even today the *Catholic Encyclopedia*, which is wrong about things as basic as whether Alexander's paternal grandfather was a Lanzol or a Borgia, says that although he was exemplary in the execution of the duties of his office, he continued after his election "the manner of life that had disgraced his cardinalate." Thereby ignoring the fact, noted with regret by many historians, that almost nothing is known of Rodrigo Borgia's "manner of life" during the three and a half decades between his appointment to the College of Cardinals and his election as pope.

Testimony to Alexander's bad character has always been available in abundance, even in such classics as Jacob Burckhardt's *The Civilization of the Renaissance in Italy*, where he is depicted as an impacted mass of "ambition, avarice, and sensuality" and as guilty of unspecified acts of "devilish wickedness." The problem is that this testimony, though routinely accepted as true beyond possibility of doubt, has never been anything of the kind. Confirmation by contemporary sources—by known individuals who were alive when the Borgias were alive, had some sort of access to the truth, and were not grinding political, ideological, or sectarian axes so flagrantly as to destroy their own credibility—proved to be exceedingly scarce. Even after this scarcity began to be acknowledged, it was regarded not as it should have been—as an indication that the whole subject required radical reexamination—but as an oddity to be noted in passing, a trivial inconvenience.

Biographers were forced into uncomfortable and even absurd positions. Lucas-Dubreton himself, on almost the same page where he complains about the "sea of uncertainty" that is Borgia history, plunges headlong into the murk. He follows an admission that almost nothing is known of Cardinal Rodrigo's private life with details about when and where he first met his alleged mistress Vannozza, providing no sources. Much the same thing was done in the nineteenth century by the Prussian Ferdinand Gregorovius, author of an eight-volume *History of the City of Rome in the Middle Ages* along with a hefty biography of Lucrezia. As noted in the introduction to the present work, Gregorovius preceded Lucas-Dubreton in acknowledging that "nothing is known of Rodrigo's private life during the pontificate of the four popes who followed Calixtus." But this clean admission, a recognition of the need for restraint in writing about who Alexander was and what he did before 1492, is followed by a declaration that "insatiable sensuality ruled this Borgia, a man of unusual beauty and strength, until his last years. Never was he able to cast out this demon." These are outlandish charges to level at a man about whose personal life *"nothing"* is known until he is in his sixties—against whom no charges of what Gregorovius means by "sensuality" can be proved from the beginning to the end of his life.

An English historian, Sir Charles Grant Robertson, acknowledged in a published lecture of 1891 that little is known also of the woman said to have been Cardinal Rodrigo's de facto wife and the mother of any number of his children. Robertson complained that "little [is] wrapped in the almost impenetrable mystery which shrouds the private affairs of the Borgias." One wonders if it occurred to Robertson, or to any of the writers who have had so much to say about the lady in question, that perhaps the only thing making the Borgias so mysterious is the insistence on believing tales for which no sufficient evidence exists. The question of how one of the most visible and influential men in the capital of the Christian West was able to raise a large family without even his most hateful adversaries commenting on it in their letters, diplomatic reports, and other writings dissolves into nothingness the moment real evidence is requested. A more recent historian, Michael Mallett, follows the conventional line in asserting of Alexander's children that "there were certainly eight or possibly nine." He then adds, however, that even to "consider" (a curious word choice) these offspring is to be "plunged into a world of uncertainty tinged with acrimonious and often libidinous controversy." Seeing a writer and scholar as competent as Mallett resort to such vague and florid abstractions raises questions about his own confidence in whatever he was struggling to say.

In the end the worst that can responsibly be said of Alexander VI is that he is one of history's puzzles. Gregorovius came to acknowledge this and to admit his own bafflement. "All experience of psychology," he wrote, "makes us expect that the burden of sin should have made of Alexander a man dark with fear and gloom, but he stands before us cheerful and happy, ready for enjoyment, till the last days of his life." This aspect of the puzzle would disappear if Alexander could be shown to have been utterly cynical, without belief in the creed he professed and therefore exempt from any sense of sinfulness. He is often, even usually, depicted in exactly that way, but such an interpretation of his character is unquestionably false. He was a believer and a devout one, displaying particular devotion to the Virgin Mary and unqualified so far as we know in his acceptance of the teachings of the Church he led. It is at least possible that, while believing in damnation (he would be a remarkable fifteenth-century European if he did not), he was not "dark with fear and gloom" for the simple reason that he was hopeful of escaping it and saw reason to be so.

The first historian to take such possibilities seriously appears to have been the Italian Andrea Leonetti, who in an 1880 work titled *Papa Alessandro VI* raised the startling question of whether what the world had believed about his subject for almost four hundred years might after all be wrong. His book drew some praise, some of it from scholars and journals of note, but it was not translated into languages other than Italian and sank into oblivion. Something similar happened in the 1920s, when Peter De Roo, in his *Material for a History of Pope Alexander VI* (see background section on "Paternity" beginning on page 239) published five volumes of documents inconsistent with the Alexander legend, and again in the 1930s and 1940s, with the publication first in Italian and then in English of Orestes Ferrara's *The Borgia Pope*. Both De Roo and Ferrara appear to have been ignored—certainly they have been denied the dignity of rebuttal—and to have had no impact whatever.

The last small eruption of Borgia revisionism occurred almost seven decades ago in an article, "New Views upon the Borgias," written by J. H. Whitfield of Oxford University and published in the March 1944 issue of the journal *History*. Whitfield, who was at the time lecturer in Italian, devoted most of his article to a somewhat cursory but generally perceptive overview of the literature in which, over the centuries, "every conceivable crime" had been attributed to the Borgias. Whitfield describes Burckhardt's depiction of the Borgia family as a "growth of romance," apparently meaning a tumorlike thing, and explains the Gregorovius version as "animated mainly by the wish to prove his thesis of the necessity of the German Reformation." He calls the standard biography of Lucrezia, written by Maria Bellonci in the 1930s, "not honest" and says too much has been made of suspect editions and faulty translation of the diaries of Vatican master of ceremonies Johann Burchard. He notes that even writers hostile to the Borgias have found themselves forced by the evidence (or the absence of evidence) to conclude that Cesare was not involved in the murder of his brother Juan, that he and his sister and Alexander could not have poisoned Prince Cem and are not likely to have been poisoners at all, and that the pope's actions against the Roman barons and the warlords of the Romagna were not only justified but necessary, et cetera.

Turning his attention to the defenders of the Borgias, Whitfield describes Ferrara's *The Borgia Pope* as "too simple" and "too blithe," not explaining what he means. Of De Roo's five volumes he has nothing to say except that they are "frankly apologetic" (both words are exactly correct, and it is improbable that De Roo himself would have rejected either), giving no indication of having paid much attention to their contents.

Whitfield concludes that "a revision in favor of the Borgias remains to be made," that "it is no longer possible to make with impunity the old global assertions of the wickedness of the Renascence," and that, as he previously noted, "Burckhardt and Gregorovius have had their day."

On that last point he was wrong. After his article appeared, Whitfield left Oxford to become professor of Italian language and literature at the University of Birmingham, never again publishing anything about the Borgias.

Seventy years on, the "revision" that he expected remains to be made. The "day" of Burckhardt and Gregorovius persists as a long, long twilight.

About the Famous Mistresses

It would hardly be surprising, taking into account the general level of clerical discipline in the generations before the Council of Trent and his own immense vitality and joie de vivre, if Rodrigo Borgia had a full and varied sex life. One might be justified in thinking it improbable that he did not.

None of this changes the fact, or licenses us to ignore the fact, that there is no convincing evidence that he ever had anything of the kind. Nor does it rescue the stories about his having long-term relationships with two women, Vannozza Catanei and Giulia Farnese, from ranking among the most dubious elements of the whole dark Borgia legend.

We saw in "Background: The Paternity Question: An 'Apology'" following chapter 13 that Peter De Roo, in volume one of his *Material*, concludes that Vannozza's five hundred years of notoriety are almost certainly undeserved— that though she was indeed the mother of Cesare and Lucrezia and five or more other children, the father was not Rodrigo Borgia but a son of his sister. That this conclusion departs radically from the legend is of course obvious. Its credibility becomes stronger, however, when one delves into what other historians have had to say about Vannozza and discovers the confusion and contradiction that they have left for us to untangle as best we can.

Was she Spanish or Italian? If Italian, was she from Mantua or Rome? Did she become Rodrigo's mistress as early as 1460, as Ludwig Pastor tells us, or is Gregorovius correct in saying that the relationship "may have begun shortly before 1470" (in which case Vannozza could not be the mother of Pedro Luis first duke of Gandía). Was she of noble rank, or an innkeeper, or a prostitute and madame of a brothel? What was her proper name, actually— Vanotia or Giovanna? We could be helped in deciding if the writers offering their many different answers to the endless questions gave us evidence for what they assert. They rarely, almost never, do.

After *Material*, no work has explored this matter as thoroughly as Orestes Ferrara's *The Borgia Pope*. Ferrara devotes an entire chapter to Vannozza's origins and her place in the Rome of the late fifteenth century (later doing the same for Giulia Farnese). After considering the various versions of the Vannozza story that have been offered over the centuries, he arrives at a conclusion that at first can seem almost a joke. "We find," he writes, "that there must have been several of them"—several Vannozzas. He is not joking, and what he says makes sense. He observes that Vannozza was a popular nickname, that Catanei was "one of the commonest names of the time," that it is not implausible that more than one woman so named was living in Rome in the 1480s and after, and that no one of them is likely to have been doing all the things that the archives of the time show people named Vannozza to have been doing. "The rich woman [named Vannozza Catanei] who left a fortune to charitable and religious works could not be the poor woman [another Vannozza] whom the notorial document shows so concerned about her small debts. . . . The woman who kept hostelries could not be the mother of the Duke of Gandía, the Duchess of Ferrara and the Prince of Squillace." Nor, Ferrara adds, is it likely that any single Vannozza could have been for many years the mistress of the vice-chancellor of the Church, the mother of his many children, and the wife, sequentially, of at least three other men, with one of whom she supposedly had a son named Ottaviano at almost the same time that Jofrè Borgia was born. Too much material has been conflated in a story that cannot logically contain it all.

Ferrara concludes, in tones suggestive of despair, that "in all this question there is more darkness than light" and that in the absence of adequate information the only way to prove that Vannozza was Rodrigo's mistress would be to establish that he was the father of her children. Which sends us back to De Roo and the fact that Rodrigo's paternity is, as we have seen, a distinctly shaky proposition.

De Roo and Ferrara are agreed on a number of important points, and together these points form a Vannozza story that is more coherent and less fraught with difficulties than the better-known alternatives. The first is that after the death of her first husband, Guillen Ramón Lanzol y de Borja, Vannozza married a Spaniard named Domenico Arenos. The two moved to Rome in the 1480s under the sponsorship of Cardinal Rodrigo, who is likely to have been responsible for Arenos's (in Italy the name became de Arignano or Carignano) finding employment in the papal bureaucracy. In keeping with the customs of the time Vannozza did not take her children with her into her second husband's household (we saw the same thing when Lucrezia Borgia moved to Ferrara as the bride of Alfonso d'Este, leaving her son Rodrigo of Aragon in Rome). The four youngest were taken into the establishment of their great-uncle Rodrigo, where the cardinal's friend and cousin Adriana del Milà took charge of their care and they came to be known as Cesare, Juan, Lucrezia, and Jofrè Borgia.

What, in the end, is proved? Very little, where Vannozza is concerned. To return to Ferrara's words, "it is extraordinarily difficult to affirm anything whatsoever with absolute certainty." Without question it is not only difficult but impossible to say with anything like confidence that she was Rodrigo Borgia's woman, or he the father of her children.

Readers with some prior knowledge of the Borgia story (if only through the most recent television dramatization, which is to be excused on grounds that its producer denies any attempt at historical accuracy) will perhaps have been surprised by the small attention given in the present volume to Alexander VI's supposed mistress Giulia Farnese. She looms large in most accounts, as an example and victim of the pope's satyriasis.

As the story goes:

Giulia, reputed to be so fantastically beautiful that she was known to all Rome as La Bella Giulia, became the mistress of Rodrigo Borgia when she was at most fifteen years old and he nearly sixty. She was seduced or coerced into submitting not only by a monster of a pontiff but by her own greedy relatives—above all her ambitious brother Alessandro, who traded the use of her body for appointment to the College of Cardinals.

She went on to bear the pope at least one child, possibly three or even four. She did so in spite of having a young husband, the Baron Orso or Orsino Orsini, and in spite of being herself a daughter of the Roman nobility, descended from two of central Italy's most important families.

For almost a decade she reigned as unofficial queen of a papal household that was managed, in perhaps the story's oddest twist, by her husband's mother, Adriana del Milà, who after moving from Spain to Rome had married Ludovico Orsini, lord of Bassanello, and been widowed after giving birth to her son.

It is a great story, as rich in novelty and drama as it is sordid. It is, however, *only* a story and for that reason has been omitted from the main narrative of the present volume. Here, in summary, are its flaws:

As with other stories about Rodrigo Borgia's moral degeneracy and sexual excesses, this one proves upon careful examination to be supported by only the flimsiest and most dubious evidence. It is certainly true, and was no secret at the time, that Giulia Farnese became a regular at the papal court when barely out of childhood, and it is likewise true that her presence gave rise to rumors that were taken up by three contemporary writers at least. One was the diarist and gossip Stefano Infessura, whose political agenda and recklessness with the facts have been noted more than once in the present book. The others, Jacopo Sannazzaro of Naples and Francesco Matarazzo of Perugia, were essentially entertainers, professional satirists concerned not with truth but with amusing such patrons as the Baglioni warlords of Perugia, enemies of the Borgias. To use them as sources is approximately as legitimate as basing an evaluation of President George W. Bush on transcripts of *The Daily Show*. When, more than a generation after Alexander's death, Francesco Guicciardini conferred new dignity on the Giulia story by making note of it in his *Storia d'Italia,* he acknowledged that he was repeating low gossip.

A sexual relationship is not needed to explain Giulia's presence at Cardinal Rodrigo's palace or at the papal court. She had access by virtue of the prominence of the Farnese and Gaetani families (her mother was a Gaetani), and she penetrated the Borgia inner circle when she married the son of Adriana del Milà. Along the way she became a close friend and companion of Lucrezia, and she and her husband joined the social set centered on Lucrezia and Alfonso duke of Bisceglie. Though she certainly became a favorite of the pope's, it is a long leap from charming an aging cleric to becoming his mistress.

Likewise, Giulia's submission to Rodrigo is not required to explain Alessandro Farnese's promotion to cardinal. Alessandro was not plucked out of obscurity; his appointment to the Sacred College in the second year of Pope Alexander's reign shocked no one. A young man of ability and high social status (in 1534 he would become Pope Paul III, going on to achieve considerable historical importance), he had first been singled out for advancement by Innocent VIII. He became a protégé of Lorenzo de' Medici and at the time of Alexander VI's election already held the high rank of protonotary apostolic, was the Vatican's treasurer-general, and had served as a papal secretary. He was several years older than Cesare when they were among the dozen new cardinals appointed in September 1493. According to the contemporary historian Sigismondo de' Conti, his selection had been urged upon Alexander by the Roman nobility.

Though the young Cardinal Farnese became the butt of jokes, this was not necessarily because his sister was the pope's mistress. He was called "the petticoat cardinal," and this has been assumed to refer to his dependence on his sister's special position. It could as easily have reference to his connection to the clique whose central figure was Adriana del Milà. Similarly, the fact that Giulia was called "the bride of Christ" is significant only to the extent that the satirists responsible for such jibes were credible—which they have no known claim to having been.

Bella Giulia had one child only—and there is no reason to believe that that child had a Borgia father. The Borgias, as we have seen, were not only willing but eager to acknowledge and embrace illegitimate additions to the family (taking several small bastards with them, for example, upon fleeing Rome after the death of Alexander). Alexander at no point showed any interest in Giulia's child, her daughter Laura, who grew up to be married in a lavish Vatican ceremony to Nicola della Rovere, a nephew of Pope Julius II. Julius of course was the former Giuliano della Rovere, whose obsessive hatred of the Borgias makes it difficult to believe that he could have countenanced such a union if he even suspected the bride of being a daughter of Alexander VI.

The alleged role of Adriana del Milà in the Giulia story is deeply improbable.
Evidence or testimony to the contrary being nonexistent, it is fair to Adriana
to assume that she was a person of at least normally good moral character.
Both before and after his election as pope, Rodrigo Borgia (her father's first
cousin) entrusted her not only with running his household but with raising
Lucrezia and her brothers after their mother remarried and they moved to
Rome. When Lucrezia journeyed from Rome to Ferrara to become the wife
of Alfonso d'Este, the pope sent Adriana along as her chaperone. A widow,
she was devoted to her son, an only child. And yet the Giulia story requires
us to believe that this same woman participated in cuckolding her son—a
noble who does not appear to have sought advancement in the papal service
and certainly was not financially needy—and in reducing his bride, who was
barely more than a child, to a state not far removed from prostitution. If as
is often alleged Giulia was already the pope's mistress at the time of her wedding, the story requires us to believe also that as powerful and proud a figure as Cardinal Giovanni Battista Orsini, in attending the ceremony, also
acquiesced in such a vile travesty.

This is not the only psychologically improbable part of the Giulia story.
Would Alexander, who doted on Lucrezia even as he used her as a diplomatic pawn, have allowed her to grow up in a Vatican bordello and live almost as the sister of his concubine? At the time of the Este marriage, when
distancing Lucrezia from the scandalous stories then in circulation was so
essential, would he have sent her to Ferrara in the care of his personal pro-
curess? Would Giulia's kinsmen, her Farnese brothers and Gaetani uncles
and Orsini in-laws, have accepted concubinage without complaint? Or
would the pope, during the time when his passion for Giulia was supposedly
at its height, have launched the attacks that resulted in the ruin of the
Gaetani? An affirmative answer to all these questions is possible. In the absence of better evidence, however, it would be unreasonable to regard affirmative answers as *very* possible, never mind probable. To assume them to be
the true answers is irresponsible. As Ferrara says in his chapter on the Bella
Giulia question, the whole business is "ringed round with confusion and alterations of known fact."

Much has been made, by various writers, of a letter sent by Alexander VI
to Lucrezia when she was the wife of Giovanni Sforza. The pontiff blamed
Lucrezia for allowing Adriana del Milà and Giulia, after visiting her at
Pesaro, to travel to see Giulia's gravely ill brother Angelo rather than returning directly to Rome. He chastised her in the following terms:

Madonna Adriana and Giulia have arrived at Capo di Monte, where they
found her brother dead. This death has caused deep grief to Cardinal Farnese

*as to Giulia and both were so cast down that they caught the fever. We have
sent Pietro Carianca to visit them, and we have provided doctors and all things
necessary. Let us pray God and the glorious Madonna that they may very
quickly recover. Messire Joanni and you have truly not shown great respect or
consideration for us in the matter of this journey of Madonna Adriana and
Giulia, in that you let them go without our permission: you should have
remembered that such a journey, undertaken so suddenly and without our
consent, could not but cause us extreme pain. You will say that they decided
upon it because Cardinal Farnese had wished it and arranged it; but you
should have asked yourself if it was to the Pope's taste. The thing is done now,
but another time we shall look to it better and shall consider in what hands
we place our affairs.*

That this letter expresses hurt feelings could hardly be more obvious.
Whether the hurt was caused more by Adriana or by Giulia—or by Lucrezia
for that matter—is entirely unclear. To take the pope's words as proof of his
sexual involvement with Giulia is absurd. It is more sensible to interpret
them, as Ferrara does, as akin to the complaint "of an old parish priest, who
had grown difficult with age, irritable and touchy." It is entirely plausible
that what was irritating him most was the prolonged absence of the woman
he twice names before Giulia in his letter, the woman on whom he was really dependent for his everyday comfort, his housekeeper-in-chief Adriana.

And About Lucrezia's Mystery Pregnancy

Did Lucrezia become pregnant shortly after her final separation from
Giovanni Sforza of Pesaro?

If so, might the father have been a young man named something like
Pierotto Calderón, a courier in the employ of Alexander VI?

Was this Calderón murdered by Cesare? In the pope's presence?

Did Lucrezia secretly give birth to a healthy son after the annulment of
the Sforza marriage and before her betrothal to Alfonso duke of Bisceglie?

The search for answers to these questions takes one into an all-too-typical
Borgia maze—one that leads nowhere.

W. H. Woodward, in a fine biography of Cesare written more than a century ago, concludes that "it seems to be true that [Lucrezia] was *enceinte* by
the murdered man . . . but the story that he was murdered by an enraged
Cesare in the presence of Alexander VI . . . is a later embroidery of the facts."

Writing earlier, Ludwig Pastor in *The History of the Popes from the Close of
the Middle Ages* likewise decided that the claim that "Cesare stabbed Pierotto

in the presence of the pope is another story that will not bear examination." (Pastor's use of the word *another* is not without significance. Though no one could accuse him of being a defender of the Borgias—the contrary would be closer to the truth—his researches led him to the conviction that much of what has come to be believed of the family over the centuries collapses when exposed to the known facts.)

A bona fide Borgia-hater, Ferdinand Gregorovius, fails even to mention the Calderón story in the more than two hundred pages devoted to the family in his *History of the City of Rome in the Middle Ages*. Presumably he did not regard it as deserving of mention.

The extent to which writers can lose their bearings in dealing with the Borgias is perhaps most vividly apparent in Maria Bellonci's often-reprinted 1939 biography of Lucrezia. In her fourth chapter, Bellonci sets forth a detailed and romantic account of how Lucrezia and "Caldes" (as she calls him) surrendered to a passion that was all the more intense because of their understanding that it was doomed. She too describes the pope as splashed with blood as he tries to protect Lucrezia's helpless lover from a Cesare driven out of his wits by the discovery of his sister's condition. When Bellonci returns to the subject two chapters later, however, she adds the awkwardly belated suggestion that *if* Lucrezia had a child in 1498, the father *may* have been not Caldes but rather the pope. In the end she throws up her hands, complaining that "the mystery is insoluble" and appearing to acknowledge that everything she has written about it is imagined. Perhaps she had not so much lost her bearings as yielded to the temptation to squeeze as much dramatic juice as possible out of sparse material, later feeling too uneasy about what she had done to let the matter rest.

Michael Mallett, in his 1969 work *The Borgias,* takes a more responsible approach, noting only that an affair and a pregnancy were rumored and that "Calderón" was a real person and was murdered—no one knows by whom.

There being no solid basis for choosing among the various versions of the story, if choice is deemed necessary it can only be done on the basis of probabilities, and the probabilities can be derived only from what is known of the individuals involved—Lucrezia herself above all. And it is prudent, when exploring the darker facets of the legend of Lucrezia Borgia, to begin with the understanding that they are invariably unproven and that the most sensational almost always turn out to be unworthy of attention. It is advisable to suspend judgment until one knows enough about the whole of Lucrezia's life story to judge what sorts of things she does and does not seem to have been capable of doing, and enough about the world in which she lived to judge what sorts of things a young woman of her status was—if she did them—likely to get away with.

It is the opinion of the writer of the present work that if in the late 1490s Lucrezia was capable of becoming pregnant by a man unsuited by rank to become her husband, she was unlikely to do such a thing and escape without consequences.

Notes

In a book of this kind, a book of history, almost every sentence is based on some anterior source—or sources. It is the nature of the beast. To inform the reader of the origins of all the bits of information that make up the narrative would require a second volume.

Limits are necessary, choices must be made, and such rules as exist are ambiguous. In the present instance the governing principle, which the author hopes is an unobjectionable one, has been to omit source notes for:

- Those things (dates, events, statements of fact or opinion et cetera) on which the credible sources have long agreed. For example, no one disputes that Alonso de Borja was born on December 31, 1378; citing a source is pointless.

- Those cases in which all the credible sources are not agreed (whether Cesare Borgia was born in 1474 or 1475, for example), no way of establishing the truth appears to exist, and even if resolved the question could in no material way change our view of the Borgias and their world.

Even after the exclusion of such things, an author is left with a substantial responsibility: to single out those statements of fact and opinion that remain material and disputable or are sufficiently obscure that an interested reader might have difficulty finding them. And then to provide either a source for the information or the reasons for the opinion.

This responsibility is particularly weighty, in the present case, in connection with the questions raised about the character of Rodrigo Borgia/Pope Alexander VI, the paternity of Cesare and Lucrezia Borgia and their siblings, Lucrezia's alleged illegitimate child, and Alexander's alleged mistresses. Therefore these matters, rather than being confined to the source notes provided below, are dealt with separately and at length in "Examining Old Assumptions," which begins on page 419.

If there exists an infallible, unarguable way of deciding which of thousands of items merit a source note, it is not known to the author. This is perhaps especially true of a work aimed at a popular readership rather than at the academic community; it is difficult to accuse E. R. Chamberlin of being irresponsible in offering fewer than two pages of "sources and notes" with his *The World of the Italian Renaissance,* for example, or to criticize Lauro Martines for appending only five such pages to his information-rich, immensely sophisticated *Power and Imagination.* The author of the present work has attempted to find an acceptable middle ground and beyond that can only invite any readers seeking further support of what he has written to contact him via the publisher.

The Borgia Problem: An Introduction

xxviii **Nearly seven decades have passed . . .** : Whitfield, "New Views," p. 77.

xxviii **In the seventh volume . . .** : Gregorovius's statement that the "secrets" of Rodrigo Borgia's private life are unknown is in his *History of Rome,* p. 7:326. The statement that "nothing is known" is in his *Lucretia Borgia,* p. 6.

xxviii **It is much the same with Burckhardt . . .** : Burckhardt, *Civilization,* p. 78.

Prologue: One Whom All Did Fear

3   **If the visit happened . . .** : Sabatini, *Life of Cesare,* p. 447, says the tomb was destroyed "at the close of the seventeenth century." An article in the January 18, 1954, issue of *Time* says it happened in 1527. Woodward, *Cesare Borgia,* p. 375, while giving no date, rather spoils the fun by saying that the identification of the body discovered under the road at Viana as Cesare's is "conjectural only" and blames Yriarte for that identification. But Yriarte, *Cesare Borgia,* p. 222, specifically states that no such identification is possible.

4   *Here in a little earth . . .* : The translation used is taken from Sabatini, *Life of Cesare,* footnote p. 448.

PART ONE: *Alonso*
From Out of Nowhere

If there exists or has ever existed a book dealing solely or even mainly with the life and career of the Alonso de Borja who became Pope Calixtus III, the author has found no trace of it. The material about

Alonso that constitutes the foundation of Part One has therefore been drawn from a multitude of limited and often fragmentary sources, all dealing principally with other subjects. The result is probably as comprehensive an account of Alonso's career as is to be found anywhere.

At the narrow end of the completeness spectrum is the first volume of Symonds, *Renaissance in Italy*, which, amid detailed treatments of several popes, declares that "little need be said" of Calixtus and limits that little to three lines (perhaps because Calixtus's life and reign provide little of the kind of sensational material in which Symonds specialized). Burckhardt, *Civilization*, doesn't mention Calixtus at all, and Gregorovius gives him ten of the thousands of pages that make up the forty volumes of his *History of Rome*. The most extensive available treatments include Johnson, *Borgias*, which devotes fifty heavily illustrated pages largely to Calixtus, and Mallett, *Borgias*, which gives him and his reign twenty-three pages.

Chapter 1: A Most Improbable Pope

10 **Every part of the process . . . :** The College of Cardinals' gradual assumption of sole power over papal elections is outlined in Symonds, *Renaissance in Italy*, p. 59.

11 **Not that Nicholas has left them . . . :** A detailed account of the reign of Nicholas V is in Gregorovius, *History of Rome*, p. 7:105–148.

12 **The existence of the league requires . . . :** Arnaldi, *Italy and Invaders*, p. 125, touches on the Italian League as a reflection of the midcentury balance of power. Its significance is explained in Hay, *Europe*, p. 185.

14 **Coiled like a serpent . . . :** The present work's treatment of the place of the Colonna, Orsini, and other baronial families during the half-century of Borgia prominence in Rome is informed by the uniquely detailed information in Shaw, *Orsini Family*.

15 **Through three tense days . . . :** Gregorovius, *History of Rome*, p. 7:104, describes the conclave of 1447 with emphasis on the failure of Cardinal Colonna.

18 **So . . . some *other* compromise . . . :** The dynamics of the conclave that elected Alonso Borgia are explained in Mallett, *Borgias*, p. 68.

Background: The Road to Rome

20 **The records show . . . :** The early history of the de Borja family in Valencia is outlined in Yriarte, *Cesare Borgia*, p. 17, and Mallett, *Borgias*, p. 59, and presented in exhaustive detail in De Roo, *Material*, vol. 1.

21 **This assembly of the Church . . . :** Barraclough, *Medieval Papacy*,

p. 180, provides a succinct introduction to the Council of Constance, its purposes and significance.

22 **Alfonso V at twenty-one . . . :** An excellent introduction to Alfonso V and his career is in Prescott, *Princes*, p. 51.

22 **He was also intelligent . . . :** King Alfonso's joke about marriage appears in Ryder, *Kingdom of Naples*, p. 71.

26 **When Alfonso appointed him . . . :** Alonso's refusal to go to Basel is in Mallett, *Borgias*, p. 65. The significance of the council is explained in Barraclough, *Medieval Papacy*, p. 18, and Gregorovius, *History of Rome*, p. 7:32.

26 **The war for Naples appeared . . . :** Prescott, *Princes*, p. 56, deals with Alfonso V's experience as a prisoner of Filippo Maria.

Chapter 2: Surprises, Disappointments, Hope

29 **According to this story . . . :** The tale of Ferrer's prophecy is recounted in Mallett, *Borgias*, p. 61.

30 **The former Alonso Borgia . . . :** The description of Calixtus III as "peaceable and kindly" is in Johnson, *Borgias*, p. 41.

35 **Calixtus's lifestyle, always simple . . . :** The austerity of the papal household under Calixtus III is described in Mallett, *Borgias*, p. 80.

36 **Not many of the pope's envoys . . . :** Ibid., p. 71.

Background: Il Regno—*The* Kingdom

39 **It was under the Normans . . . :** "The state as a work of art" is in Croce, *Naples*, p. 81.

40 **In the fourteenth century the barons . . . :** Machiavelli's description of the Neapolitan barons appears ibid., p. 60.

Chapter 3: Pope and King, Friends No More

44 **In the very month . . . :** That Alfonso V supported Piccinino in his attack on Siena is attested by Johnson, *Borgias*, p. 46, and Gregorovius, *History of Rome*, p. 7:154.

45 **The alienation of pope from king . . . :** The information in this sentence and the six following is in Ryder, *Kingdom of Naples*, p. 81.

45 **Pressed for an answer . . . :** Calixtus's reply to Lucrezia d'Alagna is in Johnson, *Borgias*, p. 48.

45 **Before long Calixtus was warning . . . :** The exchange appears in Johnson, *Borgias*, p. 47.

50 Niccolò Machiavelli, who was still . . . : Gregorovius, *History of Rome,* p. 7:156, is typical of nineteenth-century historians in asserting without evidence that Calixtus hoped to make Pedro Luis king of Naples. Mallett, *Borgias,* p. 75, suggests that this is probably true but unimportant. Johnson, *Borgias,* p. 51, appears to be on solid ground in describing the idea as "gossip."

Background: Amazing Italy

52 The Italy for which Alonso . . . : For a detailed and insightful overview of the life, politics, and culture of the Italy of the fifteenth century, nothing compares with Martines, *Power and Imagination.*

Chapter 4: Family Matters

58 We see Rodrigo . . . : Ferrara, *Borgia Pope,* p. 25, is good on Rodrigo Borgia's early benefices, as are Mallett, *Borgias,* p. 86, and Woodward, *Cesare Borgia,* p. 11. De Roo, *Material,* vols. 1 and 2, are cumulatively comprehensive on the subject. Mallett, *Borgias,* p. 84, deals with the exemptions granted by Nicholas V to permit the young Rodrigo to depart Spain for Italy.

59 It would later be said . . . : Mallett, *Borgias,* p. 77, claims that in 1456 a number of cardinals objected to Calixtus's promotion of men "so young and so untried" to the Sacred College, but he goes on to suggest that other reasons were undoubtedly more important.

60 The scholarly diplomat Enea . . . : Piccolomini's words about the newly appointed Cardinal Rodrigo are in Ferrara, *Borgia Pope,* p. 40.

62 Alfonso V, always happy . . . : The dispute between pope and king over the March of Ancona and other properties is in Pius II, *Memoirs,* p. 95.

63 Calixtus was prodded into action . . . . The story of Rodrigo's subduing of Josias in Ascola appears in abbreviated form in Ferrara, *Borgia Pope,* p. 38.

Background: The Men in the Red Hats

66 Typically, the cardinals pledged . . . : The emergence and intent of capitulations is detailed in Hay, *Europe,* p. 278.

68 Most of them had charge . . . : Majanlahti, *Families,* p. 53, describes in detail the structure and responsibilities of the Curial bureaucracy. Mallett, *Borgias,* p. 49, is also helpful on the subject.

68   **Of the fifteen cardinals . . . :** The national origins of cardinals present
      at various conclaves are in Hay, *Church in Italy,* p. 41.

70   **The complex ironies of the situation . . . :** Gonzaga's advice to his son
      the cardinal appears in Martines, *Power and Imagination,* p. 306.

Chapter 5: The End of the Beginning

74   **"Would to God . . .":** The translation of Cardinal Piccolomini's letter
      to Rodrigo Borgia appears in De Roo, *Material,* p. 2:67.

74   **He was to report to Rome . . . :** The position of vice-chancellor and its
      place in the papal bureaucracy are detailed in Majanlahti, *Families,*
      p. 77.

77   **No one was more delighted . . . :** Calixtus's words are in Johnson,
      Borgias, p. 51.

77   **No less significantly . . . :** Illegitimacy as a barrier to inheritance of a
      crown is explained in De Roo, *Material,* p. 1:175.

78   **He pledged to "do my utmost . . .":** Woodward, *Cesare Borgia,* p. 7, and
      Johnson, *Borgias,* p. 48.

PART TWO: *Rodrigo*
A Long Apprenticeship

The three and a half decades when Rodrigo Borgia served as vice-chancellor of the Roman Catholic Church kept him at the center of the reigns of five popes and so of Italian and European affairs. Therefore his public career through all these years is thoroughly documented, and the fact that his private life generated nearly no comment in spite of his prominence is curious if his posthumous reputation for scandalous behavior is deserved.

Chapter 6: Surviving

86   **Attention now turned . . . :** Exceptionally detailed accounts of the
      conclave of 1455 are in Gregorovius, *History of Rome,* p. 7:166, and
      Mallett, *Borgias,* p. 68.

87   **What happened next . . . :** Cardinal Piccolomini's own account of his
      exchange with Rodrigo Borgia and subsequent election is in Pius II,
      Memoirs, p. 80.

89   **The new pope was a remarkable man . . . :** Piccolomini's life story is
      in Ady, *Humanist Pope,* and in Mitchell, *Laurels and Tiara.*

91   When on September 26 . . . : Woodward, *Cesare Borgia*, p. 12, gives the
       cause of death as malaria without qualification, but his certainty on
       the point is not explained.

92   As conceived by Pius . . . : The innovative character of the Mantua
       conference is explained in Gregorovius, *History of Rome*, p. 7:182.

94   One was a proclamation . . . : Ibid., p. 7:183.

94   It was prompted . . . : For the significance of the Pragmatic Sanction,
       see Barraclough, *Medieval Papacy*, pp. 183, 187.

Background: The Eternal City, Eternally Reborn

97   The Rome of Pius II's time . . . : As a source of information about and
       insight into its subject, nothing surpasses Stinger, *Renaissance in
       Rome*.

98   "The city is for the most part . . .": Latour, *Borgias*, p. 15.

98   As the historian Theodor Mommsen . . . : Mallett, *Borgias*, p. 36.

99   A chronicler described . . . : Majanlahti, *Families*, p. 42.

Chapter 7: Pius II: Troubles Rumored and Real

100   *Beloved Son, We have learned* . . . : Translations of both of Pius II's letters
       to Cardinal Rodrigo about the Siena affair are in Ferrara, *Borgia Pope*,
       p. 56.

105   There has probably never been . . . : Gaspar of Verona's description of
       Cardinal Rodrigo appears in Gregorovius, *Lucretia Borgia*, p. 9.

105   He was rather stolidly . . . : Alexander's religious conservatism is dis-
       cussed in Mallett, *Borgias*, p. 240.

106   His reputation has suffered . . . : The slanderous pamphlet is discussed
       by Pastor, *History of Popes*, p. 6:114.

106   This encouraged further . . . : Guicciardini's claim that Rodrigo Bor-
       gia was "mightily lustful of both" appears in Deiss, *Captains of For-
       tune*, p. 23.

106   Pius II in his *Memoirs* . . . : Pius II, *Memoirs*, p. 254.

107   The fare was so plain . . . : Mallett, *Borgias*, p. 229.

107   The German Ludwig Pastor . . . : Pastor, *History of Popes*, p. 5:386.

107   A twentieth-century historian . . . : Mallett, *Borgias*, p. 82.

107   Even Guicciardini conceded . . . : De la Bedoyere, *Meddlesome Friar*,
       p. 65.

107   It may have been bafflement . . . : Mallett, *Borgias*, p. 82.

108   There was a continuing war in Naples . . . : For the story of Ferrante

saving his throne with the help of the pope and the Sforzas, see Gregorovius, *History of Rome*, pp. 7:185, 197. Ady, *Humanist Pope*, p. 103, is good on the troubles in Rome that obliged Pius to return from Tuscany.

108   As the rebellious barons . . . : Ferrante's dark side is illuminated in perhaps excessively lurid detail in Prescott, *Princes*, p. 65.

109   In 1462, unable . . . : De Roo, *Material*, p. 3:71.

110   It was the discovery . . . : Gregorovius, *History of Rome*, p. 7:209.

110   He hurried to Rome . . . : Castro's words are in Pius II, *Memoirs*, p. 233.

113   He died the next day . . . : The aborting of Pius's crusade is in Norwich, *History of Venice*, p. 343.

Background: Il Papa

114   The story of the popes . . . : See Barraclough, *Medieval Papacy*, for the story of the medieval popes, and Pastor, *History of Popes*, for the Renaissance papacy.

Chapter 8: Paul II: The Poisoned Chalice

118   The conclave that followed . . . : Gregorovius, *History of Rome*, p. 7:218.

120   Therefore they made it . . . : For the capitulations of 1464, ibid., p. 7:221.

122   (If betrayal it was . . .): Stinger, *Renaissance in Rome*, p. 162.

124   Even as a young man . . . : Paul II's life story is in Gregorovius, *History of Rome*, p. 7:218, with much additional detail in Robertson, *Tyranny*.

126   But when he demanded reforms . . . : See Robertson, *Tyranny*, p. 68, for detail on how Paul's settlement with Bologna strengthened the Bentivoglii.

126   Most humiliating of all . . . : The revolt of the abbreviators and the slanders of Bartolomeo Platina are in Symonds, *Renaissance in Italy*, p. 297.

127   Negropont was a key Venetian stronghold . . . : The fall of Negropont and its importance are in Norwich, *History of Venice*, p. 347.

Background: The Inextinguishable Evil-Heads

129   *Malatesta: the word translates* . . . : For more on the Malatestas, see Jones, *Malatesta of Rimini*, and Prescott, *Princes*, the three chapters beginning on p. 278.

131   "I am Sigismondo Malatesta . . .": Ady, *Humanist Pope*, p. 194.

Chapter 9: Sixtus IV: Disturbing the Peace

134   **Della Rovere seemed a perfect choice . . .** : Della Rovere's career before his election is in Gregorovius, *History of Rome*, p. 7:242.

138   **The selection of Rodrigo Borgia . . .** : Rodrigo Borgia's mission to Spain is described in unparalleled detail in De Roo, *Material*, vol. 2, and also receives extensive attention in Ferrara, *Borgia Pope*, p. 71, and in Mallett, *Borgias*, p. 93.

141   **Rodrigo moved on to Castile . . .** : Cloulas, *Borgias*, p. 48, is exceptionally good on Cardinal Rodrigo's activities in Castile.

142   **Having earlier accused Rodrigo . . .** : For Cardinal Ammannati-Piccolomini's accusations about and communications with Cardinal Rodrigo, see Ferrara, *Borgia Pope*, p. 65.

147   **Still in Milan . . .** : The alleged plotting of Sforza and Cardinal Riario is discussed in Burckhardt, *Civilization*, p. 75.

Background: War, Italian Style

148   **Most of them were . . .** : For further information about the *condottieri* and their place in Italian history, see Deiss, *Captains of Fortune*; Prescott, *Princes*; and Mallett, *Mercenaries*.

Chapter 10: Innocent VIII: Plumbing the Depths

156   **And so was hatched . . .** : Cronin, *Florentine Renaissance*, p. 254.

158   **He summoned Lorenzo to Rome . . .** : The conflict between Sixtus and the league supporting Florence is told in detail in Gregorovius, *History of Rome*, p. 7:261.

159   **When a hard-pressed Venice . . .** : The terms on which Venice made peace with the Turks in 1479 are in Norwich, *History of Venice*, p. 357.

159   **Lorenzo bet everything . . .** : An account of Lorenzo's trip to Naples is in Hibbert, *House of Medici*, p. 152.

161   **The withdrawal was hailed . . .** : The occupation of and subsequent withdrawal from Otranto is in Stinger, *Renaissance in Rome*, p. 114, and Norwich, *History of Venice*, p. 357.

161   **A Christian counteroffensive . . .** : Gregorovius, *History of Rome*, p. 7:266, offers the opinion that attacks on Constantinople and Greece could have succeeded.

162   **He said they could have . . .** : Venice's "savage attack" on Ferrara, and the political context, are treated at length ibid., p. 7:268.

163   **Rome exploded in an orgy . . .** : Ibid., p. 7:287.

164 **This was Rodrigo's fourth . . . :** Interestingly varying accounts of the conclave of 1484 are in ibid., p. 7:287; Pastor, *History of Popes*, p. 5:233; Woodward, *Cesare Borgia*, p. 20; and Mallett, *Borgias*, p. 97.

165 **Cibo's roots contributed . . . :** Cronin, *Florentine Renaissance*, p. 262; Pastor, *History of Popes*, p. 5:350; and Gregorovius, *History of Rome*, p. 7:290.

165 **Other signs of favor followed . . . :** De Roo, *Material*, vol. 2, is comprehensive on the benefices granted to Rodrigo Borgia by Innocent among other popes, and he contradicts what is said in Mallett, *Borgias*, p. 102, about the purchase of the duchy of Gandía for Pedro Luis Borgia.

165 **The tragedy opened this time . . . :** The destructive consequences of Alfonso duke of Calabria's visit to Rome are described in Prescott, *Princes*, p. 72, and Gregorovius, *History of Rome*, p. 7:293.

166 **Thus, when Alfonso later . . . :** Innocent's continuing difficulties with Naples are detailed in Pastor, *History of Popes*, p. 5:274.

168 **The character of their marriage . . . :** Caterina's lament that "you cannot imagine the life I lead" is in Prescott, *Princes*, p. 117.

168 **The extent of his commitment . . . :** The troubles confronting Innocent as 1491 ended are discussed in Pastor, *History of Popes*, p. 5:311, and in Elliott, *Imperial Spain*, p. 90.

PART THREE: *Alexander*
Pope at Last

The great challenge for anyone examining the reign of Alexander VI is to decide which of the vast number of things said about his personal life and conduct during his papacy (including the many examples of which there is no record predating his death) should be regarded as at least possibly if not certainly true. One work is indispensable in this regard: Peter De Roo's five-volume *Material for a History of Pope Alexander VI*, which offers incomparably more documentation and analysis than any other source. Ferrara, *Borgia Pope*, whose conclusions echo De Roo's and undoubtedly are to some extent based on them, is useful as a succinct introduction to the key questions.

Chapter 11: The Best Man for the Job

173 *I am Pope!:* Ferrara, *Borgia Pope*, p. 109.

173 *I! I am Pope!:* The anonymous and influentially slanderous pamphlet

in which this version of Alexander's supposed exclamation first appeared is discussed in De Roo, *Material*, p. 2:336; Pastor, *History of Popes*, p. 6:113; and Hibbert, *Borgias and Enemies*, p. 37.

174   He wrote—and influenced . . . : The accusations of simony are in Guicciardini, *History of Italy*, p. 13, and challenged by De la Bedoyere, *Meddlesome Friar*, p. 86; Mallett, *Borgias*, p. 117; and De Roo, *Material*, p. 2:339.

174   And that the 1492 conclave . . . : Quoted are words from Guicciardini, *History of Italy*, p. 13.

174   He could be ridiculously . . . : Hibbert, *Borgias and Enemies*, p. 61.

181   From the point at which . . . : Symonds, *Renaissance in Italy*, p. 312.

182   Even as intransigent . . . : Infessura's words are in Latour, *Borgias*, p. 31.

185   In one of these missives . . . : Ferrante's complaints to Spain about Alexander are in De Roo, *Material*, p. 4:74.

186   "Rest assured," López replied . . . : Ibid., p. 4:76.

191   "He is small and ill-made . . .": Contarini's description is in Ferrara, *Borgia Pope*, p. 184.

192   At the end of 1493 . . . : The Briçonnet mission to the papal court is in De Roo, *Material*, p. 4:163, and Gregorovius, *History of Rome*, p. 7:359.

Background: Madness and Milan

194   All the Visconti and Sforza . . . : Prescott devotes more than fifty pages to the history of Visconti in *Lords* and almost as many to the Sforza dynasty in *Princes*.

195   "Do you not know, you fool . . .": Prescott, *Lords*, p. 299.

Chapter 12: The Coming of the French

206   There survives a unique . . . : The Ferrarese ambassador's description of the adolescent Cesare appears in Gregorovius, *Lucretia Borgia*, p. 57.

208   He was at least . . . : Burckhardt, *Civilization*, p. 28.

208   Other support was needed . . . : The favors bestowed on various Borgias by kings of Naples are in Woodward, *Cesare Borgia*, p. 59.

210   It was typical of the relaxed view . . . : Pastor, *History of Popes*, p. 5:427.

211   They brought with them . . . : The revolutionary effects of the new artillery, including its contribution to the quick collapse of Naples, are in Taylor, *Art of War*, pp. 83, 132.

212   His troops marched under standards . . . : De la Bedoyere, *Meddlesome Friar*, p. 117.

212   That the arrival of the French . . . : The French invasion's immense consequences for the future of Italy are outlined in Martines, *Power and Imagination*, p. 277.

214   If it is true as alleged . . . : Strathern, *Artist, Philosopher*, p. 72, states that Ascanio Sforza persuaded the Colonna to seize Ostia for the French.

216   He told the assembled . . . : King Charles's demands of the Florentines are in Symonds, *Renaissance in Italy*, p. 429.

217   "The triumph of France . . .": Alexander's warning about the consequences of the French invasion are in Woodward, *Cesare Borgia*, p. 71.

218   Also necessary, he noted . . . : Cronin, *Florentine Renaissance*, p. 285.

218   Charles, he says, is "young and . . .": Ferrara, *Borgia Pope*, p. 193.

Background: Florence: An Anti-Renaissance

220   He gave early evidence . . . : Savonarola's words are in Cronin, *Florentine Renaissance*, p. 269.

Chapter 13: The French Depart

232   In short order they formed . . . : The terms of the Holy League are in Pastor, *History of Popes*, p. 5:467.

232   When a new round of appeals . . . : Ibid., p. 5:469.

233   With him went also . . . : The extreme estimates are by Gregorovius, *History of Rome*, p. 7:396, who says twenty thousand mules, and by Cronin, *Florentine Renaissance*, p. 287, who says five thousand.

234   Something worse than wailing ladies . . . Gregorovius, *History of Rome*, p. 472.

236   The ensuing battle of Fornovo . . . : A clear and detailed account of the battle is in Mallett, *Mercenaries*, p. 242.

236   When it was over . . . : Prescott, *Princes*, p. 25.

236   The result, hastily arrived at . . . : The Peace of Vercelli is in Norwich, *History of Venice*, p. 378.

Background: The Paternity Question: An "Apology"

240   A rare exception is Michael Mallett . . . : Mallett's *Borgias* describes De Roo's work as a "vast collection" (p. 325) and as a "vast apologist work" coated with "whitewash" (p. 329).

240 He says forthrightly . . . : De Roo, *Material*, p. 1: xi.

242 The four young Borgias . . . : Ibid., p. 1:132, and Ferrara, *Borgia Pope*, p. 168.

243 Gregorovius, interestingly, says he . . . : Gregorovius, *Lucretia Borgia*, p. 13.

243 The author of the present work . . . : Genealogical information about the Borgias of Spain is in Imhof, *Genealogie viginti*, pp. 19–28.

244 Various documents supposedly . . . : De Roo's exploration of the forgery question is in *Material*, pp. 1:447–529, and is followed by eighty pages of documents and extracts from documents.

244 De Roo devotes eighty-three pages . . . : The statement about a bull of legitimization being the "fabrication of some criminal ignorant of the habits of the Roman Curia" is ibid., p. 1:417.

245 Typical are a 1493 ambassador's letter . . . : De Roo's extensive discussion of the use of such terms as "son" and "nephew," "daughter" and "niece" begins ibid., p. 1:420.

246 A Spanish royal brief . . . : Ibid., p. 1:197.

Chapter 14: A Shattering Loss

252 One of them would remember . . . : Mallett, *Borgias*, p. 145.

259 Ascanio Sforza for one . . . : The Sforza cardinal's clash with Juan Borgia is in Bellonci, *Lucrezia Borgia*, p. 93, and Pastor, *History of Popes*, p. 5:493.

260 "The duke of Gandía is dead . . .": Woodward, *Cesare Borgia*, p. 113.

260 Of the Orsini he said nothing . . . : Reasons to suspect the Orsini are in Pastor, *History of Popes*, p. 5:506, and for not suspecting Cesare are in the same work, p. 511; Woodward, *Cesare Borgia*, p. 114; and Mallett, *Borgias*, p. 154.

261 He announced that he was creating . . . : The work of Alexander's reform commission and the lack of result are in De Roo, *Material*, p. 3:171.

264 This was made freshly apparent . . . : The arrest of Alexander's former secretary and confession to forging documents are in Gregorovius, *History of Rome*, p. 7:432.

264 He was now fully formed . . . : Paolo Capello's words are in Bradford, *Lucrezia Borgia*, p. 18.

Background: The Young Ones

265   Everything known about Cesare's eldest brother . . . : Extensive infor-
       mation about the first duke of Gandía is in Ferrara, *Borgia Pope*, p. 166.

266   Cesare, financially independent . . . : Cesare's early life is in Wood-
       ward, *Cesare Borgia*, p. 24.

Chapter 15: Valentino

272   For him to submit . . . : The quote appears in the detailed account of
       Alexander's handling of the Savonarola affair in Pastor, *History of
       Popes*, p. 6:7.

273   "Oh prostitute Church . . .": Ibid., p. 6:17.

273   On May 12, yielding to demands . . . : Pastor, *History of Popes*, p. 6:19.

282   But beyond that, he promised . . . : Louis XII's benefactions are in
       Woodward, *Cesare Borgia*, p. 132.

284   "Are you aware, monsignor . . .": Pastor, *History of Popes*, p. 6:63.

PART FOUR: *Cesare*
Caesar or Nothing

It is evidence of the stagnation of Borgia scholarship that, a century after its publication, W. H. Woodward's *Cesare Borgia* remains not only unsurpassed but unchallenged as a source of information on its subject. Yriarte, *Cesare Borgia,* is superior in its treatment of Cesare's final career in Spain.

Chapter 16: The Landscape Changes

300   "Should I have to perish . . .": Caterina's words are in Breisach, *Ca-
       terina Sforza*, p. 207.

304   Learning of this . . . : Mallett, *Borgias*, p. 177.

Chapter 17: Conqueror

325   At a point when . . . : Castellini's description of Lucrezia is in Bellonci,
       Lucrezia Borgia, p. 187.

331   One historian has suggested . . . : Whitfield, "New Views," p. 79.

Chapter 18: "Longing for Greatness and Renown"

337 **Cesare is *loved by his soldiers* . . . :** This translation of Machiavelli's famous and variously translated words is in Strathern, *Artist, Philosopher*, p. 105.

338 **Of the almost preternaturally . . . :** Gregorovius, *History of Rome*, p. 7:452.

338 **The historian Pandolfo Collenuccio . . . :** Sabatini, *Life of Cesare*, p. 241.

338 **In a flash of almost . . . :** Strathern, *Artist, Philosopher*, p. 90.

344 **The two talked all night . . . :** Bellonci, *Lucrezia Borgia*, p. 241.

345 **A retainer of Francesco Gonzaga . . . :** Strathern, *Artist, Philosopher*, p. 117.

346 **"I cannot conceal my fears . . .":** Prescott, *Princes*, p. 175.

347 **On September 2, in bidding . . . :** Strathern, *Artist, Philosopher*, p. 119.

347 **He helped to hold her down . . . :** Gregorovius, *Lucretia Borgia*, p. 282.

Background: Superstitions: Another Side of the Renaissance

380 **We want to think of it . . . :** Purcell, *Great Captain*, p. 183.

381 **The Gian Galeazzo Visconti . . . :** The examples are all from Prescott's *Lords*: Gian Galeazzo Visconti on p. 322, Ludovico Sforza on p. 146, and the complaint about the latter on p. 208.

Chapter 21: Alone

387 **As a priest at the Vatican . . . :** Bellonci, *Lucrezia Borgia*, p. 261.

394 **The Florentine authorities . . . :** Villari, *Machiavelli*, p. 357.

396 **"He spoke with words full of poison . . .":** Strathern, *Artist, Philosopher*, p. 289.

397 **The duke had a plan . . . :** The size of Cesare's remaining military forces is in Villari, *Machiavelli*, p. 361.

397 **He intended to "prevent . . .":** Strathern, *Artist, Philosopher*, p. 293.

398 **Another newly minted cardinal . . . :** Soderini's words on Cesare are in Villari, *Machiavelli*, p. 361.

399 **Cardinal Lloris . . . :** Mallett, *Borgias*, p. 249 and 251, Strathern, *Artist, Philosopher*, p. 293.

399 **At one point . . . :** Strathern, *Artist, Philosopher*, p. 299.

405 **Evidently he remained . . . :** Ibid., p. 366.

407 **Now recovered from his injuries . . . :** Quote is ibid., p. 367.

Aftermath

The literature on Lucrezia Borgia is, for the most part, as credulous and unjustifiably sensational as it is extensive. Bradford, *Lucrezia Borgia,* is the best biography and unquestionably superior to everything that precedes it. Bradford does not, however, consider the paternity question or even acknowledge that such a question might exist, and neither De Roo nor Ferrara appears in her otherwise impressive bibliography. Ferrara, *Borgia Pope,* is good on the Borgia family and its relations after the death of Lucrezia.

410   **In almost all ways** . . . : Gregorovius, *Lucretia Borgia,* p. 159.

411   **But as the Borgia biographer** . . . : Mallett, *Borgias,* p. 262.

413   **Her descendants, like Lucrezia's** . . . : Ibid., p. 260.

414   *When he fell sick* . . .: Gonzaga's account of the deathbed scene is in Bradford, *Lucrezia Borgia,* p. 200.

417   **Considered by many** . . . : Gregorovius, *Lucretia Borgia,* p. 281.

Examining Old Assumptions

420   **Because to let go** . . . : Lucas-Dubreton, *Borgias,* p. 57.

421   **As noted in the introduction** . . . : Gregorovius, *History of Rome,* p. 7:326.

422   **An English historian** . . . : Robertson, *Cesare Borgia,* p. 11.

422   **A more recent historian** . . . : Mallett, *Borgias,* p. 101.

422   **"All experience of psychology . . ."**: Gregorovius, *Lucretia Borgia,* p. 290.

424   **Did she become Rodrigo's mistress** . . . : Pastor's opinion is in his *History of Popes,* p. 5:361. "Shortly before 1470" is in Gregorovius, *History of Rome,* p. 7:327.

424   **"We find," he writes** . . . : That "there must have been several" Vannozzas is in Ferrara, *Borgia Pope,* p. 147.

425   **Ferrara concludes** . . . : Ibid., p. 152.

427   **He was several years older** . . . : Conti's assertion about pressure to make Farnese a cardinal is in Pastor, *History of Popes,* p. 5:417.

428   **As Ferrara says** . . . : Ferrara, *Borgia Pope,* p. 154.

428   *Madonna Adriana and Giulia have arrived* . . .: Ibid., p. 158.

429 W. H. Woodward . . . : Woodward, *Cesare Borgia*, p. 125.

429 Writing earlier, Ludwig Pastor . . . : Pastor, *History of Popes*, p. 6:128.

430 In her fourth chapter . . . : Bellonci, *Lucrezia Borgia*, p. 108.

430 When Bellonci returns . . . : Ibid., p. 180.

Bibliography

Abullafia, David. "The Crown and the Economy Under Ferrante I of Naples (1485–94)." In *City and Countryside in Late Medieval and Renaissance Italy.* Edited by Trevor Dean and Chris Wickham. London: Hambledon Press, 1990.

Ady, Cecilia M. *Pius II, The Humanist Pope.* London: Methuen, 1913.

———. *The Bentivoglio of Bologna: A Study in Despotism.* London: Oxford University Press, 1937.

Arnaldi, Girolamo. *Italy and Its Invaders.* Cambridge, Mass.: Harvard University Press, 2005.

Aston, Margaret. *The Fifteenth Century: The Prospect of Europe.* London: Thames & Hudson, 1968.

Barraclough, Geoffrey. *The Medieval Papacy.* London: Thames & Hudson, 1975.

Bellonci, Maria. *Lucrezia Borgia.* Translated by Bernard and Barbara Wall. London: Phoenix Press, 2000.

Binns, L. Elliott. *The History of the Decline and Fall of the Medieval Papacy.* London: Methuen, 1934.

Borgia, Lucrezia, and Pietro Bembo. *The Prettiest Love Letters in the World.* Translated by Hugh Shankland. Boston: David R. Godine, 1987.

Bradford, Sarah. *Lucrezia Borgia.* New York: Penguin, 2004.

Breisach, Ernst. *Caterina Sforza: A Renaissance Virago.* Chicago: University of Chicago Press, 1967.

Burchard, Johann. *At the Court of the Borgia.* Edited and translated by Geoffrey Parker. London: Folio Society, 1963.

Burckhardt, Jacob. *The Civilization of the Renaissance in Italy.* Translated by S. G. C. Middlemore. New York: Modern Library, 2002.

Chamberlin, E. R. *The Fall of the House of Borgia.* London: Temple Smith, 1974.

———. *The World of the Italian Renaissance.* London: Book Club Associates, 1982.

Chambers, D. S. *The Imperial Age of Venice, 1380–1580.* London: Thames & Hudson, 1970.

———. *Popes, Cardinals and War.* London: I. B. Tauris, 2006.

Champion, Pierre. *Louis XI.* Translated by Winifred Stephens Whale. Freeport, N.Y.: Books for Libraries Press, 1929.

Cloulas, Ivan. *The Borgias.* Translated by Gilda Roberts. New York: Franklin Watts, 1989.

Collison-Morley, L. *The Story of the Borgias.* London: George Routledge & Sons, 1932.

Commynes, Philippe de. *Memoirs.* Edited by Samuel Kinser. Translated by Isabelle Cazeaux. Columbia: University of South Carolina Press, 1973.

Croce, Benedetto. *History of the Kingdom of Naples.* Chicago: University of Chicago Press, 1970.

Cronin, Vincent. *The Flowering of the Renaissance.* London: History Book Club, 1969.

———. *The Florentine Renaissance.* London: Collins/Fontana, 1972.

Dandelet, Thomas James. *Spanish Rome, 1500–1700.* New Haven, Conn.: Yale University Press, 2001.

Deiss, Joseph Jay. *Captains of Fortune: Profiles of Six Italian Condottieri.* London: Victor Gollancz, 1966.

De la Bedoyere, Michael. *The Meddlesome Friar: The Story of the Conflict Between Savonarola and Alexander VI.* London: Collins, 1957.

De Roo, Peter. *Material for a History of Pope Alexander VI, His Relatives and His Time.* 5 vols. Bruges: Desclée de Brouwer, 1924.

Edwards, John. *Torquemada and the Inquisitors.* Stroud, Gloucestershire: Tempus, 2005.

Elliott, J. H. *Imperial Spain, 1469–1716.* New York: St. Martin's Press, 1964.

Fernandez, Henry Dietrich. "The Patrimony of St. Peter. The Papal Court at Rome c. 1450-1700." In John William Adamson, ed., *The Princely Courts of Europe: Ritual, Politics, and Culture Under the Ancien Régime, 1500-1750.* London: Seven Dials, 2000.

Ferrara, Orestes. *The Borgia Pope, Alexander the Sixth.* Translated by F. J. Sheed. London: Sheed & Ward, 1942.

Gilmour, David. *The Pursuit of Italy.* London: Allen Lane, 2011.

Green, V. H. H. *Renaissance and Reformation.* London: Edward Arnold, 1964.

Gregorovius, Ferdinand. *History of the City of Rome in the Middle Ages,* vols. 6–8. Translated by Annie Hamilton. London: George Bell & Sons, 1909.

———. *Lucretia Borgia: According to Original Documents and Correspondence of Her Day.* Translated by John Leslie Garner. New York: D. Appleton & Co., 1909.

Guicciardini, Francesco. *History of Italy and History of Florence.* Translated by Cecil Grayson. New York: Twayne, 1964.

Hale, J. R. *Machiavelli and Renaissance Italy.* London: English Universities Press, 1961.

———. *Renaissance Europe.* Berkeley: University of California Press, 1977.

Hale, J. R., J. R. L. Highfield, and B. Smalley, eds. *Europe in the Late Middle Ages.* London: Faber & Faber, 1965.

Hare, Augustus J. C. *Walks in Rome.* 17th ed., rev. New York: George Routledge & Sons, n.d.

Hay, Denys. *Europe in the Fourteenth and Fifteenth Centuries.* London: Longman, 1966.

———. *The Church in Italy in the Fifteenth Century.* Cambridge: Cambridge University Press, 1977.

———. *The Italian Renaissance in Its Historical Background.* Cambridge: Cambridge University Press, 1977.

Hibbert, Christopher. *The Rise and Fall of the House of Medici.* London: Penguin, 1979.

———. *The Borgias and Their Enemies, 1431–1519.* New York: Harcourt, 2008.

Hughes, Robert. *Rome.* London: Weidenfeld & Nicolson, 2011.

Imhof, Jacob Wilhelm. *Genealogie viginti illustrium in Hispania familiarum.* Leipzig: Gleditsch, 1712.

Johnson, Marion. *The Borgias.* London: MacDonald, 1981.

Jones, P. J. *The Malatesta of Rimini and the Papal State.* London: Cambridge University Press, 1974.

King, Margaret L. *The Renaissance in Europe.* London: Laurence King, 2003.

Krautheimer, Richard. *Rome, Profile of a City, 312–1308.* Princeton, N.J.: Princeton University Press, 1980.

Larner, John. *The Lords of Romagna.* London: Macmillan, 1965.

Latour, Anny. *The Borgias.* Translated by Neil Mann. London: Elek Books, 1963.

Laven, Peter. *Renaissance Italy, 1464–1534.* London: Methuen, 1966.

Law, John Easton. "City, Court and Contado in Camerino, c. 1500." In *City and Countryside in Late Medieval and Renaissance Italy,* edited by Trevor Dean and Chris Wickham. London: Hambledon Press, 1990.

Leonetti, Andrea. *Papa Alessandro VI.* Bologna: Tipografia Pont. Mareggiani, 1880.

Le Roy Ladurie, Emmanuel. *The Royal French State, 1460–1610.* Translated by Juliet Vale. Oxford: Blackwell, 1987.

Lev, Elizabeth. *The Tigress of Forli.* Boston: Houghton Mifflin Harcourt, 2011.

Lotherington, John, ed. *Years of Renewal: European History, 1470–1600.* London: Hodder & Stoughton, 1988.

Lowe, K. J. P. *Church and Politics in Renaissance Italy.* Cambridge: Cambridge University Press, 1993.

Lucas-Dubreton, J. *The Borgias.* Translated by Philip John Stead. London: Staples Press, 1954.

Machiavelli, Niccolò. *Selected Political Writings.* Edited and translated by David Wootton. Indianapolis: Hackett, 1994.

MacKenney, Richard. *Renaissances: The Cultures of Italy c. 1300–c. 1600.* New York: Palgrave Macmillan, 2005.

Majanlahti, Anthony. *The Families Who Made Rome.* London: Chatto & Windus, 2005.

Mallett, Michael. *The Borgias: The Rise and Fall of a Renaissance Dynasty*. London: Bodley Head, 1969.

———. *Mercenaries and Their Masters: Warfare in Renaissance Italy*. Barnsley, South Yorkshire: Pen & Sword, 2009.

Mariéjol, Jean Hippolyte. *The Spain of Ferdinand and Isabella*. Translated by Benjamin Keen. New Brunswick, N.J.: Rutgers University Press, 1961.

Martines, Lauro. *Power and Imagination: City-States in Renaissance Italy*. New York: Vintage, 1980.

———, ed. *Violence and Civil Disorder in Italian Cities, 1200–1500*. Berkeley: University of California Press, 1972.

Mattingly, Garrett. *Renaissance Diplomacy*. Harmondsworth: Penguin, 1973.

McNeill, William H. *Venice, The Hinge of Europe 1081–1797*. Chicago: University of Chicago Press, 1974.

Mitchell, R. J. *The Laurels and the Tiara: Pope Pius II, 1458–1464*. New York: Doubleday, 1963.

Noel, Gerard. *The Renaissance Popes*. New York: Carroll & Graf, 2006.

Norwich, John Julius. *A History of Venice*. London: Penguin, 2003.

Parry, J. H. *The Age of Reconnaissance*. New York: New American Library, 1964.

Partner, Peter. *Renaissance Rome, 1500–1559*. Berkeley: University of California Press, 1976.

Pastor, Ludwig. *The History of the Popes from the Close of the Middle Ages*, vols. 4–6. London: Kegan Paul, 1898.

Pius II. *Memoirs of a Renaissance Pope*. New York: G. P. Putnam's Sons, 1959.

Potter, G. R., ed. *The Renaissance, 1493–1520*. Cambridge: Cambridge University Press, 1961.

Prescott, Orville. *Princes of the Renaissance*. London: George Allen & Unwin, 1970.

———. *Lords of Italy*. New York: Harper & Row, 1972.

Procacci, Giuliano. *History of the Italian People*. Translated by Anthony Paul. London: Penguin, 1991.

Purcell, Mary. *The Great Captain: Gonzalo Fernandez de Cordoba*. London: Alvin Redman, 1962.

Reston, James, Jr. *Dogs of God*. New York: Anchor Books, 2006.

Robertson, Charles Grant. *Cesare Borgia: The Stanhope Essay for 1891*. Oxford: B. H. Blackwell, 1891.

Robertson, Ian. *Tyranny under the Mantle of St. Peter: Pope Paul II and Bologna*. Turnhout, Belgium: Brepols, 2002.

Ryder, Alan. *The Kingdom of Naples Under Alfonso the Magnanimous*. Oxford: Clarendon Press, 1976.

Sabatini, Rafael. *The Life of Cesare Borgia*. Boston: Houghton Mifflin, 1930.

Setton, Kenneth Meyer. *The Papacy and the Levant, 1204–1571*. Philadelphia: American Philosophical Society, 1976.

Shaw, Christine. *The Political Role of the Orsini Family in the Papal States, c. 1480–1534.* Unpublished Ph.D. thesis, Oxford University, 1983.

Showerman, Grant. *Eternal Rome.* New Haven, Conn.: Yale University Press, 1925.

Simon, Kate. *A Renaissance Tapestry: The Gonzaga of Mantua.* London: Harrap, 1998.

Stinger, Charles L. *The Renaissance in Rome.* Bloomington: Indiana University Press, 1998.

Strathern, Paul. *The Artist, the Philosopher, and the Warrior.* New York: Bantam, 2009.

Symonds, John Addington. *Renaissance in Italy,* vol. 1. New York: Modern Library, 1935.

Taylor, F. L. *The Art of War in Italy, 1494–1529.* London: Cambridge University Press, 1921.

Thomson, John A. F. *Popes and Princes, 1417–1517: Politics and Polity in the Late Medieval Church.* London: George Allen & Unwin, 1980.

Tracy, James D. *Europe's Reformations, 1450–1650.* New York: Rowman & Littlefield, 1999.

Villari, Pasquale. *The Life and Times of Niccolò Machiavelli,* vol. 1. Translated by Linda Villari. New York: Greenwood Press, 1968.

Whitfield, J. H. "New Views upon the Borgias." *History* 29, no. 109 (March 1944), pp. 77–88.

Wilson, Peter H. *The Holy Roman Empire, 1495–1806.* New York: St. Martin's Press, 1999.

Woodward, William Harrison. *Cesare Borgia.* New York: E. P. Dutton, 1914.

Yriarte, Charles. *Cesare Borgia.* London: Francis Aldor, 1947.

Index

G. J. MEYER is the author of four previous books, including two works of history: *A World Undone: The Story of the Great War* and *The Tudors*. He has degrees in English from St. Louis University, which he attended on a National Merit Scholarship, and the University of Minnesota, where he was a Woodrow Wilson fellow. While working as a staff writer at the *St. Louis Post-Dispatch* he was awarded a Nieman Fellowship in Journalism at Harvard University. He has taught literature and writing at colleges and universities in Des Moines, St. Louis, and New York, and now lives in Wiltshire, England.

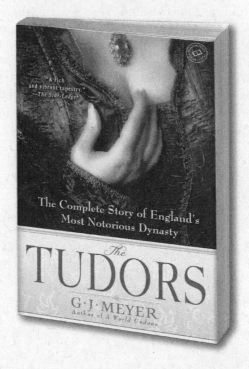

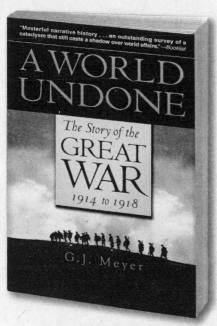